# THE WORLD ON EDGE

# THE
# WORLD
# ON
# EDGE

EDWARD S. CASEY

Indiana University Press

This book is a publication of

Indiana University Press
Office of Scholarly Publishing
Herman B Wells Library 350
1320 East 10th Street
Bloomington, Indiana 47405 USA

iupress.indiana.edu

♾ The paper used in this publication meets the minimum requirements of the American National Standard for Information Sciences—Permanence of Paper for Printed Library Materials, ANSI Z39.48–1992.

Manufactured in the United States of America

Library of Congress Cataloging-in-Publication Data

Names: Casey, Edward S., [date] author.
Title: The world on edge / Edward S. Casey.
Description: Bloomington : Indiana University Press, 2017. | Series: Studies in Continental thought | Includes bibliographical references and index.
Identifiers: LCCN 2016034881 | ISBN 9780253025586 (cl : alk. paper) | ISBN 9780253026095 (pb : alk. paper)
Subjects: LCSH: Boundaries (Philosophy) | Knowledge, Theory of. | Perception.
Classification: LCC BD392 .C37 2017 | DDC 117—dc23 LC record available at https://lccn.loc.gov/2016034881

1 2 3 4 5 22 21 20 19 18 17

*FOR MARY*

*YOU ARE NO LONGER AT THE EDGE OF MY WORLD*
*BUT AT ITS VERY CENTER*

# CONTENTS

# ACKNOWLEDGMENTS

Many hands and many minds went into the making of this book. I am profoundly grateful to each person who has been part of the process. With Dee Mortenson, I discussed the book's core conception a decade ago, and from that point on she has been nothing but enthusiastic. Quite indispensable has been Lissa McCullough, my good friend who became my closest reader and critic at every phase to the final moments.

It is an extraordinary situation when a teacher has received such help as I have from my own students. At every stage, I have benefitted immensely from the energetic assistance they have given me. Andrés Colapinto provided close critique of early versions of the manuscript, often leading me to reconsider my claims and to make very different ones. At a crucial moment, Adam Blair took over the securing of permissions and the selection of the book's illustrations with finesse and impeccable aesthetic judgment. Also fundamental were the detailed remarks given by Julia Sushtyka and Wesley Mattingly, each of whom brought distinctively different perspectives to bear on my writing. I am indebted to Jennifer Carter for her insights into the deeper logic of the caress. Kriszta Sajber advised me wisely and in detail regarding my treatment of the split self. Randy Dible intervened at a critical late stage when his special gift for locating obscure references proved especially timely. Remarkably apt observations, as to both style and basic content, were made along the way by Donald Landes. Brady Heiner pushed me to consider social and political implications that I might have ignored otherwise. Katherine Wolfe made telling comments at several important moments. Kyle Tanaka and Stephen Bourque, both from the master's program at Stony Brook, helped substantially.

Fellow faculty members at Stony Brook and elsewhere have been invaluable interlocutors as well as perceptive readers of this book. These include eminent musicologist Judith Lochhead as well as my treasured colleagues in the philosophy department, among them Megan Craig, Anne O'Byrne, Robert Crease, Eva Kittay, Mary Rawlinson, Lorenzo Simpson, Gary Mar, Harvey Cormier, Lee Miller, Don Ihde, Donn Welton, and Eduardo Mendieta (now at Pennsylvania State). I thank Megan Craig warmly for generously allowing me to use one of her recent paintings as the cover of this book. Remembered here fondly and with gratitude is Hugh Silverman. The late Peter Manchester was a primary inspiration to me throughout, thanks to his sheer brilliance as well as to his exemplary fortitude in the face of serious health issues.

Friends and colleagues from elsewhere supplied me with insights from their diverse points of view. Fred Evans of Duquesne University and I have exchanged thoughts on voice, place, and edge over the past twenty years: originally my student, I now regard Fred as not only a peer but also a mentor in many respects. To Glen Mazis, I am indebted for many years of animated dialogue on topics ranging from philosophy to poetry, and many things in between; he has helpfully commented on parts of this new book. David Morris of Concordia University has been consistently one of my most astute readers, often understanding me better than I understand myself. I have learned much from discussions with Jeff Malpas of the University of Tasmania. Several former doctoral students from Stony Brook who have become stellar figures in the field have been especially helpful in my recent career; these include Brian Schroeder and Tony Steinbock. Irene Klaver first pointed me to the importance of boundaries in her doctoral research. I am also grateful to Tanja Staehler for so carefully tracking my work and suggesting new directions.

Colleagues and friends from other fields remain essential to my work. Artist and art theorist Eve Ingalls kept me honest when it comes to what I say about art, while Kent Bloomer and I continue a dialogue about art and philosophy that we have been sustaining for decades. Fellow members of the Friday Night Painters, especially Parviz Mohassel and Christina Maile, have been inspiring forces throughout. Alberto Perez-Gomez, leading architectural theorist, has been a model of the deeply interdisciplinary approach to which I aspire in my own work. Theologian extraordinaire Tom Altizer remains an enduring presence in my life and work: his fearless iconoclastic thinking releases new energies.

Conversations with Eugene Gendlin concerning the paradoxes of edges were invaluable. To the wisdom of Bruce Anderson, MD, I owe more than he can ever know.

I have learned a great deal from the recently printed volume dedicated to my work that was planned and edited by Donald Landes and Azucena Cruz-Pierre. Each essay in that collection acts as a signpost of where my thought has come from and where it should now be going. *The World on Edge* is in many respects a response to the authors of that volume: to each I extend my deep gratitude.

Friends in philosophy who remain insightful conversation partners include David Carr and David Kleinberg-Levin. My first teacher in philosophy, Richard Bernstein, sets an especially encouraging example of writing and teaching philosophy well beyond standard retirement age. Drew Leder has been a guiding spirit ever since he was an undergraduate student of mine at Yale. His pioneering action of teaching philosophy in Baltimore prisons has inspired my reflections on the edge aspects of solitary confinement.

To Bruce Wilshire, my departed friend and original thinker, I express my deep gratitude for his example of steering one's own course in philosophy, however unfashionable or untimely that course may seem to be.

Special thanks to Bram Briggance for his gift of the original map of northern Mexico, "Carta Geográfica del Estado Chihuahua," which figures importantly in chapter 1 of this book.

Eric Casey added invaluable comments in two areas of his expertise: ancient languages and modern music, especially jazz. His mark is most evident in interlude 4, which treats edges in music.

I am grateful for the support of administrators at Stony Brook who generously granted me research leaves during which most of this book was composed: Paul Armstrong, James Staros, Nancy Squires, and Sacha Kopp.

Mary Watkins was the guiding force throughout. This project got off the ground when I first joined forces with her in Santa Barbara, and during our time together there and in New York she has offered her wise counsel and selfless loving support.

# PRELUDE

No doubt we must edge our way through narrow doorways and along knife-edge paths.
  —Luce Irigaray, *Speculum of the Other Woman*

We strangely stand on,—souls do,—on the very edges of their own spheres, leaning tiptoe toward & into the adjoining sphere.
  —Ralph Waldo Emerson, *Harvard Journals and Miscellaneous Notebooks*

This book pursues the thesis that edges are constitutive not only of what we perceive, but also of what we think and of the places and events in which we are situated. Edges do much more than demarcate or delimit spatial spread or temporal extent, being a formative force of their own. I shall maintain that the role of edges is central to the drama of experience at every level—perceptual, practical, cognitive, aesthetic, emotional, intersubjective. Far from being a negligible aspect of ordinary experience, they are an extraordinary and quite constructive (though also at times destructive) basis of this experience.

Yet edges have been almost entirely overlooked in previous philosophical accounts of human experience. At most they are noted and then passed over in favor of abiding philosophical preoccupations such as the nature of truth, the verification of knowledge claims, or the evidential nature of sensory perception. The nature of edges has been quite literally marginalized. But what if edges are not merely incidental aspects of perception? What if they are distinct presences in their own right—indispensable not just to perception but also to many other kinds and parts of our experience of the world? Edges, I contend here, are essential to being a thing or a thought, a place or an event—and, by extension, a person or an artwork. Without edges, none of these could be what they are. Edges contribute to the peculiar character of that which they constitute, its status as *this* rather than *that*. Nothing distinct or finite can emerge except as edged—and edged in a specific manner that helps to form its unique identity.

## I

As I look out across the remarkable rock formations thrusting up from the Pacific Ocean near Moro Bay, California, catching my eye is a ledge whose jagged upper edges are sharply etched.

FIGURE 1.  Cliffs at Moro Bay, California. Author's photo.

These starkly displayed edges seem to be poised as if awaiting something momentous—as in a vigil for some unknown future, despite being so ancient that the details of their origins are known only by geologists. Standing out in this place, they stand in for these concealed origins. In their exposed state, they are overt and outgoing; as material entities, they are closed in upon themselves. In the first capacity they open themselves out to sea and sky; in the second they draw back into the earth from which they have emerged.

The rock edges cut a dramatic figure, at once brash and fragile. Extruding from high cliffs, they cut incisively into the air while rising from the depths of the surging waters. Even as they thrust themselves upward in their sheer physicality and angularity, they are open to whatever the local weather and the changing seasons and the ever-changing tides deliver.

At this moment in mid-March, the rock edges appear to gesture toward Japan, which sustained a catastrophic tsunami a few years ago, creating waves that reached all the way to this central California coastline. Arrayed before me, the rocks stand like solemn sentinels, pointing to the disaster from the eastern edge of the vast body of water that separates the United States from Japan. These rocks belong to the single massive edge that is the California coastline: they are edges upon that edge. This coastline is not just the westernmost periphery of the United States; it is also the farthest edge of one side of an entire continent. Here North America comes to a particular point that is marked by disparate edge phenomena that vary from marshlands to beaches, from cliffs to rocky inlets such as the one I now stand before. "From sea to shining sea"—these familiar words remind me that I am indeed standing at land's end, westward from which there is nothing but oceanic depth upon depth, until the shores of Hawaii, Japan, and China are reached. The whole North American continent is framed by the colossal edges that make up its eastern and western coasts, between which plains and mountains, prairies and lakes, present very different edge structures. Everywhere we look, everywhere we are on earth, we find ourselves in the midst of ancient and abiding edges of land and sea.

In truth, we live at all times and in all places in a teeming edge-world, replete with edges of every description—not only the rugged edges I confront at Moro Bay but also the many everyday edges by which we never fail to be surrounded, in cities as in open landscape. There is no escaping edges anywhere, no way out or back into an edgeless world. Such a world does not exist, and we would be foolish to seek it. The closest we come to an experience of edgelessness is in a pervasive fog or in our prenatal life in the womb. Once born, our life consists of one encounter with edges after another—some benignly supportive, others obstructive, but others distinctly traumatic—and as we grow up we move into increasingly complex and demanding edge circumstances. Much emanates from edges: energy, definition, profile, outreach. Much begins with edges, whether in painting, politics, or poetry, and everything ends with edges: every thing and every event terminates in edges, including the event of death as the ultimate edge of our life.

## II

After my brief trip along the California coast, I am writing at a familiar table in the Coffee Cat café. This modest scene of edges is no less revealing. As my attention concentrates on words—to express what I am just now thinking—I am *not* attending to the specific edges of my computer or the table on which it rests, much less to the edges of the room I am in. The computer, table, and room are instances of instrumental things that I count on for their "reliability," in Heidegger's word, their accessibility as things ready to use: *this* table, *this* computer, *this* open space— so much so that I take them for granted and do not attend to them as such. They withdraw from my attention even as they subtend my writing and make it possible. But the edges of my laptop and of the table on which it sits are not just externalities that act to limit material masses. These edges have a presence of their own that actively shapes the surfaces of the table and the computer, containing and configuring them.

Edges, then, bear up and bear out that which they edge. *Bearing up* points to the way that the edges of an instrument such as my computer supports my life as a philosopher who wishes to capture his thoughts in a format that can be easily retained and retrieved. More generally, once the edges of any particular thing are established in perception, they help us to discern it as that very thing; they act to situate it in the midst of what we experience. They bear it up. *Bearing out* refers to an effect of moving out laterally through the edges, which act to extend any given surface outward. Here, the directional "up" of support is supplemented by the "out" of extension in space. Bearing out brings with it a paradoxical effect: as external, edges act to give shape to things yet also to relate them to their surroundings. In this way, edges make emphatic that which they serve to define, whether this be a thing or an event. At the same time, as falling away from centrated perception, edges direct attention to whatever lies outside them in the environing circumstance in which they, and that which they delineate, are set. In both capacities, they act to bear out.

Although edges are effective as demarcating and delimiting (as in my work space in a café), they can also be quite porous and resilient. Even edges that serve to contain may also, in certain other respects, serve to open up. Right here in Coffee Cat, the walls furnish limits, holding in heat and light, while through the doors and windows air flows and views are seen. On the coast near Moro Bay, the rock ledge at which I peered is an opaque barrier in its erect fortitude, even as the rest of the scene was composed of open domains (the beach, the ocean).

Further afield, we find much the same twofold distinction obtaining in the edges of Tahrir Square in Cairo, where several years ago antigovernment protestors moved in from all over Egypt only to be confronted by militant supporters of the Mubarak government. In this tumultuous scene, the formal borders of the square itself (as determined by the position of buildings and sidewalks around the square) remained intact even as they were crossed and recrossed by the crowds, while through the passageways near the square—the contiguous streets and alleyways—thousands of people surged and retreated. Thus an event that captured the attention of the world was configured by edges of diverse sorts. Not only did this extraordinary event defy the settled belief that the long-term reign of a dictator was there to stay, but in objecting to his regime masses of Egyptian people also converged in a mixture of intense enthusiasm and violence that put virtually everyone on edge, literally and figuratively.

We live in an uneasy world in which human beings teeter on the brink, not knowing what to expect the very next moment. This is a world of high risk, not only when coming into a wholly new setting—where we do not know our way—but even when remaining in familiar, seemingly secure circumstances. Everywhere the world, inner as well as outer, presents itself as a congeries of competing edges. Ongoing daily experience bristles with edges, many of which interfere with each other; only rarely do we find ourselves in circumstances in which conflictual edges are lacking. When this does occur, we are surprised and grateful for the surcease, savoring the moment when the edges seem to fit together in a coherent pattern. But we are also aware of the transitory character of such a moment; we know how difficult it will be to sustain it.

The presidential election of 2016 was a striking case in point. Donald Trump's unexpected victory over Hillary Clinton constituted a sudden volte-face in which the latter's widely projected win—forecast by many pundits and ordinary people— vanished in the course of one evening. By 11:30 p.m. on that evening (November 8, 2016), it was manifest that Trump had triumphed by a large margin, to the joy of his supporters and the chagrin of Clinton's advocates. Here, time itself was set on edge: the confidence of a political prediction shared by millions of Americans was undermined in a matter of hours, and a very different future for the people of the United States, and for many abroad, opened in all its vast uncertainty.

For the most part, the world as we experience it is a world on edge, one that puts us on edge time and again. From these examples—the mundane table's edge in Coffee Cat, the dynamic ocean's edge sculpting jagged rock formations at Moro Bay, the volatile edges of Tahrir Square filled with insurgent bodies, the upending of the 2016 presidential election—we can infer that even if there is an identifiable genus we can call *edge*, the species of which it is composed are quite varied, with none being paradigmatic for the others.

## III

One question that will occupy us is whether edges are *something*, some kind of thing, or whether they are, rather, *nothing*—or perhaps *next to nothing*. Edges have a curious way of always giving out, coming to naught, ending, or about to end. Consider how the edge of the table on which I am writing belongs securely to the physical object of which it is the edge, being *its* edge and not the edge of anything else. Yet in this very capacity, it designates the exact place where the table itself is ending, coming to lack material presence. Past its edge, the table does not exist and is nowhere to be found. Is the table's edge something physical, thus thing-like, or is it nothing, or is it in an indeterminate middle state that signifies the process of *becoming nothing*? (I return to this issue at length in the postlude.)

One always has a certain perspective on an edge, a "take" on it that is susceptible to a quick reversal, of thing to nonthing (and back again), of seeing up close to seeing beyond (and the converse). This reversal does not derive from an edge's being sharp or precipitous, but rather because the very character of an edge involves a certain disequilibrium, occasioning sudden shifts of perception or action in its proximity. Edges, for all their ordinariness, enact *enantiodromia*, Heraclitus's word for sudden reversal into the opposite.

What makes being an edge so paradoxical, at once something definite (as defining the perimeter of something) and yet so subject to change (as coming to nothing)? One answer is that edges are transitional in their basic character and in our perception of them. Except for decorative edges, they do not invite lingering, neither visually nor by way of inhabitation: who (other than a zealous ascetic) would want to live on the edge of a cliff or on top of a pole? Edges mark an abrupt turn from one surface to another, or from one part of something to another part, or from one phase of an event to another. No wonder our look does not remain long with them but characteristically sails past them, finding its way elsewhere. Every edge and every perception of an edge is on the way to elsewhere, on the verge of going somewhere else. And this is so even though edges also serve to establish the extent or spread of a given thing or place or event: its current closure.

Edges trace out "lines of flight" in Deleuze and Guattari's sense of the term; they are quasi-linear structures that are inherently mobile rather than fixed. Not only my eye or body or mind is in movement in their presence, but they—the edges themselves—are also on the move in their own way, no matter how integral they are to things that are meant to be unmoving (like the table at which I am now seated: it is bolted to the floor). There is a visual pas de deux under way whenever we encounter edges, which at once draw our glance and yet disappear from every look; they are mercurial in their evanescence, making their way between several things and several places or events. Like the statues of Daedelus, they are ever on the move—ever eluding us. Yet they also act to enclose and close off.

The peculiarities to which I have just pointed are expressions of the endemic uneasiness occasioned by edges. Edges bring with them a characteristic anxiety of the uncertain and the precarious. Not only in being literally at the edge of a high precipice but in heavy traffic when we try to avoid collisions with the edges of other automobiles. In composing this prelude, I am putting myself on edge— the opening edge of this book, exposing myself to the doubts of skeptical readers. Such specific forms of edge anxiety (the root of "anxiety," *angst*, signifies a narrow channel with closely fitting edges) are instances of the more general anxiety felt by our immersion in a world of edges from which there is only rarely an effective, much less a lasting, exit. Given its complexity and uncertainty, its sheer liminality, yet also its pervasiveness, this is a world that we characteristically seek to evade at almost every opportunity, preferring the reassurance of the central mass of things and the familiar core of places and events. We gravitate to the heft and bulk, the easily identified center, of material objects and live bodies, of settled places and consistent events. Yet we overlook the edges of these same things at our peril. This book argues that it is better to confront them directly and to acknowledge and describe them on their own terms.

## IV

*The World on Edge* pursues the more exact description of edges in four ways. I begin by examining two great classes of edges: borders and boundaries. These are operative in many edge situations, both by themselves and in combination with other kinds of edge. (I treat a series of these other edge-types in three interludes in part one in order to impress upon the reader the multiplicity of edges in their striking variety.) In the same first part, I discuss differences between edges and limits, edges and surfaces, as well as the distinctive sort of edges that pertain to places and events. In part two, I compare naturally given and humanly constructed edges, contrasting the edges that emerge in the experience of wilderness with those that surround human beings in their constructed environments (especially gardens and parks but also city streets and neighborhoods) while taking the edges of landscapes as something of a middle term. In part three, I consider the edges of our own bodies, edges that are psychical rather than physical (emphasizing phenomena of falling apart psychologically), and the edges of earth and sky. In following this threefold path, I aim to show how edges pervade our inner as well as our outer lives, and how they arise in the interaction between human beings and what surrounds them: in bodies and minds, things on the earth and sights in the sky. For in truth edges are everywhere: as far we can see and as close as we can touch.

Scattered throughout the book are brief studies of various particular edge circumstances that call for their own treatment. In this vein, I consider such disparate items as cusps and traces, picture frames and veils, while thinking as well about edges in music and an assortment of problematic edges ranging from the edges of cells of solitary confinement to the edge of doom. My aim in these briefer forays—which supplement the main descriptive chapters—is not to cover *every* sort of edge but to do at least minimal justice to the array of edges that impinge on human beings, whether contingently or by internal necessity. For edges abut, enclose, draw down, and open out our lives.

## V

Edges are endemically elusive, quickly disappearing from the very perception that notices them to begin with. In view of this elusiveness, I shall pursue edges in this book by recourse to *peri-phenomenology*, that is, the description of ostensibly peripheral phenomena: *peri-* signifies going "around" or "about" with an element of risk taking. This is the approach I took to the human glance in *The World at a Glance*, a book that is in effect this book's companion. There I attempted to show that glances deliver an entire meshwork of structures that ramify through visual experience of many kinds. Glances open up a world that is apperceived within and beneath the robust perceived world. This is a world in which surprise emerges spontaneously in moments of alert apprehension. In peri-phenomenological investigations, one finds directions out by indirection. By deliberately seeking out the peripheries of thoughts and things, places and events, acts of glancing move into outskirts where the not-yet-apprehended comes to light. The further one goes in this exterocentric direction, the more will glancing be solicited (so as to discern subtle structures) and the more will as yet unnoticed edges and surfaces come to light.

The bond between glances and edges is especially intimate. Edges, as Merleau-Ponty put it, "flay our glances."[1] They call for glances, but they also undo them by showing their limitations and their inherent partiality. For the most part, however, edges and glances collude with each other, often in complicated ways. Each is a creature of the indirect, the eccentric, and the extraneous. This is so even though glances issue from the percipient organism, while edges adhere most saliently to the surfaces of perceived things and to the outer parts of places and the phases of events. As exiguous and evasive, however, glances and edges alike call for concerted peri-phenomenological investigation.

All too often, edges have been considered literally "superficial" features of things and events—contingent structures that possess little if any interest of their own, as if they were mere externalities in comparison with the central substance of things. My aim in this book is to show that, on the contrary, edges are integral to the ongoing experience of the surrounding world and its disparate contents, as well as to the internal worlds of feeling and thought. They are neither expendable nor trivial, as is tempting to assume when we confine them to the task of literally terminating things, places, and events. To put exclusive emphasis on any such purely functional role is to denigrate the intrinsic force of edges, their deeper sense, and their inherent vibrancy.

Edges are much more than the delimited endings of things and events: merely marking where they drop off. Their effects of closure, though undeniably operative, fail to capture the full range of the dynamics of edges. Edges actively shape events as well as places and things and psychical events; they are not just emblems of expiration but open many sorts of things to intricate interactions with their immediate as well as their far surroundings. Taken in their full measure, edges are constituent members of entire place-worlds and whole worlds of thought, each of which possesses temporally as well as spatially specified features. Once brought more fully into the light, edges can be seen as leading denizens of both kinds of world as well as constituents of other worlds—notably of body and psyche, earth and sky—so much so that all these worlds are to be regarded as edge-worlds.

Every world comes to us edged, irremissibly and multifariously so. It comes laced with edges, textured by them. These edges form an armature, an ever-ramifying network, for all that we experience. This book takes its beginning from the acknowledgement of this fact—this fate—from which there is no effective escape. From there it explores the larger significance of edges.

I write this book from my conviction that it is time to bring into our individual and collective lives a fuller consciousness of the dense immanence of the edge-world. I will attempt to awaken this consciousness by bringing edges to our more complete attention—from which a much wider edge-awareness and edge-understanding can emerge. As with imagination and memory, place and glance—topics I have treated in earlier writings—this book aims to restore to edges the concerted attention they deserve.

I finish this book on the very eve of the inauguration of Donald Trump as the forty-fifth president of the United States. As the edge of one political era draws to an end—that of Barack Obama during the last eight years—the edge of another opens. In this moment of transition between two very different political regimes, much is uncertain, much is unknown. Many fear what will happen in the next four years, and for good reason. Whatever does come to pass in times ahead, we can be sure that the profile of the new administration will be palpably different from that of its predecessor. The stakes are high: the well-being of millions of Americans is at risk, and the effects on the larger world (both human and otherwise) hang in the balance. Whatever one's doubts and fears, one can only hope that the edges of people's lives and of the communities to which they belong will not be hardened by the rancor of discrimination and exclusion—that they will not exhibit the rigidity of closed and unyielding borders and will show instead the elasticity and permeability of open boundaries. Even if this does not happen—or does not happen for some time now—we must remember that concerted attention to constrictive edges brings with it one decided gain. Where and when edges harden and sharpen, people gather, resistance is generated, creativity is sparked, and new ways of being with one another emerge.

New York City, January 19, 2017

## Notes

1. Maurice Merleau-Ponty, "The Philosopher and His Shadow," in *Signs*, trans. Richard McCleary (Evanston: Northwestern University Press, 1964), p. 181. I have slightly altered the translation.

# PART 1

# Sorting Out Edges

# Preface to Part One

In part one, I undertake close descriptions of certain basic sorts of edge in order to set forth a nomenclature on which author and reader can converge—which is important in view of the nebulous niche that the term *edge* inhabits in the collective linguistic consciousness of English speakers. In common usage, "edge" signifies such things as "the outermost part of an object" or "the abrupt termination of something"—casual meanings that unduly restrict the idea of edge, leading us to overlook the fact that there is a plurality of edge types, each of which calls for its own description. I take up a number of these in the first chapter of this part and in three interludes; they range from borders to boundaries, rims to margins, gaps to picture frames, cusps to veils. The descriptions I give are designed to convey the diversity of edges that form part of human experience. The interludes, in particular, detail the considerable range of edges that human beings (and other animals) routinely encounter in their respective life-worlds.

A second chapter in this part takes up two pairs of terms: edges and surfaces, and edges and limits. The first pair exhibits a mutual indissociability; just as there is no surface that does not have an edge of some sort,[1] so there is no edge that does not belong to some kind of surface. The second pair, edges and limits, manifest a basic difference in kind despite their being run together in ordinary language. I argue that we need to recognize this difference in kind if we are to do justice to what is uniquely true of edges.

On this clarified basis, the last chapter of this part extends the scope of edges to include edges of places as well as events. Every place has its characteristic edges, beyond which it is no longer that place, or any place at all. The same holds for events; these, too, run out, and they do so in time as well as space: *where* and *when* they come to an end, *there* is their edge. Not only is this extension of edges to places and events descriptively demanded, it has the merit of expanding the scope of what counts as an edge beyond the edges of finite *things*. In this context, I contest the hegemony of things (material substances, reified particulars, res extensa) that has dominated Western metaphysics since Aristotle. Places and events are ontological domains that call for their own accounting and recognition as distinct realms of being. A crucial aspect of this accounting and recognition is that any given place comes with its own edges, without which it wouldn't be *that* place. Similarly, events come edged in certain unique ways that I spell out, emphasizing the temporal parameters of such edges—which is not to deny that the edges of places also have historical depth.

Beyond making crucial peri-phenomenological distinctions, the three chapters and three interludes of this part of the book seek to immerse the reader in edge phenomena. This means gaining a concrete sense of what being an edge is like, and in particular how any given edge both configures and concludes that *of which* it is the edge. By employing close description, I attempt to draw the reader into the *edge-world*: that world in which edges are determinative even if not always conspicuous. This is none other than the very world that human beings and other living things inhabit; it is an intrinsic dimension of their life-world, their place-world. For there is no world that does not come edged in multiplicitous ways. Were edges lacking, there would be no way to determine where one thing or place or event concludes and another starts. And if everything were plenary and undifferentiated—if all were one edgeless mass—there would be no sense of being in a world; indeed, there would be no world at all. It follows that *there is no world without edges and that every world is an edge-world*.

An immense variety of edges goes into constituting the surrounding world, despite a given edge's delimited appearance—an appearance that is in effect a *dis*-appearance. An edge is just where something gives out: a paradox of perishing to which we shall have occasion to return more than once. But what is undeniably slight, being lesser in extent than that which it edges, turns out to have a force and influence of its own.[2] Edges are instances of augmented returns from what is presented or appears as diminutive (as when something begins to give out at its edge). They constitute a variation on what I designated as the Logic of the Less in my earlier study of the glance. According to this logic, what seems to be of minor import is seen, upon closer analysis, to be indispensable to existing in the worlds in which we and other sentient beings dwell.[3]

In becoming oriented in the world we inhabit, we cannot do without edges any more than we can do without our bodies or brains. We could not get anywhere or accomplish anything without them. They are a formative presence in our experiential lives despite their endemic vanishing and their marginal status in virtually every epistemology and ontology in Western systems of thought.

### Notes

1. I say "of some sort" to allow for apparent anomalies such as that found in the Möbius strip, which I discuss in chapter 2.

2. Edges are not always diminutive or slight: certain Constructivist sculptures bristle with edges as the most prominent feature of these works, and border walls constitute one continuous edge. But such exceptions only prove the rule that for the most part edges are recessive and nonconspicuous.

3. See "Concluding Thoughts" in Edward S. Casey, *The World at a Glance*, where I identify several variants of this "Logic of the Less," whereby from the less the more results—often to paradoxical effect. I return to the above formulation in the postlude to the present book, where I argue in detail that it is another way to express what I consider a "heterodox" of the edge-world.

# ONE

# Borders and Boundaries

Boundary (*horos*) is the primary cause of bodies.
—Iamblichus, cited by Simplicius in *Aristotelis Physicorum*
*Libros Quatturo Priores Commentaria*

Borders are clearly demarcated edges that serve to distinguish one place (region, state, territory) from another. An international border, such as the one between the United States and Canada, is an obvious instance, but so is the footprint of a building, the building's precise profile on the ground. The precision of borders— the fact that they can be traced out by a simple line (the "borderline")—is a function of their having a shape regular enough to be describable in geometric terms (as straight, curvilinear, and so on) while also being easily projected (for example, envisioning a given borderline as traversing rugged terrain). Thanks to this dual aspect, the one ideal and the other imaginary, borders often approach a certain formal perfection, as when the founders of a city decide just where the city limits should be. Borders are often the basis of such representations as maps afford: for example, a map of the state of Kansas after its statehood was established in 1861, as it borders on Colorado to the west and Missouri to the east. Cartographic representations make clear that the comparative abstractness of both the imaginary and the ideal dimensions of a border readily invite literal delineation, the exact determination of where public or private lands (or bodies of water) begin and end.

Boundaries, in contrast, resist linearization; they are inherently indeterminate, porous, and often change configuration. This is most easily observed in the case of a bioregion—say, the edge of a desert that alters its exact shape with passing seasons and climate change. But boundaries also characterize human habitations. Where exactly does "southern California" begin and end? How are we to determine the precise extent of New York City's "lower East Side"? Of course, efforts at mapping places and regions, civilized or wild, are made all the time. But most attempts at cartographic representation involve significant simplification of the terrain; the strict borders they depict in the form of continuous lines are an imposition on an indeterminate and often unruly situation on the ground.

A boundary, despite its apparent imperfection vis-à-vis a geometric ideal of perfect linearity, has the advantage of being directly perceptible: it is a literal part of the actual place for which it forms the edge. The place itself can be natural—a desert, a river—or artificial, insofar as it is created, shaped, and reshaped by human beings: such as a planted forest in Utah or a neighborhood in Minneapolis. Either way, the boundary belongs to the place or region as its outer edge. It is an inherent and nondetachable part of it: where the "of" of "part of" is a subjective genitive that signifies *belonging to*.[1] The boundary of the forest or the city neighborhood belongs to the forest or neighborhood, not to what surrounds it. And yet the same boundary also opens outward into other sectors of the landscape or city, being continuous with them rather than closed off from them.

## I

We may usefully contrast border and boundary by recourse to a single example: the Mississippi River. Considered as a natural phenomenon, this river has continually shifting boundaries: it swells and shrinks, depending on the season and the weather. Even when it is comparatively stable, its precise shape is difficult to make out: just where does its outer edge begin or end? When the river is ensconced in its accustomed banks, we can plausibly say that this edge is found in these banks. But the banks themselves alter shape, position, even their entire identity—notoriously so when spring rains cause extensive flooding or hurricanes suddenly raise water levels. Furthermore, in many stretches the banks are barely discernible or have been overlain by wetlands in the form of marshes or floodplains. The latter, which are no less boundaries than are the banks, are still more indefinite in form, and are rarely included in cartographic representations. In their passion for accuracy, such representations prefer the simplicity of continuous single lines, hence the characteristic remove of these representations from the local landscape by the assumption of a bird's eye view far above it. Seen from a sufficient height, even the massive Mississippi increasingly resembles a line drawn in planiform space. But the closer one comes to the river itself, the less likely a strictly linear representation is able to capture its natural coursing and seasonal variability.

I imagine myself floating in the air high above the Mississippi: at first I grasp the river below as a sinuous serpentine line cutting across the surrounding land, making curvilinear incisions into it. Descending slowly in imaginary space, I notice the river broadening, beginning to look like a ribbon on the land. This ribbon continues to augment in diameter as I drift downward toward it; before long, I begin to perceive the outreaches of the river—its winding width, changing shape, and present extent. No longer does it resemble any kind of line, nor can any line claim to adequately represent these boundaries in their intrinsically amorphous edging. By the time my descending body touches down into the river itself, I glimpse the banks directly opposite me at eye level. As I sink into the muddy waters, my body enters the river's flowing mass and I lose track of any definite edge, except for the river's surface glimmering above me as I sink further down into the waters, returning to the surface only when I must come back up for air.

From this brief thought experiment one realizes the futility of representing the edge of an ever-mutating river by a perfectly regular, one-dimensional line. This is not to deny that for various practical purposes, linear representation has its uses: it is economic in means, instantly readable as an image, and it is entirely appropriate to employ in representing a border, joining forces with its inherent geometrism. But it is precisely the indefiniteness of a boundary that resists linear representation and calls for a more appropriate means of indication, one that respects the permeability of natural entities like river banks and marshlands, their immersive (and submersive) powers. Let us not be tempted too quickly to replace the indeterminacy of boundaries with the alluring determinacy of elegantly depictive lines! We should not submit unthinkingly to the hunger for securing "simple location" (in Whitehead's term). Such location is suitable only for a border—as when the Mississippi is considered the legal border between various states (say, Missouri and Illinois); only then does the sparseness of linear representation have a point and a purpose. Otherwise, it is literally out of place.

## II

How, then, do we do justice to the dynamic character of a boundary? We may grant that naturally given contours can, by sufficient abstraction, give rise to regular geometric shapes. In "The Origin of Geometry," Husserl sketches out such a process of geometrization in the land surveys of ancient Egypt. The evolution of proto-Euclidean geometries can be traced from these surveys, which gave bare descriptions of the natural features of rivers and deserts.[2] But this genealogy of geometry does not address the more difficult question of the intrinsic shapefulness of the earth's land and water masses. What forms inhere in them *in their own right*? Husserl himself provides a crucial clue in a passage of *Ideas I*, entitled "Descriptive and Exact Sciences." There, Husserl distinguishes between the demands of exact sciences that involve formal eidetics—such as Euclidean geometry, which employs constructed or projected figures—and genuinely descriptive undertakings such as phenomenology, which must take account of the imperfect and irregular shapes found in ordinary perceptual experience. (Husserl's own examples of the latter are "notched," "umbelliform," "scalloped," and "lens-shaped.") These shapes, asserts Husserl, are *"essentially, rather than accidentally, inexact and consequently* also non-mathematical."[3] In contrast with "ideal" shapes, such as the perfect circle or rectangle, these shapes are inherently "fluid" and "vague,"[4] and can only approach the ideal limits that belong to ideal shapes—and more generally, to ideal essences— "without ever reaching them."[5] Nevertheless, such shapes possess "the firmness and the pure distinguishability of generic concepts."[6] They can be named and described as such in their very indefiniteness. Thus "the vagueness of such concepts, the circumstance that their spheres of application are fluid, does not make them defective."[7] Indeed, "morphological concepts of vague configurational types" are not only grasped directly within sensuous intuition and describable on this basis, but in certain areas of knowledge they are "absolutely indispensable," and in these same areas they are "the only legitimate concepts."[8]

Despite the seeming complexity of Husserl's formulations, his proposal is straightforward when carried over into actual experience. Boundaries, as I have here described them, constitute a domain of experience in which indefinite non-linear shapes are *intrinsic* to the phenomena of this domain, and are thus valid descriptions of these shapes. Rather than being dismissed as degenerate geometric formations, such shapes "must be taken as they are given."[9] They are given precisely as inherent parts of a domain such as "water" or "earth." They belong to such domains and must be included in any adequate description of them, including one that focuses on the visual or tactile forms of the corresponding phenomena.

If it seems counterintuitive to reduce the waters of the Mississippi to a line, this is because the line belongs to one order of things—that of ideal shapes and formal essences—while the river belongs to another order, that of shifting shapes and a "fluid" sphere of application, thus to a domain that is intrinsically and not just contingently vague. *Vague* itself means "wandering or straying," from its primary root in Latin *vagus*, a root that is also the source of *vagrant*; but from its French linguistic cousin, *vague*, wave, it refers to the same elemental water world as does the term "fluid." Indeed, the two etymological sources conjoin, since it is of the very nature of water to wander—to find its way through the places of least resistance, filling up or overflowing whatever shapes these places possess. This indicates that we should respect the vagueness that belongs intrinsically to the landscape world of places and regions, whose edges are boundary-like. Boundaries lack the determinacy of borders, but they act as fully effective edges of and between natural spaces.

## III

In telling contrast, borders lend themselves readily to linear representation, easily submitting to eidetic (literally "formal") analysis of the kind that characterizes the Euclidean era of mathematics. In their distinctness and clear definition, borders are subject to streamlining of the sort we observed when we imagined viewing the Mississippi River from far above, and (even more so) when it is considered the legal border between the states it serves to separate. In this rarified realm, ideal shapes and their associated formal essences have free reign, allowing geometricians and cartographers, real estate agents and politicians, to conspire to one end: to make the demarcation of a border as precise as possible. In pursuit of this common interest, the vague has no effective role to play; indeed, it is considered distracting, so it is characteristically avoided. To make room for vagueness is tantamount to admitting defeat in such diverse but affiliated enterprises as mapmaking, nation building, state making, and the demarcation and sale of property.

The alliance between ancient survey mapping and modern real estate practices is not accidental: in the world of modern Western capitalism, a land survey is
used to determine individual or corporate ownership, as in, for example, "cadastral
maps." The purpose of a cadastral survey, first undertaken by the ancient Romans
and continued in early modern times in England and elsewhere in Europe, was
to represent "the extent, value, and ownership of landed property"—the primary
purpose being to give a basis for taxation per capita. A *cadastre* (the word derives
from *capitum*, head, as in "per capita") is a survey map of a region on a scale "sufficiently large to show accurately the extent and measurement of every field and
other plot of land."[10] To this end, exact linear representation is clearly of great advantage, given the comparative clarity and simplicity of continuous lines. A cadastre is in effect nothing but a congeries of such lines, almost all of them straight.
These lines trace out shapes that are geometrically regular in the manner of rectangles and squares. The state sometimes prescribes such regular geometricity as
such—notably in the fateful 1785 Land Survey of the United States directed by
Thomas Jefferson. In this case, new counties in the just-opened territories of the
Middle West, starting with Ohio, were divided into perfect squares—unless a river
or other natural feature got in the way and a compromise had to be made, as was
often the case.[11]

Or take a map of an entire region, such as the mid-nineteenth-century "Carta
Geográfica del Estado Chihuahua," showing the "northern portion" of the state
of Chihuhua as well as the "southern boundary of New Mexico." (See Figure 2.)

The two primary portions (*partidos*) of this map show mountains (the Sierra
de la Burros, the Mogallon), lakes (Langusing de Guzman, Laguna de Santa Maria),
a water source (Ojo de Vaca), and several rivers (Río de Gila, Río Grande del Norte,
Río Mimbres, Río Pecos). In addition, there are names of cities or towns (Ysleta,
Paso, Robledo) and of the overall represented regions (Partido de Galeana, Partido del Paso, the two northernmost parts of Chihuahua). These topographical
features and named places and regions are indicated in various linear patterns—
ciliated foot lines at the base of the mountains, double lines for the Río Grande del
Norte and the Río Pecos, wavy lines for the two lakes. In the case of the Río Mimbres, a single broken but regularly curving line suggests that the trajectory of this
river was not fully known at the time. In contrast with these variously configured
linear patterns, all of which curve and bend to some degree, there are several perfectly straight lines: most eminently, the southern border of what was then New
Mexico, perfectly horizontal but broken into a series of dots; and three continuous
parallel lines of latitude along with four continuous meridians of longitude, each
marked by the exact degree it embodies. These eight lines create a grid, a framing
device (reinforced by a rectangular margin, painted yellow, around the entire map).
It is by means of the grid, *in terms of it*, that the various topographical entities and

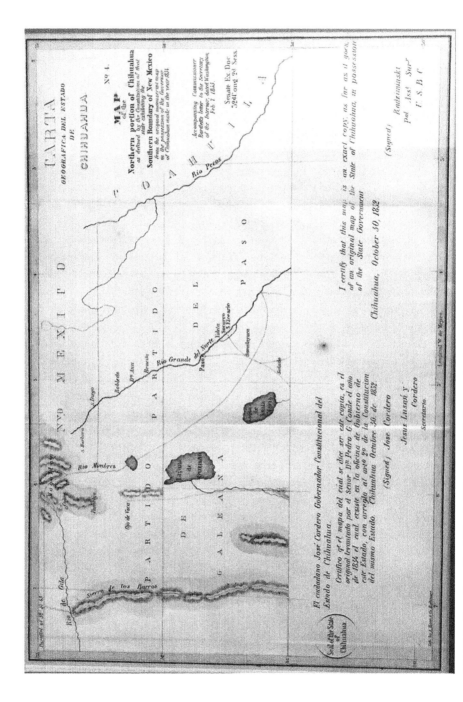

FIGURE 2. *Carta Geográfica del Estado Chihuahua* (1852). From author's collection.

places and regional names ("toponyms") manifest themselves—as if through a transparent cartographic window onto their geographical reality.

In effect, the Carta Geográfica del Estado de Chihuahua of 1852 presents to us three kinds of cartographic content: the state-sanctioned, historically delimited southern limit of New Mexico in relation to the two northern Mexican provinces; the location of a number of cities; and various landscape features rendered through several representational conventions. The first content reflects its historical and official origins by means of the perfect rectitude of the line that depicts the border; the second is a matter of pinpointed loci to which the place and regional names are attached; the third retains an element of topographical specificity, especially in the case of the iconic images of rivers, mountains, and lakes. The map as a whole has four main compositional elements, two imagistic and two verbal: on the one hand, a literal borderline and various boundaries of natural phenomena (mountains, rivers, lakes); on the other hand, toponyms (not only of cities but of entire regions, provinces, and states) and various descriptive words. For example, the title and contents of the map in the upper-right-hand corner, along with statements by representatives of the two respective governments below the central image, both attest to the validity of the map as an "exact copy, as far as it goes," of an original map first created in 1834 but certified (and presumably updated) in this version of 1852.[12]

I give this rather detailed analysis of diverse compositional factors not only to indicate how complex even a comparatively simple map can be at the level of representational means: the pictorial and the symbolic, image and word all commingling to one end.[13] More important for our purposes is another mixture: that of border and boundary within one and the same layout. Borders are present here in several formats—most conspicuously, the New Mexico border presented in a horizontal dotted line, but also the borderlines at stake in the lines of latitude and longitude. Each of these is traced in a perfectly straight line—a line that, in the case of the intersecting meridians and parallels, makes up regular rectangles. Boundaries, in contrast, are depicted by icons that morph the character of the local landscape, whether in following out the contours of rivers or the profiles of mountains or the peculiar shapes of lakes. Variations in mode of representation are permitted, indeed encouraged: broader rivers are represented by parallel curving lines, the height of mesas is indicated by quasi-parallel foot lines at the base of a flattened top area. The area around the map presents another kind of boundary, a margin that is an integral part of the map's overall presentation.

Two basic points emerge from this brief analysis of the Carta Geográfica del Estado de Chihuahua. First, boundaries, although nonlinear in their alliance with natural features, can be *represented* by linear means—where "represented" means literally *given representation*, as if delegated to do so (as we speak of a "representative" in Congress). In this map the linearity is softened in the case of the mountains by the addition of a pale blue watercolor wash over and around them (not visible in the figure), as if to say that linear representation, though necessary, is not sufficient in their case, and indeed can be misleading.

Second, borders and boundaries, despite their differences, can be copresent in the same cartographic space. In this space, they realize a certain complicity. But they do so precisely, and only, to the extent that each is represented (designated as well as delegated) in that space. Borders and boundaries coexist in a common medium of representation thanks to their differential deployment of linearity, a linearity that is as integral and pronounced in the case of borders as it is subdued and secondary when it comes to boundaries.[14]

We see much the same mixture of borders and boundaries in the case of intrinsically ambiguous entities such as frontiers and territories and borderlands: each of these exists in relation to an existing border, yet each is boundary-like by virtue of its mutability and its close bonding with natural features.

Frontiers are comparable to margins in being bands at the edge of exploration and expansion; in their continual relocation, they are changing entities that assume the very shape of the landscape they at once delimit and occupy. Frontiers present themselves as being open-ended, and in this respect as boundary-like, especially in the direction of their outward movement. But in their varying historical avatars, frontiers make at least implicit reference to already existing borders, those away from which a given frontier is moving.[15]

In contrast, territories are fully contained by their outer edges. Even so, they are located outside better known and longer-established regions. They are not fully developed and are typically not yet fully mapped, being filled with uncharted boundary phenomena. In the American usage of the term, territories have not yet attained statehood, as in the case of the Kansas-Nebraska Territory in the 1850s: a territory that in becoming two separate states after 1860 entailed establishing fixed borders for each, including one contiguous border.

Borderlands are open regions that are complex combinations of an exactly determined existing border (around which they cluster) with the informality and imprecision of a natural boundary.[16] They resemble peripheries, which are more or less indefinite marginal areas that make at least covert reference to the geometric precision of perimeters (themselves constituting a species of border).[17] But a borderland is a cultural as well as a geographical entity. It is a place—often two places on either side of a border—that house whole populations; for example, the borderlands that have grown up around the United States–Mexico border and that offer distinctive mixtures of Mexican and American ways of life that vary in keeping with their location along this border.

It becomes evident that borders and boundaries each come in multiple forms, some of which combine features of both, including linear representations of several sorts. Between "border" and "boundary," construed as polar terms, there are many intermediate edge situations—an indefinite plurality of them. Borders can incorporate boundaries into their constitution, as happens with the Río Grande del Norte in the case of the United States–Mexico border. By the same token, certain boundary situations incorporate reference to borders—as we have just seen in the case of borderlands, which are arrayed on both sides of a given border.

## IV

Borders and boundaries are major ways in which we encounter the edges that surround places and regions (sometimes within them, too). This is why I am devoting most of an entire chapter to their description. They are complementary in relation to each other; borders serve to delimit and to define, whereas boundaries act to ground, to receive, and to open. Borders are literally aporetic ("without opening") insofar as they are posited as continuous and lacking gaps. Not surprisingly, they are typically linear in conception and representation. Boundaries are only linear as represented in maps; they surround parts of the earth, water, and other substances (animal bodies, manufactured goods, even thoughts), acting as their permeable outer edge. Boundaries are porous and vulnerable, changing size and shape with time and circumstance, hence their characteristically indefinite form: they are literally *amorphic* ("without-form"). Despite these basic differences, boundaries and borders both remain forms of containment: each acts to enclose a place or region—a theme to which we shall return in chapter 4. This reflects the fact that most edges are *enclosive*; this includes frames, margins, territories, peripheries, perimeters, and rims—all of which act equally, but differently, to contain that of which they are the edge. On the other hand, gaps, rills, ridges, folds, creases, frontiers, borderlands, thresholds, and verges *disenclose*; they emerge on the surfaces of those things or places where they appear, giving figural form to these same surfaces. Borders close in and close off; boundaries open up and open out.

Cutting across borders and boundaries, as well as other kinds of edge, is a very different kind of distinction: functionality versus decoration. Some edges are esteemed mainly for their utilitarian value, such as rims of tires, gutters on roofs (another kind of rim), frontiers, and verges that lead us to a determinate thing or place. Others are prized mainly as embellishment: decorative picture frames, wainscoting around a dining room wall, folds that enhance a fabric's presentation. Sometimes the two concerns come together in one set of edges: for example, in the colorfully painted rim of a porcelain plate, the ornamented margins of a medieval manuscript, the threshold of a temple or other sacred space.

Borders are almost always instrumental in character. Their effectiveness often depends on how well they are demarcated or recognized, enforced or patrolled, depicted or misrepresented—all of which draw on instrumentalist criteria. Boundaries, in contrast, resist reduction to practical usages; for the most part, they are inherent features of already existing phenomena, natural or cultural, and as such lend themselves to a diversity of employments, only some of which are practical while others are aesthetic, as when we admire the horizon as the sun sets. Borders are artifacts of explicit human designs, individual or collective; they are imposed structures, whereas boundaries emerge from what is already given, whether this is the edge of an open plain or of a neighborhood long in the making.

## V

Borders and boundaries possess a special force and power. They are not only useful—borders in a more focused way than boundaries—but they also often act to determine entire histories: personal, institutional, regional, even global. This is so despite the abstractness of borders (their status as imagined or ideal) and the indefiniteness of boundaries. These features, basic as they are, pale before the deep and lasting effects of both sorts of edge: effects that can shape the destinies of whole peoples, as in the case of walls that exclude immigrants—or in the "water wars" that characterize an era of increasing water scarcity, when issues of real estate and land use, as well as state borders, are often at stake. The very intransigence and intransitivity of borders—their status as *instituted*—along with their resistance to easy alteration act as a forceful historical determinant. Beyond any explicit intention of keeping historical events strictly delimited, borders give rise to an ever-broadening wake. Part of this wake includes the rigors of having to cope with their presence (for example, the necessity of dealing with the border fences erected recently in eastern Europe to exclude people fleeing from Syria) and part of it from an accumulating history of the subtle effects of a given border on many concrete aspects of ongoing life (as, for instance, the mixture of ethnic and national populations that come to reside on the opposite sides of a given border, such as East and West Germans before 1989, or Palestinians and Israelis since 1967).

Boundaries spawn their own momentous aftermaths, and they do so despite their intrinsic porosity and vagueness. Rather than being a mark of weakness, these very qualities may become a source of strength—a strength no longer of resistance or exclusion but of conveyance and facilitation. Boundaries allow, and sometimes abet, movements across or through them that might not otherwise be possible. This has been the role of the Río Grande del Norte in the case of the United States–Mexico border: its protean, shape-shifting character (thus its character as a boundary) aids in crossing the border itself at certain times of year (when it runs dry in summer, it can be directly traversed on foot). In remote regions of China, the Great

Wall fell prey over time to bushes and trees that could be used to scale it, in effect turning that famous border into a boundary that gave access instead of preventing it.[18] In each of these cases, what was at first an exclusionary border situation gave way to boundary states that offered modes of passage through them.

Other kinds of edges may also have significant deferred effects, especially if their scale is large enough; for example, the Pacific Rim has influenced trade and travel, colonization and migration throughout the history of human inhabitation and exploration. But in contrast with borders and boundaries—which at any scale give rise to expansive effects—such sequelae are comparatively exceptional. At a more modest scale, the impact is largely limited to the immediate circumstances of which they are part: my writing on a particular table in my favorite cafe, for example, or the frame around the Braque still life I most admire in the Metropolitan Museum, or the cut over which I place a bandage. Nothing comparable to an entire *Wirkungsgeschichte* ("history of effects," "effective history") is to be found in their case. This is just what we might expect in view of such edges being constituent parts of actual physical objects—thus being part of a determinate and delimited materiality that does not obtain for borders and boundaries, whose effects often exceed their status as ideal or material respectively. This exceeding takes the form of a widening wake in the course of the history to which they give rise and in which they come to figure as integral components.

## VI

Edges occur in a number of different forms and possess distinct purposes. Sometimes edges are quite regular, such as the circular rim of an aluminum can or a perfectly rectangular painting frame; sometimes they are very irregular, as with a gash in the flesh or a bomb crater. Sometimes, however, edges display a combination of intentionally perfected form and casually imperfect shape. Certain earth works are conspicuous instances of this latter kind of hybridity. *Spiral Jetty* (1970) by Robert Smithson, for example, has for its central design an elegant spiral form, but this form is rendered dense by the fact that the Jetty itself is made of crushed stones, with the result that its actual edge is uneven and far from perfectly geometrical, as any visitor can attest.

Though created wholly from rough rock and set out into the Great Salt Lake, *Spiral Jetty* is not only a natural-cum-geometric entity, but is also informed by a cosmological vision on the part of its creator. As Smithson writes, "Following the spiral steps [of the Jetty] we return to our origins. . . . [In this work] the prehistoric meets the posthistoric."[19] Here we witness a fusion of the cultural with the natural, not wholly unlike what we have noted in the Geographical Map of the State of Chihuahua. In Smithson's celebrated earthwork both dimensions are basic to its construction—indeed, to its very conception and our understanding of it.

FIGURE 3.  Robert Smithson, *Spiral Jetty* (1970). © Holt-Smithson Foundation/Licensed by VAGA, New York. Photo George Steinmetz. Courtesy Dia Art Foundation, New York.

We shall return to the interaction of the cultural with the natural in chapters 5 and 6. My concern here is with something different: the power of edges to influence the character and structure of what lies far beyond their physical extent—not only what is beyond their immediate context but also what lies much farther afield. Smithson's work inspired an entire movement, that of "earth art" (or alternately "land art"), which far exceeds the literal dimensions of the *Spiral Jetty* itself but for which this work has become iconic.

The effects of edges go both ways: not only outward into the wider world but also inward into the very things or events or places they circumscribe. They are inherently constitutive of that of which they are the edges by a movement of implicit ingression from the surfaces they configure into the very inner being of what lies beneath the surface, whether this be a metal can, in the case of a perfectly circular rim, or an entire mountainous area that has manifestly irregular edges. Even short of such inwardizing influence, edges possess a special power to reflect what is interior from their very exterior positions, suggesting what is within from their situatedness without. The edges of the waves that I observe rolling onto the beach on which I stand adumbrate the deeper patterns of underwater currents that I cannot literally see but that I infer to be lurking there. The wrinkles of my friend's face tell me something about the life he has led—how stressful it has been or how exposed to the sun he was in his daily work. "Reading faces" often consists of looking closely at physiognomies and seeing a life history etched in the edges displayed on faces. These edges, which are outer boundaries of the face, are uniquely expressive of that history: they contain it by condensation, as it were.

I am certainly not maintaining that edges determine all that is distinctive in what they qualify, whether in the form of a sequel or in the interiority of a given thing, event, or place. Critically formative as edges are, they have their own limits of influence. Other things are equally and sometimes more determinative: for example, the kind of matter of which something is composed. The rocks and earth that make up the main mass of mountains have a force and being of their own— as do the crushed rocks from which Smithson created *Spiral Jetty*. Nevertheless, I recognize the same mountains by their characteristic profile, and I savor Smithson's masterpiece thanks to the helix formed by its spiraling edges.

## VII

Borders and boundaries, along with frontiers and borderlands and territories, all belong to the *real*, whether the real in its ideality (borders as cartographic projections, perimeters as forming perfect circles and squares), the historically constituted (borders as established by treaties), the materially real (things and places), or composites of nature and culture (as in the case of frontiers, territories, and borderlands).

In view of their unrefusable reality, it would be a mistake to imagine that edges depend for their existence on our interaction with them. We must not be tempted by any subjective idealism in their case, as if by looking at or touching them we bring them into being. Such basic sensory actions as these (along with hearing, given that we can hear edges of sound) enliven, open, and explore what delineates the near and far side of surfaces: they bring us to the edges of things, places, and events. They go right up to them by attending to the surfaces of which they are the edges and activating their presence. The senses animate and enhance certain edge-bearing phenomena, as when my eye traces out the contour of the lamp before me. They help to set forth such phenomena, putting their inner and outer edges into sensuous relief. In these ways and others, they alter their character as experienced. But they do not bring these edges into existence, nor can they banish them from existence, either.

In the end, edges are the endings of whatever lies around and under them, the endings of what *is there*, even if it is just barely beyond me (as with the edges of the table on which I am writing) or even if it is located within me (as when I think certain thoughts having characteristic contours). Edges are not merely literally there (*einfach da*, as Husserl liked to say), nor do they exist exclusively as determinate matter, nor are they there only as the outermost parts of something (for they can be part of their inner structure, as we see with folds and creases). Edges are arrayed and disposed in complex and nuanced ways that painters often strive to capture, as did Cézanne in his still lifes, which emphasize the outlines of things along with their colorifically qualified in-lines. Edges are indeed *there*: they are out there and in there. We attest to this whenever we say of a thing or situation, "there are edges here." The *"there are"* of this last expression is an ontological operator that affirms not just that certain things exist in space and time, but also that they *are*, they *have being*. This is to say that *there are edges* insofar as there are also things and places and events, including events of thought whose edges mark the moment and take the measure.

Edges, then, are not things or events or places, but integral parts of all of these these—components of them, constituent parts. As the German language would put it, *es gibt Rande* ("there *are* edges")—however much we may interact with them by complicating and decorating them, specifying and signaling them, using them or abusing them. If our intervention alters them, it alters *them*. There is a stubborn realism of the edge that is the other side of its very evasiveness, its resistance to being pinned down or being declared simply located as just here, just there. An edge not only drops off into a void; it *trails off*—departing from its own surface but also from our perception of it—even as it evinces the dense matter of the events, things, and places of which it is the edge.

A given edge is not only *"for-us* an *in-itself"* in Merleau-Ponty's formula.[20] It is also something *with-us*: at our level, congeneric with our lived body and our living thought. As Merleau-Ponty also says, "[I] follow *with my eyes* the movements and contours of the things themselves . . ."[21] The withness of my body—to which thinkers as diverse as Hume and Whitehead and Nancy have attested—consists in my witnessing of the edges of things in the midst of their motion or stability. Such witnessing is a form of serious play: playing with things at the end of our look or touch or hearing. Such play, which is equivalent to apperceptual work, is to be considered a form of "deep play."[22]

But the matter is more complex than meets the eye (or hand or ear). It is certainly not one-way—just a being of things with us or us with them. It is both at once: two-way, a matter of intimate *interbeing*. My edges meet up with yours as well as with the edges of things or events; and your edges, along with those of things and events, meet up with mine. The outer edges of my body, in particular of my eyes and hands and ears, rejoin those of the denizens of the visual and tactile and audible world. Not surprisingly so, if indeed my flesh belongs integrally to what Merleau-Ponty calls "the flesh of the world."[23] The environing world is composed of conjunctures that connect bodies and things, places and events, peoples and animals, across hollows and divergences. Among these conjunctures, edges are especially prominent members, being found at (and often *as*) "the joints of the opaque body and the opaque world [where] there is a ray of generality and light."[24] As exemplary instances of these joints, edges offer inroads into that of which they are the edges.

Every edge is in effect double-jointed. At the most abstract geometric level, an edge is an angle formed by the meeting of two lines or surfaces at a common point. Because the angle thus formed may be regarded as convex in the case of edges (concave in the case of corners), room is made for the insertion of the edge into more encompassing wholes composed of things, places, and events that have their own edges—finally, into the entire circumstance to which the edge belongs and to which it brings its distinctive presence. Moreover, that into which a given edge is inserted can embrace it back: as when I stretch out my arms to put them around a friend walking toward me whose arms are already reaching out toward me.

An edge asks to be embraced, if not by my whole body, then by my eyes or hands (and sometimes my ears). What matters is less the exact form of the engagement than the fact that there is connectivity between edge and lived body— that they become complicit (literally, "folded together"). In such engagement, the contribution of each is approximately the same or at least mutually fitting, belying claims that one is more real than or prior to the other. There is an edge-to-edge interaction among equally real corporealities that ex-tend to each other—that come right up to the thresholds formed by each other's edges. The result of this reciprocal (even if not perfectly symmetrical) interaction is a *mysterium coniunctionis*, a mystery to the extent that the engaged entities are often of very different kinds—human and nonhuman, human and animal, human and inanimate—and not only a pair of human beings in each other's familiar company. For this reason, the deepest shared structure is not that of *Mitsein*, "being-with others," as per Heidegger's early anthropocentric assessment. Nor is it only the bodily being-with to which I pointed just above. It is a more profound *with* or *co-* that obtains between members of widely different regional identities: tables and chairs, cabbages and kings, myself with a person of another gender, animals of different species. This with-structure assembles and connects diverse beings across, and in, their very differences.

"The *co-* defines the unity and uniqueness of what is, in general."[25] This is Jean-Luc Nancy's formulation of what is axiomatic in the situation to which edges lead us. The edge-world is a world of co-presences: a plenary world in which edges, rather than taking us into abyssal depths (as early modern models of empty space would encourage us to think), become complicitous in acts of spontaneous apprehension. Such acts animate and alleviate the surrounding world, which does not consist in material plenitude alone. "Presence is impossible except as co-presence," adds Nancy.[26]

Of primary significance is the deeply intertangled co-presences that characterizes the entire edge-world, not only in the form of borders and boundaries but also in the formats of all the other edges under discussion in this book. Such co-presence characterizes the circumstance in which edges meet, our own along with those of virtually everything we encounter. They meet in a distinctive with-world, an interplace of edges. To be in this world is to be in its embrace and to embrace it in turn. Not merely successively but *all at once*. This last phrase, which Aquinas reserves for God's knowledge of the created world "all at once" (*totum simul*), and Husserl for the absolute flux of inner time-consciousness, which operates "simultaneously" (*zugleich*), should be extended to the place-world as coinhabited by edges and the sensuous bodies that coexist with them. In this world, what matters most happens all at once—in the moment, at the place, in the event where these edges and bodies coinhere. It is there that generality and light are to be found—thanks to an illuminative ray that moves from eye to edge and back again—and there, too, that a transfer between hand and edge emerges in a transaction of touching that is the haptic parallel of this ray.[27]

## VIII

Not only do we glance at edges—a topic I treat further in chapter 9—we also gaze at them. This is especially true of perceiving border walls, which call for the more prolonged looking that belongs to gazing. Standing at La Frontera in Nogales, I can be so overwhelmed by the sheer height of the walls, topped with fierce barbed wire, that I find myself staring off into space as a reaction to the formidable obstacle posed by the wall. Consulting a map that represents this same border situation, I find myself scrutinizing the cartographic image that sets it forth: an abstraction from the intense reality of the landscape before me. Both of these responses—looking away, scrutinizing—count more as gazes than glances in their profound differences.[28] Of course, I could also glance in either instance. If I were seeking to scale the wall, I would glance around to see if border guards were in my vicinity or if surveillance cameras were trained on me, and am likely to forego looking at a map given the high risk of the situation.

In many less urgent circumstances, a bare glance at edges will do. I glance casually at the familiar edges of my car as I enter it or at the curbs of the street through which I drive. Only if there is a conspicuous ambiguity—is that a dog about to race across the same street?—do I take the time to scrutinize the edges of what confronts me. But if I dwell overmuch on the content of a centrated look, I am likely to miss more subtle details of what is before me: say, another automobile that is just pulling out from the side of the street. To catch this, a quick glance may suffice.[29]

Many edges escape our active attention and remain unthematized in our everyday dealings with them. But in truth we cannot afford to overlook them, since their presence may be quite definitive, telling us what is now happening or about to come and informing us about what is dangerous or detrimental at the time: a bleeding wound, the crumbling edge of a precipice on which I stand, the sharpened edge of a knife in the hands of an angry and disturbed person. Called for here is a special edge-alertness whose ally is the discerning glance.

## IX

A final question: how are we to relate borders and boundaries to various other edges such as rims, thresholds, and frames? Given the considerable range of borders and boundaries, do they not merge, or at least overlap, with these other sorts of edges? Are not many rims forms of border, or at least very border-like? Do not many frames serve as borders for the paintings they surround? And are not thresholds often boundary-like? The natural groupings of these various kinds of edges—and others still to be discussed in interlude I—suggest a more complex circumstance than my treatment of borders and boundaries in this opening chapter has allowed us to envision. In particular, is there not an affinity between certain sorts of edges? And if the affinity is in fact substantial, we cannot assume that the edges under discussion in this book as a whole exist in splendid isolation from each other.

The question is not just one of taxonomy—a matter of sheer nominalism, a game of names. Instead, it is a question of essential kinds, *eidé*—not formal kinds located in a separate Platonic heaven, but concrete patterns that are consistently repeated and instantiated in the actually experienced world. Such patterns constitute *material kinds*, being sorts of things that the natural world contains and proffers—and that culture incorporates, complicates, and sublimates. The fact is that edges as we experience them fall into these kinds. Moreover, even though edges often appear in a spatial configuration, they have a temporal character as well: as ephemeral or as long lasting. They are in time just as they are in space.

This bears out Plato's contention in the *Timaeus* that space (*chôra*) stands outside being (the realm of *eidé* or forms) and becoming (the domain of generation). For Plato, space is a matter of necessity (*ananké*), and in this assertion he takes a first step toward recognizing that space has its own intrinsic structures, its characteristic ways of existing and presenting itself. But these ways are not only spatial but temporal as well. Edges, regarded as belonging to the realm of *chôra*, are not static. For *chôra* is the matrix or receptacle of becoming. It instantiates both space and time regarded as fundamental cosmic parameters.

Plato offers a second, even more valuable clue to understanding edges as embodying eidetic kinds: in the eidetic realm itself, the forms of things mix with each other. As he insists in the *Sophist*, the "great kinds" of things such as existence, sameness, difference, rest, and motion, combine significantly and yet without confusion between them.[30] One thing can be the same as something else in certain respects, yet differ from it in other regards, and it can fully exist throughout the simultaneous exhibition of such relations of sameness and difference. A given thing, despite having very disparate formal properties, does not thereby lose its identity. This identity (what it *is*) is complicated but not compromised by the copresence of several great kinds in its determination.

Plato's model of combinative forms is directly relevant to the circumstance of edges. Various kinds of edge (and I emphasize *kinds*) can coexist equably within a single concrete instance, whether that instance is a material thing or a particular place or even a singular event. These types of edges, however different they may be in genesis or structure (and thus in descriptions of the sort I shall be giving) are compatible with each other—borders with rims, boundaries with frames and thresholds, and so on. Still more radically, features of one kind of edge may qualify an edge that, regarded by itself, belongs to a different kind: thus there are rims (normally crisply regular) that are boundary-like in some respects (as with the ragged edges of North Rim of the Grand Canyon), just as there are thresholds that are border-like (insofar as they are critical turning-points) and frames that serve as borders (as with simple metallic frames of paintings). It is difficult to deny such overlapping or even merging of edge types, and nothing is compromised by doing so; indeed, there is every reason to acknowledge it outright.[31]

We not only can but also *must* acknowledge the intertanglement of the various kinds of edge that I have identified; for it is thanks to their interweaving that a given edge is rarely reducible to being a transparent exhibition of a preexisting type, as if this edge exemplified just this one type. For purposes of simplification, it may be convenient to proceed as if this were the case—and I do so myself at several points in this book. But in descriptive fact, the matter is more complex and more interesting. To admit this is not to descend into descriptive taxonomic chaos; it is to discern an abiding order in the midst of complexity. Even as embodying several sorts of edge, a given edge will as a rule exemplify one primary or most salient form of edge. In the case of the Berlin Wall, for example, we recognize it as marking a strict border between East and West Germany, even though its surfaces became boundary-like when they were employed for lively protest art prior to 1989. The North Rim is similarly understood as the northern terminus of the Grand Canyon, yet in actual physical and perceptual fact it is nothing like a strict container. It is only rarely that we can remain with a single pristine level or kind of determination. We must be prepared to recognize an interplay of edge types in any given event or thing or place. For with virtually all edges we are addressing a plurality of recognizable shapes and intrinsic powers that constitute a dense scene of topomorphic possibilities. In this pluriform scene, no single edge or set of edges can claim a privileged status—not even those I have designated in this chapter as "borders" and "boundaries," despite the extensive applicability and broad presence of these latter in the unfolding of human experience.

Any particular edge we encounter exhibits the active coinherence of several different kinds of edges, and this coingredience goes deeper than mere surface resemblance would suggest. Not that such intertwining of kinds is peculiar to edges alone. Commixtures of kinds obtain for many other sorts of things, ranging from automobiles to butterfly reserves, from single skiffs to entire seascapes: each of which is irremissibly multiplex in its eidetic analysis. But edges exemplify this intertwining in an especially compelling way, and they do so whether they are edges of places or things or events.

## Notes

1. I have in mind the contrast between *Moment* (inherent part) and *Stück* (discrete piece). See Edmund Husserl, *Logical Investigations*, III, "The Logic of Wholes and Parts." We shall have occasion to return to this nomenclature later in this book.

2. See Edmund Husserl, "The Origin of Geometry," appendix to *The Crisis of European Sciences and Transcendental Phenomenology*, trans. David Carr (Evanston, IL: Northwestern University Press, 1970).

3. Husserl, *Ideas Pertaining to a Pure Phenomenology and to a Phenomenological Philosophy; First Book: General Introduction to a Pure Phenomenology*, trans. F. Kersten (Hague: Nijhoff, 1982), p. 166 (italics in original). Such shapes, appearing spontaneously in perceptual consciousness, lack a "genuine mathematical manifold" that would allow their mathematization (p. 165). For further discussion, especially concerning the claim that only a "mathematically definite manifold" allows for formal-logical axiomatization, see section 72, "Eidetic Sciences: Concrete, Abstract, 'Mathematical.'" Strictly speaking, only formal (e.g., Euclidean) geometry and arithmetic count as mathematical sciences for Husserl. Phenomenological description can attain "eidetic" yet never strictly mathematical status: "phenomenological eidetics" must be contrasted with "mathematical eidetics." (On this latter contrast, see section 71, "The Problem of the Possibility of a Descriptive Eidetics of Mental Processes." See also sections 12, 15, 16.)

4. Ibid.

5. Ibid., p. 167.

6. Ibid. Most of these words are in italics.

7. Ibid., p. 166; "vagueness" is italicized.

8. Ibid. "Morphological concepts" is italicized in the original. Note that phenomenology as a descriptive eidetic discipline is precisely a case in point. One part of Husserl's otherwise remarkably clarifying claim has to be qualified, namely that the "morphological concepts of vague configurational types" are "nonmathematical." This would be true only if we restrict the mathematical to the purely arithmetic or the rigorously geometric (e.g., to Euclidean geometry). This restriction was respected by Husserl, true to the mathematics of his day. (Concerning this restriction, see *Ideas, Book One*, sections 71–74.) I shall invoke morphological concepts at several points later in this book, especially in my discussion of vagueness in "A Last Lesson," part 4.

9. Ibid.

10. Both entries under "cadastral" in the *Oxford English Dictionary*, edition of 1971.

11. For further discussion, see the chapter "Rectangularity and Truth," in my *Representing Place: Landscape Painting and Maps* (Minneapolis: University of Minnesota Press, 2005).

12. The conjoint attestation is a backward gesture: why would a map made almost twenty years earlier require legitimation at this later point? In between was the settling of the American-Mexican border in the wake of the bloody war of 1848. There is no direct trace of this war as such in the map, but one can speculate that an affirmation of the southern New Mexico border was called for in 1852, when the two representatives of their respective countries met in Chihuahua and together signed this document, which is said to have accompanied Commissioner Bartlett's letter of 1853 to the Secretary of the Interior. The dotted character of this border—on which I comment further just below—may indicate that it was newly established after the Mexican-American war. In any case, it is at once a state and a national border, given its position in cartographic-geographic space. For further discussion of the United States–Mexico border situation, especially with an eye to issues of immigration, see Edward S. Casey and Mary Watkins, *Up Against the Wall: Re-Imagining the U.S.–Mexico Border* (Austin: University of Texas Press, 2014).

13. For a more complete discussion of these means, see Casey, *Representing Place: Landscape Painting and Maps*, chapter 7, "First Considerations."

14. Words also join borders and boundaries in the same project insofar as they are written or printed. They possess their own kind of linearity, that which constitutes individual letters and words but which is also implicitly present in the invisible horizontal line that subtends a given word or phrase employed in the map.

15. On frontiers, see the excellent description in Katherine Bradford's dissertation from Pacifica Graduate Institute, "Creating Mythic Frontiers: A Cultural and Depth Psychological Analysis" (2006).

16. On borderlands, see Jerome S. Bernstein's book, *Living in the Borderland: The Evolution of Consciousness and the Challenge of Healing Trauma* (New York: Routledge, 2005). See also the imaginative extension of the same term to include spaces of political change and psychical renewal in the work of Gloria Anzaldúa, *Borderlands/La Frontera: The New Mestiza*, 3rd ed. (San Francisco: Aunt Lute Books, 2007), and the further extension of Anzaldúa's reading of borderlands to the situation in Eastern Europe in Julia Sushytska, "What is Eastern Europe? A Philosophical Approach," in *Philosophy, Society, and the Cunning of History in Eastern Europe*, ed. C. Badatan (New York: Routledge, 2012).

17. Unlike a brink or verge (which is always on *this* side of an area), a periphery is on the far or later side. In contrast with a frontier or a territory, it clings to that side, being just beyond it. In these respects, it is closely comparable to a fringe.

18. On the complex fate of the Great Wall, see Arthur Waldron, *The Great Wall of China: From History to Myth* (Cambridge: Cambridge University Press, 1990). Indeed, it is questionable whether the Great Wall was ever the intact, formidable, single entity one hears about in superficial histories of China. John Hay has this to say about the very conception and structure of the Great Wall: "The period of most intense wall building was in the late sixteenth and early seventeenth centuries in the late Ming, when the north was increasingly

threatened by the nomads. Even then, the so-called 'Great Wall' was an erratically developing scheme involving several related walls—and certainly not symbolic of any nationhood" (Hay's introduction, in John Hay, ed., *Boundaries in China* [London: Reaktion Books, 1994], p. 12).

19. Robert Smithson, "The Spiral Jetty," in Smithson, *The Collected Writings*, ed. J. Flam (Berkeley: University of California Press, 1996), pp. 148 and 151.

20. This phrase is first formulated in Merleau-Ponty's *Phenomenology of Perception*, trans. Donald Landes (New York: Routledge, 2012), p. 74: "we must rediscover the origin of the object at the very core of our experience, we must describe the appearance of being, and we must come to understand how, paradoxically, there is *for-us* an *in-itself*" (his italics).

21. Merleau-Ponty, *The Visible and the Invisible*, trans. Alphonso Lingis (Evanston, IL: Northwestern University Press, 1968), p. 146; my italics.

22. See Diane Ackerman, *Deep Play* (New York: Vintage, 1999), especially p. 16: "Thrown free of one's normal self [in deep play], a person stands in another place, on the limits of body, society, and reason."

23. On the flesh of the world, see Merleau-Ponty, *The Visible and the Invisible*, pp. 248ff.

24. Ibid., p. 146. On "junctures," see p. 153. Concerning folds, hollows, divergences (*écarts*), see chapter 4, "The Chiasm."

25. Jean-Luc Nancy, *Being Singular Plural*, trans. Robert D. Richardson and Anne E. O'Byrne (Stanford: Stanford University Press, 2000), p. 39. See also his statement that "the with is strictly contemporaneous with all existence, as it is with all thinking" (p. 41).

26. Ibid., p. 62. Such co-presence is "neither a presence withdrawn into absence nor a presence *in* itself or *for* itself" (p. 40). If this is true, we must abandon the Hegelian and Sartrean categories of *in itself* and *for itself*, thing and consciousness. The *coniunctio* is so profound that even this very basic metaphysical difference no longer obtains, or, if it does, only in the compound format of an *in-itself for-itself*.

27. On visual rays, see Casey, *The World at a Glance*, chapters 5 and 7. There is an acoustic equivalent: from edge of sound to ear and back again.

28. See Casey, *The World at a Glance*, especially the afterword, "Glancing vs. Gazing."

29. For this reason, I have argued for an active alliance between glancing and *apperception*—not construed in Leibniz's or Kant's sense of self-conscious awareness at a transcendental level but as literal "ap-perception," (i.e., perception *at* a primary perception) thus at its fringes. See ibid., pp. 476–79. I return to this theme in part 4 below.

30. See Plato, *Sophist* 254 b–d; on the "mixing" (*methexis*) of existence, sameness, and difference, see *Timaeus*, 35a–c.

31. Eugene Gendlin has helped me to see more clearly the way in which eidetic or typological distinctions, far from being final or absolute, may harbor possibilities of commixture. In his example, a rim not only rounds off or terminates a physical thing but may also open onto a larger environment much as a boundary often does (conversation of April 1, 2008, Spring Valley, New York). A classical instance of this is found in Wallace Stevens's poem "A Jar in Tennessee," in which a single glass jar on a Tennessee hill opens onto an entire world surrounding it.

# A Panoply of Edges

> You learn the most by watching the edges.
> —Inuit saying

> It turns out that the closer you look at the edges of things the more
> they mimic the incredible diversity apparent without magnification.
> —Paul Shepard, *Coming Home to the Pleistocene*

In this first interlude, I offer descriptions of edges frequently encountered in everyday life. Characterizing a broad range of our experience, they provide useful contrasts with each other, being closely related yet structurally very different. Rims, for example, are paradigmatic outer edges, while gaps emphasize the spaces that open up between preexisting edges while having their own edges. Folds and creases are representative of passively given edges, typically found in something preexisting, whereas margins are instances of edges that are at once active (in structuring our perception of what they surround) and yet highly ambiguous in status upon closer examination. In such cases and others, we are presented with an array of distinctions suggesting that edges are as various as they are elusive.

Let me assure the reader that my strategy at this early point is not to describe every significant species of edge, nor is it to give a complete description of each of the edges here discussed. I instead single out certain salient and exemplary types of edge—leading instances, as it were. With these in mind, the reader can extrapolate to other forms in which edges exist.

Some edges are more conspicuous than others. Among the most prominent are brinks and precipices: for instance, the promontory at Morro Bay from which I looked far down into the Pacific Ocean. It was as if the central California coast had become one enormous high edge—to which I had no choice but to cling. Other kinds of edges are less dramatic but still deeply influential in our lives. We do not have to search for them—*they find us out* thanks to a certain orienting and governing force they possess on their own: the edges of the room I was in this morning, the edges of the road along which I now drive, the edges of the beach I shall soon come to. Still other edges are more reclusive and need to be coaxed into the daylight of fully manifest presence. I shall start by describing several such comparatively inconspicuous edges.

# I

*Folds* and *creases* are edges that have a broadened or flattened shape. Instead of being etched sharply, as are precipices or brinks or rims, they are more or less smooth in their configuration. They typically characterize fabrics and textiles, and like the latter, they tend to be flat or gently rounded (whereas paper edges are often more acute). Moreover, they are found *in the midst of* such materials, as is indicated by expressions such as "a fold in" or a "crease in"—where the *in* signifies being contained within something more encompassing like a tablecloth or bedspread. Just as these latter are stretched out *over* something, such as a table or a bed—or, in the case of a curtain drape, *down* from a curtain rod—so creases and folds reflect the same basic directionalities that characterize the materials that include them. The folds in curtains are vertical; those in a table cover lie flat. Each runs in the direction to which the material in which it inheres is itself disposed. A crease or a fold is in effect an *inner edge* that is a feature and function of the material in which it is visible to the eye or palpable to the hand. It obtrudes from this material or intrudes into it, however slightly. (Were it to obtrude too abruptly, it would no longer be perceived as a fold or crease but as a freestanding structure.)

*Margins* and *verges* are characteristically broader and flatter than folds or creases; and, in contrast with these, they are not situated in the midst of their material base but alongside it. Thus they are not inner but outer edges. Each kind of edge lies in an outlying area that flanks a primary thing or event or place. A margin lies *around* a more or less central region—on virtually any side of it and often surrounding it (as in the case of a margin on a printed page). In this respect, it is like a perimeter but not constricted to a linear format. A verge (like a brink or threshold) is located *before* such a region: at (or as) its point of physical or visual entry. We go *from* a verge into something else; hence we say "being on the verge of . . . ," that is, being about to do something, to get underway, to happen. In contrast, we go *into* a margin from that of which it is the margin. (Similarly, we proceed from a center into a fringe; but a fringe is normally narrower than a margin. It is a more fully peripheral presence.) If a verge is frankly preliminary and tends to vanish as soon we pass through it, a margin is ongoing; it stays there—every time we open a book, every time we look into the edge of the perceptual field (as Husserl first insisted).[1] Like brinks, verges belong mainly to a temporal process of being-about-to-do X or Y—while margins are primarily spatial entities: they are there-around. (Closely related are fringes and precipices, which are also mainly spatial.)

The various edge phenomena I have just described contrast starkly with *rims*. Whereas folds and creases, margins and verges are characteristically spread out—distended, as it were, albeit in distinctively different ways—rims possess a certain intensity and economy. A fold or margin is pliable in its extent or shape and often seems to have a life of its own in relation to its underlying material (as with the many creases that occur in the surface of a paper bag,[2] or with the considerable variability in page margins). A rim is much more tightly bound up with its physical bearer. It conveys the sense of being just what it is, without needing to be a scrap more, of going this far and no farther, extending just to its very edge and as that edge itself. For this reason, a rim is often representable by a line, the paradigm of economy in the realm of the represented. Like a line, it is located in a definite portion of its material substrate, in the very outermost part; indeed, it *is* that outermost part. A rim is the very externality of something, the place where it comes to a definite end, while remaining nonetheless continuous with that *of which* it is the rim. (There are no inner rims, strictly speaking. The rim of a pencil holder inside a computer bag remains the outer rim of that holder.)

Familiar examples include the rims of ordinary physical objects (like the outer edge of a mirror or a frying pan) or places (the rim of a swimming pool, a low-lying wall that marks the outer edge of a public park, or the North Rim of the Grand Canyon). Each of these embodies the three criteria I have just invoked: their rims are located in an exterior position vis-à-vis the rest of the thing or place; they inhere in it, being an intrinsic part of its physical or spatial being; and each serves as the very point where it comes to an end, being its effective terminus. It follows that none of these rims is added onto the thing or place, as if it were a mere supplement. Each is ultimate in the sense that no other edge lies beyond it: the rim is nothing but the outer edge that it is.

The shape of a given rim is integral to the identity of the place or thing for which it serves as a rim.[3] This shape serves as the determinative form of the material that makes up a given thing or place. As Dominic Lavoie laconically puts it, a rim is an edge that "arises only from presence"[4]—that is, from the intimate com-presence of its shape with the material substance it delimits. Each of these dimensions, the formal and the material, calls for the other, and their collaboration results in a configuration that has the distinction of being an edge that is unique to the entity it qualifies. A rim clings tightly to its thing or place; it concludes that very thing or place.

In terminating the materiality of something, a rim almost always does so as surrounding an *opening*. It is double-edged: it is the edge of a thing or a place as well as that of an empty space—and both at once. The rim belongs equally to a material particular and to an empty space within that particular (where such emptiness can take several forms: for example, an empty can, a hole, or a puncture in a surface).

Consider another example: the entrance to a mineshaft, which is located where the surface of the earth has been broken open in order to excavate down into its depth. The entrance's rim not only determines the shape of the opening, it is also where the opening begins, just as it is also where the shaft inside ends. In either case, empty space is configured by this rim: on the one hand, the inner space of the shaft; on the other, the open space of land and sky. This same rim, even if not marked as such, is an edge where the mine shaft and earth's surface and the sky above conjoin. The simpler its structure, the more effectively does it provide this conjunction: were there to be too much complexity of structure at the mine's entrance, the very being of the rim would be compromised. This suggests that for rims that serve a practical purpose—and most rims do just this, with the exception of decorative rims—the less elaborate their shape the better.

Contrast such a rim with the rills and ridges that are found within the same mine shaft. These configure the walls and ceiling of the mine, whether by natural formation (the very character of the rock, mineral, and earth inside the mine) or by the effects of mining itself (the blasting and digging that create many mine shafts from within). These forms are noticeable to the hand or eye, as is the opening of the mine itself. But they characterize the internal surfaces of the mine and not its external entrance. In this respect, they are closely akin to creases and folds: all three are located in the midst of a material medium, and thus count as inner edges, unlike the rim of the entrance, which is a resolutely outer edge. But, like lamellae in a desert, and in contrast with fabricated things like textiles and paper, rills and ridges inhere mainly in parts of the natural world. In the case of a mine-shaft, they accrue to the ceiling and walls of an excavated cavity. Like ribs in a vertebrate body, they enclose but do not terminate; they are features of the cave's internal space, being located around miners as if protecting them (or sometimes, as in a mine collapse, endangering them). Although they encircle the mineshaft as excavated in the earth, they do not open onto the larger landscape of earth and sky: this happens only at (and as) the opening's rim. In other words, the walls and ceiling of the mine surround but do not terminate. They offer circumambience, albeit of a partial nature. (Complete circumambience is realized only in a situation without egress, as in a submarine or airplane that, when in motion, can have no open external apertures.[5])

A rim like that at the mineshaft's opening marks the moment of exit from the walled-in circumstance that is found inside the mine. The opening's rim signals that the internal surface of strict enclosure, "circumclosure," we might call it, has reached termination, the point where "dis-closure" begins—where an enclosed internal space gives way to a space exposed to another element or medium (sky and earth in the case of the mine shaft; various forms of soil or rock or water in other cases, as when a deep cleft in the bottom of the ocean gives onto open watery depths that are distinguishable from the closed-in depths found in the cleft itself).

Also operative in this circumstance is a peculiar *turning*, which is effected by the way internal rims (made up of ridges and rills within the shaft) give way to an external rim (embodied in the cave's entrance): a diversion of direction as it were (from in/around to up/out) or, equally, a conversion of function (from holding in to leading out). This diversion/conversion is two-way: as when we imagine going into the mine shaft, thus transitioning from being outside to being inside—in contrast to coming out once again. The edges proffered by the pertinent surfaces are indifferent to which direction of movement is actively pursued; neither direction is intrinsically favored, much less required. Reversibility of in/out obtains, as when miners enter and leave the same shaft at shift changes in the day or night.

Turning of some sort is always happening where rims are at stake. For miners at work, the walls regarded as internal rims *turn around* them at a certain angle of enclosure; when leaving work by the shaft's opening, these same workers experience the same walls as *turning out* toward the world of air and sky—and, by further implication, toward the domestic home-place to which they will return after their labors. At the same time, there is a *turning away* from one modality of edging to another: a literal deflection outward upon exiting—or else a turning inward in returning to work, thanks again to the inherent bidirectionality of the circumstance. These two modalities often meet in an area of transition from one to the other—an area that may be so subtle as to pass unnoticed, yet is sensed tacitly in the bodies of those who work in the mine, for instance, when miners going into the shaft for a new work shift pass by the weary bodies of those coming out.

It is evident that rims serve to structure entire work worlds. But they figure into many other contexts as well: eating (most utensils possess rims), drinking (every glass has a rim), and in erotic play. Indeed, in the latter case, "rimming" is the name of a particular practice. It refers to a form of erotism often considered taboo—touching and circling the outer edge of the other's anus with one's tongue. It is as if the rectum here plays the role of an erotized shaft that goes deep into the interior of the lived body, just as a mine shaft delves into the earth. Both are unillumined by natural light; both enter into the entrails (of the human body, of the earth); both are considered "dirty." Yet one belongs to work, the other to sexual foreplay.

Freud said famously that happiness is to be found in *Lieben und Arbeiten*, and it is perhaps not altogether surprising that love and work both maintain close relationships to rims, especially those that serve as openings.[6] In each, openings are experienced as thresholds: either as the entry/exit from the workplace (not only in the case of mines but also of factories and offices), or as a highly sensitive area of mucous membrane that is an exciting fillip to eroticism (not only anal but also genital and buccal). But where employees look forward to leaving the place of work at the end of the day or night, lovers enjoy entering (or being entered into) through each other's bodily orifices from their outer edges—and lingering there for a while. In the case of work, one enters and leaves the established and socially sanctioned workplace through its outer edge (entrance to the mine, the door to the office, and so on). In making love, one plays on and around fleshy edges as gateways to corporeal depths—whether of the anus, vagina, penis, or mouth. In every instance, a rim of some significant sort is in play, and a considerable part of erotic pleasure (as well as satisfaction in work) consists in experiencing a rim as a threshold to be crossed and savored in the crossing itself.[7]

## II

Let us next consider *gaps*. These take many forms, from mere rips, rifts, and ruptures to fissures, holds, and entire abysses. But every gap, whatever its exact character, is interruptive: it breaks open what would otherwise be a smooth surface or a continuous transition between surfaces, and it often does so in a jarring manner—unanticipated, calling for a renegotiation of our expectations. Even if not unbridgeable, a gap is unbridged at the moment in which we encounter it: it "gapes open," as we say.

Bridged or not, vast or tiny, natural or artificial, every gap comes edged. This much is evident. More difficult to grasp is the fact that every gap *is itself an edge or set of edges*; indeed, it creates new edges where none existed before. This latter claim complicates our usual opinion that a gap as such is nothing, a nonentity, just a bit of empty or open space. But a gap functions as formative of edges for that which surrounds it as well as having its own edge structure. Indeed, its very nonsubstantiality is what makes this double edging possible. If I am walking in the countryside and suddenly come across a deep hole in the earth—a hole that opens into the earth and disappears into limbo—I am suddenly stopped in my tracks. The hole, though a spatial vacuity, acts as an obstacle in my path, blocking my direct forward progress.[8] It presents itself as a break in the securely traversable land on which I am walking, giving to it an interruptive edge that it does not possess as a continuous stretch of earth. All the while the hole itself has an edge of its own: this is where it comes to assume the shape it has for my perception of it.

The edge of a gap contrasts with that afforded by a rim. Whereas a rim is typically a continuous, unbroken contour—think of the rim of a teacup and the saucer on which it is placed—the edge provided by a gap is a creature of discontinuity: it is entirely a function of a chasm, a discontinuity in an otherwise continuous surface. If the saucer on which I place my cup is broken, the pieces into which it falls now have gaps between them. These gaps serve as spaces between the separate pieces, which have their own edges—these latter remain rims, each belonging to a separate broken part. Yet beyond the generation of these new edges are those of the spaces between the broken pieces. In another parlance, these latter would be called the edges of "negative space," that is, the edges of a spatial interval or void that has its own integrity and presence. A gap is just such an interval or void that induces new edges for things that, broken or not, possess edges. The gap has its own edges: those of the space between the broken pieces. Thanks to its interruptive character, a gap creates a new species of edge: an edge of the space that now opens between parts of a thing formerly intact. (The same obtains for a place, as when an earthquake opens a gap in the formerly continuous surface of the earth.)

The edges of a gap are characteristically irregular—rough, ragged, jagged. The adjective "gappy" refers to the unevenness of a gap's edge, an edge whose irregularity is part of its very identity. The irregularity of a gap's edges suggests something awkward or odd, "out of line," "out of kilter." This is why we often presume that a gap has been forcefully or violently formed: skewed, torn open, wrenched out of shape. To be filled with gaps disappoints any expectation of plenary presence. It suggests that something untoward is being presented to us—as when Freud refers to memories that have been forcefully bowdlerized by calling them "gappy" (*lückenhaftig*, "full of gaps," *Lücken*). The irregularity of a gap's edges underscores this untowardness, whether it arises as pathological effects in the psyche construed as "smooth mind,"[9] or as wounds to the body (as in "gaping wounds").

A gap, physical or otherwise, consists both in its own irregular edges and in the edges it induces for that which it has rendered discontinuous by its separative action. These two kinds of edge, one irregular and the other discontinuous, merge in the experience of a given gap: to trace the edges of this gap is to trace both the edges of that which it serves to separate as well as the negative space it creates. But the two sorts of edge remain distinguishable, since the former belong to the gap itself and the latter to that which surrounds it. Together, they constitute a holey space that is an affront to the ideal of a seamless whole—a whole without a break or gap. A gap is like a rent in the fabric of a sheer surface that would have been undisturbed without its intervention. It resembles a defiant gesture that undercuts the flow of time as well as the continuity of space; I pause in my walking before the hole in the ground, and I have to go out of my way to get around it. The gaping space and uneven edges of the hole undercut the rhythm of my walking and undermine its continuity. (This is not to deny that in other contexts gaps exhibit creative potential, as in Heidegger's notion of the "rift design" [*der Riss*] that is the fissure where "earth" and "world" configurate in their very differences.[10])

In short, while a rim is nothing but an edge of some particular thing (and doubtless for this reason rims are often taken to be paradigmatic edges), a gap is both *edged* and *edging*. It is the former as constituted by its own uneven edges and the latter as bringing about a new edgeful configuration for that which is interrupted by the gap itself. This difference does not mean that there cannot be gaps in rims—as in an archipelago of discrete islands that form part of an oceanic rim (such as the Pacific Rim) or in a bicycle wheel that has been broken apart. Such hybrid cases only demonstrate that gaps as a class of edges collude with a broad diversity of different edge phenomena, including rims. In this respect, rims are more restricted than gaps, since rims obtain mainly for physical things and actual places (for which they serve as the unique outer edges), while gaps exist between things and places as well as within them.[11]

## III

Lest we get lost in the details of close description, let me here distinguish between *active* and *passive* edges. Active edges are dynamic in that they refuse to stay within prescribed limits and instead forge their own path. A striking instance of such edges is found in the evolving edges that reflect the interests and practices of a given person or group of persons—say, the way that I establish my own "turf" in East Harlem as a salesman setting up my route in view of potential customers; or the way that Puerto Rican culture burgeons in the same region, spreading from block to block, as one bodega opens, then another. In neither case is there a strict preexisting limit that I can or must observe; as salesman, I try to "penetrate," indeed to create, "new markets." If I am an ordinary resident of East Harlem, I join my neighbors in preferring to shop at certain bodegas that are congenial to my tastes (or that suit my pocketbook) and are located in a certain area of town whose own perimeter is not strictly determined (who can say exactly where East Harlem begins or ends?). Thus my actions as a salesman or an ordinary shopper generate ever-altering edges in this part of Harlem, as in many densely inhabited places. These edges reflect my habitual actions—my characteristic ways of moving through local space. But they are also occasions for change as they change their exact location over time. They are the indeterminate perimeters of my proximal life-world.

It is a very different situation when I respect existing edges, taking them as established or given, neither questioning them nor pushing them back. Here the edges are what they are—and where they are—by virtue of a history or a tradition that has set them down as such. Thus the edges of Central Park, first established in the early 1860s, have not moved since that time and are unlikely to budge in the future. In my nomenclature (as discussed in chapter 1), these edges are "borders" rather than boundaries, and as such they resist modification: standing before them, we are encouraged to be comparatively passive, to take them as already there.

Much the same difference is found in the contrast between rims and gaps. Almost all rims are constituted from already given materials: they come to us as inherent parts of a given thing (my favorite coffee cup) or the surrounding landscape (the rim of the mesa in Billings, Montana, the upper surface of which serves as the runway of the local airport). Rarely do I seek to alter a rim—unless I am a ceramicist in the process of making a pot, or an earth artist altering the shape of a natural formation in the landscape. For the most part, I take rims for granted: I accept them as they are given to me in their manifest form and function.

In the case of gaps, however, the situation is different. Even if some gaps are edged in ways that make them virtually permanent (such as the edges of the high cliffs in Yosemite Valley, or a crack in the ground opened up by an earthquake in Point Reyes, California), in other cases I am called to make a difference to them: to put a patch on a torn sweater, or to sew up a surgical wound. In the case of the patch, I cover up the gap in the fabric by stitching the patch over the edges that define the tear itself. In the second case, the edges of the surgical wound are encouraged to merge over the wound in the process of healing. Both instances suggest that the edges of gaps share with boundaries a capacity for significant alteration in character and constitution. Indeed, we noted already that gaps themselves actively constitute new edges for the things that they force apart; they contribute edges to these things—edges that are defined by the negative space that has opened up in their midst.

Rims are border-like in their comparatively fixed character—as the material embodiment of edges that are determinate in several important respects—while gaps possess edges that are more likely to be boundary-like in their protean proclivity for changing shape and size in accordance with the interests and intentions of human and other animal beings, and in their capacity for adding edges to the situations of which they are part, thanks to the expansive action of negative space. Given this difference, we can say that while rims are mainly passive presences, gaps serve as active or transformative forces.

It follows, further, that folds and creases are to be considered passive edges insofar as they are the direct expression of the fabric or other material of which they are made and whose configuration they model. The same is true for rills and ridges, which are strictly bound to the physical substrate that they configure. These two facts contribute to the basic assumption that most edges are either inherent in given things and situations, or have come to settle there—if not forever, then for the foreseeable future. This fits with our spontaneous tendency to say that edges serve to define, in whole or in part, that of which they are the edges—where I am taking "define" in the literal sense of providing the terminus or end (*finis*) of someone or something.[12]

Despite their formal and functional differences, the various edges treated in this first interlude contribute to the edgework that is essential to the formation and presentation of things, places, and events. Such edges work and play at the extremities so as to bring what is centrally presented—as image, scene, happening—into an identifiable format: something we recognize and with which we can interact effectively. Edges of many sorts help to make the surrounding world accessible and intelligible even as they complicate it. They help make it into an edge-world, the coherent core of every life-world.

I have here described a small set of edges with varying degrees of attention. These include folds, creases, rims, gaps, verges, and margins. Where the first five are located primarily in the physical world and are features of that world, margins are decisively shaped by cultural constraints—as are frames, which we shall examine in interlude III. But each of these different sorts of edge can be analyzed in terms of its comparatively active vs. passive aspects; these aspects cut across them all, though rarely in exactly the same way.

All such differences are telling: they indicate that edges are highly various in basic kind, characteristic shape, and overall function. The edge-world is essentially multifarious, refusing to be reduced to just one kind of constituent. Edges are not just everywhere, their roles vary decisively from one situation to another. They are at once creatures of unique circumstances while helping to make these circumstances what they are.

## Notes

1. For further analysis of verge, with special attention to its deeper philosophical implications, see the chapter titled "On the Verge" in John Sallis, *On the Verge* (Chicago: University of Chicago Press, 2007).

2. The complexity of such creases is brought home when one attempts to make a careful drawing of the creases on an ordinary paper bag: an instructive exercise that formed part of Josef Albers's legendary course in drawing at the Yale School of Art and Architecture in the 1950s, which I attended as an art student.

3. There are no rims of events, which may terminate abruptly but not in a separately identifiable outer edge that would be the equivalent of a rim. This applies to aural events, which have boundaries but not rims in the strict sense I am here discerning. On aural spaces, see the obituary story about Max Neuhaus, the environmental composer who created special sound environments in public spaces( e.g., at Times Square). Neuhaus is quoted as saying that "the sound creates a space for itself with definite boundaries" ("Max Neuhaus, Who Made Aural Artwork, Dies at 69," *New York Times*, February 9, 2009).

4. Dominique Lavoie, "The Fecundity of the Impossible: Phenomenology at the Edge," unpublished essay of 2001, Graduate Program, New School for Social Research, p. 9.

5. No wonder experiences of claustrophobia arise just here, in enclosures to which one is involuntarily confined. I return to this situation in a discussion of solitary confinement in the epilogue.

6. If lips of all kinds are considered rims, lovemaking can be seen as continual rimming: from kissing to oral sex performed on a woman to anal rimming for both sexes.

7. It remains a striking fact that "rimming" describes, strictly speaking, only one form of erotic play. But this gerund appears to be the only circumstance in which the English noun "rim" has been actively verbalized, as if to reflect the fact that this activity is positively valorized in its audacity of behavior and its comparative rarity.

8. For a thorough discussion of the topology of holes, see Robert Casati and Achille Varzi, *Holes and Other Superficialities* (Cambridge, MA: MIT Press, 1994).

9. I take the term "smooth mind" from Western Apache lore. See the discussion of smooth mind by Keith Basso in *Wisdom Sits in Places: Landscape and Language Among the Western Apache* (Albuquerque: University of New Mexico Press, 1996), pp. 130–34, 136, 138–39. I return to smooth mind in this sense of the term in the afterword/foreword.

10. Heidegger distinguishes his sense of rift from that of a mere "cleft": where the latter merely divides, a rift "carries the opponents [i.e., earth and world] into the source of their unity . . . it brings the opposition of measure and boundary into their common outline. . . . The rift-design is the drawing together, into a unity, of sketch and basic design, breach and outline" (Martin Heidegger, "The Origin of the Work of Art," in *Poetry, Language, Thought,* ed. and trans. Albert Hofstadter [New York: Harper, 1971], p. 63). Conceived thus, the rift gives rise to "figure" and thus to truth in art: "The strife that is brought into the rift and thus set back into the earth and thus fixed in place is *figure, shape, Gestalt.* [It is a matter of] truth's being fixed in place in the figure" (p. 64, italics in original). In my nomenclature, cleft and rift are two modes of gap—the one regarded as merely literal, the other as realizing a creative potential within what is otherwise a sheer break in the continuity of a given surface.

11. The direction of this last paragraph, including the example of a broken bicycle wheel, arises from a suggestion of Andres Colapinto.

12. On the complications of *finis*, especially as applied to one's own death regarded as a final boundary of life, see Jacques Derrida, *Aporias: Dying—Awaiting (One Another At) the "Limits of Truth,"* trans. Thomas Dutoit (Stanford: Stanford University Press, 1993), especially part 1.

# TWO

# Edges and Surfaces, Edges and Limits

It is time to discuss two parameters that are basic to edges of every kind. The first parameter concerns the relationship between edges and surfaces; the second bears on the difference between edges and limits. The fact is that most edges inhere in surfaces of some kind, even if we rarely pause to understand how they do so. And we tend to think that edges are some kind of limit, without reflecting on what this means. Each of these relationships is complex and requires our attention.

## I

In addressing the relation between edges and surfaces, two preliminary observations are in order. First, it is a very rare surface that has no edge. An exception is the surface of a perfect sphere, which never comes to an end, much less to an abrupt edge.[1] Even a Möbius strip, which sports a single surface on which a self-connecting line can be traced without crossing over any edge, is composed of a continuous band having its own discernible edges. Second, it is difficult to find—or even to imagine—an edge that is not the edge of some surface or that does not have a surface attached to it somehow: as, for instance, the rim of an aluminum can, whose cylindrical outer surface terminates with this rim as an upper edge. This holds true for all physically realized edges, which we tend to regard as paradigmatic in this context as in so many others. This does not require, however, that the surface be even or smooth; this is certainly not the case with the horizon, an edge that hovers over a variegated landscape seen in the distance.

Why this bond between surface and edge? Two remarks are in order. First, unless they are infinite in extent, surfaces need to end somewhere. Where they end, just there is their edge. This edge marks the very place where the surface comes to a halt. Ordinary examples abound. The surface of the table on which I now write ends in a circular edge that defines and closes off this surface; the sidewalk just outside the café in which I am writing comes to an abrupt end in the curb that is the effective edge of its flat concrete surface.

Second, edges have to be the edges *of something*. If two primary such somethings are (physical) things and (landscape) places, it is noteworthy that both of these possess surfaces. Indeed, they occur *as* surfaces. We would not know them or have access to them if they did not present themselves in and through the appearing of their surfaces. To claim that something is appearing to us, yet has no surface by which it presents itself, is in effect to talk of a nonthing or nonplace: its status can only be that of a noumenon—a being of mind or spirit—that has no phenomenal manifestation. To be a perceived *phenomenon* at all is to have a finite surface we can grasp by our senses. And (again with the exception of a sphere) to have such a surface is to have to have an edge that terminates it, closes it off.

More generally, we can say that surfaces serve as the crucial third term or mediating factor between things and places and their respective edges. (I leave aside the situation occasioned by events.) Phenomenal or presentational surfaces act to convey such things and places to our notice, bringing them under our look or to our touch. This suggests a triadic, hierarchical structure something like the one shown below.

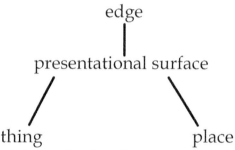

FIGURE 4. Edge in relation to surface, thing, place.

This bare schema embodies a general rule: *just as there is no finite thing or place without an edge, so there is no edge except that of some surface.* A double embedding is at play—not only this:

edges > surfaces > things/places

but also this:

things/places > surfaces > edges

## II

What is a surface such that it can have edges? What are edges such that they are the edges of surfaces? To address these questions, let us consider surface and edge in more detail.

*Surface.* We rarely pause to consider what a surface is, thinking of it as an in-different feature of physical things (sometimes of land or sea as well). I shall take it to be the locus of a thing's or place's presentation: where (and for the most part as) it appears. It is that part of things, including land- and waterscapes, where inherent or transitory sensory qualities come forward to meet our glance or gaze or touch. We have access to these qualities through our sensoria, which are aware of surfaces during all waking hours—so efficiently so that we rarely pause to scrutinize a given surface in order to know what color, texture, or gloss it has. In a glance or with one stroke of our fingers, we know just how brittle or rough it is, how resilient, or how refractive of sunlight.

A given surface is always of finite extent, and with rare exceptions it is open to our spontaneous apprehension or concerted inspection. (The exceptions concern buried surfaces such as tectonic plates or those found in long-closed mines.) Indeed, the surface is just where, within its given limits, something or someplace is *open to perception*—thus also where it is maximally exposed. Things and places *show themselves through their surfaces*. As manifestational, a surface is a source of knowledge about that of which it is the surface—knowledge that is an indispensable clue to the nature of the thing or place it covers. But the very same surface is a point of vulnerability: its manifestness can be its undoing, as when prolonged exposure to the sun causes melanoma in human skin.

A first general rule of surfaces, then, is this: *their being resides in their appearing*. But no appearing goes on forever, neither in time nor in space. Not if time and space are finite as experienced—necessarily so, as Kant first argued rigorously. (Their putative infinity, of theological provenance, became a scientific construct, whether in Newtonian physics or in special relativity theory—in which "spacetime" is held to be infinite.) This is to say that there is no appearing of a surface that goes on forever in its literal extent: the surface of a perfect sphere doesn't end, but it is certainly finite in the space it occupies. A surface does not continue indefinitely, not if it figures into human experience. If I am standing under the hull of the ocean liner *Queen Elizabeth II*, I take in its metallic surface in one continuous arc, seemingly without end. But only seemingly; if I retreat further back on the dock on the Hudson River, I soon realize that this massive surface tapers off at the prow that is pointed into the heart of Manhattan to the east. And if I were to stay transfixed in my looking at this same sweep of surface, no matter how patient I might be, there will come a moment when I must leave the scene. Even Andy Warhol's film of the Empire State Building as seen from a single point, interminable as it seems to the viewer, breaks off after eight hours and five minutes. The surface of this iconic building, elevated in space as it is, comes to an end in a top story, and its presentation in the temporal medium of film cannot go on without concluding at some point, even if the film itself were to be viewed repeatedly.

A paradigmatic case of the finite spatiotemporal closure of a surface is that of our own body. Its surface is provided by the skin, which is continuous insofar as it wraps around the mass of muscles and tendons, bones and ligaments. The skin does not terminate abruptly, yet it is notably finite—having just the extent of the living body for which it furnishes such a snugly fitting container: it is a "boundary" in the sense explored in chapter 1. Yet it is not perfectly smooth: it harbors several orifices, into which the skin ingresses without ever breaking off completely, except in cases of cuts and open wounds, "gaps" in my nomenclature. (Even these possess their own species of minimal continuity: there is never a complete break in the sack of the skin, not even in amputation.) My body, being mortal, is enfleshed by a surface that lasts little longer than I survive as a living organism and does not extend any further than the body mass it encloses. Being thus finite in two basic dimensions, my body's skin comes edged, or let us say *scalloped*. (For more on the body's surface, see chapter 8).

What, then, is a surface such that it can have edges? My short answer is that its phenomenal appearing requires edges as accomplishing its finitude in space and time.

We must also ask: What are edges such that they are the edges of surfaces? What enables them to be the closing acts of the appearing of any surface, whether this be the surface of my diminutive body or that of the enormous *Queen Elizabeth II*? Edges are structured—whether by design or contingently—in ways that allow them to bring a surface to a stop, whether gently or abruptly. This happens by their intervening to shape that surface in a way that alters the character of the surface itself: if not by terminating it, then by changing its directionality and texture. For example, the edge of a city street constitutes an interruption of its given surface, either by marking the end of the pavement or by interposing a curb. Either way, an effective edge breaks up the horizontal plane of the street, bringing it to an effective end.

There is no fixed upper or lower limit to the degree of deviation in a surface that is required for an edge to intervene upon that surface: much depends on the materials that make up the surface, on conventions of construction (in the case of manmade surfaces) or configuration (as these shape the surfaces of landscape), or even on my own perceptual sensitivity (such as how alert I may be at a given time). Depending on which of these factors (or their combination) is paramount in a given circumstance, edges of certain distinct types emerge that act to close down or close off a given surface. Those effective for the *Queen Elizabeth II* diverge markedly from those of the pier at which she is docked; the sleek contours of the former contrast with the rough rectangularity of the latter. Yet each is appropriate for the overt purpose of the physical thing whose surfaces it bounds, and in this case also for their interrelation. In other cases, there is a manifest disparity in the conjunction of edges that belong to different surfaces that have no shared function or common destination: each seems to possess a separate destiny or trajectory. When the same ocean liner passes the Statue of Liberty on an outgoing voyage to

England, for example, the edges and surfaces of the ship and those of the monument pass each other by in their very differences.

As with the ocean liner, its pier, and the Statue of Liberty, many edges have to be quite rigid if they are to be part of the functionality of the thing or place that they edge. But they do need to *configure* somehow with the surfaces of these things or places: they have to fit the figure or shape of the surface and, in particular, to collaborate with it in bringing it to closure—as we see in the graceful edges that round off a ship's hull that facilitate movement through deep waters with their fitful edges. If they act against the interests of the thing or place, they are rebarbative and threaten to undermine these interests. In that case, they fail to configure themselves with the surface in question: they do not fit the surface in such a way as to bring it decisively to its end state as surface—as that very surface. The latter calls for a certain kind and form of edge, depending on the character and constitution of the surface itself; in fact, it is required if it is to come to an end, as it must at some point, given its finitude of spatial and temporal spread. Edges must be such that they allow this spread to diminish and cease. Thus they enable it to end as that particular surface with its unique material properties (its tensile strength, resistance, specific gravity, and so on). They must take account of these properties if they are to perform as efficacious edges, just as they must also take account of the environment or medium in which the surface they edge is to function.[2]

In short—a surface is something whose inherent delimitation in space and time is marked by the edges that realize its closure; and edges, for their part, must possess a pertinent configuration such that when they are conjoined to a given surface they can act to close it off effectively.

## III

The relationship between surface and edge also has to be considered in the form of two propositions that extend the preceding analysis in a direction very different from more formal ways of discussing the relationship, such as that of J. J. Gibson, who states that a surface is "a set of faces meeting at dihedral angles, that is, edges and corners."[3]

The first proposition is as follows: *The edge is all but the shadow of the surface.* By this I do not mean the literal shadow cast by an object. Rather, I refer figuratively to a "shadow" of anything that is cast forward (or backward) that is indissociable from the original object. Shadowlike is the fact that wherever the surface goes, the edge goes with it: just as my own visual shadow in sunlight follows me in every step I take. Here, I am proposing that we conceive of the edge as that into which the surface of something (a thing, a place, even a psychical process) is projected—its local destiny, as it were. The surface meets its fate in the edge in which it ends: it moves forward into it by way of an implicit dynamic that has no equivalent in strictly physicalistic terms. (We can just as well imagine this happening in other ways—that is, the edge as accruing to a surface from behind, or from underneath or above, or from still other angles and directions.) At stake here are two implicit intentionalities of a thing or a place: that of its surface outward into its edge, and that of this edge as carrying forth this same surface into the immediate environs. These are two aspects of the circumstance that complements the way in which edges shadow forth surfaces.[4]

Also shadowlike is the fact that the edge, in contrast with the surface, has no substance of its own. A surface, after all, is the face that something of substance, whether a thing or place, turns outward to the world. Hence the very word surface means literally "on the face"; it is thus the surface of some depth. "A visible," as Merleau-Ponty puts it, is "the surface of a depth, a cross section upon a massive being."[5] This "massive being" is a literal substance, something that "stands under"; in this respect, a surface can be considered the pellicle of what underlies it, its shell as it were. Its fate is ineluctably linked with that which is subjacent to it: "insofar as substances persist, surfaces persist."[6] At the same time, surfaces are in contact with their surroundings—in particular, through the medium (air, water, and so on) in which they are located.[7] As the outer layer of a substance, a surface is an intermediary between that substance and the environing medium.

Most strikingly, the edge of a substance (whether of a thing or place) is the very moment when substance and surface alike lose their density, texture, reflectance, and other properties—when they "go out of existence."[8] They do this by becoming edge. This edge is shadowy in that it is the very diminution of the surface—there where it runs out for good, definitively. At its vanishing point, the edge is thinner than paper-thin, thinner even than graphene, since it is finally a formal feature of the surface of which is it the edge: hence Gibson's temptation to define it as a species of dihedral angle.[9] Where the surface and its underlying substance are both material in a significant sense and the medium is insubstantial (air is no kind of thing), the edge represents the place where surface and substance alike cease to be robustly material: it is the moment of diminishing and vanishing materiality. But it is not yet wholly immaterial or insubstantial, being more the shadow of matter than its substance. After all, it is still attached to a surface and thus closely coordinated with it. With surface, it is contiguous, chockablock. Like a shadow, an edge is undetachable from a surface.

The second proposition to be considered is the following: *The surface is the edge enlarged*. The imaginative dynamics of matter and substance allow us to reverse this thought experiment. We can also think of the edge as growing into the surface, being aggrandized there, thereby gaining mass and substance from this incursion. The edge undergoes involution into the very surface of which it is the edge: joins forces with it, merges with it, *becomes it*.

If the first proposition has to do with a process of *extromission*, sending out, this is a matter of *intromission*, sending in. The edge is forcefully sent into the surface. So radically is this the case that the edge, in effect, *disappears into the surface*: it is nowhere to be found there, being lost in it and rarely leaving any trace there. One can imagine this as an event of sheer dissolution where the edge merges into the surface, losing its identity as edge in order to become surface. It is as if the edge has been flattened out in the surface—so radically so that not even its shadow is left. If the edge can be conceived as the shadowing-out of surface, the surface can be considered in turn as the shadowless incorporation of edge.

Despite the striking differences between these two propositions, taken together, they indicate that, in the case of surface and edge, *each becomes the other*, albeit differentially and by a reversal of imaginative directionality. Edge and surface come and go out of existence from and into each other. This means that (once more, with the exception of a sphere) each is sine qua non for the other: without surface, there can be no edge; without edge, there can be no surface. In short, edge and surface are convergent, covalent, and corequisite. This is so despite their salient structural and functional and material differences—and despite the dissymetries that result from their having opposed vectors when they are imagined as extruding from or entering into one another.

## IV

Now we can begin to address edges in relation to limits. In everyday experience—and the ordinary discourse that reflects it—we refer to *edges* and *limits* almost interchangeably. We say, "I'm at the limit of my energy," when we could just as well claim, "I'm at the outer edge of my energy." Or we think of the "limits" of our knowledge of a given topic as if this knowledge were defined by the "outer edges" of what we know, where we veer into what we do not know. Perceptually or experientially, to stand at the "city limit" is difficult to distinguish from standing at the "outermost edge of town." Yet these casual pronouncements do reflect a conceptual difference. To speak of the *limits* of energy or knowledge or cities is to invoke something determinate and often quantitative, thus measurable—the city limit, for example, is specified in meters or miles—whereas in referring to the *edges* of these things, we do not imply anything so definite, much less measurable. Hence the need to qualify the use of *edge* with adjectives like "outer" or "outermost" in order to bring the word into line with *limit*. At the least, this suggests that *limit* has a discrete semantic kernel, calling for few qualifiers, if any, whereas *edge* is ambiguous enough to require them. This indicates that limit allows for a stricter definition and a more rigorous discussion than does edge. But to say this is to call for a more concerted discussion of the difference between edges and limits.

Whatever is the case in everyday talk, edges should not be confused with limits—at least not with limits taken in the strict sense of something non plus ultra ("that beyond which not")—something that cannot, or should not, be transgressed. This is the sense that Kant invokes when he writes of "religion within the limits of reason alone" and, more generally, of "the limits of possible experience." For Kant, these are limits that are determined entirely by the demands of pure reason in the former case, and by the criteria of pure understanding in the latter. In their legislative function, these regnant faculties dictate the outer bounds of coherent experience and knowledge. Whatever happens within the limits they prescribe must conform to the categories of understanding and not exceed the proper scope of reason. Nothing indefinite, nothing incoherent, nothing edgy permitted here! Whatever happens must fall squarely within these limits. Limits so conceived provide both aegis and law, *domos* and *nomos*, a conceptual home and a rational wall, a sheltering structure and a situation without exits. There is no going beyond such limits; there is only staying within them. Their untrespassability is determined in advance, mandated by the requirements of reason and the rigors of understanding.

It is just because of their tight enclosure, however, that such limits themselves call for transgression—as Kant recognized in the case of the mathematical and dynamic modes of the sublime. The sublime defies the limits, the *Grenzen*, set forth by the architectonic of pure theoretical reason. Experiences of the colossal scale and sheer might of natural forces take us beyond epistemic limits by suspending their authority so as to allow for the sheer projection of what is nowhere given in sensuous experience. In doing so, they point the way toward another relation to limits, one that consists more in contesting than respecting them. Not only do these experiences involve trespassing, they also suggest that limits of the sort invoked by Kant, despite their rigorous delimitation, point beyond themselves: by their very mission of holding so much *in*, a transgressive sense of something emerging from *without* emerges. This is not a matter of a chink, a flaw in the wall of reason, but of a limit immanent in the wall itself that calls for its own surpassment. Such a limit tempts us to look beyond its very delimitation, to suspend its appointed task of strict containment, and to cease its iron hold on what is permitted in possible experience.

Not only in extraordinary experiences of the sublime, but in everyday encounters with limits as well, we project beyond them. We find ourselves on the other side of formal or rational limits by virtue of the very act of positing them—even by just talking about or thinking of them (as I am doing here by writing about them). We are precipitated into their far side even as we are told that we are restricted to being on their near side. Here, vision becomes active clairvoyance, a special mode of "tele-vision" or *seeing into the distance*.[10] We envision the very things that Kant wanted to exclude: the nonphenomenal, the nondeterminate, the paralogical, the excessive, and the monstrous. Perhaps it was just because Kant sensed so strongly, and suspected so greatly, what lies on *die andere Seite* that he required human beings to stay strictly on *dieser Seite*. The very stringency of his sense of limit, that of the cognitive or conceptual non plus ultra, brings with it a longing for knowing what lies beyond the tidy limits of orderly experience. These limits resemble the "narrow defile" invoked by Freud when he began to confront the strange and disturbing prospect of dream-life in its full sweep.[11] A defile such as a mountain pass imposes quite specific local limits, but by the same token, it can also open suddenly beyond these limits. But the mountain pass contains concrete hints as to what lies beyond: it concretely adumbrates what is to come. No such adumbration occurs in the case of formal limits, whose other side requires supplementary actions of sheer projection.

When we do project beyond formal limits—in the manner of Kant's positing of the dynamic and mathematical sublime—we are in effect exploring a new *dimension* rather than the continuation of a perceived edge (as in the case of the defile). Such a dimension opens onto rather than closes down; it opens onto an expanse in space or time. Limit thus construed is the opposite of a rim; which is strictly bound down to the material thing it is the rim of—a literal part of it and inseparable from it. In contrast with a rim, a limit that allows for its own transcendence is, literally, *de*limited ("off the limit"). A parallel point holds for the border, whose primary function is to demarcate and delineate. But beyond every border, al otro lado, a whole landscape opens—that is, something both passable and porous, something that is more boundary-like than border-like. Following this analogy (and keeping in mind that rims, borders, and boundaries are all species of edge), we get to this analogy:

limited : delimited :: border : boundary

Whereas formal limits and borders are *enclosing* and *enclosed*—or purport to be such—concrete limits and boundaries that invite their own eclipsing are *open* and *opening*. The opening itself is not necessarily into the irrational or the unknown, as Kant feared; much more likely, it leads into the diffuse dimensionality of the place-world. Limit as undelimited takes us without rather than keeping us within. It takes us somewhere else than where it purports to keep us officially: at an absolute end, a final termination. It is no longer the embodiment and enforcement of the non plus ultra but rather is the *plus* of the *ultra* itself, the eclipsing of *the ultra* via the undoing of the *non plus*. It does things differently than do strictly conceptual limits—where stringencies and strictures abound—and in this way it allows us to experience the world differently as well.[12]

## V

Dennis Schwendtner, a piano tuner from Denver, remarked to me that he thinks of edges in music as existing on the far sides of limits—they are the places where the formal limit of a chord, octave, or other interval is pushed to the point of no longer counting only as that octave or chord. Reflecting on this passing remark (in response to my question, "how do you think of edges in your work?"), I realized that limits are entities of another order from edges: they are definitory, ideal, legal, statutory, and institutional. Of themselves, they do not change—not because they are physically enduring, but because they are not subject to the usual determinants of change and becoming that obtain for material things and historical events. Limits belong to the *being* of a given phenomenon—to its very identity, status, or definition. As encountered, they are always already established, laid down; once established, they hold their position until replaced by another limit, one that claims to be more accurate or that meets other identifiable needs. Limits do not alter their character or state. This is so even if they may also invite transgression, especially when they are perceived as intransigent; and in some cases they even collude in the transgression itself.

Edges, in contrast, are inherently capable of alteration, and often call for this expressly. At one level, they change because the very terms by which they are defined may be modified: say, for example, the terms of a political treaty that define the exact position of an international border—a situation I address elsewhere.[13] Or else, at a still more concrete level, the exact shape of a material container is altered with use (blunted, crumpled, creased), with the result that its contour changes shape. Indeed, the very edges of my personal identity can be altered when I undergo a traumatic event—an act of violence, the death of a loved one, and the like. I "come out different," as we say, without understanding just how this has happened.

Though they may be conscripted into the service of idealities (as happens with perfectly straight borderlines), edges themselves *accrue to the actual*. Again, this occurs in diverse ways. Rims are edges of something physically real; they are as real as that of which they are the rim. (I am taking "real" to be a modality of the materially actual, one of the major ways in which it is concretized.) The edges of psychological states are borders of these states (as in "borderline personalities"), being the ways these states dispose themselves in patterns of behavior and thought. Despite being internal and psychical, they are as actual as the edges of material things. Each of these various kinds of edges changes when the underlying state, either material or psychological, changes. (I return to psychological edges in chapter 9.)

In none of the instances I have just alluded to—rims, borderline psychological conditions, and material things—is anything like conceptual or geometric limitation possible.[14] With edges we are not in the realm of idealities or formalities; we are in the region of actualities and becomings, where everything is subject to change. The informality of edges here contrasts with the formality of conceptual limits. If there is any geometry operative here, it is an informal geometry of the sort that Husserl (as noted in the previous chapter) designated as "morphological."[15] His examples of morphological concepts are revealing: being notched, umbelliform, and so on. Each of these shapes is constituted by an edge that is more or less informal, that is, rough or "raw." To be notched is to exhibit cuts that are not perfectly regular, just noticeable or palpable enough to number if we so wish. An umbelliform plant shape is fanlike yet presents itself in no perfectly repetitive pattern: variations are embedded in the shape itself. The same is true of the fractal formations of many coastlines. Variant in detail, these formations nevertheless embody an overall progression that can be mapped and discussed as such. They manifest an informal consistency that belongs to their respective edges themselves. Their material actuality is edged, but it is not strictly limited as it would be if they were to exhibit an ideal geometric shape determined by axioms, postulates, and definitions (as in Euclidean geometry).

How do edges and limits relate to each other? Dennis Schwendtner's casual but perceptive observations are again pertinent. He said that edges are located *on the other side* of limits, somewhere just beyond their sheerly formal and fixed positions. This suggests that edges hover around limits in their vicinity but not as part of them, much less *as* them. Different as edges and limits are as to *kind*, they nevertheless maintain a certain relationship *in space*, a partnership in localization, as well as *in time* (that is, when related to events). The uncompromisable differences in their ontological status (one being actual, the other ideal) do not preclude their being related to each other in a given spatial or temporal field—and related in quite specific ways. These ways are captured by such phrases as "edging over the limit" or "edging across the limit." These adverbial phrases, signifying diverse directions and movements, point to the elasticity of edges as enacted concretely in relation to limits. It is telling that limits themselves do not engender or suggest any such adverbial proliferation; in the primary phrase by which we refer to it— "at the limit"—the word *limit* stands by itself as an austere monosemantic marker.

Despite their various differences at eidetic and concrete levels alike, limit and edge are intimately related to each other. A given limit can cut across the edges with which it is associated, while these same edges may cluster in turn around this limit. Imagine limit as a perfectly flat surface, across which other surfaces play at various angles. The effect is that of being two-dimensional, as we can see in figure 5 just below.

Here, limit is envisioned as a formal plane—the single such plane—that subtends an open-ended set of informal shapes, each representing a particular way

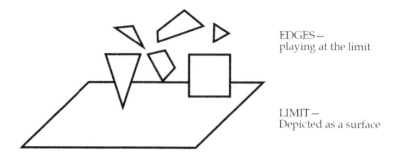

FIGURE 5. Edges impinging at a limit.

of being an edge. It is as if the former is a plane of immanence in relation to the latter construed as discrete transcendences, employing these terms in the senses discussed by Deleuze and Guattari.[16] Here, limit is imagined as a formally consti-tuted plane on which many things and events, and many *kinds* of things and events, happen at the same time. It is like a sheer surface where idealities are at home, while upon and around it play a congeries of actualities. Ideal identities inhabit the formal plane, but the shapes that intersect it at various angles are actual singulari-ties. The former is the site of limits, the latter of edges. Yet in their very disparity, each calls for the other; each accomplishes what the other cannot.

## VI

Let me draw an analogy from the realm of concrete bodily practice: yoga. In this practice, the perfect or final, "finished" pose contrasts with the stages of learning through which the practitioner passes. These stages, which fall short of the per-fect pose, are nevertheless part of the practice and cannot be bypassed or excluded. They are the equivalent of edges in my nomenclature, and it is striking that yoga instructors employ this term spontaneously in their teachings: "hold it at the edge," "don't go over the edge."[17] The ideal pose itself can be conceived as the limit in relation to which practitioners fall short in their halting approximations: they are edging toward this limit of perfection.

By "fall short" I do not mean to imply a regrettable failure, but rather two things: First, I point to the various passing postures as particular moments in which the practitioner is experiencing her or his own bodily positions as forming singular poses, however imperfectly realized. These positions can be experienced as diffi-culties or even warnings; but they are also moments of discovery—of finding out how it feels to be *underway* at various stages, which has its own pleasure and value. Indeed, it is sometimes said that in yoga "perfection lies in the journey, not the des-tination."[18] Here perfection as an ideal limit is suspended in order to encourage moving toward it via imperfect bodily edgework. Second, in such a journey there can be a sense of edge as more-than-physical, a place where the practitioner moves from body to mind, from a corporeal state to a mental realization. It is as if one goes *over the edge*—that is, over the halting somatic edge of a given bodily position toward another kind of edge, a periphery as it were, with which the first is never-theless closely affiliated. This is not a move to the ideational as such, that is, to a set of discrete thoughts (memories, anticipations, ideas, and so on); it is more like a transition to the psychical dimension of one's being.[19] In this dimension, there are distinctive edges as well—nooks and crannies of the mind, as it were, momen-tary pausing places, way stations at the psychical level.[20]

I point to the practice of yoga as a praxiological analogue to what has been mostly disembodied in my previous examples of limits and edges. If limits are mat-ters of determinate or formal perfection—lending themselves to delineated depic-tions (as with stick figures that exemplify various yoga postures)—edges are too intrinsically alterable to be reduced to any such privileged idealizations. Not only are there always several postural edges in relation to a given limit but there are also several *sorts* of such edges, and still more importantly several possible edge actions (edging forward, edging back, relaxing, and the like). There is no one right way of taking up the postural edges that constitute a given position, for these edges are part of the very medium of the multiple becomings of the yoga practitioner's body in time and space. They issue from many such becomings even as they help to constitute them in turn. This is in marked contrast to the limits around which they cluster. These limits are insistently ideal, there being only *one* ideality of a certain kind: one *2*, one equilateral triangle, one perfect yoga pose of a given kind (such as "the plank" or "downward dog"), and so on. A limit belongs ineluctably to being in its formal and identitarian oneness. An edge, in contrast, is actual and multifarious, always altering, ever becoming.[21]

## VII

At first glance, it might seem as if the distinction between limit and edge is, if not arbitrary, then at least contingent and thus dispensable, easily replaceable by other distinctions (such as endpoint vs. intermediate moment); however, this is not the case. A formal-ideal limit represents a genuine asymptote around which edges cluster as multifarious neighbors. But a given limit needs edges as much as the latter require a limit. Taken by itself, a limit would be merely abstract—an isolated single term, unreachable (invisible, untouchable) as such. Taken by themselves, edges would be merely diverse, an indeterminate swarm of disparate elements. This is not to say that limit is the common term, much less the Form or Idea of which edges would be the mere instantiations or species. Quite to the contrary! Edge and limit both retain their own integrity—one formal, the other informal—even as each calls out to the other to illuminate it by way of contrastive differences. It may help, indeed may be essential, when attempting to grasp what edges are like to know what a limit is, both in general and in particular cases; and it is indispensable to the process of conceiving limit to have experienced a multiplicity of edges that cluster around that limit. The one is not the mere manifestation, much less the realization, of the other; rather, each relies on the other to be more fully realized itself—both on its own and in its very difference from the other. In brief, it is a matter of "reciprocal presupposition," in Deleuze's term;[22] each term presumes the other's effective presence, as neither could be adequately grasped without allusion to the other. Here, the rule is, *no edges without a limit that superintends them; no limit without edges that complicate it and populate its otherwise empty ideal space.*

For the most part, this coeval status of edges and limits has been covered over in Western thought. All too often, opposition has obscured the shared reliance of the two terms on each other. Furthermore, this reliance has often been reduced to the derivation of one term from the other, as in certain forms of Platonism. Such derivation has taken the place of cooriginarity or equiprimordiality; ontogenesis has obscured the bipolarity of corequisiteness.[23] Thus, edges are all too often regarded as mere modes of limit—and limit is taken as the archetypal term in relation to which edges are mere ectypal castoffs.

The temptation to identify a single concept and deem it paramount in a given region of experience or discourse is intrinsic to metaphysics in its specifically Western forms. We see this same temptation in late medieval and early modern efforts to make space the supreme term—so supreme that place is nothing but its adventitious avatar; or to regard the gaze as the supreme exemplar, with the glance as a merely casual act of vision. I have argued elsewhere on phenomenological grounds that both of these moves are grievous mistakes. The attempt to subordinate edge to limit is just as misguided and needs to be replaced with a very different model of their relationship. This book seeks to set forth such a model based on close description.

## VIII

The plot thickens, however, when we realize that edges belong to things in places, and limits accrue to space. This belongingness is asymmetrical. We get to places from edges only through a series of successive steps. Edges belong first of all to surfaces, while surfaces make up the exteriority (and sometimes the interiority) of physical things—and things, in turn, inhere in places. So we have a series of nested terms that goes something like this:

edge > surface > thing > place

We do not go straight from edges to places, except where places have their own edges—a situation I take up in detail in the next chapter. In the case of physical things, edges are embedded in a sequence with at least two intermediate members: surfaces and things themselves. Much the same intermediation occurs in the case of events, which feature complex concatenations of edges: those belonging to people and contexts as well as to things. In almost every instance, edges are parts of parts of parts of . . . Thus edges take us ineluctably into the mereological realm, where parts are the primary objects of study.

Limits, in contrast, concern wholes, that is, the formal totalities to which they belong. For this reason, they align themselves with space, assuming that space (in contrast with place, always particular and plural) is itself one whole: one space, infinite and unending. A limit is a moment of space, not a part or piece of it (drawing again on Husserl's distinction between *Moment* and *Stück*).[24] A limit, itself ideal in status, is an integral aspect of space, a feature of the latter's very being as abstract, empty, self-identical, and homogeneous. Thus there is a very close relationship between space and limit. The fate of space is to provide limits to its various parts, not edges. When one measures the total number of cubic feet in an apartment, the exact number is abstract and refers to purely posited volumes, "chunks of space"[25] that are contiguous with each other in an ideal, unperceived space; but the apartment itself, as a material place, has edges (walls, doors, windows). The fate of place is to be filled with concrete things and events whose ingredients are concretely and variously edged.

Like a limit, a gaze is allied with spatial wholes—in this case, with studied views and full panoramas. The gaze is an ally of the spatial objectification that is endemic in scientific thought, as we see so tellingly in Foucault's study of the "medical gaze."[26] This characteristically modernist way of looking presupposes the subsistence of a pure form: an idealized anatomical body, for example. Gazing seeks what is steady and unchanging and can be contemplated indefinitely. Glances, in contrast, affiliate themselves with momentary situations—looking at *just this, right now.* Like edges, glances join forces with things having surfaces, even if they continually detach themselves from one surface to move to another. Where gazes seek out a single definitive pattern within a unified space of looking, glances, in their restlessness, shift between momentary perches as they continually alter their focus in a particular place.

In these various ways, then, we can discern affinities between three pairs of terms—limit/edge, space/place, and gaze/glance—despite significant differences in ontic domains and precise modes of operation within these domains. Each calls for a specifically peri-phenomenological description: an approach that is sensitive to the outer parts of things and places, to their exteriorities, peripheral regions, or their "outtards," as we can call them. Peri-phenomenology requires a special form of attentiveness that goes straight to the exoskeletal structures of things and places—the very prominences and structures that attract our spontaneous glances.

## IX

It is doubtless true that the very formality of limit—its inherent ideality and strict identity—contributes to its presumed hegemony over edge: the sense that limits are definitive and final, whereas edges are "merely" empirical and heterogeneous. Reinforcing this hegemony of limit is its implicit monism in contrast with the inherent plurality of edges (their coming in many kinds and their tendency to concatenate endlessly).

Limits are natural allies of metaphysical thinking of a classical cast—given that there is an ancient alliance between form (or essence) and metaphysical thinking. Metaphysical presence is intensely formal, whether this be in the guise of Platonic Forms, Parmenidean being, the Plotinian one, or the Aristotelian divine mind that thinks itself thinking. In each of these cases, the formal factor is triumphant: it establishes the rules of the metaphysical game, determines its risks and stakes. Above all, it *sets the limits* of conceptualization, hence it is not surprising that the very language of "limit" comes forward in later metaphysical contexts in close concert with "form" itself. Examples of this include the differential limit in the calculus invented by Newton and Leibniz, and the limits of human understanding and reason in Hume and Kant. It is striking that in each of these paradigmatic modernist instances, there is only *one* such limit or set of limits: only one asymptotic limit in differential calculus, one set of limits of human understanding (as in Hume's rule that *all* ideas are copied from impressions and are thus delimited by them in their content) or of reason (the limits of possible experience that are trespassed in inflated ideas of God, freedom, and immortality). This indicates that there is a rigorous relationship between the *form*, the *one*, and the *limit*. Each of these terms—and other affiliated terms, such as "space," "ideality," "condition of possibility," "ground," and "God"—lends itself to hegemonic positionality in the great chain of Being. In that chain, places and edges are ipso facto subordinate members insofar as they lack formality and oneness, pure ideality and rigorous limitation.

And yet edges, like places and glances, possess a disruptive force that contests this very hegemony and threatens its supposed priority. The very diversity inherent in these three phenomena endows them with a power that is efficacious by virtue of their very subaltern position. In their multiplicity and heterogeneity, they set their own standards and invoke their own criteria—standards and criteria that are no longer tributary from the putatively primary terms of limit, space, and gaze. They have a power and a presence of their own, and they operate on their own terms.

Like every glance, the perception of each place and each edge constitutes an event, and is thus able to bring surprise with it—surprise that is capable of unsettling predominant concepts and systems of thought. For the surprising emerges from the other side of every edge; it is also what the glance delivers, just as it arises from the insistence of a place or an event.[27] We glance at the edge, aware that it harbors the unexpected—not only as what is concealed from present perception but as the not-yet-happening: the event-to-come. Edges, like places and glances, are creatures of becoming, not fixed instances of being. Just as places complicate space, and glances undercut gazes, so edges contest limits: they diversify limits from around and under and beyond them, immanently, even as limits present themselves as fixed and transcendent. Such is the sub rosa subversive force of edges that their subordination under the presumed priority of limits is resisted and undone by the very character and operation of edges themselves. Formally imposed limits are deconstructed by the teeming energy of the very edges that cluster about them.

It is tempting to think that edges and limits are equiprimordial in their differences; both are required, neither is prior, and each is complementary to the other. But if forced to choose, it would be more accurate to say that of the two terms, edges are primus inter pares, first among what is otherwise equal in the playing field constituted by limits and edges. They are first insofar as ongoing experience depends upon them directly; we navigate the world by way of the actual edges we find there. The same cannot be said of limits, which are not encountered but posited or presumed; as such, they exist elsewhere than in the immediately surrounding world of places to which we belong as sentient creatures.

## X

This is a book on edges. Throughout it, my primary effort is to acknowledge and underline the insistence of edges in the course of experience as well as their sheer multiplicity in terms of shape and number. In this chapter, I began by clarifying the relationship between edges and surfaces; after this, I brought out various ways in which limits contrast with edges. My thesis has been that in relation to edges, limits figure as secondary. Even when sternly proclaimed to be necessary, limits remain the phantomic others of edges: their conceptual counterparts in the domain of formality and ideality.

There is no end to the proliferation of edges that we come upon—and that come upon us. We exist in a plenum of edges that constitute a veritable world of its own, an edge-world. This is so despite the fact that any given edge is composed as much of what is not directly before us as of what is. Like the "adumbrations" (*Abschattungen*) that for Husserl constitute the outer profiles of physical things, edges shade off (in the literal meaning of *ab-schatten*) into the shadows of demi-presence. Their concealed parts are held in abeyance even as their manifest parts are given to us in plain perception; but the concealment is only ever partial, for we sense already in a given edge what it opens onto, even though we are rarely certain as to just what this may be. Edges are ports of entry into the not-yet-known, which is itself becoming known. Limits, in contrast, are wholly withheld from sensible experience: they are presupposed, not sensed; imposed, not given. Thus they cannot be presented as such: only their representations or signs reach our direct awareness. Nevertheless, human beings are drawn to actively imagine their other sides, as we have seen in the case of the mathematical and dynamic sublime as conceived by Kant. Here the limit gives rise to the open dimension of the undelimited.

Edges are elusive, vanishing from the very perceptions in which they first appear. Edges escape us on every side, sliding as they do into the outback of perception. Think only of the way they attach to the outermost surface of a given thing or place, typically being only partially within sight or imperfectly subject to touch: we catch sight and feel one part of an edge, while the rest of it flees our alert eye and agile hand as it veers out of range into nebulous peripheries. Only a peri-phenomenology, alert to these peripheries, is able to detect and describe them accurately. Nevertheless, even as they withdraw into the perimeter of perception, edges form a major part of our sensory awareness. We take them in, noting them and dealing with them, and we are given crucial clues as to what lies on the other side, "over the edge." This is concretely adumbrated rather than posited or projected as in the case of the other sides of strictly formal limits.

Edges, in truth, are neither fully present nor strictly absent. For this reason, they represent exceptions to the paradigm of metaphysical presence that, as Derrida has argued, has dominated Western metaphysics from its origin. In possessing this exceptional status, edges join the company of certain other phenomena that exhibit a like ambiguity of presence: notably writing (Derrida's focus in his early work), the human body (as Merleau-Ponty insists in his discussion of the phantom limb phenomenon), and the human face (emphasized in Levinas's ethics). This ambiguity contrasts starkly with limits, which are at once strictly absent from the deliverances of concrete perception and yet accessible as such to cognition and formal intuition. Limits are forever beyond "the bounds of sense," whereas edges emerge from within these bounds and help to concretize and complicate what appears there, even as they also mark its very evanescence.

## Notes

1. Of course this is not true of the earth, whose imperfection as a globe is in part due to its very possession of manifold edges on its surface—depressions and protuberances of many sorts—though its failure to have one definitive edge is arguably what drove early mariners and mythmakers to posit such an edge by imaginative extrapolation: namely, the edge where it was rumored that the earth suddenly drops off.

2. The same is true of psychical edges, even if the properties of the latter are characteristically less distinct or measurable, as qualitative traits take the place of quantitative determinations. They are the edges of that which is more of a process than a settled thing or place—hence they share the fluidity of this process, being subject to continual transformation. More on this in chapter 9.

3. James J. Gibson, *The Ecological Approach to Visual Perception* (Hillsdale, NJ: Erlbaum, 1986), p. 29. Surface is defined this way: "The surface of a substance has a characteristic texture, reflectance, and layout." Note that for Gibson "an *edge* is the junction of two surfaces that make a convex dihedral angle" (p. 308; italics in original). A corner, in contrast, is "the junction of two surfaces that make a concave dihedral angle" (p. 308).

4. For further on the "material intentionality" of edges, see the postlude.

5. Merleau-Ponty, *The Visible and the Invisible*, p. 136.

6. Gibson, *The Ecological Approach to Visual Perception*, p. 22.

7. On Gibson's model, the earth's surface is the interface formed when two of the three major components of the earth's environment (solid, liquid, gas) conjoin. See *The Ecological Approach*, p. 16. More generally, surfaces "separate substances from [their] medium" (p. 32). The paradigmatic medium is air, but anything that allows for the free movement of plants and animals within it counts as a medium: thus water for fish and seaweed.

8. Ibid., p. 307: "A surface is when its substance evaporates or disintegrates; a surface *comes into existence* when its substance condenses or crystallizes" (italics in original). But we can just as well say that it is the surface itself that undergoes these radical ontological changes.

9. On graphene, see John Colapinto, "Material Question: Graphene May Be the Most Remarkable Substance Ever Discovered. But What's It For?" (*The New Yorker*, December 22 and 29, 2014). Graphene is known as the thinnest substance ever generated: it is a layer of carbon that is literally one atom thick.

10. On *tele-vision* in a nontechnological sense, see Merleau-Ponty, working note of March 1961, in *The Visible and the Invisible* (Evanston, IL: Northwestern University Press, 1968), p. 273.

11. "When after passing through a narrow defile, we suddenly emerge upon a piece of high ground, where the path divides and the finest prospects open up on every side . . ."; Sigmund Freud, *The Interpretation of Dreams* (New York: Avon Books), p. 155.

12. For an alternative but closely akin view of limit, see Jean-Luc Nancy, "Banks, Edges, Limits (of Singularity)," trans. Gil Anidjar, *Angelaki*, vol. 9 no. 2, August 2004, pp. 41–52.

13. See Edward S. Casey and Mary Watkins, *Up Against the Wall: Re-Imagining the U.S.–Mexico Border* (Austin: University of Texas Press, 2014).

14. Borders may be ideal in their conception and projection; but as actualized—as in border walls—they are subject to manifold vicissitudes and manipulations in the material and political worlds.

15. For more on morphological concepts, see "A Last Lesson" in part 4.

16. See Gilles Deleuze and Félix Guattari, *What Is Philosophy?* trans. H. Tominson and G. Burschell (New York: Columbia University Press, 1994), chapter 2. When the authors say that "concepts are like multiple waves, rising and falling, but the plane of immanence is the single wave that rolls them up and unrolls them" (p. 36), they could well have been speaking of edges rather than concepts. Note that the plane of immanence is virtual in status—where "virtual" is contrasted with "actual" in keeping with Bergson's distinction.

17. I refer to Heather Tiddens's explicit wording in her yoga instruction in Santa Barbara, California—an instruction from which I have benefited over the past decade.

18. As recounted by Kavi Patel, Iyengar instructor, New York City, March 19, 2015.

19. I am employing "psychical" in Collingwood's sense of the term: a level of life that hovers between feeling and thought and that is coextensive with consciousness and imagination. See his *Principles of Art* (Oxford: Clarendon, 1938), especially part 2.

20. For more on psychical edges, see chapter 9.

21. This is why it makes sense to speak in actual yoga practice of "going to your edge" (versus *the* edge), "not going over your edge," "hovering at the edge," and other such informal expressions.

22. See Deleuze and Guattari, *A Thousand Plateaus*, trans. B. Massumi (Minneapolis: University of Minnesota Press, 1987), pp. 108, 140–41, 145, 146.

23. I take "co-originarity" in Nancy's sense of the term in his *Being Singular Plural*, p. 31. It echoes Heidegger's basic term *gleichursprünglich*, "equiprimordial," as employed in *Being and Time*.

24. See Edmund Husserl, "The Logic of Wholes and Parts," in *Logical Investigations*, III.

25. This phrase refers to Merleau-Ponty, "Eye and Mind," trans. Michael B. Smith in *The Merleau-Ponty Aesthetics Reader: Philosophy and Painting*, ed. Galen Johnson (Evanston, IL: Northwestern University Press, 1993), where he writes that the lived body is not "a chunk of space or a bundle of functions" (p. 124).

26. See Michel Foucault, *The Birth of the Clinic: An Archaeology of Medical Perception*, trans. A. M. Sheridan Smith (New York: Pantheon, 1973), and my discussion of this book in *World at a Glance*. Differences between the glance and the gaze are set out in the afterword to the latter book, entitled "Families of the Glance and the Gaze," pp. 482–91.

27. See Jean-Luc Nancy, "The Surprise of the Event," in *Being Singular Plural*. See also Edward S. Casey, "Glancing at the Surface of Surprise," forthcoming in a collection edited by Anthony Steinbock.

# Cusps, Traces, Veils

Our foray into how edges relate to surfaces and limits was an exercise in distinguishing edges from these two latter terms, which present themselves as closely related to edges, yet in the end prove to be quite distinct from them, both in terms of concrete descriptive detail and by way of the larger stakes at play in these distinctions. I shall now single out three edge phenomena that, in addition to their own inherent interest, allow us to catch sight of how edges and surfaces, and edges and limits, come into play in particular instances.

## Cusps

Although a cusp is neither rigid and linear (as is the rim of a sardine jar), nor flattened out (as is, say, a beach or a sidewalk), it has a definite determinacy, signifying "a pointed end; apex; peak" (*Webster's Collegiate Dictionary*, 1944 edition). Thus both the moon and certain teeth of carnivores are cusped (as in the cusp of the moon and bi*cusp*ids); they have edges where they sharpen to a point, come to a peak. But the point or peak need not inhere in a physical object; it may connote the peak of an event that is reaching culmination. A cusp, unlike an isolated sheer point, can have an extent of its own, and in this respect it is akin to a brink or verge; but where the latter are characteristically preliminary or provisional, being structures of the *about-to-happen* (about to do *x* or *y*), a cusp is the final phase of a process of accomplishment or development (something already happening). This is what we mean when we speak of "being on the cusp"—riding high on a series of happenings while now moving into a future phase of this same series.

From these several descriptions, it is evident that a cusp is often something spatiotemporal, an edge that is becoming in time as well as in space (and in place, for it creates its own place even as it becomes something other than itself). Thanks to its spatiotemporality, a cusp is frequently construed as a sign, a beacon or bellwether, of things to come: "being on the cusp *of x* or *y*." The *of* is not merely intentional (as in "consciousness of *z*") or partitive (forming part of something) but an active "of" that belongs to something in the process of becoming significantly different than it was. A further nuance is that being on the cusp often has to do with something auspicious or promising, such as a breakthrough or a dramatic development. We say, "she was on the cusp of a new discovery."[1]

Let us not ignore the frequent oceanic reference at play in the attribution of cusps: namely, the crests of breaking waves, the moving ridges where the top of a wave breaks as it arches over and down (and sometimes backs up from under), the very last moment in which the wave is held together as one entity before dissolving into amorphous spume.[2] In this elemental context, a cusp is the final shape of a long-gathering wave, an interfusion of various water currents—just as human innovators often build on the amassed work of immediate predecessors. Much as one cusped wave gives way to another, the innovators bring this previous work not just to completion but also to a new level of attainment, enabling the work to move on to a new stage—to another wave of novelty that will have its own cusp.

An oceanic cusp that is more than a fixed ridge is a *rolling edge*, an edge that moves just ahead of its material mass in an ongoing process of becoming. Such a cusp draws directly from what has gone before: this is its material condition of possibility. But it is the bearing-forward that is most emphatic in the cusp phenomenon. It is doubtless for this reason that we single out this literally progressive dimension in our customary ways of invoking the cusp. To be "on the cusp of success," for example, means to be almost there, nearing it, all but fully and manifestly successful. A cusp, far from being a straight edge, is flexible in the manner of the crest of a wave, where the crest itself is neither rigid nor strictly linear. It is ever changing and as porous as it is tenuous: no sooner does it appear than it begins to disappear, as when a single wave begins to crash in the immediate wake of its cresting. In these several ways, a cusp is much more like a boundary than a border: it does not exclude or inhibit; it does not form a partition but a pattern—an open pattern of incessant change that, nonetheless, assumes an identifiable shape. An indeterminate blur cannot serve as a cusp, even if a cusp may disappear into such a blur upon its completion. At play here is always and only *this* cusp with *these* identifiable phases and velocities.

A cusp may be regarded as located between a verge and a margin. It is not always at the start of something, *before* it, as is a verge; unlike a margin, it is not situated wholly *around* something. A cusp manifests either the end of a process, as with the last phase of a breaking wave, or the opening of a new phase of a happening, or it can embody the two together in such close concert as to be perceptually indistinguishable.[3] A cusp also differs from a verge or margin in that it belongs integrally to that which it qualifies, whereas verges and margins are separable from that with which they are contiguous. Still another difference concerns the respective durations of these three phenomena. While margins are comparatively enduring—lasting at least as long as the text or image they surround—verges and cusps tend to be time limited. Cusps are more momentary than verges, which can last for a considerable while: I can be on the verge of a discovery for a long time, whereas I can be on the cusp of the same discovery only shortly before it happens (or fails to happen).

Each kind of cusp identified here—whether humanly created or naturally situated—represents the edge of some sort of surface, whether the roiling surface of an ocean or the smooth surface of a scientific paper in which a breakthrough is announced. A cusp is an edge of such surfaces when that edge is coming to a culmination on or of these surfaces. It is an especially intensely configured edge characterized by its comparative brevity in time and paucity of presence in space. In these very respects, it contrasts with a formally constituted or historically instituted limit, which is imposed from without and meant to last indefinitely. There is an inwardly generated character to cusps that defies their exact determination from without. As John Stuart Mill observed in his remarks on tides, their precise shape and duration are never entirely predictable; they always exceed or fall short to some degree of what tidal charts prognosticate.[4] If the charts state limits—what should be the case, ideally—the phenomenon of "to some degree" acknowledges the factor of edge.[5]

## Traces

A trace, for being such a seemingly monolinear entity—typically one line, one mark, one cut—is surprisingly complex. Or, more exactly, it is *duplex*. A trace is cut *into* a surface (incised there) or marked *on* it (inscribed). But in both of these two basic forms, it always brings with it or creates two sides—*this* side of the trace and *that* side, as well as several pairs of directionalities: above and below, right and left, inner and outer. It is inherently bilateral and paired: there is no trace that does not possess at least two sides and a number of two-fold directionalities.

Other bivalencies obtain. A trace can be continuous, yet it can also be interrupted at various places and still count as a single trace (as in a dotted line). We can trace *out* by creating outlines, but we can also trace *in* (when we pursue inlines, the inner structures of something). A trace can be inherently meaningless—something entirely abstract, as with a pure arabesque—or intensely meaningful, as in cursive script. At the level of linguistic expression, traces have both noun forms ("a trace") and verb forms ("to trace"). These redoubled structures reflect the basic doubleness of a trace's materiality (including its perceivability) as paired with its putative meaning. Its materiality and its meaning are not so much two sides as two *levels* of a trace's presence: what is sensed and the sense it has. This bilevel status can obtain in several media: as writing and its signification, as articulate sound and its sense, and as bodily gesture and import.[6] Traces also occur as the edges of letters, words, or entire sentences; and, in the literal sense, they emerge as edges of drawn or printed marks on a page or other such spaces, as, for example, on engravings and etchings.

In his *Grammatology*, Jacques Derrida questions the primacy of these various binary terms as adequate accounts of written traces, positing between them or, more exactly, preceding them, an action that defies description in these exclusively dyadic terms. Derrida calls this prior action *différance*, and it consists in a deferring and differing activity that refuses to be confined to the binary choices we have so far considered. Instead of inner versus outer, for example, in the case of *différance* the outer is already located in the inner and vice versa. More importantly, there would be no sense at all if the sensible (the spatial, the outside) were not already actively insinuating itself into written signs, such as letters and words and phrases. The latter require their own typographic space: the space of tracing. In such space, matter and meaning are always already intertwined.

Derrida claims that the very vehicle of *différance* is the activity of tracing—as this occurs in the form of a proto-writing (*archi-écriture*) that is the propelling force of *différance* itself. This is to give to tracing more than merely participial standing: it is to ascribe to it the moving power to generate significant phenomena in many domains, beginning with verbal language but extending to art, the political, and beyond. As a generative force, tracing (*tracement*) is thus no longer reducible to the binaries I first cited. It is an event of the first order that is responsible for the very production of significance in all these domains. When considered from a formal standpoint, it may be analyzable into certain duplex features such as matter and sense, but it resists such analysis when account is taken of its intrinsic nisus, its propulsive power.[7]

The paradox of the trace as treated by Derrida is that something diminutive in format, nothing but a line, nevertheless possesses enormous semiotic potential. The merely momentary harbors the momentous—indeed the monumental: symbolized by Derrida as a pyramid regarded as isomorphic with the first letter of the alphabet, *A*. How can this be? Derrida resists any strictly explanatory account: he would have us savor the situation in which proto-writing, the action of a primal tracing, is the effective agency of *différance* and makes it possible. This gives traced and tracing edges an extraordinary power in the realm of meaning that brooks no compromise—a power that is not possessed by any of the separate members of various binary oppositions, such as matter/form and mind/body, nor by their sheer combination.

That something diminutive thus portends something momentous I call the Law of Augmented Return—augmented in relation to a diminished base.[8] In the current case, something as definite in shape as a finite trace, an inscribed edge, conveys indefinitely extensive meanings, none of which has determinate extent, outline, or limit. Thus an identifiable and recognizable unit or vehicle—identifiable and recognizable by its characteristic edge—adumbrates a nimbus of connotative meanings that are the disseminative effects of *différance*. Indeed, if the vehicle itself were altogether ambiguous, if it were edgeless, it could not do its work of signifying these various meaning-laden regions. It is only from the trace as a focal starting point, an ampliative edge, that capacious ranges of signification can open outward by way of augmentation.

What is further distinctive about the trace regarded as an edge is that it is almost always the effect of a prior action: the stroke of a pen, the mechanical motion of a printing machine, the kinetics of the face, the striating movement of a glacier over a boulder. In each of these cases, traces are the direct result of an efficient cause; they are the very deposition or record of the hand or the machine, of a facial expression or a glacier's slow advance or retreat. In cases of direct transcription or transmission, no intermediaries figure as such. Or, more exactly, even if a given process involves facilitations or mediations of several sorts, all that finally matters in the production of a trace is that the last pertinent effective force leave *its* trace in the form of an edge. The North Rim of the Grand Canyon is formed from many ancient geological strata, most of which have eroded, but the last of which we now witness in the North Rim regarded as a set of multilayered traces of their continuing presence. So, too, with other complex phenomena, such as the United States–Mexico border, or many artworks that are built up from dense layering in the manner of a palimpsest (as we witness in late J. M. W. Turner seascapes or in the action paintings of Jackson Pollock, where we see a direct display of the decisive gestures that created the artwork itself; see figures 7 and 8 in interlude III).

This suggests in turn that the action of tracing—making traces, by whatever means—is what matters most in the generation of these several kinds of edges. This proto-action is the relevant *Ursache*, the relevant causal force, or more literally the "primal thing." It is allied with becoming and qualitative change—with process and production, moving and being moved, marking and being marked. Let us say, then, that *the trace is the effective edge—in space and through time—of the act of tracing itself.* It is the expression of becoming as it is deposited in a given place.[9] It is what becoming becomes insofar as it leaves a sign of its presence in the form of a discrete mark. It is the external edge of this becoming, its outer imprint, its manifest mark on the surface of that which underlies it.

A trace is therefore the mark of the action of tracing, its insignia or signature. As such, it is both the physical effect of tracing (and sometimes the psychical effect, as in traumatic memories that are tantamount to psychological scars) *and* the sign of the tracing's having happened, having become. Whether the action of tracing is datable or not, what matters is that it counts as a process that brought about the trace or set of traces we now behold on a certain surface. It is just here, in this basic difference between effect and sign, that the bivalence of the trace takes its rise. Thanks to Derrida's intervention, we can appreciate this bivalence as the product of a process rather than as the primary level of the phenomenon. At the primary level, there is the ur-action of tracing, itself an expression of becoming; at subsequent levels, there are the traces left on surfaces as the depositional marks of this basic action.

It has become abundantly evident that the relationship between traces and surfaces is very close. Traces would not take effect—they would not occur, nor would they be noticed—if they did not present themselves on some surface. Jet trails aside, there are no traces in thin air. The rule is, *no trace without a surface*, whether this be a page, a canvas, a wall, or film screen. But it must be noted that traces are typically *internal edges* in relation to a given surface, positioned there in such a way as to be legible or as least apperceivable. In this, they differ from the edges that terminate surfaces, the outer edges of these surfaces.

By the same token, traces regarded as edges cannot be confused with limits in the sense discussed in chapter 2. The exact manner in which these edges are inscribed or incised is subject to considerable variegation in keeping with different styles of handwriting, disparate typefaces, and discrepant instruments for marking. We witness here once again the inherent variability of edges in contrast with the inflexibility of formal limits, such as those posited by semantic and syntactical rules. These rules order the presentation of meanings that emerge from coherent clusters of words (phrases, clauses, sentences). Such rules are in effect limits that superintend the meanings generated by the tracing of legible marks. To be legible, these marks must be traced in such a way as to be readable as letters and words. This tracing—whether done by hand or a printing press or a computer—results in a set of edges with orthographically recognizable shapes: the reader must be able to construe a certain set of edges as forming the letter *A* and another set as *N* in order to grasp the two letters together as forming the preposition *an*. Otherwise, there is considerable freedom of variation in the formation of the marks themselves, that is to say, in the disposition of their edges.[10]

## Veils

We assume that veils mainly cover up and cover over—that they hide something from view. Certainly so. Yet they also reveal—at their edges. Edges are not the mere termination of veils, their cutting-off point, their ending. They are *there where something is shown or, if not shown, where it can be inferred*. Whether by direct manifestation or by way of indication, the edges of veils show just enough to inform (say, what color of skin a veiled person has) or to suggest (what lies under the veil).

But this is not to say that we are speaking of the usual part/whole relation, according to which a part counts as a part only insofar as it belongs to a whole— as if the edges around a veil show an integral part of something whole that lies, entire and intact, under the veil. The veil has taken one whole thing—the whole face, the whole body, the whole statue or icon—away from our sight but it gives us something special in return: a set of uniquely informative edges.

It is to the edge of the veil that our eye is often drawn, and sometimes our hands, too (as in "lifting the veil"), not necessarily to grasp or possess what is on the other side, but more often to get a sense of what is there—to come to know it, at least in a preliminary way. I am speaking not only of the outer edge of a veil, its fringe, but also of inner edges such as bulges and creases that act to intimate what is under the veil. In both cases, surface figures twice. Not only as the surface of that which is veiled (the skin of a human body, the surface of a jar over which a veil has been thrown) but also as a secondary surface: a surface-upon-a-surface. The internal and external edges of this latter epi-surface are suggestive with regard to what lies under the veil. Having little else to go from, we start from these edges as clues to what lies under the veil.

The essentiality of edges to veils is borne out by the fact that an edgeless veil would be no veil at all; it would be like a Borgesian world map that is exactly co-extensive with that of which it is the map, every point of the map touching its geographic equivalent on earth, with nothing left over—a map that is a complete wrap-over with no gaps and no outer edges. In fact, an unending veil—a veil with no edges, at once altogether smooth and unending—would not count as a veil. For it would not act to veil anything under it. A veil allows us to see what is veiled through, indeed *in*, its edges: what is veiled is *there*, *it itself*, a captive of its own edges, even if all of it, or most of it, is concealed. Despite the veil, or *in the veil*, we are privy to the veiled thing itself.

Veils are peculiar in that they enter into our awareness mainly by means of their *texture*, a texture that is at once visible and palpable. Veils are characteristically created from cloth that is made, manufactured, woven. "A man of the cloth," we say, referring to the masculine analogue of a woman's religiously "taking the veil," both of which veilings tend to be black cloth as if to symbolize the way the official costume is designed to conceal human flesh.

Veils exist between two extremes: complete transparency and full covering, the former being manifestly secular (as in strip-tease shows), the latter characteristically religious. In complete transparency (not veiled at all, or with a veil that is fully transparent) what is veiled is fully revealed. When something is fully covered with an opaque veil, the veiled thing (whether a sacred relic or the human body) is withdrawn from the realm of appearance. Yet precisely as covered, it may retain an aura of powerful presence.

Fanon remarks in "Algeria Unveiled" that Algerian women's veils are not merely coverings imposed upon them: they can empower a woman by allowing her to be actively looking while being mostly removed from others' looks. Beneath the burka, freedom of movement reigns, unbeknownst to the onlooker. Deployed in

FIGURE 6. *Voiles*, drawing by Ernest Pignon-Ernest; featured on cover of Jacques Derrida
and Hélène Cixous, *Voiles* (Paris: Editions Galilée, 1998). Courtesy Editions Galilée.

this way, the veil can become a force of resistance, especially in colonialist regimes:
"the woman who sees without being seen," remarks Fanon, "frustrates the
colonizer. . . . She does not yield herself, does not give herself, does not offer herself."[11] It is to be noticed that such free movement and inherent resistance occur
most actively at the outer edges of the veil, where the veiled woman's eyes are
active. Such concealed looking acts to undermine a hegemonic regime that would
like the eyes of its subjects never to stray.[12] The veil in such a circumstance is not
just closure or covering; it provides disclosure, opening. It opens through its own
edges—*at* these edges and even *as* these edges.

   In certain cases, the actual edges of veils rejoin the actual edges of flesh or of
other physical things over which they are draped. Take the drawing above, which
is featured in Hélène Cixous and Derrida's *Veils*.[13]

   Notice how the outer edges of the knuckles and fingers of the hand here nes-
tle under the lower edges of the cloth lying over them. The two sets of edges are
closely juxtaposed—those of the veil and those of the hand. The flesh (and fingernails) of the hand and the upper folds and texture of the overlying cloth are
intimately related: they are presented as *touching* each other at their edges. These
edges act to define the shape of the cloth and the exposed part of the hand respectively—two very different entities are here conjoined through their proximity to
each other: flesh to cloth, cloth to flesh, in a contiguous coupling. Their fate is conjoint, intertwined—not just in this image, frozen as it is forever in visual stasis, but
also in any situation in which veiling brings cloth and flesh together.

"Everything will flower at the edge,"[14] writes Derrida in his essay "Parergon." A *parergon* is a by-work that is *around* or *alongside* something else, the work proper (that is, the work we identify and name as such). But these two locative adverbs—around, alongside—in turn imply the presence of edge, whether graphically depicted or purely imagined. A veil is a *parergon* of a special sort; instead of framing, or acting as ornamentation, it valorizes the very thing it veils. Beyond its own decorative interest (often woven into the design of cloth), it brings the veiled thing forward in its very unavailability to perception, as if to say, here, under this veil, is something of considerable interest—whether this "something" is an icon, a human body, or a painting (as was customary in late-nineteenth-century art openings). The interest is underscored precisely by its being withdrawn from view (and thus, by implication, from touch as well). But a hint or a peek is offered by the internal and external edges of the veil itself. These edges are ways into what is veiled, indirect and allusive as they must be. They are also ways *out*—ways that the veiled thing comes out to enter into our perception. In the case of veils, everything flowers at the edge because the edge is a double-edged affordance that moves back and forth between veil and veiled thing. The veil's edges give access, however circuitous, to whatever has (been) withdrawn as veiled.

Edge to veil, veil to edge: the two terms act together in closely collusive pairings that are not only occlusive but that also bring about a circumstance in which much is shown by what is not shown—shown or at least suggested by edges that are those of the veil itself. These same edges belong to the surface of the veil, marking the places where the veil figures what cannot be directly seen or touched. A veil is *all surface*, a surface draped over another surface, that of the veiled thing. Its edges furnish an isthmus between the two surfaces—their common channel and the transition from one to the other. Here, the collaboration of surface and edge reaches a point of conjunction in which the external edges of the veiling surface intimate the structure of the surface of what lies on their other side, even as the internal edges (the bulges and bumps) of the same veiling fabric suggest other aspects of what is concealed from sight and removed from touch.

Limits are present here in a special way. No longer formal as in the case of written language, they enter as the limits of socially acceptable behavior in a given culture. This is not only true of Islamic culture—where the veiling of women is so prominent—but also of every human society that "draws the line" between acceptable and unacceptable exposure. Nudity—how much, if any, to reveal—is often a pivotal issue when it comes to veiling the human body. The question of how much flesh to show tends to be pivotal in religious traditions that enforce strict veiling procedures with respect to covering and uncovering people as well as venerated objects. Veils collude with these various social and religious strictures, enforcing (and sometimes complicating) them in multiple ways. These strictures constitute cultural limits, and they are enacted decisively by prescribing the exact placement of the edges of mandated veils. In such a situation—where the mode of veiling is dictated by formal rules—*much converges at the edge.*

Not only are traces, veils, and cusps related to each other through the various intricate ways in which each combines edge and surface—and often edge and limit, though "limit" takes on very different forms in the case of traces and veils—but they are also related in other ways. Oceanic cusps, despite having distinct kinds of edges, act as both veils and traces in certain respects: they are at once traces of the dynamics of deeper currents and tidal forces while also veiling them from the naked eye. Similarly, a trace can be considered a veil insofar as it does not manifest its full meaning all at once; much remains concealed and calls for the concatenation of other traces and ongoing interpretations in order to be understood. It is also a cusp of sorts if we think of a written or drawn trace as culminating a line of thought or a trajectory of visual intuition, taking either of these to a conclusive, albeit momentary, point.[15] At the same time, a veil is like a trace in that it shows the bare contours of that which is veiled in its folds, even as it discretely reveals a part of what is veiled through its external edges. A veil can be imagined as analogous to a sheet of paper that carries traces for those who know how to read it, even if it is not made of paper but typically from a fabric of some sort. A veil is also like a cusp to the extent that the covered body or thing comes to a crest in the distinctive shapes assumed by the covering veil.

Each kind of edge at stake in this interlude exhibits a falling off that ends in the dissolution or disruption of the most prominent edge-structure. The cusp of a wave dissolves into the water around and under it; a veil eventually falls away from what it acts to conceal; and a trace loses its status as a bearer of determinate sense as it gives way to other traces that possess other meanings. The edge-structure of each is precarious; there is no guarantee of continuation, much less of permanence. The becoming that underlies all change reclaims these edges; their longevity is limited, and their duration is doomed. While they last, however, they are significant presences in the edge-world in which human beings are enmeshed. And they are such despite the fact that cusps are typically natural, while traces and veils are highly conditioned culturally. But these differences of provenance and effect in no way undermine the deep-lying similarities between cusps, traces, and veils.

### Notes

1. Note that here we find conspicuous instances of the opening-out feature of edges that stand in contrast to the closed and fixed character of limits. The very term *breakthrough* suggests transgressing established limits.

2. Wesley Mattingly points out that oceanic currents (and thus waves) are themselves deeply influenced by the moon's procession and precession, producing tides on Earth. Thus one cusped phenomenon gives rise to another (communication on October 27, 2013).

3. This point did not escape John Dewey, who wrote that "when . . . each step forward is at the same time a summing up and fulfillment of what precedes and every consummation carries the expectation tensely forward, there is rhythm" (*Art as Experience* [New York: Perigee, 2005.], p. 179). Rhythm occurs when the diphasic aspect of a cusp phenomenon—at once regressive and progressive—is repeated several times in a certain pattern.

4. For Mill's remarks on predicting tides ("tidology"), see J. S. Mill, *A System of Logic, Ratiocination, and Induction: Being a Connected View of the Principles of Evidence, and the Methods of Scientific Investigation* (Cambridge: Cambridge University Press, 2012 [1843]), esp. chapters 10 and 12.

5. In ordinary parlance, we employ another sense of being on the cusp in which it means that one is on the forefront of one's historical moment. This usage is especially useful in describing the avant-garde of an artistic or social movement—virtually identical with being on "the cutting edge." The placard of a recent art show at the Los Angeles International Airport (LAX) provides an example: "the cusp between painting and cartooning (explored between awkward paint, pixilated dots, and a graceful line) is tested, transgressed, and ultimately claimed under different personal banners. . . . This is at the edge of being in between figuration and abstraction" (placard for the show "On the Cusp," LAX, June 2015).

6. On gestural sense, see my essay "Meaning at the Edge of Gesture," an unpublished essay that draws upon the work of Eugene Gendlin; this essay was presented at a special session on Gendlin's work at the annual meeting of the Society for Phenomenology and Existential Philosophy in New Orleans in the fall of 2014.

7. For Derrida on trace and *différance*, see his early writings, especially the essay "Différance," in *Margins of Philosophy*, and chapter 2 of his *Grammatology*.

8. See the postlude below and "Concluding Thoughts" in Casey, *The World at a Glance*.

9. I am taking becoming in Bergson's sense in *Time and Free Will*, chapter 2, and the extension of it in Deleuze and Guattari, *A Thousand Plateaus*, passim.

10. In all this, I have left aside the internal relations between traces themselves. These are far from unimportant: they constitute the full phenomena of linguisticality and (if Levinas is correct) of ethicality as well. But my effort has been to single out traces as such, one by one as it were, and to regard them as distinctive kinds of edge. A different analysis would be required to specify the networks formed by already constituted traces: whole statements, indeed entire languages, as well as complex ethical actions. Here I have limited myself to capturing a sense of what is peculiar about traces considered as singular effects brought forth by the event of inscribing edges in a receptive medium.

11. Franz Fanon, *A Dying Colonialism*, trans. H. Chevalier (New York: Grove, 1965), p. 44.

12. Stephanie Damoff, a student of mine, writes, "I found myself thinking of some Naguib Mahfouz novels I read many years ago. I seem to recall in the Palace Walk trilogy that there was some kind of grille over the windows, or perhaps a balcony, through which the women of the house could look out at the world, but they could not be seen from the

street. This grille is called the *mashrabiy'ya*. Another kind of veil, another type of edge between inner and outer, public and private" (e-mail communication on April 7, 2008). Damoff here points to the variety of veiling structures and practices in Islamic culture, which is far from monolithic in its prescribed rules and which leaves considerable leeway in the employment of certain veils, for example, the hajib in contemporary Iran. (Conversation with Amina Tawasil, November, 2016, New York City.)

13. The drawing is by Ernest Pignon-Ernest and appears in Hélène Cixous and Jacques Derrida, *Veils*, trans. Geoffrey Bennington (Palo Alto: Stanford University Press, 2001). It figures on the cover, and a more complete image of it is presented in the center of this same book: here the veil is shown continuing to the right but with no further hint of the body underneath. This constitutes the basis for the figure as reproduced here.

14. Jacques Derrida, "Parergon," in *The Truth in Painting*, trans. Geoffrey Bennington and Ian McLeod (Chicago: University of Chicago Press, 1987), p. 81.

15. On this last point, see Rudolf Arnheim, *Visual Thinking* (Berkeley: University of California Press, 1969).

# THREE

# Edges of Places and Events

The cold smell of potato mould, the squelch and slap
Of soggy peat, the curt cuts of an edge
Through living roots awaken in my head.
    —Seamus Heaney, "Digging," in *Death of a Naturalist*

From an initial consideration of material things, with their rims and frames, gaps and margins, along with other sorts of close-in edges such as borders and boundaries, we moved to the relation between edges and surfaces, and then edges and limits. We saw how the latter two pairs of terms are ingredient in grasping the particular edges found in traces, cusps, and veils, selected as three sample edges from the vast array of the edge-world. Let us now delve into the capacious domain of places and events in their edge-bearing and edge-generative powers.

By moving to places and events, I am departing from the usual view that edges belong exclusively to things. This view is as ancient as Socrates, who claimed that an edge is "the limit of a solid."[1] This implies that edges properly accrue to things regarded as solid substances—three-dimensional objects that are material in their constitution and settled if not fixed in their shape and size. I take this to be tantamount to the literal *reification* of the edge-world, tying edges down to concrete physical things, an object-obsessed approach to edges that amounts to what Merleau-Ponty calls "the freezing of being."[2] Certainly, many edges do pertain to physical objects—as is clearly the case with the automobile with which I drive and the computer with which I write—but do *all* edges inhere in material things? This chapter will explore the hypothesis that this is not the case, and that there are at least two significant classes of edges that do not attach to physical objects, or not to these alone. These are the edges belonging to places and events. Sections I–VI below take up how edges accrue to places, while sections VII and VIII explore their inherence in events.

This is not to say that edges are ever wholly detached or free-floating. Every edge is the edge *of something*: if not of a discrete material thing, then of non-things like events and places, even if these latter are themselves composed in part of physical things that have their own edges.

I

When I am in New York City on 110th Street, on the block just west of the Frederick Douglass Memorial, I find myself in a very definite place, peculiar to that part of the city, with its own atmosphere, diverse population, and local street scene. Living on this block as I do, I recognize certain rhythms of pedestrian and traffic movement, including the way the wind courses through the street. I am also familiar with the patterns of sunlight and shadow that fall on the street in several configurations at different times of the year. None of the phenomena I have just mentioned—automobile and bodily rhythms, wind and light patterns, local population, and the overall atmosphere—is a concrete material *thing*, and yet each belongs to the place in which I find myself.

In this same place, physical things are certainly also present: the human bodies and cars that generate the rhythms I feel, the traffic lights and signs, parking meters, street curbs, the buildings that line this visual canyon, the people I encounter on the street, and much more. Each of these things certainly has its own edges, which differ from thing to thing. The edges of the parking meters and street curbs are blunt in comparison with those of street signs; those of the buildings vary from acute to molded, depending on the architectural style of the building. The edges of the people passing by on the street range from angular to bulbous, with very diverse fringes (of hair, clothing, hands, shoes). Everywhere I look, I see not just things but the edges of those same things—highly variegated but altogether appropriate for each thing I see.

Yet this same place has its own edge, *the edge of the place.* How is this to be described? It is tempting to do so by a phrase such as "the southern edge of Harlem on its west side." This edge so designated is largely a construct of city planners and urban historians—and of mapmakers who depict regions of New York City in coherent cartographic space. Members of each of these three groups are at a definite remove from the place itself. The urban historian depends on a certain temporal distance to be able to claim that certain groups of people have settled there at given moments in time. The city planner, though aware of the pertinent urban past that preoccupies the historian, is intent on projecting a future for this place—how it will fit into a civic space that will improve living conditions for the inhabitants of the various neighborhoods making up this part of Manhattan. The cartographer presents an image of how the city is configured in the present, at the moment when a city map is published. But this convergence between the current reality of the city and its more or less isomorphic representation in a map cannot undo the spatial distance between the cartographic image and the urban reality it purports to represent. The historian, the city planner, and the cartographer all discuss or depict a given place from a position outside that place—from their offices or studies or libraries. They conceive and depict the edges of this place from another place, another location.

Those who inhabit or daily traverse the place itself, by contrast, know the edges of the place up close—from within their own experience. They know them as belonging to a "near sphere," to use Husserl's term for a space that is as proximal as it is familiar. The edges of the place they know are not manifested primarily by written words or printed images—by history, or plans, or maps—but by their specific daily *experiences*. The place's edges are delivered by these experiences rather than by images and words. Such experiences are in turn a function of the lived body and, more particularly, the "habitual body" in Merleau-Ponty's expression. They arise from the repeated movements of the place-dweller's body, from his or her customary walking through the place and the associated looking at it (smelling it, touching it, hearing it, navigating it), as well as from the memories that linger from these walks and looks. Not just history but *historizing* is here at stake: the way the lived bodies of inhabitants create their own history in space, their own place in time—and their own edge-world on the basis of both.[3]

Let me get specific by citing my own experiences on the south side of 110th Street, where I reside. The building where I live forms one very particular edge of the street scene I have described, and it does so in two respects. Experienced from inside my apartment, it acts as a threshold from which I view the street below as I gaze down on it; this same threshold converges with my bodily location at or near the windowsill. But when I go down onto the street to do errands, I sense the same building from the outside as a single massive façade with pronounced outer edges (the building's overall profile) and internal edges (those of discernible floors and windows).

This building's facade is not the only edge-bearing denizen of this place, of course; across the street there is an architectural twin that has the same overall dimensions. This other building makes up the northern edge of 110th Street as one walks west from the Douglass memorial. Unlike my own building, I experience it only from the outside and from below—from the street. Its exterior seems distinctly *other*. My own building, containing my residence, feels familiar, and its external and internal edges are at once deepened and softened in comparison with the building across the street to the north. As an integral part of my current life, these edges seem less formidable and more forgiving than those of the building that is its exact physical counterpart. This demonstrates that edges cannot be reduced to their physical dimensions but reflect the lived historicity of the occasions on which they are perceived.

In this circumstance, I experience a *modulation of edge* that is especially characteristic of places—a modulation that itself may take many forms in terms of color, texture, height, shape, architectural style, and so on. Unlike rims, which tend to be repetitive and standard for the physical things to which they pertain, the edges of places have multiple aspects—even when they are of the same basic type (here, two symmetrical buildings facing each other, each a slight variation of the other). This multiplicity partly derives from the fact that the edges of places are often difficult to pin down exactly; it is also a function of the fact that the experience of being in a place is indispensable to the way its edges present themselves. In the case I have just described, the differential modulation of the two sets of edges—those of my building versus those of its twin—arises mainly from how my residence in one of these buildings provides a very different experiential base.

Still other edges are at stake in this particular place: those of the sidewalk and street under my feet, the shops at street level, the sky under which I move. In the case of sidewalks, for example, edges are experienced as slight unevennesses in the surfaces on which I walk. They belong entirely to the material from which these surfaces are constructed: asphalt and concrete. These edges are creatures of the material medium that intervenes between my moving body and the earth underneath. In contrast with any edges the earth itself might possess—those of rocks or naked ground—the edges I feel underfoot on 110th Street are altogether artificial. This artificiality is not just a fact of their generation or history but also something I actively sense as such, something I *know* to be the case with my lived body itself. Such corporeal knowing (*connaissance du corps*, as Merleau-Ponty puts it) is integral to my experience of the place I am in and thus part of its primary identity for me.

Other artificial surfaces and edges abound in this urban place. As I lift my gaze from the pavement, I notice the doors and windows of stores and shops—Central Market, Amrita Café, Dorita cleaners, a bicycle-rental store, and a boutique for the care of toe- and fingernails. The edges in these modest-scale structures are entirely rectilinear and they intercalate closely with each other: the vertical edge of the café is chockablock with the edge of the cleaners next to it, which is contiguous in turn with Lila's Nail Care. Everywhere I look, juxtaposition is the order of the day. I find myself in a fabricated world where everything has been crafted by implements or is itself an implement (such as the doors to these stores). This is the domain of the ready-to-hand (in Heidegger's term), that is, of things manufactured for practical employment: tools, clothes, sandwiches, cups, bicycles, and bottles. On 110th Street, these things are made available at street level, where they are delivered or displayed. In the busy place-world of local stores and cafés, a tight mosaic of edges reflects even as it supports a commercial life in which accessibility is indispensable: all this forms a densely configured mosaic, from which there seems to be no escape.

Nevertheless, escape lies close at hand. All I need do is to look up—straight up. When I do, a generous canopy of air and light opens above me: I see the sky. I am conscious of its sheer vertical height; it is so high up that nothing exceeds it—nor can it be measured as such. It is a striking instance of "the Vertical," Heidegger's term for the ultimate dimension that links earth and sky. In its sheer transcendence of the street below, the sky would seem to lack edges—in stark contrast with the apartment buildings and commercial establishments that sport so many salient intersecting edges. But is this so? The sky is not a surface in any usual sense, certainly; it is too diaphanous for this, and it has an indefinite depth that defies metric determination. Even in this nebulous situation, however, we can discern edges: namely, those belonging to clouds and other atmospheric phenomena, as well as those where the sky's visual appearance is intercepted by buildings that cut across it at acute angles. These latter edges stand out all the more on a cloudless day: they are an intrinsic feature of the presentation of the sky as seen from below.[4] Their exact identity seems ambiguous: do such edges belong to the upper parts of the buildings or to the sky itself? In fact, they belong to *both*; they are instances of edges so intimately shared that we cannot say to which of their bearers they finally belong.

Here, we come upon quite a basic structure—let us call it the *edge/edge relation*—that is by no means confined to the way the sky is profiled against high buildings. Other instances of this relation include edges arising from the occlusion of one object by another: say, those formed by the way a parked car is seen against a building as I walk across the street, or the manner in which the sign of the former Esso gas station on the corner of 110th Street and Frederick Douglass Boulevard was set against the bare brick wall of the apartment building adjacent to it on the east. Indeed, everywhere we look we see congeries of edges that are the outcome of such occlusions: walking in Central Park, just across the street to the east, I observe the way tree branches cut across my view of the rock protuberances behind them, spontaneously forming a new set of edge/edge relations with each change of position I take. In these instances and many others, we see evidence that edges as experienced do not cling to single things or places alone but arise in the interface between two or more things or places, and from there ramify throughout entire cityscapes and landscapes.

The edge/edge relation in general takes several major forms. In certain cases, it signifies the *sharing* of edges that are clearly distinguished, as with the chockablock edges of stores next to each other on W. 110th Street; sometimes the edges are so deeply merged that we cannot tell them apart, as when a table top is made from pieces of wood so finely glued together as to be indistinguishable; and sometimes the edges are distinctively different, yet such that we cannot easily say to which thing or place the edges belong (as with the example of buildings profiled against the sky). Still, other edges are not shared in any of these three senses but nevertheless closely *collude*. Here the leading instance is found

when the edges of something interact with its immediate background, spawn-
ing awareness of edges in this background (a building as profiled against a car,
or high rocks in Central Park as seen through tree branches). Here edges are
grasped *through* edges. Typically, these edges are tributary from a primary
object, as we witness in the edges of shadows cast on the street from the bodies
of pedestrians.

Places are peculiar in that *all their edges exhibit edge/edge relations*—every edge
of a place is interactive with other edges rather than independent or freestanding. There is no edge of any place that does not emerge from the way that place
is situated in its own larger environs and thus in relation to a plethora of other
edges in these environs, including those of the particular things that populate it.
With rare exceptions, the edges of a place interact with those of the surrounding
world in manifold and subtle ways.[5] Here we are at an opposite extreme from rims
and frames, which have the status of edges mainly because of their inherence in
discrete single objects; for such objects, edge-edge relations may occur, but if so
they are secondary or supplemental. In the case of edges of places, all of them are
interactive with other edges—those of its own occupants as well as those of other
places and what is in them.

## II

But let us return to the scene on 110th Street to address another aspect of this particular place. Not only the sky above but also the vistas opening at both ends of this
street allow it to breathe in a special way. These vistas to the east and west are like
glass walls in that I can see *through* them and can take in contents differing markedly from those found in the immediate street scene itself. City parks beckon at
each end of the street—Central Park in the east, Morningside Park to the west.
The distinctively different appearances these parks present provide welcome relief
from the closely configured reality of the immediate street world of 110th Street
in between the two parks.

These appearances exhibit a blend of edges more sinuous and supple than any
that characterize the buildings, pavements, and streets that make up the rest of
this south Harlem scene. Such edges are not as constant as those of constructed
things; they change with the seasons and display different colors and shapes, textures and volumes than we find in the built world. The diverse edges that structure
the comparatively open space of the parks is such that the two ends of this urban
scene are experienced as beckoning to me, offering an exit from an otherwise unre-
lieved metropolitan street scene. At the same time, the edges of this scene concatenate with the edges of the two parks to form a complex nexus of edges that,
despite their many formal differences, are experienced as belonging together in
one and the same urban situation.

In the end, different as both the sky and park dimensions of this place are from those that characterize the buildings and sidewalks, all these factors cohere as components of the experienced place: they *coinhere*. If human beings have any doubt about this, they need only consult the many birds (seagulls, herons, hawks, robins, sparrows) that fly freely around the sundry parts of this same scene, whether naturally given or humanly devised. Their agile movements act to stitch the various parts together, constituting one continuous world—as if to complement and complete the way a single glance can sweep through the same scene and take it in as one continuous place.

Important for our present purposes is the fact that the edges of the two parks exemplify a basic trait of placial edges: their capacity to reach out into their environs in subtle ways while also conveying a sense of their own character and content as places. Such edges are open textured and porous. Not only do they define or enclose a place, they also extend that place into what lies around it—they take it into the circumambient space.

## III

Several sorts of edge conspire in the making of a single place. To be a place at all is to possess a multiplicity of edge types. To call places "open textured" as I did just now is to contrast them with *sites*, which are spaces determined in strict terms by the closure effected by imposed or imputed edges, which tend to be rectilinear (as in building sites).[6] Moreover, where a material thing tends to feature one consistent kind of edge (that of the rectangular step of a ladder or the margin around a printed page, for example), a place characteristically possesses a variety of edge-types. Though there are more complicated places than the corner of W. 110th Street where I live, this particular place proves to be rife with edges of disparate sorts—so many, in fact, that my description of it could continue indefinitely. A proliferation of edges inheres in any given place, more so than for any given thing in that place.[7]

A place is an especially powerful catchment area of edges, absorbing and exhibiting a variety of them—natural and artificial, conspicuous and understated, fully presented or only adumbrated. This reflects the fact that *a place has no single definitive edge*, no set limit in any strict sense. To have a definite edge is a basic feature of sites, by contrast; but places—and regions, which I construe as complex collocations of places—are not so restricted. Consider how places we designate by phrases such as "Gramercy Park" or "Battery Park"—or regions like "Midtown Manhattan" or "the financial district"—refuse to be characterized as stopping or starting at a certain precise point, whatever city maps may claim. By the same token, when places and regions intersect, they do so in diffuse ways that defy definite, much less complete, description. South Harlem merges into the Upper West

Side across Morningside Park, which acts as a buffer zone between these two regions, at once connecting and separating them. Yet no local inhabitant is likely to say that South Harlem extends only to a particular point—say, to Manhattan Avenue but not one yard beyond. In Morningside Park (which abuts Manhattan Avenue), Harlem residents mix with Upper West Side residents and Columbia University students. Such intermediary or liminal spaces abound in cities. Their existence makes it difficult to establish a strict border between two or more parts of the city. It is notoriously difficult to specify, for example, just where city neighborhoods begin or end. (We shall return to neighborhoods in chapter 7.)

In short, the edges of places are more like boundaries than borders. They share with boundaries an inherent openness and vagueness of spatial extent. These two qualities are here present in such elementary phenomena as being able to walk back and forth between different places in a city with comparative freedom—with many opportunities for entry and exit: from South Harlem I can approach Columbia University by any number of streets ranging from 110th Street to 120th Street and across the multiple walkways of Morningside Park. It is as if places and regions provide many points of access, some newly evolving, some of more ancient vintage—in direct contrast with sites, whose very definition and existence depend on the maintenance of tightly contained and rigid limits that resist change. Such limits resemble borders much more than boundaries.

We are thus presented with a situation of double parallelism when it comes to the presence of edges of places and regions:

> edges of places / regions > boundaries
> edges of sites > borders
> [where ">" signifies "are like"]

But to say that the edges of places and regions are like boundaries, and those of sites like borders, is not to say that such edges simply *are* boundaries and borders without remainder. We must be cautious when it comes to establishing the parallelism of traits. Such parallelism, while striking, does not amount to identity. In fact, we are here talking of two different levels of analysis: on the one hand, edges of places / regions versus those of sites; on the other, two basic kinds of edge. Edges of places and regions evoke boundaries and those of sites suggest borders, but the relation is not symmetrical; it is not the case that boundaries are always (or only) evocative of places or regions, or that borders allude only to sites. The reason for this is straightforward: borders and boundaries are edges not just of places but also of many things (artworks, colors, persons, groups, security walls between nations, and so on) and of events as well (the creation of an artwork, migration across an international border). The pertinent differential factor is not that of comparative abstractness or ideality—as it is when we compare edges and limits—but that of the *respective inherence of edges* in that to which they properly belong, whether this be a place, a region, a thing, or an event.[8]

## IV

Despite its fuzzy fringes, which facilitate close links to a larger constructed or natural environment, a place is always a whole of some sort, at some scale; it is equivalent to *this* part of the world, *this* neighborhood, *this* street scene, *this* hotel lobby. It may not have a proper name or toponym, but is still an integral, intuited *something*: a place is never sheer vapor, or mere myth; it is not nothing, nor does it come from nothing. The fact that it comes always with edges means that it cannot be entirely nebulous: even fuzzy edges give a certain definition and shape to a place. Indeed, its very identity as a place comes in significant measure from its being distinctively edged. Its edges are not just where a place fades out or ends. Prominent as the ending of a place may be, especially when marked as such, a place's edges also convey the basic character of the place itself, its physiognomy as well as its ingression into a larger encompassing world. Such edges are not merely the exoskeleton of that place but are also an integral part of its very being, essential to its being the place it is.

This is no more—but also no less—mysterious than the fact that our personal identity has everything to do with our bodily presentation, which is itself conveyed by the visible edges of our flesh: edges that constitute our contour as we present ourselves to others and to ourselves.[9] We often recognize these same others in turn by the profiles they assume: by the set of edges they project in their bodily bearing, along with (and as an active part of) their gestures, posture, gait, and so on. Often a single glance at their profile allows us to identify them without further inference, remembrance, or reflection. Likewise, we instantly identify a place by its characteristic shape; even if much else is obscure in our perception of that place, its edges stand out and allow us to recognize it as just that place. Thanks to the pattern formed by edges, we find the gestalt familiar: "I must be on upper Broadway, around 112th Street, close to Le Monde Café," we say to ourselves, even as swirling snow obscures the scene around us while walking in that part of the city. Despite the density of the atmosphere, we are usually able to discern enough edges to figure out where we are: say, the edges of the long green awning that is a familiar mark of that same café, the pattern formed by the distinctive vertical glass windows, and so on.

The multivalency of the edges of a place synchronizes with the monovalency of its ongoing identity. Otherwise put, the character of a place is presented and maintained through its edges: not despite them—as we might imagine if we consider edges to be merely obstructive or trivial—but because of them. Edges constitute the distinctive "cut" of the place they bound. Their manyness—both of kind and in number—gains coherence in the oneness of a given place, while the one-ness benefits from the multiplicity that subtends it. We encounter here a version of the ancient conundrum of the One and the Many: no One without a Many for that One, no Many without a One for this Many. As may be inferred from Parmenides's and Plato's discussions of this conundrum, the One would be stultified—would be formal and fixed—without the intervention of the Many. For its part, the Many would be merely dispersed were it not for the unifying force of the One.

There is a lesson here for the relationship between a given place and its edges. It would be all too easy to reduce place to the formality and definiteness of site were it not for its many absorptive and expansive edges; without these edges, a place could not accommodate the mutations of history or the physical processes to which it is subject—mutations that are essential for any place to be a continuing and vital presence. By the same token, without a sense of singularity holding it to-gether, a place dissipates into its environs and loses its identity as *this place*—with the result that it is no longer distinguishable from other places, as happens so often in suburban sprawl, where tract after tract and house after house mime each other. Singularity here disappears into sameness. In such situations, edges are mainly con-ventional or functional delimitations, such as streets that demarcate blocks from each other. Such edges fail to delineate a characteristic gestalt that allows us to dif-ferentiate one block from another as a singular place over time, despite the many changes to which it is subject.

The indefinite and multiple edges of a place require the main mass of that place—its heft and bulk—for these edges to be effective in giving it shape and out-reach, while the place in turn requires these edges, if it is to be sufficiently pliable, to be capable of change of the sort that environmental or historical mutations entail. We have here two corequisite factors, one bearing on sameness and the other on difference. Once the conundrum of the One and the Many is brought into the realm of historical and material becoming—where the same and the dif-ferent are always at stake—it applies with surprising aptness to something that was of little direct interest to Parmenides or to Plato: the edges of places.

## V

By emphasizing the complex fate of edges when they are ingredient in a place, I do not mean to overlook one very particular dimension of such edges: their instru-mental character. In Heidegger's nomenclature (already invoked), edges belong to the realm of the useful or ready-to-hand (*zuhanden*): a predicate that obtains for the edges of places and not just for things, as Heidegger presumed.[10] Consider the way that one street intersects another, forming an "instrumental complex" (as Sartre put it) whose edges are perpendicular to each other, as obtains on 110th Street in New York and in many suburbs. The actual shapes of such edges need not be formally geometric or strictly grid-like; indeed, slight irregularities may contribute to their greater utility, since these allow for the give-and-take of ordinary usage. A road that surrounds a particular place has edges that are rendered less than rigid by the roadside areas where tires can be changed, telephone calls placed, or naps taken by sleepy drivers. Edges of roads, even those designed to be perfectly straight, depart from geometric perfection and lend themselves all the more effectively to multiple instrumental use.

Edges of places very often act as orientational, guiding us from one place to another: say, from 110th Street into Central Park. Even though it is by means of edges that we often make our way in the surrounding world—thanks to their acting as effective signposts—not every edge of a thing or a place has an explicitly orienting character. Some placial edges are prized for their aesthetic value, as in the decorative hedgerows around gardens. Still others are valued for their determinate formal or objective dimensions—thus for their very indifference to art and work alike. These are valued for their sheer regularity of shape or size: say, the town square in its very squareness. Whatever the instrumental, aesthetic, or formal value of edges of places, these edges remain resolutely part of the place they describe—distinguishable from the place, yet integral to its existence and identity.

## VI

We may take it as a basic truth, then, that edges belong to places, which are as much edged as are things. I shall close my treatment of such edges with an analysis of two aspects of their belongingness, two inherent directionalities.[11]

*Terminus ad quem* ("end toward which"). From a given place or set of places, edges begin, spreading out from there—not so as to interdigitate with other edges in an instrumental fashion (as when the edges of a wrench engage the head of a recalcitrant bolt) but such that the edges of one place are sources for the edges of other places, the generative contours for entire place-worlds. I had this phenomenon in mind earlier when I alluded to the way that the two public parks near W. 110th Street seemed to call out to me as I glimpsed them: they were edges *toward which* my look was drawn. But a comparable outreaching occurs in wholly natural settings as well. Creosote bushes in southern Nevada desert regions grow densely together up to a certain level of elevation and then abruptly stop. From that discernible line of termination a new area opens out, one that lacks such bushes and is comparatively barren. One place, marked by thick creosote growth, leads the eye onward to a contiguous place bereft of such growth, the clearly discernible edge of the first area opening onto the prospect of the second, which is its effective *terminus ad quem.*

Only a few miles away from this particular scene, a wall on the far west side of Las Vegas marks the limit of local construction; on its other side, a dry

gulch is found, and just beyond that, an uncultivated reserve of hills and mountains of intense coloration and convoluted configuration. An entirely artificial
wall—positioned to mark the outer limit of a local subdivision in the sprawling
suburbs of west Las Vegas—cedes place to wild landscape, traversed only by a
single access road. In this way, the edges of two places—one wholly natural, the
other a matter of concerted effort—manifest the respective characters of these
places, their status as "wild" or "constructed." Thanks to their contiguity, their
edges are linked in the way they abut each other, even if dramatically different in aspect and appearance. One kind of place gives way to another through
an implicit directionality that moves from a constructed edge outward toward
a wild place. One's eye is led from the wall to the open area as if guided by an
invisible force.

Terminus a quo ("end from which") is a place that not only reaches out to another place through its outer edges; it also serves as the ground for the further perception of other places. From being there (or projecting myself there in vision), I
move to other areas. The emphasis is now not upon these other places as the des-
tination of my look but upon the *edge from which* I move (if only in vision) to these
other locations. The directionality is not *toward* but *from*.

An example of edge as a terminus a quo comes from the same desert place-
world I have just described. A few years ago I participated in a silent vigil at the
Nevada Test Site—a desolate stretch of land devoted to nuclear and other kinds
of bomb testing that is pockmarked by nearly one thousand past explosive tests,
some above ground and some underneath. The protesting group I joined was
allowed to assemble in one predesignated place, just outside the main entrance to
the test site—an entrance ironically named "Mercury."[12] As we gathered together
in a circle early one morning, we were keenly aware of the place in which we were
confined—both by the barbed-wire fence to the east and by the view of the test
site beyond it. The merest glance took one right up to this fence, then through it
to the buildings and other structures of the test site. We were looking into the test
site *from* a determinate viewing place: from its edges outward. Our conjoint perception arrived there from here, where *here* signifies the enclosing edges of a carefully confined stretch of viewing space.

Both of the two basic edge situations I have identified were at play at the
test site. The terminus ad quem names the transitional moment in which one's
gaze moves *to* or *toward* the edges of another place, such as from the edges of the
barbed-wire fence to those of the buildings of the test site. The terminus a quo
emphasizes the edges of a place *from* which one observes the edges of another
place: in this case from the viewing area outward. Instead of being smoothly transitional (as when my view went into the hills west of Las Vegas), in the case of
the test site my look went to another place *despite* being confined by the place in

which I was located. I arrived at this other place from within the prohibitive enclosure of a first place, from behind the barbed wire fence.

This contrast is complicated by the fact that the same edge can serve in both capacities. The edge of the creosote growth in my first example can at once be both a terminus a quo and a terminus ad quem; as the former, it serves as a base for looking beyond it, but as the latter it is something toward which I look in the first place even if my look then moves on. The same is true for the other edge situations just mentioned. For instance, the fence that edged the protest area was a launching point *from which* I and others looked to other buildings of the testing area. But the same fence also served as a confining structure when I first focused on it upon arriving. In each instance, a place's given edge can be seen for its own sake even as it can also serve as conveying my look to the edges of another place or area.

The Janusian character of these edge modalities tells us something significant about the role of edges in the place-world. The fact that the two modalities (the to-which and from-which) that I have just identified can characterize one and the same edge indicates a special feature of edges belonging to places as well as the intimate ties that exist between the edge-world and the place-world—a close collaboration in which these two worlds are conterminous, even if they never completely coincide. It shows that edges of places can be outgoing even as they also serve to enclose and delineate a given place. They take us out of the place where we are even as they determine the manifest shape of that same place. If Iamblichus could say that "boundary [*horos*] is the primary cause of bodies," we can affirm that the edges of places, most of which are boundary-like, *are deeply formative of these places*: shaping them, forcefully our apprehension of them, and bringing them into their own determinate being even as they allow room for their own transcendence.

## VII

We need now to take a crucial further step and consider the relationship between edge and *event*. To start with, let us first note that place and event both act to undermine the primacy of space and time, those twin colossi of early modern philosophy and science. For each contests the hegemony of monolinear, successive time by opening out multiply into history—not just in the form of datable, narrativizable "historical events" but also insofar as every event and every place (and often the two together) have ongoing resonances, whether in a particular place (say, what is now happening in Grand Rapids) or over a stretch of time (the ever-lingering effects of the Vietnam War). Both event and place also act to undermine the idea of a homogeneous, monolithic space insofar as each, respectively, differentiates itself into multiple happenings and into a number of discrete locales and region. As a consequence, each resists reduction to the dates and simple locations by which we designate them for reasons of convenience or scientific measurement. A place is more and other than the topographic site by which it is located in the world-space of meters and miles, and an event is likewise something more and other than its occurrence in the world-time of clocks and calendars. Each ramifies beyond the limits that define these spatiometric and chronometric units.

To extend my narrative of the Nevada test site: this same place exfoliates into historical events because of the central role of nuclear bomb testing in the post–World War II era—the test site is both a place in the Nevada landscape and an event in the history of nuclear proliferation during and after the Cold War. The truth is that both events and places (and not events alone) are historical, where the word *historical* refers to peculiarly human ways of inhabiting space and time: ways that are at once concrete and multiple, yet singular in each individual case, and that are subject to eventual recounting and reckoning as to their larger significance.

Place and event converge further in that both possess an essential factor of *surprise*. In their continually changing character, places can surprise us when we return to them after an interval. But events are surprising all the time. Every event, in its unfolding, contains an element of the not-yet-known in the form of what is still to come. No matter how well we think we understand it, each event harbors possibilities of taking other turns than we had expected—thereby yielding the surprising. This is so much the case that, as Nancy contends, "the event surprises or it is not an event."[13] If this is so, it is due largely to the edges inherent in any event; these edges trace its outermost periphery, at least in part concealing what is coming next. In the oncoming of the edges of events, the surprising lurks.

A major basis of such surprise derives from the occlusiveness of edges. As the outward parts of surfaces (I here set aside internal edges) and to the degree they are nontransparent, edges conceal what lies on their other side: the edge of the window curtain in my apartment obscures my full view through the window onto 110th Street. Edge occlusion obtains for temporal as well as spatial edges. Such occlusion arises when a feature of the unfolding of an event in time acts to obscure other parts of that same unfolding. Thus the "retentions" (in Husserl's term) that stream back and down from contemporary events may act to cover over what is next to emerge; the same holds true for "protentions."[14] In both cases, the surprise of the event consists in the fact that what is to come is not fully revealed but always at least partially obscured by what is now happening. Nevertheless, what is coming is often adumbrated by the edges of what is occurring in the present: something is revealed despite its concealment by these same edges.

The surprise that arises from events, delivered from just beyond their retentional or protentional edges, need not be shocking, nor need it be a matter of deep wonder. It is usually encountered by the merest glance. Glances play over the surfaces onto which they are trained, flitting over them and touching their edges intermittently.[15] When this happens, something surprising is likely to arise: as I gaze out through the large glass windows of the café Le Monde—windows that constitute an external spatial horizon—I see someone going back into her car unexpectedly after having just come out of it as well as someone walking who suddenly reverses course. These are only mildly surprising events, but perceptual life is made up of them as well as occasional major surprises.[16]

Surprise, then, is what comes from *just around the edge of an emerging event*. Whether the pertinent edge is primarily spatial or temporal—or, as in the case of full-fledged events and places alike, irrecusably historical—the surprising enters into my ken as I come into its vicinity. The situation of surprise is always interactional: it is not just a matter of what comes to me, but also of how I come to it. The surprising presence of the toponym "Mercury" appearing on a sign in the Nevada desert did not announce itself from nowhere; it arose in relation to *where I was myself placed*. Driving north on Highway 95 from Las Vegas, I failed to perceive it on my right because a group of hills hid it from my sight. After having overshot the location, driving back south I suddenly saw the whole test site laid out before me: I was now looking down into a vast valley that had been obscured by the hills I passed on the way north. The spatial view I sought opened up to my surprise, but only after I had taken extra time and gained new perspectival reach in finding it.

Just as space and time collude continuously in the generation and experience of an event, so what appears in a place connives with my place-of-viewing in the upsurge of surprise. The surprise itself is a function of the adumbrative powers of the pertinent edges of the place-world as it is enlivened by the events that animate it. The edges of events interact with those of the occupants of the place-world, including stationary things in that world, such as hills and trees. One set of edges coordinates with another—evoking the edge/edge relation to which I pointed earlier. Thanks to this intermingling of edges of places and edges of events, surprise emerges all the more forcefully.

Places and events, which we tend to consider as disparate occupants of the life-world, are closely linked in ongoing experience. The edges of both are at once *occlusive* and *disclosive*, concealing and revealing. Just as edges can conceal the presence of certain things and places and events, they can also act to disclose this very presence once they have been circumvented. Surprise happens when the edges of a single thing or place or event that act to obscure what is to come give way suddenly to the emergence of what now lies unconcealed: enclosure gives way to disclosure, obscuration to revelation, the unknown to the known (though sometimes also to a new unknown).

## VIII

In searching for what is most characteristic of the edges of events, I turn to consider an event commemorating those who were lost in the inferno of 9/11, an event that emerged spontaneously the day after the disaster, in Union Square, just a mile or so north of Ground Zero. Shocked and stunned, thousands gathered in the square, where many photographs of those still missing were pinned to hastily assembled fences or taped to the marble walls at the base of the equestrian monument at the south end of the square. It was a matter of coming to terms with an event whose proportions were so gigantic and whose larger significance so unknown that it exceeded any customary ways of understanding it. In part, coming to Union Square was motivated by an impulse to share one's confusion and grief; at the same time, those who came were searching for the meaning of 9/11— what did it portend, both in itself and for the future of the nation and the planet? I was not then living in Manhattan but on Long Island; I had taken a train into the city on the day after the world-historical event. I heard that people were gathering at Union Square at Fourteenth Street, just east of Fifth Avenue, and found myself impelled to join them, not knowing what to expect.

The spectacle at Union Square was unlike any other I had ever attended. A somber mood hung over the occasion as people filed quietly along the inner lanes of the square. No one was speaking—except at the extreme southwest corner of the square, where some were debating how to interpret the disaster and what to do in its wake. I have never been among so many human beings where such eloquent silence prevailed—a silence not enforced but shared by tacit consent (there were no designated or self-designated "leaders," nor were there any police). The people themselves were from every walk of life and income level, brought together by a deep wish to commiserate in each other's company. As daylight faded, streetlights came on and gave a garish aspect to the scene. Music stemming from a small group of flute players rose plaintively from the northern side of the square. It was a moment of collective mourning—and of public memory in the making.[17]

The edge aspects of this moving event were telling. To begin with, the edges belonging to the place conspired perfectly with the occasion. The outer edges of the square consisted of open sidewalks that acted as buffer zones from the heavy ongoing traffic. These edges also provided space for those who preferred to be onlookers rather than participants. From this outer spatial edge a number of access points offered entry into the square's interior, as did the whole southern side—including a major subway station, low balustrades, and various entry paths. Crisscrossing the square were internal walkways whose comparative narrowness gave a sense of firm enclosure, yet whose winding shapes, "edged" carefully on both sides, encouraged a kind of walking meditation. These inner lanes sanctioned and supported the absorbed slow-paced walking in which the majority of those present engaged, including myself, keeping in step with each other in an unrehearsed processional format, a moving cortege.

The internal and external edges of this public space were protective and reassuring, while at the same time making possible the kind of movement that amounted to a spontaneous missa solemnis. These crisply delineated edges contrasted starkly with the smoldering edges of the collapsed Trade Towers just to the south—edges that had lost all definition in the devastation to be found there: the acrid smoke from the towers still hanging heavily in the air at Union Square.

And the event's own edges? The contrast between the disastrous event of the day before and the solemn after-event at Union Square was significant. The destruction of the towers happened all at once, as if from nowhere: it was an apocalyptic moment whose temporal edges were fiercely compressed and starkly definitive. The world watched in horror when the towers, having been struck by the two hijacked planes, collapsed one after the other in a matter of minutes. These minutes were clocked in world-time in a dense procession of lethal explosions, uncontrolled flames, and human beings diving to their deaths. Each such moment had its own acute undilutable edge. This condensed nexus of unthinkable tragic events was reverberating in the minds of those who walked solemnly in Union Square: the tragedy of the day before was an absolute edge of world-time— "absolute" in that what preceded and what followed it were forever changed by the event itself—an event that acted as an unavoidable source point for the events of the next day and for many years afterward.

On the day after, the temporal edges of the event of 9/11 were drawn out and down: out into history, down into the moving bodies of the commemorators at Union Square. The edges of the apocalyptic event itself (composed of a myriad microevents) haunted these bodies as they gathered and walked in gravely flowing duration. Those present in the square felt we could continue the vigil all night— perhaps for days on end (as some, in fact, did). The last thing in my mind was what clock time it was; I thought nothing of the train schedule or when the last train to Long Island would depart. I was not just drawn into the drama but was also at one with it; I existed entirely in the moment of being with others who were as stunned as I by what had happened the day before.

If there was a sense of a more encompassing edge of time, it was that of history in the making; but of this historical horizon those present had only the dimmest sense. It was as if the edges of the Now, which had become impossibly compressed on the morning of the day before, were being slowly distended, spreading outward like tentacles toward a very uncertain future. Those of us at Union Square the evening of the day after were already part of that future in its barest opening phase, all the while feeling ourselves suspended in a temporal haze, a pensive moment of mourning. Having no way to know what was going to emerge at the level of world events, we sank all the more deeply into the current moment. If the event of 9/11 was monstrously immeasurable, the event at Union Square was strangely measured. It was as if the slow pace of the communal walking within defined spatial confines effected a meting out of time and space in which the participants were taking the measure of the cataclysmic event of the previous day—thereby allowing it to become a collective memory held within the minds and bodies of the commemorators rather than remaining a shattering event located exclusively without in an external, indifferent world-time.

It will be noticed how the temporal edges of what happened at Union Square on September 12 rejoined those of the placial edges of this happening: the two sets of edges interleaving in still another instance of the edge/edge relation that we have seen to be so formative in other contexts in which place figures. The curvilinear edges of the walking paths of Union Square joined forces with the dark temporal texture of the occasion, opening onto an unknown futurity that would affect many millions of people, not only in the United States but also abroad.

Contrast this intensely somber scene with the much less momentous one I recounted earlier—my walk on W. 110th Street, in which Central Park and Morningside Park were prominent presences. These public parks acted to frame the bare action of walking along the street extended between them; welcome as these parks were in this intensely urban setting, I did not feel an urge to enter them, being content to keep them as optional openings at the two ends of the street scene. But when I approached Union Square Park, two miles to the south, late in the day after 9/11, I felt I had no choice but to enter the park and to engage in what was happening there. The park was not merely a beckoning horizon of possible visitation but also a magnet for collective action that I and many others felt deeply drawn to join.

From the foregoing analysis of the evening after 9/11, we can say that the edges of events have the following properties: they fit within an ongoing flow of temporal becoming, being part of this flow but also acting as eddies and currents within it, as it were. The event at Union Square was a slender current within the raging cascade of the tumultuous week that stretched from Monday, 9/11, through to the next Monday—and indeed for long afterward. Its spatial and temporal edges spelled out a moment of pensive pausing in the midst of what was otherwise a massive impersonal flux. Joining up with others was not just an act of commiseration or empathy; it was also a first step in making sense of the tragedy of 9/11. It was an event in a tidal wave of response that carried away everyone in the region, the nation, and much of the rest of the world.

Ever shifting in their shape, edges of events exhibit a varying temporal range that fits between a beginning and an end; we designate the extent of this range by phrases such as "starting with the sunset," "until late at night," and other similar locutions. At the same time, each event exhibits a distinctive duration of its own—its specific course of manifestation—which we describe by saying things like "all evening" or "for several hours." The outer edges of commencing and terminating act to enclose this unfolding of time: an unfolding that has its own phases with their own internal edges. None of these instances of the edges of events is measurable in precise quanta of world-time. If chronological units of date and time are attached to them—such as "9/11," "meeting at Union Square tonight at 8:00 p.m."—these act as bare designators, never as adequate descriptors.

When it comes to the edges of events, we are no longer talking of retention or protention (the nuanced inner horizons of time-consciousness) but of basic temporal phases of beginning, lasting, and ending. These phases are apparent in the experience of events as happenings within whole life-worlds that are shared or shareable with others (unlike time consciousness, which is always mine or yours alone). Each of these phases has its own characteristic kind of edge that forms part of the temporal becoming of an event.

> *Starting phase.* As events get underway, they display an edge that is forward tending, initiatory. As the Union Square event began, there must have been a palpable sense of something significant getting underway: something *to come.* No single action needs to be here at stake, nor anything dramatic; it can be as inconspicuous as several people beginning to walk together. Their walking in silence along the pathways of the park would be enough to constitute the initiation of the event about to gather force.

> *Durational phase.* As others joined in, the event got more fully underway. Things were in midcourse when I arrived and entered into the durational thickness, which was open-ended, having no precise starting or ending point of its own; it was simply *ongoing.* Any thought of how long it had been going on, or how long it would last, was only of indirect interest; what mattered was being part of the gathering—especially its processional, which was in the form of a circular, self-rejoining pattern.

> *Ending phase.* It is especially notable that there was no upper limit to this event; not only was no such limit announced, but had it been it would have seemed intrusive and arbitrary. Normally, Union Square closes at midnight, as signs posted on the gates of the park announced; but on this occasion no such terminal moment was observed. Those of us still there just kept on walking and thinking and listening. If we left at a certain moment, it was for personal

reasons and had nothing to do with the ending of the event itself, which tapered off gradually sometime in the middle of the night— just when I don't know, as I had left by then—nor did it matter to the existence of the event as a whole, which was in the process of becoming a current within that moment of history.

It ensues that eventmental edges are at least threefold in character, and not surprisingly so given the triple dimensionality of temporal unfolding itself (past, present, and future). Each of the phases I have just identified has a certain character and an inherent nisus. The fact that these phases of eventmental edges are indefinite in extent in no way diminishes their force or effect in the ongoing stream of experience: a stream that is composed primarily of events or event-like happenings. On the contrary, their comparative amorphousness, their immeasurability, is just what we should expect, given that events themselves are not quantitatively determinable occurrences in *Weltzeit* ("world-time," Heidegger's term for the kind of time that is specifiable as present-at-hand), but rather are unique happenings in entire life-worlds. These life-worlds are themselves complex congeries of human beings, animals, inanimate things, vegetation, the earth, the sky, and so on. The differential destinies of the denizens of life-worlds mean that the events of which they form part are not isolable from each other. Such events are *intereventmental* in character: they form "concrescences," using Whitehead's term, for the unique configurations they manifest. The edges of these ongoing events—each of which exhibits the threefold edge structure I have described above—are intensely interactive: as were the edges of 9/11 and the Union Square event that was its irrepressible sequel.

It is becoming evident that the edges of events are comparable to those of places in that both kinds of edge are interactive through and through; the edge-edge relations of each, whether considered internally or externally, are manifestly multiple—indeed, integral to the very structure of events and places themselves.

## IX

There is a larger lesson to be learned regarding the edges of places and events. These edges keep locations and happenings—which make up so much of our daily experience—within a scale that suits the range of our own activities and energies. Were we to know nothing but infinite space or time, we would be floundering; we would not know how to find our way about or what to do there. Edges of the sort I have been discussing orient us in our everyday lives, much in the manner of the walkways at Union Square that gently guided mourners the evening after 9/11. Such edges direct our perception and motion, allowing us to deal discerningly with a finite life-world. *No place, no event, is not finite, and there is no unedged finitude.* Only

infinite space or time can claim to lack edges. Hence the celebrated medieval saying, repeated by Nicholas of Cusa, Bruno, and Pascal, to the effect that the universe
is an infinite sphere in which "the center is everywhere and the circumference nowhere."[18] Down here below, however, we live in a finite sphere with many insistent
circumferences, thanks to the proliferation of edges that accrue to things, events,
and places. Even though they may frustrate us, these edges keep us honest. They
let us know that the world in which we live on earth is something continually ending. The life-world is an edge-world from start to finish.

The edges that surround us, far from being merely restrictive, can be distinctly
liberating. As Lacan says, "nothing creative appears without urgency."[19] This urgency stems from the way that edges, spatial and temporal alike, pervade our lives,
leading us to realize that constructive coping emerges from within the very challenges that edges frame and present. In their very finitude and modes of closure,
edges of events and places encourage, and often enhance, innovative actions and
issue in unprecedented works. No wonder that artists need studios, scholars use
desks and seek cells, actors thrive on stages, scientists flourish in laboratories. Creative artists and thinkers, and many ordinary people as well, benefit from being in
workplaces alive with edges, where discipline goes hand in hand with inspiration.
The restrictive spatiality of such places and the delimited time within which creative work often has to happen there can summon the extraordinary.

## X

It cannot be denied that the edges of places and events alike are often *closed* and
*closing*; in effect they turn away from the local surrounding and serve to keep a
place or event contained within itself. But the same kinds of edges are sometimes
also *open* and *opening*; in this capacity, they are porous in their constitution and
open out into the environing world in which they occur. In possessing these contrastive directionalities, such edges are in effect clavicular: like the two prongs of
the collarbone or "clavicle," they are of roughly equal tensile strength. They may
begin a given place or event, but they can just as well end it. In one case, they
open a place or inaugurate an event; in the other, they close off that place or terminate that event.

Another clavicular characteristic of the edges under discussion in this chapter
is that of being in space or in time. Sometimes these edges present themselves as
spatial (for example, as *in* versus *out*) and sometimes as temporal (*during* versus *before* or *after*). But even if the edges of places lend themselves most easily to spatial
specification and those of events are most often temporally cast, in the end every
edge of every place and every event is spatiotemporal.[20] The spatiality of a place is
situated *in* the duration of that place. So too the temporality of an event emerges
*from* that event's very locatedness in place. Just as we cannot hold space and time

apart in the case of placial and temporal edges, so we cannot separate event and place themselves from each other in any definitive manner. For there is no event without place (*somewhere* to happen), nor is there any place that does not itself incorporate, or at least implicate, an event (something that *happens*). This means that the edges of places and events, though descriptively different in the ways I have discussed in this chapter, are not only compatible but also actively cooperative.

The edges of places and events, different as they are in detail, interact so intimately that it is often difficult to keep them apart. The event of 9/11 is a case in point: we cannot altogether separate the temporal edges of this event from the placial edges of the locus of its happening. They are distinguishable upon analysis but inseparable in historical reality. The same obtains for the after-event in which I participated at Union Square: the placial edges of the latter concatenated closely with the shapes of the commemorative action that took place there on September 12. These two internally related situations exemplify the ongoing collusion between placial and eventmental edges. Elsewhere as well, indeed everywhere in human experience, these edges form indispensable coconstituents of the life-worlds we inhabit.

The interaction of placial and eventmental edges has another dimension: that of their shared *incrementality*. Whereas the edges of a thing are tied to that one thing, the edges of events and places act to link the parts of each. By this I mean that such edges follow out, and contribute to, the extent of a place and the course of an event. A place is a conjunctive entity, made up of multiple items that are interrelated in one common setting; its edges respect this coadunative property. An event unfolds, and its edges reflect the unfolding itself. In both cases, edges follow out of a place or an event incrementally—part by part, phase by phase—even as they also coalesce among themselves to become the edges of that place or of that event.

Things, events, and places show themselves to be complicitous with each other thanks to their interconnective edges. The edge of a discrete material *thing*—the *horos* or "boundary" to which Iamblichus pointed—is the edge of something situated *in a place*: this thingly edge is situated in the matrix of edges provided by that place. And every place, with its various edges, is in turn part of an ongoing *event* that has its own edges. The edges of an event are intimately interwoven with the edges of the place where the event happens and with the edges of the things found in that place. Thanks to the edges of each, the edges of all interact in polymorphic patterns that have everything to do with how we experience the world and how we live our lives.

Imagine yourself to be a Mexican migrant who is attempting to get into the United States to find work—work that is not available in your own country. As you make your way on foot to La Frontera, the United States–Mexico border, your body has had to come to terms with arid stretches of land in the far north of Mexico, bereft of water and filled with cacti and snakes and wild animals. Your increasingly exhausted body struggles as you force yourself to move with increasingly falter-ing steps across a torrid landscape. Your bodily energies may be forthcoming in less trying situations, but they are all too soon depleted when you are on the point of complete exhaustion and daily dehydration.

Assuming that you succeed in getting to the northern part of Mexico, you will soon come to the border itself, marked by an impenetrable concrete or iron spike wall, patrolled by border police, and lit by powerful klieg lights at night. Your bodily movements are literally arrested by this wall. Up against this barricade, you cannot proceed further. The wall is a formidable material thing, and it is set in a specific place—that defined by the United States–Mexico border. Coming up against it is an event: the event of being stopped dead in your tracks. Such an event has an outer edge that is distinctively border-like: the stoppage has been imposed from without, it assumes the form of an interdiction ("no passage!"), and it is indifferent to the local topography. The placement of the wall has cut short the event of your cross-ing. The edges of your failing body come up against the rigid surface of the wall in a static edge-to-edge confrontation. The edges here at stake are not only those of your body or the wall; they also belong to the event of your having come to this impasse. They constitute the edges of the arrested movement of your body as it encounters an unyielding obstacle. They are the edges of an event of sheer blockage.

In this circumstance—all too common in this historical era, not only in Mexico but wherever walls have been built to block the forward movement of migrants—we witness graphically the way that the edges of places and events can act to close off, stopping a hopeful migrant from further movement, in contrast with other occasions on which the same edges serve to open up: say, when a different migrant has the good luck or the money to possess the documentation that will allow him to pass through an official checkpoint at the wall. The same massive Thing in the same stationary Place, the place of the wall, can prohibit the Event of traversal; but it can also permit legal movement across it. By the same token, all the effective edges in this multiplex circumstance—those of the wall (thing), the border (place), and the moving body (event)—are at once spatial and temporal. The edges of the wall and the border, spatial as they are in the perception of the migrant and in rep-resentation (say, on a map), are also historical in their provenance. By the same token, the edges of the migrant's body are spatial as shaped flesh and temporal as bearing a life history. The edges of places and events rejoin those of dead matter and live bodies to form a situation in which movement is for the most part fore-closed and only rarely facilitated. Our own lives, albeit often in less dramatic fash-ion, continually confront comparable circumstances in the edge-worlds to which we already belong or which we come upon as new.

## Notes

1. Plato, *Meno* 76a. The exact statement is that "shape [itself a form of edge] is that in which a solid terminates, or, more briefly, it is the limit of a solid."

2. Merleau-Ponty, *Phenomenology of Perception*, trans. C. Smith (New York: Routledge, 1962), p. 63: "The notion of geometrical space, indifferent to its contents, that of pure movement which does not by itself affect the properties of the object, provided phenomena with a setting of inert existence in which each event could be related to physical conditions responsible for the changes occurring, and therefore contributed to this freezing of being which appeared to be the task of physics." (Don Landes's translation speaks instead of "the determination of being" [New York: Routledge, 2012], p. 55).

3. The "lived bodies" here in question are not completely individuated entities but have always already incorporated social mores and structures into them by way of the deeply-lying habitus that Pierre Bourdieu has identified as formative of the corporeal social subject. See Bourdieu, *Outline of a Theory of Practice*, trans. Richard Nice (Cambridge: Cambridge University Press, 1977), especially chapter 2.

4. I am always seeing the sky from some place underneath, and this is so even when I am situated much higher up myself, on top of a building or on a mountain; only if I were to leave the earth's atmosphere altogether would the sky cease to present itself as above me. Note that the sky's immeasurability—key to its mathematical sublimity for Kant—does not remove it from the world of edges: it is another aspect, virtually another dimension, of this world. (I owe this last line of thought to Katherine Wolfe.) I return to the edges of sky and clouds in chapter 10.

5. These exceptions are precisely those in which a place comes to such an abrupt limit that it is prevented from merging with its surroundings. In an urban setting, this is found in certain parts of lower Manhattan in which one's sense of being surrounded by buildings is so dense that there seems to be no way out from under their formidable presence. Even here, the sky offers a way out—if only by providing a bare splinter of light. But a basement or a strictly windowless room, as in solitary confinement in prison, yields a circumstance of such strict enclosure as to preclude edges that stem from the felt or seen relationship between this place and its surroundings. On this latter situation, see the epilogue concerning edges as experienced in solitary confinement.

6. For further discussion of site versus place, see Casey, *Getting Back into Place: Toward a Renewed Understanding of the Place-World*, 2nd ed. (Bloomington: Indiana University Press, 2009), pp. 258–60, 267–70, 362–64. On space as homogeneous and isotropic, see Casey, *The Fate of Place: A Philosophical History* (Berkeley: University of California Press; reprint, 2013), chapters 5, 6, and 9.

7. Exceptions include a complex machine made of many parts, each having its own different set of distinctive edges: for example, Alan Turing's early computer models. The capacious character of a place supports the coexistence of a considerable number and variety of edges.

8. The alert reader will notice that there is a certain convergence between "border" as I'm using this term and "limit" as discussed in the last chapter. Both possess a certain

continuity or sameness compared to the changing actualities of boundaries and nonformal edges. Even so, a given border is historically generated—as in the case of the border between the United States and Mexico—whereas a limit as I am using this term (e.g., as in differential calculus) is a sheerly formal entity and posited as such without regard to such concrete variables as features of a given landscape or the course of a certain history. See chapters 1 and 2 for further discussion.

9. Our silhouette is an extreme version of this phenomenon, as when a friend "picks me out" from others as I advance toward her in the dark. For a discerning discussion of silhouette, see Jean-Luc Nancy, *Being Singular Plural*, trans. Richard D. Richardson and Anne E. O'Byrne (Stanford: Stanford University Press, 2000): "People are silhouettes that are both imprecise and singularized, faint outlines of voices, patterns of comportment, sketches of affects . . ." (p. 7). On bodily edges, see chapter 8, "At the Edges of My Body."

10. See *Being and Time*, trans. John Macquarrie and Edward Robinson (New York: Harper, 1962), sections 15–18; on usefulness or "reliability," see "The Origin of the Work of Art," trans. Albert Hofstadter in *Poetry, Language, Thought* (New York: Harper, 1971), pp. 28–39.

11. I have discussed this distinction in a different way in "Do Places Have Edges?" in *Envisioning Landscapes, Making Worlds: Geography and the Humanities*, ed. Stephen Daniels, Dydia DeLyser, J. Nicholas Entrikin, and Doug Richardson (New York: Routledge, 2011); and in "Edges of Places," in *The Intelligence of Place: Topographies and Poetics*, ed. J. Malpas (New York: Bloomsbury Academic, 2015), pp. 23–38.

12. I say "ironically" since Mercury is the Roman name for Hermes, the Greek god who was known for moving swiftly over crossroads marked by Herms, the signposts that consist in single phallically shaped stone shafts.

13. Jean-Luc Nancy, "The Surprise of the Event," in *Being Singular Plural*, p. 167. It follows that to speak of "the surprise of the event" is to utter a "tautology"; in other words, every event brings with it "the unexpected arrival (*sur-venue*) of the thing itself" (ibid.). In my interpretation, this arrival is ushered in by the edges of the event in the form of its currently known contour.

14. It is an open question as to whether the edges of protentions are inherent in them or are a function of what lies beyond them (i.e., the unknown oncoming event). As Andrés Colapinto asks in reference to an earlier version of this passage, "Is it really the *limit* of protention that *occludes* what is to come? Isn't it precisely *because* what is to come is not visible that our protentions have a limit in the first place? This would mean that unknowability constitutes edges, not that edges create unknowability by occlusion" (e-mail communication of August 10, 2011; italics in original). To this I would say that unknowability in its full scope is composed of two factors, the occlusion effected by edges and the fact that what has not yet happened is not yet visible (audible, tangible, etc.). Each contributes, but each exists on a different plane: the invisibility belongs to the part of the unfolding event that has not yet come into our ken, the occlusion to that which has already appeared as it masks what is to come. Edges exist between these two planes, thus are integral to the full phenomenon of events' unknowability. See also in this connection the astute paper by Elizabeth B. Behnke, "Bodily Protentionality," in *Husserl Studies* 25 (2009), pp. 185–217.

15. See Casey, *The World at a Glance*, especially chapter 7 and "Concluding Thoughts."

16. It is to be noticed that no surprise can arise except in relation to a prior anticipation: I had expected that the woman who went right back into her car would stay out of it.

17. I have written on this last aspect of the same situation in "Public Memory in the Making: Ethics and Place in the Wake of 9/11," in *Architecture, Ethics, and the Personhood of Place*, ed. Gregory Caicco (Lebanon, NH: University Press of New England, 2007), pp. 69–91.

18. Even if often attributed to Nicolas of Cusa (1401–64), this saying derives from "The Book of the XXIV Philosophers," a pseudo-Hermetic text of the twelfth century. Giordano Bruno and Blaise Pascal cite the same saying centuries later without attribution. The roots of the saying have been traced back to Plotinus: see his *Enneads* VI, 4–5.

19. Jacques Lacan, *Écrits*, trans. Bruce Fink (New York: W. W. Norton & Company, 2006), p. 201. In my citation, I have altered "created" to "creative."

20. To bear out this claim, I would extend the analysis of events as temporally triphasic to places, which possess the spatial equivalent of starting/lasting/ending. My justification for doing this is that space and time are themselves ineluctably intertwined in the conjuncture of places and events.

# Frames in/of Painting

### I

Certain edges are able to alter their status from actively dynamic to passively inscribed or observed (or vice versa). This mutability is especially evident in the case of *frames*. For a given frame (such as that of a painting or photograph) can impose itself on us as inalterable (as seeming to be "exactly right" or "what is called for") or it can solicit our intervention, not just to praise or criticize it but to change it if we have the means to do so. Hence the temptation to be finicky about finding just the right frame for a given painting. Fitting or not, frames are themselves an active force inasmuch as they act to modify our perception of the artwork they surround. The bivalence of frames has led Derrida to conclude that frames are "beyond passivity and activity alike."[1] Or we might say rather that they are capable of being *both* passive and active in their presence and effects: passive in that they are already there, part of our perception of what they surround, active insofar as they alter this same perception.

The "picture frames" of paintings (to which I shall here restrict discussion) are bivalent in other ways. For one thing, they provide edges for what they enclose, yet they have their own edges. As the outer edges for a painting, they encircle—or more usually, "enrectangle"—the primary focal area of the artwork. At the same time, they are themselves enclosed at *their* outer edges by the surface of the wall against which they appear. These same outer edges are in effect enframed by the wall space on which they are hung, while the artwork proper (the painting itself) forms the inner edge of the same space.[2] There is a two-way vector at work here: the outside of the frame pulls toward the surrounding space, the inside toward the painted entity within. Each respective edge is the source-locus for the appropriate vector, the place from which a visual dynamism moves outward or inward. Altogether, a given frame constitutes, in Merleau-Ponty's phrase, "the inside of the outside and the outside of the inside."[3] It is inside and outside at once, though in different respects in each case. In this redoubling, frames resemble gaps, which we have seen both to determine edges for what surrounds them and yet to have their own edges. But the action of frames is more complex and subtle than this.

A picture frame is not just a go-between that exists between the pictorial space of a painting and the space environing it. This it certainly is: a via media for these two kinds of space, their *truchement* as the French say, their mediating bond. But it is also *its own space*, a peculiar space, a *triton genos* ("third kind"), neither purely figurative nor merely locatory. It is its own between, as if it mediates itself; it is like an it-self that is also a for-itself. It is not merely a delimiting presence or a neutral place, and much less is it a mere void in the manner of a gap; beyond its vectorial in-and-out dynamics, it constitutes a dynamic space of its own.

How does one describe the edge formed by the frame? It is neither pictorial/representational (except in rare cases to be considered below) nor is it practical/instrumental (except in the negative sense of providing a place for the artwork to come to an emphatic closure). It does not simply "stand out" or "efface itself" (as Derrida explicitly proposes), as if these were exclusive alternatives.[4] Instead, it does both of these latter things. To the extent that we notice it at all, it stands out; yet, as we begin to focus on the painting it encloses, it becomes increasingly peripheral and begins to merge with the visual background of the experience. In between, however—an in-between that is not to be measured in any definite number of spatial or temporal units—it has a life of its own, which our look takes in by a single sweeping glance. This glance glides between its edges as surely as we go from one edge to another in everyday life outside of art. The edges of the frame at which we glance constitute a species of "smooth space" in Deleuze and Guattari's sense of this term, by which they mean a nonhomogeneous, nongridded, open space in which our vagrant look assumes the role of the nomadic "legwork" these authors single out as constituting smooth space proper. (It is more appropriate to speak of "glancework" in the context of paintings.[5])

Even if the space of the frame varies considerably in width or length, it does have its own integrity, its own mode of presenting itself as a visual field. Just as "there is no natural frame," so there is no essence of frame: "*there is* frame, but the frame *does not exist*."[6] It does not exist *as such*, as an instance of one kind or type of frame, but it is *there* as constituting a spatial region of its own. In the sort of spontaneous apperception here happening, we do not focus on the frame as a separate material entity (this would be a frame that "exists") but on the framed entity, for which the frame acts more as a field than an object ("there is" frame, in that it is felt as present but not as an altogether discrete entity).

Another curious feature of picture frames is that even if they bring the artwork for which they are made to a new level of presentational being, they are not necessary for a given painting. We know that painters can decide to do without any frame: Mondrian and de Kooning eschewed frames, considering them a distraction from their paintings. The ordinary viewer of art can also do without a frame, as usually happens when we look at art reproduced in books or on posters or sent

FIGURE 7. Joan Míro, *Femme entourée d'un vol d'oiseaux dans la nuit* (1968) acrylic on tarpaulin. Fundació Joan Miró, Barcelona. © Successió Miró / Artists Rights Society (ARS), New York / ADAGP, Paris 2016.

to us electronically in a jpeg file. Here the image is typically presented against a blank background, and this suffices for its viewing. It is thus indeed true that a frame *need not exist*—exist as such, as a self-declared frame. But its actual absence does not eliminate all framing effects. The bare edge of the canvas or sketch paper may assume the role of frame; this edge is simultaneously an outer framing factor for the artwork *and* the place where the wall impinges, both at once. When Mondrian famously said that the straight black lines in his mature paintings were meant to "go on to infinity," he meant that they are to be imagined as traversing the literal edge of the canvas, moving into the environing space, and extending onward indefinitely. But something like this holds true for many other kinds of painting: we sense that Constable's hills stretch under and beyond the edges of the ornate nineteenth-century picture frames in which they were often ensconced. The literal presence or absence of a wood or metal frame need not curtail the visual dynamics of the edge of paintings or other visual artworks. Take, for example, the above striking painting by Joan Míro.

In the absence of an external physical frame, Míro playfully creates an internal frame by painting a single line around the central image; this line serves as a frame inside the painting that is part of the painting itself. This inner frame is all the more striking insofar as it is trespassed, almost defiantly, by several bold black brushstrokes in the lower right corner of the painting.

An example like this suggests two lessons. First, any frame, internal or external to the painted image, provides an opportunity to enhance the presentation of this image. Second, an inner frame such as we find in Míro's work effects what Gadamer designates as an "augmentation of being."[7] It brings the artistic interest of the painting to a new level of realization that it could not achieve without the positive intervention and intermediation of such a frame. Rather than containing

FIGURE 8. Howard Hodgkin, *Autumn in Bombay*, (2010–2014), oil on wood. © Howard Hodgkin. Courtesy the artist and Gagosian Gallery.

and limiting the central image of the painting (as in many traditional frames), this inner frame helps to animate the painting as a whole: from within, as it were.

Another variation is visible in a painting by British painter Howard Hodgkin. Here the inner frame is furnished by a matt placed around the center of the work—a matt that is in effect a rectangular margin. This latter is painted over with pronounced dabs of paint. These dabs assert their right to move unhesitatingly over this inner frame. The specific space of this marginal frame not merely surrounds the central content of the artwork but also allows for its extension onto this frame's surface and beyond. This is to *enact art on its own edge*—to carry it into the space of its own self-generated interior frame. It is as if both Hodgkin and Míro recognize the augmentative potential of internal framing, capitalizing on this potential by carrying the painting proper right into this self-inscribed framing and embracing it as an integral part of the painting as a whole.

In addition to the augmentative and resonative virtues of such internally located frames—virtues also evident in those cases where the painter carries the central painting onto its outer *physical* frame (as happens notably with Seurat and Marin)—there is still another variation: the deliberate breaching of the physical frame as if rebelling against its confinement and foreclosure. In such a case, we witness an attempt to overcome the frame not just by omitting it altogether, as with Mondrian, or by interpolating an internal painted frame, but by depicting the outer frame as broken open, as in a striking work by Tim O'Brien. (See figure 9.)

In this painting, it is as if water in its sheer wild surging-forth threatens to overcome the civilization of the frame, here presented in a highly conventional

FIGURE 9. Tim O'Brien, *Realism* (1996), oil on panel. Collection of the Museum of American Illustration at the Society of Illustrators, New York.

nineteenth-century format save for its lower edge, which is overwhelmed with the gushing of water. Not only does the depiction here overrun the outer edge of a fully framed traditional seascape, but it thrusts an entire ship and the surrounding water out of an otherwise conventionally represented implacement of ships on water. The shock effect acts like a deconstruction of physical frames, suggesting that the sea is here taking revenge on its containment in tepidly painted seascapes. In a case such as this—as in others in which the outer material frame is forcibly breached—we witness not just a tension between the natural world in its sheer elemental physicality and the artificial containment embodied in a picture frame but also an act of revolt against "the world as picture"—in Heidegger's phrase for the fate and affliction of the modern age.[8] The cunning of O'Brien's work is that it is the *represented* content (i.e., of the wild water) that is imbued with the force to destroy the actual physical frame that is designed to contain it. Representation itself overcomes conventional framing, normally a major ally of representation itself.

The sources of this subversion of traditional framing are to be found in two basic dimensions of any material picture frame—dimensions that can act to incite rebellion. First, every such picture frame represents a disconnect between the artwork for which it serves as a frame and its immediate environs; no matter how intimately related it may be to the content of the work, every picture frame enforces a certain stoppage, a spatial arrest between the pictorial (the represented or expressed) and the actual (the literally seen, the physically constructed). The frame breaks the spell into which aesthetic experience puts us, as if to say: *the magic stops here*. It brings the artwork to a peremptory closure, for at the outer edge constituted by this frame the spectator is de facto excluded from the experience that the artwork itself as image has induced. Artists like O'Brien, Hodgkin, and Míro contest this exclusion, each in his own innovative way.

Second, the status of every frame is highly ambiguous, as we have seen in the exploration of its paradoxical aspects: at once inside and outside, possessing an intermediate space of its own, *being there* yet not *existing* like other physical objects. A frame, insists Derrida, is "neither essential nor accessory."[9] Given the extent to which human beings prefer certainty and simplicity for the most part, it is difficult for them to tolerate for long the paradoxical aspects of a picture frame: namely, its being neither/nor (neither painting nor nonpainting) while also being both/and (painting and nonpainting). Hence the natural association of frames with veils: just as a veil hides-yet-reveals, so a frame encloses-yet-releases.[10] It is not surprising, therefore, to find that certain paintings have been literally veiled. Upon its first exhibition, for example, Frederick Church's celebrated "Heart of the Andes" was presented with velvet curtains at its edges looking like nothing so much as veils. Such framing by veils at once softens the disruptive break between the work and the exhibition space—"takes the edge off" that break—while concretely symbolizing the ambiguities of the intermediate space of a frame. The Metropolitan Museum's recent reexhibition of this same painting by Church in its original heavily veiled presentation convincingly demonstrated the subliming of a frame's hard edge by veiling it in soft velvet. Rather than extending the painting directly into an internal frame in the manner of Míro and Hodgkin, or onto an external physical frame as with Marin and Seurat, the place of the frame was assumed by a curtain acting as a veil.

## II

Rims, I said in interlude I, are often taken to be edges par excellence. We accept them as such, as definitive in their own way—think again of the North Rim of the Grand Canyon—and thus, in contrast to frames, we are rarely motivated to alter or decorate them. Much the same is true of gaps, especially with respect to the empty space they proffer: the fissure, the rupture. This empty space is given, and we are rarely motivated to ornament or otherwise alter it (unless we need to bridge it so as to traverse it). In both cases, there is a practical factor that discourages enhancement by means of decoration. Just as we typically *use* rims (bringing the rim of a coffee mug to our lips), gaps call us to cope with them (driving around a pothole in the street). By contrast, picture frames are primarily aesthetic in function and are rarely valued for their sheer instrumentality. They are also more complex in their bearing; like many kinds of edge, they serve to contain, but they also set off or set up, extend and enhance the artwork they act to enclose, augmenting it and sending out resonances into the surrounding visual field. As a result, we are strongly tempted to construct or decorate frames that suit the style of the pictorial image they surround: Baroque, Rococo, art deco, or high modern.

Moreover, whereas we speak of framing in the natural world mainly by metaphoric extension from the art world ("the horizon framed the landscape"), so conversely we talk of rims and gaps in the cultural world mostly by extension from their primary presence in the physical world ("population gap," "the outer rim of human habitation"). But conventional picture frames are in fact both physical and cultural. This is part of their deeply ambiguous status, and is doubtless reflected in our ambivalent attitudes toward them: Are they frivolous or required? Can we do without them? Another aspect of the ambivalence is this: just as the physical world can present what is not (yet) possible in the cultural world, so we can do things in the latter that exceed what the natural world can ever bring forth on its own, unassisted.

Rims and picture frames, despite their manifest differences, can both be considered instances of *works*—products of human efforts to shape or "work" matter so as to realize certain human purposes. (Sometimes the working is that of nature, as with the North Rim.) Each kind of edge is an *ergon* in the original sense of this Greek term: a "work" that is realized and that has definite consequences. In a term already invoked in interlude II, we can say that a picture frame is a *parergon*, a literal "by-work" that is located at the fringes of an actual painting. As a by-work, it exists *in addition to* the painting it surrounds, supplementing it. It does so as something seemingly superfluous, thus something we might do without. Nevertheless, it plays a formative role in the circumstance. How is this so?

Immanuel Kant, who first introduced the term *parergon* into aesthetic analysis, appraises frames of artworks in an intensely skeptical mood, asserting that they tend to be nothing but frivolous appendages, thus to be ranged alongside garments (qua mere finery) or compared with elaborately sculpted columns and the fancy windows of governmental buildings. It is notable that we gain access to such by-works, whether they resemble windows or columns, via their most significant edges. Kant writes, "Even what we call *ornaments (parerga)*, i.e., what does not belong to the whole presentation of the object as an intrinsic constituent, but [is] only an extrinsic addition, does indeed increase our taste's liking, and yet it . . . does so only by its form, as in the case of picture frames, or drapery on statues, or colonnades around magnificent buildings."[11] On Kant's stern view, both "form" and "extrinsic addition" characterize the edges supplied by picture frames. But Derrida, building on this dismissive remark of Kant's in his *Critique of Judgment*, argues that, far from being merely adventitious additions to artworks, *parerga* are constitutive of the works themselves. These latter are not just supported or supplemented by frames or columns or clothes; they depend on the presence of these *parerga* to be or become what they are. The by-work, and thus its edges, are integral to the work itself, which cannot do without it.

One way to understand the value of the *parergon* is to distinguish between "decoration" and "ornament," which are easy to confuse with each other in ordinary English usage. What is tempting to discount as merely decorative in the case of frames (as well as garments and architecture)—such is Kant's austere stance in *Critique of Judgment*—is to be regarded very differently when we see it as genuine ornament. An ornament, though certainly pleasing to the eye (or hand, or foot), is integral to what it ornaments, the work itself. It sustains an organic relationship with the work that may not be necessary in any strictly material or instrumental sense of the term (as rims are to bicycles and teacups) but that nonetheless has *importance* for it—to use the term that Whitehead argues is a crucial metaphysical category.[12]

Derrida is here on the right path: though not necessary, picture frames regarded as ornamental edges are not just accessory either. If they are supplemental, they are so in Derrida's special sense of the term: crucial to the very phenomenon they supplement, formative of it in their very ambiguity and variability. Thanks to picture frames, the by-work *works*; it helps to bring the work itself (notably, the artwork), if not into being in the first place, then into its most complete mode of realization—where "most complete" means not merely finished but aesthetically effectual. Cézanne held that a painting should be as complete as possible at every stage, even if it is never finished.[13] By "complete" he meant such as to work aesthetically, making sense to the eye. In the various degrees and kinds of a painting's completeness, a picture frame may well figure as a very distinct part of its completeness—usually, in a very late stage and frequently by the intervention of someone other than the artist himself (the dealer, the curator, the legal heir). Just how the frame comes to be joined to the physical painting matters far less than how it matters to the *work of art*—its import for the presented image as such. In the most propitious cases, it serves to complete this image and not just to decorate it.

When it matters to the painting as a constructive contribution that helps the work to be fulfilled at its own edge, the picture frame is a genuine *parergon*. In its very position as external to the work, a frame can fill out the work itself, thereby bringing it to a degree and kind of completeness not otherwise attainable. This action is at once work and play: work as active shaping of matter, play as happening in an unprogrammed and spontaneous manner. Seurat's and Marin's physical frames (onto which these painters continued their painterly motifs) stand out for being more playful than the focal areas of the paintings they surround, even as they contribute effectively to the presentation of these areas. In this way, the work of the frame extends creative play to the work itself. No wonder frames need to be *right next to* paintings, for it is from there, at the very edges of the work, that they can work their parergonal magic, an ornamental magic that is complementary to, and supportive of, the major magic of the work itself in its primary presented image. In their play, frames help the work to work; in their work, they help it to play. Frames work and play at the edge—*as* the edge and *from* the edge.

### Notes

1. Jacques Derrida, "Parergon," in *The Truth in Painting*, trans. Geoffrey Bennington and Ian McLeod (Chicago: University of Chicago Press, 1987), p. 77.

2. In Derrida's phrase, a frame is a "hybrid of outside and inside" (Derrida, "Parergon," p. 63). In other words, it is a hybrid that is an "outside which is called to the inside of the inside to constitute it as an outside" (ibid.). Derrida adds that such a hybrid is nevertheless no mere compromise of inner and outer: a frame is a hybrid that "is not a mixture or a half-measure" (ibid.).

3. Maurice Merleau-Ponty, "Eye and Mind," trans. Michael Smith, *The Merleau-Ponty Aesthetics Reader: Philosophy and Painting* (Evanston: Northwestern University Press, 1983), p. 126. Merleau-Ponty is here discussing the art image. Strikingly, what he says of the lived body is also pertinent to frames: this body is "the outside of its inside and the inside of its outside" (*The Visible and the Invisible*, p. 144). The similarity of the two citations from Merleau-Ponty (one being the grammatical reverse of the other) suggests that the body is a framing factor—that it actively mediates between our subjective intentionality and the environing world. It is "existence as congealed or generalized" (Merleau-Ponty, *Phenomenology of Perception*, p. 169). For more on body and edge, see chapter 8.

4. Derrida claims both of these things: "the [frame regarded as a] *parergon* stands out [*se détache*] from the *ergon* (the work) . . . from the milieu, it stands out first of all like a figure on a ground . . . but the *parergon* is a form which has as its traditional determination not that it stands out but that it disappears, buries itself, effaces itself, melts away at the moment it deploys its greatest energy" ("Parergon," p. 61).

5. On smooth space, see Gilles Deleuze and Félix Guattari, *A Thousand Plateaus: Capitalism and Schizophrenia*, trans. Brian Massumi (Minneapolis: University of Minnesota Press, 1987), chapters 12 and 14.

6. Both citations in this sentence are from "Parergon," p. 81 (italics in the original).

7. Hans-Georg Gadamer, *Truth and Method*, trans. Joel Weinsheimer and Donald G. Marshall (New York: Continuum, 1989; second edition), pp. 468 ff.

8. See Martin Heidegger, "The Age of the World Picture," in *The Question Concerning Technology and Other Essays*, trans. and ed. William Lovitt (New York: Harper and Row, 1977).

9. Derrida, "Parergon," p. 63.

10. For more on this double action, see the description of veils in interlude II.

11. Immanuel Kant, *Critique of Judgment*, trans. Werner S. Pluhar (Indianapolis: Hackett, 1987), p. 72 (italics in the original).

12. See Alfred North Whitehead, *Modes of Thought* (New York: Free Press, 1966), Lecture 1. For a comprehensive and insightful account of ornament (vs. decoration) in architecture with implications for all the arts, see Kent Bloomer, *The Nature of Ornament: Rhythm and Metamorphosis in Architecture* (New York: Norton, 2000).

13. I here paraphrase Merleau-Ponty's discussion of Cézanne in "Cézanne's Doubt," trans. Michael Smith, in *The Merleau-Ponty Aesthetics Reader*, pp. 63–64: "It is Cézanne's genius that when the overall composition of the picture is seen globally, perspectival distortions are no longer visible in their own right but rather contribute, as they do in natural vision, to the impression of an emerging order." The point is a variation on Baudelaire's claim that "a complete work [is] not necessarily finished, and a finished work [is] not necessarily complete" (cited in Merleau-Ponty, "Indirect Language and the Voices of Silence," in *The Merleau-Ponty Aesthetics Reader*, p. 88).

# PART 2

# Constructed versus Naturally Given Edges

# Preface to Part Two

We now move to a very different distinction in the edge-world: that between artificially generated edges and those that are given spontaneously in natural settings. The former are brought forth by human endeavor, whether individual or collective. These are the edges that surround us and impinge on us in houses and cities, on streets and airplanes. They tend to be angular, but even when not, they are manufactured with human aims of comfort, utility, or beauty expressly in mind.

In contrast stand the edges we encounter in wilderness areas, in undeveloped open landscapes, or in wild countryside outside city limits. Such edges are brought forth by natural gestation according to the ways of nature that we know only partially, even as we propound scientific laws to explain them. Despite the generality of these laws—which obtain for all natural processes—when immersed in the natural world we are brought into contact with edges that challenge us by their sheer variety and often seem to serve no obvious purpose. Whatever edge-structures we encounter here have their own being and character. Kant said that "Nature likes to be specific"[1]—a statement we can take as emblematic for much of the material to be discussed in this middle part of the book, which focuses on how specific edges inform natural settings such as wilderness areas, landscapes, and waterscapes of several sorts. Specific as well are the intermediate edges that are characteristic of the cultivated spaces of gardens and parks, which I shall contrast with characteristic edges of urban spaces to be found in streets and neighborhoods.

To describe edges as they emerge in the experience of nature should not be taken to mean that the situation of edges in the natural world is altogether distinct from that obtaining in human historical and cultural worlds. In discussing the differences between natural and artifactual edges, we shall be led to recognize their close relationship, sometimes to the point of interfusion. An example is the Tijuana Estuarine Reserve, a restored wetland that is integral to an understanding of the fate of edges in the city of Tijuana and in the section of the border wall that separates it from the United States. The same wall that makes crossings from Mexico into the United States so difficult for migrants—thanks to its hard, unremitting edges—also wreaks major damage on the natural edges of the estuary just to the north of the wall.[2] This is a telling contemporary instance of the intersection of nature and culture in a local edge-world—in this case, to highly detrimental effect. In other, less charged, circumstances we observe variations of such intersection.

The ensuing discussion begins by teasing out differences between artifactual and naturally given aspects of a specific locus on an island off the coast of Maine: Sand Beach, taken as paradigmatic for the meeting of land and sea as experienced in a given place. Similarly, human gardens and public parks are seen to exhibit a delicate equilibrium of the natural and the constructed in the creation of special places of leisure and reflection. Beyond the reappearance of the basic edge-types of borders and boundaries throughout this new part, we shall encounter novel forms of edge that configure the experience of landscapes and seascapes—for instance, the edges operative in the horizon, sky, and earth, each of which I explore further in chapter 10.

After a focused treatment of the difference between natural and artifactual edges in chapter 4, I turn to a full consideration of wild edges—those farthest from human intervention and influence—in the fifth chapter. Chapter 6 takes up the nuanced situation of landscape and seascape as exemplary instances of places and regions with edges that we like to believe are natural but whose full appreciation and assessment require a significant cultural sophistication. Finally, in chapter 7 I explore the juxtaposition between the altogether artificial edges of cities (as in buildings and sidewalks) and those obtaining in the parks and gardens that punctuate urban landscapes, resulting in a complex amalgam of highly diverse edges. Filling out this discussion is a consideration of the role of edges in the streets and neighborhoods that make up city spaces.

An interlude between chapters 5 and 6 takes up the very different question of the edges experienced in listening to music.

## Notes

1. See, for instance, Immanuel Kant, *Critique of Judgment*, trans. Werner Pluhar (Indianapolis: Hackett, 1987), pp. lvii, 25. This statement is my gloss on what Kant calls "the law of the specification of nature."

2. For a more complete account of this complex circumstance, see Edward S. Casey and Mary Watkins, *Up Against the Wall: Re-Imagining the U.S.–Mexico Border Wall* (Austin: University of Texas Press, 2014), chapter 3, "Tijuana: The Wall and the Estuary."

# FOUR

# Natural versus Artifactual Edges

> The distinction between the two planes (natural and cultural) is abstract: everything is cultural in us (our *Lebenswelt* is "subjective") (our perception is cultural-historical) and everything is natural in us (even our perception rests on the polymorphism of the wild Being).
> —Merleau-Ponty, working note of May 1960

It is tempting to contrast edges that are naturally given, generated by the natural world independently of human presence, with those that are artificially produced, that is, brought forth by explicitly human efforts. Important as the contrast is—I have already employed it in passing at several points—we shall find that it cannot be sustained indefinitely; a point will be reached where the two categories of edges will be seen to converge and even to merge in significant ways. They will also be seen to be implicated with borders and boundaries in ways to be detailed below. Before reaching these complications, however, I want to consider the differences between natural and artifactual edges on their own terms.[1]

## I

*Natural edges* are those given without the influence of direct human intervention. They range from the fracture patterns inside rocks to the outer edges of these same stones to the profile of an entire mountain range—say, the Himalayas as seen from the southern plateau of Tibet (in this case, the edges pertain to an entire region). They inhere in undiverted rivers and unaltered mesas, uncultivated plains and undulating shorelines formed from the interplay of ocean and beach. They are also found in beaver dams and coral reefs. Everywhere we look, even in the midst of humanly generated edges, we catch glimpses of edges uninfluenced by humankind. As I drive along US Interstate 80 going south from Vallejo, I am in heavy traffic that proceeds from one densely populated community to another— from Hercules to Pinole, from San Pablo to El Cerrito, from Berkeley to Oakland. Just south of the Carquinez Bridge, I find myself in the midst of an oil refinery situated on both sides of the highway. Looking through the fumes and flares emitted by the refinery, I spot Mount Tamalpais in the far distance. It rises in serene detachment, as if untouched by the population and pollution of the San Francisco Bay region in which it is set. It presents itself as purely *there*: out there, over there, up there. In the haze of the late afternoon that clings to it, I make out this mountain's imperial presence *through its edges*—those of its summit and upper sides, which together constitute a coherent contour for the body of the mountain itself. Within this literal outline, the mountain presents itself as a monochromatic gray-blue plane that shows no internal differentiations: no traces of rocks or rills, trees or cliffs or fields. It is as if the mountain as a whole has been subsumed into its own continuous external edge.[2]

Noticeable in this experience is the fact that an apparently unsullied natural edge appears *despite* the urban and suburban congestion that surrounds it lower down on every side of the state park within which it is set—a park that, on its west side, borders on the Pacific Ocean. There is a sense of uplift in being able to perceive, if only in a glance, such a magisterial natural presence in the midst of so much human sprawl and traffic. The same was true, albeit less dramatically, in my perception of swatches of vegetation alongside Highway 95 north of Las Vegas when I was searching for the Nevada test site. There, too, the edges of parts of the landscape presented themselves as independent of the incursion of a major highway through their midst—and as if indifferent to the testing of nuclear weapons nearby. Such experiences might lead us to suppose that natural phenomena, with their characteristic edges, are quite independent of human intervention, and that they exist on their own. This is surely true at fundamental levels, for instance, that of their physical constitution or biochemistry, their quantum mechanics, or their early evolutionary history. In themselves, are they not integral parts of the natural world that in no way call for human presence, indeed that often seem to defy it in calm disdain?

Yet the undeniable fact is that natural phenomena and their edges, even if independently generated, enter the human world at almost every turn. The edges of Mount Tamalpais and the Las Vegas landscape came to my attention only as I was moving in an automobile through their midst. Or, to cite a more fateful example, the underground aquifer on which the Las Vegas metropolitan complex depends is being contaminated by the nuclear waste that has seeped into it insidiously since nuclear testing began at the testing site in the late 1950s. This aquifer, though formed in the course of geological evolution altogether apart from the history of human beings, is now infused by nuclear waste that human beings have produced. At the same time, the air that circulates over this same geographical region is filled with hydrocarbons that come from electrical plants as far away as Los Angeles. The same is true of Mount Tamalpais, whose considerable height does not allow it to escape the acid rain that falls everywhere in the western United States.

Quite apart from these human-induced environmental hazards, the very presence of the state park in which Mount Tamalpais is located represents another incursion of humanity into the natural world. This park was established to preserve natural things like this very mountain, but this happens *only on the terms* established by the park authority: the traffic it allows, the campgrounds it provides—not to mention all its rules and regulations. The mountain's pristine status is only *"as if untouched"* in my earlier phrase. What is very tempting to take as an uncompromised natural formation is in fact deeply compromised, if only we consider the environmental, historical, and cultural worlds in which this formation is implaced—worlds that themselves overlap and interpenetrate at many points. Although first appearances may lead us to think otherwise, the land north of Las Vegas as seen from Highway 95, like the mountain glimpsed to the west as witnessed from Highway 80, is in fact a nexus of the natural and the artifactual in complex intertanglements. If the land and the mountain exhibit their own natural edges, they do so only as enclosed in and traversed by edges that are culturally and historically determined. Finding things with purely natural edges is not as easy as we might at first imagine; even when we can locate such edges, they are pervaded or surrounded by a matrix of other edges that are humanly constructed and serve human purposes.

To find natural edges that are truly unentangled with the machinations of modern industrial civilization—machinations whose shadows reach into every corner of the earth, from Papua New Guinea to Ladac, from Amazonian rain forests to sub-Saharan Africa—it appears that we must have recourse to the deep interior of particular material things, given that my leading examples so far have been the *outer* edges of a mountain and a landscape. The interiors of natural things, in contrast, like the earth or a simple stone, fiercely retain their inherent edgefulness: so fiercely so that it often takes a catastrophe to eliminate or even modify this feature. The material things that have been subjected to nuclear explosions at the Nevada test site—soil, rock, water—have indeed been affected in their inherent fault lines, their crystalline structures, their intact material composition. But short of such destructive events, ordinary material things—patches of soil, naturally occurring stones, living things such as trees or bushes, animals of many sorts—retain their internal pattern of edges, often over long stretches of time. Part of our fascination with such things—as expressed, for example, in a passion for rock collecting or for taking soil samples—has to do with their enduring possession of their own uniquely configured internal edges. This fascination extends to entire mountains regarded as mega-entities with a profound interiority that is disturbed only by such comparatively rare events as earthquakes or volcanic upheavals. The interiority here at stake possesses an invisibility that is the other side of their own visibility—that can be said to make this visibility itself possible.[3]

Thus, we must move not just to material things but more particularly to their inner structuration if we are to find exemplary cases of naturally determined edges that are independent of human influence. Such structuration has an independence and durability that are not easily found elsewhere—not in those external edges that are directly exposed to the impact of other things and events, and certainly not in places whose edges are far more vulnerable to trespass and dissolution than many of the things that populate them. Indeed, fully natural edges are to be found in abundant supply in the most ordinary things: the rocks I pick up by the roadside, the trunk of the tree that offers me shade. Each of these has a resistant internal core that subtends its outer surface and its inherent external edges. But if the outer surface and its edges are especially vulnerable to humanly generated destructive forces, it is a fact that what is found in the core of many material things is nevertheless subject to contamination by humanly generated toxins and poisons, many of which are themselves invisible and thus work all the more insidiously.

This core is not to be confused with atomic and molecular structure, which underlies everything that belongs to the constructed as well as to the natural world and which by itself does not serve to distinguish things from places, even though atomic structure does serve to distinguish generic *kinds* of physical entity: cabbages from kings, ferns from fireplaces. The *core*, as I am construing this term, is the inner physical structure of the material thing: an abiding structure that manifests itself in phenomena like friability, crystalline formation, and other ways of being constituted in accordance with preestablished edges. The core is a physical structure that can be identified by the kinds of edges it contains and which, once made accessible, are visible and tangible. This is so even though in their fully natural state such a structure and the edges associated with it are invisible and intangible, hidden from eye and hand alike. Yet they are persisting presences that make up a given kind of material thing from within. Think, for example, of the ten or so kinds of fracture patterns possessed by rocks. These patterns exist in ordinary rock specimens and become evident only when the latter are struck open by force. Once that has happened, the inner edges come to light; they leave their concealed state to manifest themselves in a now-visible configuration. In the absence of such fracturing, they continue to exist intact and unseen. Even if circulating greenhouse gases eventually affect even the sturdiest of external surfaces—through chemical corruption—the edges of inner structures deep within physical things maintain an integrity of composition throughout all but the most devastating forces and events. They stay the same—within—and in this way they are exemplary of edges that are resistant to influences, human or otherwise, impinging from without. The inner edges of living animal bodies and of plants are in contrast much more vulnerable to invading influences, as we see in the case of viral or bacterial disease. For this reason, I am taking the interior of rock formations rather than the inside of organic bodies as paradigm instances of independently existing natural things that possess their own edges.

Material things, especially rock formations, retain their internal edges with an impressive constancy. One wonders, in fact, whether this sturdy inner configuration of edges, amounting to a literal *Selbständigkeit* (German for "independence" but literally "standing by itself"), contributes to the promotion of such things to the status of full-fledged substances, as we find in philosophers as diverse as Aristotle and Descartes. For such thinkers, inanimate physical things such as rocks or stones count as exemplary because they are to be considered as strictly independent, both in existence and in concept: they are, in Descartes's words, "conceived through themselves alone," with the result that "a thing that exists in such a way . . . needs nothing else in order to exist."[4] (Living things, from micro-algae to plants and animals, though entirely natural, are less convincing as instances of sheer material substance, given that they are manifestly dependent on other living beings that, together with them, coinhabit entire environmental systems.)

In the last chapter, I objected to the privileging of things over places and events. This privileging can now be seen to derive support from extending such definitional and metaphysical formulas as I have just cited to inanimate physical things, in this way valorizing them over other aspects or parts of the life-world, including other living things as well as places and events. In insisting on the neglected importance of places and events in terms of their characteristic edges, however, I do not want to overlook the very different sense in which material things, especially those that are not alive, do indeed have a distinctive standing in the world of edges. This standing stems from their capacity to contain naturally generated edges within themselves—a decidedly nonmetaphysical and nondefinitional power that comes, rather, from their being material substances that possess certain internal edge structurations. To recognize this, however, is not to give priority to things over places and events within the world of edges in general. It is to underline the importance of naturally occurring edges in the core of things—a core that in the case of inanimate things is almost altogether independent of the corrosive presence of human beings.[5]

## II

Let us now consider, by way of contrast, *artifactual edges*. These are edges that have been made by human beings or, if not outright produced by individual humans, are recreated, reshaped, or otherwise bear the mark of human intervention. *Artifactual*, after all, literally means made by art, according to the *Oxford English Dictionary*—"made by or resulting from art or artifice; contrived, composed, or brought about by constructive skill, and not spontaneously." Even though the artifactual is here placed in opposition to the natural, it can also be a substitute for it (as in prosthetic devices) or else, as in representational art, it can be the very likeness of it. In this last case, we see that the artifactual may include the contrived in the form of the pictorial: thus what is "merely made up, the factitious; hence, feigned or fictitious." In all these instances, practical or pictorial, the artifactual is a matter of "displaying special art or skill." More generally, following these semantic clues, we can say that artifactual edges are those that result from human activity. Such edges include those that are accidental by-products of such activity, in contrast with those that are intended as such. The fact that my examples will be drawn from the latter class of things does not mean that we should overlook the unintended products of human activity—including all those that are cast off and discarded.

The following are examples of artifactual edges we have already touched on:

Rims and perimeters. Leaving aside natural rims (like the Grand Canyon's North Rim), the rims of cans, jars, and other manufactured containers are exemplary artificial edges, since they are constructed with the sole aim of effectively holding their contents, whether these be stewed tomatoes or strawberry jam. The shape and function of such rims are determined entirely by aims of efficiency, utility, reliability, or beauty as these are required by human design and the technology of manufacture and commerce. Something other than the very matter from which they are constructed, something that modifies their already given bodily character and aptitudes (say, of glass or metal), must be invoked to understand their construction, say, tight storage or decorative attraction. This stands in contrast with natural organisms, whose guiding aims (of nourishment, growth, reproduction, and so on) are internal to their bodily materiality. Much the same is true for perimeters, whose artificiality consists in being geometrically determined and composed from carefully constructed lines drawn around a central mass. If the artifactuality of rims is largely functional (a matter of efficiency), that of perimeters is formal and linear in the construction of an outer edge for a given thing or place.

Borders. The same artifactual functionality obtains in the case of borders. This is true both at the level of their concrete demarcation—by fences and walls, for example—and at the level of their cartographic representation. Both levels embody the artifactuality of edges in straightforward ways: the first in the choice of materials (concrete, steel, barbed wire) and their positioning on the land; the second in the explicit goals of accuracy, reigning paradigms of cartographic depiction, suitability for archiving, and the like. Edges in maps are especially revealing in

this respect. In contrast with manufactured edges, such as the
rims of cans, these edges (usually in the form of lines or colored
areas) refer to something beyond that of the manifest image they
present: namely, a particular place or region, of which graphically
delineated edges purport to give a trustworthy representation.[6] This
reference, however, is complicated in at least two ways: historical
and conventional. Virtually every map incorporates and reflects
particular historical events—for instance, the immediate aftermath
of the Mexican-American War of 1848 in the case of the *Carta
Geográfica del Estado Chihuahua*.[7] Furthermore, the map itself can
be of historical significance—for example, by its use in legitimating
certain claims, reinforcing existing national borders, in the didactics
of teaching North American history, and similar things. By the
same token, any cartographic map is a reflection of the conventions
of mapmaking that prevail at the time of its construction. These
conventions include the use of continuous versus dotted lines,
pictographic signs of lakes and mountains, and the lettering
that allows certain features to be named (cities, rivers, mountain
chains)—not to mention the inscriptions that serve to legitimate the
map itself, its intended purpose, as stated in its corners or margins.
Here convention converges with history: one form of artifactual
construction confirms and reinforces the other.

Rims, perimeters, and borders share a common recourse to
linearity. Lines are highly economic means of representing, indeed
*being*, an edge: they compress the three-dimensionality of the edges
of things and places into two-dimensional strokes or traces; they
hover between point and surface by connecting at least two points
across a single surface. Lines certainly occur in nature, ranging
from those left by receding glaciers on the surfaces of boulders
to rutilated gemstones to those evident in the internal fracture
formations discussed above. In contrast, artificially engendered
linearity has the peculiarity of being imposed on surfaces for
particular cultural and technological purposes: the glacier has no
choice but to leave its traces as it moves across massive stones, but
the linear representations of the *Carta Geográfica* were chosen with
the express goal of updating an earlier map in light of the outcome
of the recent war between Mexico and the United States.[8] So,
too, the circularity of the rim of the can of stewed tomatoes I am
about to open has been imposed upon it for overtly practical and
commercial purposes.

Artifactual edges, then, stem from a process of imposition upon matter—an imposition itself shaped by historicity, convention, utility, and sometimes aesthetic norms. Such imposition is by no means limited to the linearity of edges that figure into the construction of artificial containers and cartographic maps. Lines constitute an economic, but by no means an exclusive, way to instantiate or represent artifactual edges. Also effective are three-dimensional objects that embody and reinforce artifactual edges in various ways. I have in mind such things as walls, fences, and surveillance towers, notably as these exist at many security check points, such as those at international borders. They may be arranged in a linear pattern, but they are not constituted by lines as such; they are physical objects that make use of contrived edges in the absence of definitive directions from the natural environment— even if they sometimes reinforce such directions (as, for example, when a wall is built alongside an existing river). Although fences and walls are not reducible to linear design, they can be quite effective in imposing order—in this instance an *institutional order*. Such order is especially prized and pursued in a nation-state that commits itself to the strict regulation of immigration—as in the walls constructed between East and West Berlin, Israel and Palestine, at various places in southeastern Europe, and at many locations along the United States–Mexico border. In cases such as these, the imposition of artificial edges is particularly concerted, reflecting fiercely maintained aims of exclusion and control. Further discussion is called for here.

*Borders, borderlines, border stones.* Three-dimensional objects like walls and other barricades materialize borders, literally grounding and strengthening them, rendering them fit for such "de-fensive" (literally fending-off and fencing-off) purposes as self-protection and security. But the deep alliance that exists between artifactual edges and borders is also evident in much earlier forms of construction: for instance, in "boundary stones" (in Mesopotamian *kudurru*, in ancient Greek *herms* and *horai*). Boundary stones have two remarkable features. They are created from materials belonging to the natural environment, and they are discontinuous in their distribution: no strict stone-to-stone contiguity is required, since by being spaced out at regular intervals they can constitute an effective borderline, an imaginary line that connects them. It is notable that precisely such "marker stones" (as they are also sometimes called) served as the official designators of the Mexican–American border in an earlier era. Most of them are still there, but in many stretches of the current circumstance at La Frontera they have been incorporated into the concrete-and-metal walls and barbed-wire fences that now traverse the desert landscape of the American southwest. The blunt edges of native stone have given way to the sharp edges of corrugated metal: natural stone has ceded to artifactual steel.

The stone itself was taken directly from the natural world— in a largely unchanged state, as is seen most dramatically in the case of boulders, prized precisely for their sheer bulk—and then brought directly into an institutional world by being positioned in an intentional series of similar such stones, with each sometimes outfitted with a plate announcing its precise position in this series. Hybrid phrases like "marker/stone," "mile/stone," and "boundary/ stone" convey their bivalent status: the "stone" deriving from the natural realm, the "marker," "mile," or "boundary," being culturally constructed. Once selected and put in place, a given stone counts as a constituent member of the string of stones that, taken as a whole, traces the borderline: the *gran línea*, as it is called in the case of the United States–Mexico border.[9] (For this reason, "boundary markers" are better named "border markers.") As Patricia Price says, "There really is no border on the border. . . . Only borderlining."[10] Whereas boundaries remain permeable, allowing for or even facilitating traversal, borders are prized for their impermeable continuity: for leaving no gaps, either on the ground or on a map.

This brief discussion demonstrates how closely artifactual and natural edges can collude in given circumstances. With boundary stones we witness a situation in which a given natural object—a heavy stone or boulder—is conscripted to become part of a carefully constructed barrier that materializes an international border. Other examples come to mind: Ellis Island is both a natural phenomenon, a land mass at the head of the New York harbor, *and* a place where millions of immigrants from Europe and elsewhere were examined and processed on their way to becoming US citizens. In contrast with the impenetrable wall at La Frontera, Ellis Island, had no wall. As an island, it needed no such protective barrier. It erected its own internal barriers in the form of forced inspections of those who had come to the United States from abroad. Until the late nineteenth century, most European immigrants were admitted (except for those with serious diseases); but by the 1920s strict immigration controls were enacted, severely limiting the admission of Southern and Eastern Europeans and others. Even if such strictures were less fiercely exclusionary than those at Angel Island after 1882 (the year of the Chinese exclusionary act) or at La Frontera since 1994, Ellis Island constituted a de jure border rather than a welcoming boundary, a place of highly conditional hospitality.[11]

Situations of genuine welcome often rely on a collusion between open passage and artifice. The most ordinary doorway, which serves as the basis of minimal domestic hospitality, is constructed from carpentered edges in its lintel, door panels, door handle, and other elements. This indicates that border edges are not inherently repressive. It is when these edges are built with a certain will to keep out or keep in—to exclude or to protect—that they act as alienating or incarcerating forces. Between borders and artifactual edges there is an ongoing collusion: after all, borders are constructed and institutionally sanctioned entities, whether in the form of borderlines or border walls. Conversely, between boundaries and naturally generated edges there is a frequent alliance. We witness this wherever the edges of vegetation leave open spaces through which various animal species can pass easily: situations to which we shall return in chapter 6.

This is not to deny that some naturally given edges are inherently closed and hostile to life: think of the edge of a raging tsunami or the edge of an advancing desert. In their forceful determinacy, such natural edges are more akin to borders than to boundaries. Conversely, artifactual edges can contribute to a boundary situation—as in the case of a threshold constructed as a welcoming space or with sluices that help salt and sea water to circulate and mix more freely in estuaries.

We must resist any simple identification of artifactual edges with borders, and of natural edges with boundaries, despite an understandable temptation to affirm these alliances. The determination of borders can make use of natural materials such as stones (as with boundary stones), just as boundaries can incorporate objects with artificial edges in their construction (directional markers posted along a path in the wilderness, for example). We witness in such cases and others a striking instance of the congruent overlapping, and sometimes the actual merging, of terms whose origins, material constitution, and primary modes of application are distinctively different.

### III

So far, I have contrasted artifactual with natural edges. I have made a first pass at describing their characteristic differences while also exploring ways in which they combine forces. On the one hand, there are such things as the outer edges of mesas and mountains and canyons, and the inner edges of the deep structures of material things (such as crystalline and fracture patterns). Such edges are "natural" insofar as they are given and not fabricated; they proceed entirely from natural processes of formation and evolution. On the other hand, there are the frankly artificial rims of tires and football stadiums; the front edge of the car we drive (the bumper), and of the paneling in our living room; as well as the frames of paintings on the wall and the lintels over the front and back doors in that same room. All such edges are brought into existence by human construction and design. We live in and with both kinds of edge, natural and artifactual, whether experienced in alternation or simultaneously. But in this era of advanced technology and sophisticated natural science, and if we are not living in a rural area, we find ourselves more often in the midst of artifactual edges than natural ones: in the course of a single typical day, I move from the rectangular metallic edges of the mirror in which I glance at my slowly awakening face to the rounded edges of the toaster on the breakfast table; one hour later entering the rectangular subway doors on the C-line train and then peering through the glass edges of the shop windows that stud the interior of Penn Station. Even if I do not attend to any of these edges in a concerted way, manufactured edges are pervasive in virtually everyone's life in a modern city. If we are so often "on edge," this psychological state may reflect the massive facticity of living in a largely artificial, highly contrived edge-world. In this world, there is no getting around the angularity and enclosedness of the artificial edges in which we are immersed at every turn; to get past by one set of edges is only to encounter another differently configured set.

Despite the urban experience of encountering constructed edges everywhere about us, the fact is that we often experience natural and artifactual edges together and in complex and often subtle combinations: the edges of the nature trail that, though cleared for human use, nevertheless follows the lay of the land; the razor's edge as it meets the stubbled surface of my cheek; the edges of the airplane wing that cuts through the air in aerodynamic patterns that affect the speed and elevation of the aircraft. Indeed, it is more the exception than the rule when we find ourselves in the midst of nothing but artifactual edges. Commixtures are much more common than we might think, even in urban settings: when I am riding the C line in Manhattan, I am enclosed by artificial edges, yet on a subway car I cannot help but notice the bodily edges of my fellow passengers: the edges of their faces, necks, and hands. By the same token, I am only rarely surrounded by exclusively natural edges: as I look into the sky from the mountain I have just climbed, I see the line of a jet contrail high above me, and at my feet is litter left by hikers who preceded me. We tend to remember experiences of full submersion in a scene of natural edges—such as being lost in a dense forest, scuba diving near the ocean floor—precisely because they are exceptional.

Of special interest are those cases in which the two kinds of edge not only mingle but become continuous: in which the edges of things and places and events are both artifactual and natural. This situation is not just one in which such edges join forces across their differences—in arbitrary alliance or contingent compromise, as with boundary stones—but rather one in which a given edge is both natural and artifactual at once.

As an example of such uncompromised compresence, let us consider a *city limit*, in which the artificiality of a statutory edge conjoins with the naturally proffered edges of the surrounding landscape, the two fusing in the one entity designated as "city limit." I have in mind two cases in point: one in Topeka, Kansas, and the other in Las Vegas, Nevada. In Topeka, where I grew up, the city limit was, as we put it, "on the edge of town." This last phrase, which comes to the lips so readily, indicates that a given *city limit*, taken as a legal entity, is not to be confused with the edge of the countryside that opens up beyond this limit. As a *limit*, the former exists as posited by an institution (here, the municipality of Topeka); whereas the *edge* of the countryside is naturally given. Yet the artifactual and the natural converge here in a manner that, despite allowing us to distinguish them in terms of their origin and mode of givenness, renders them inseparable from each other. In the case of the Topeka of my youth, the city limit and the edge of town helped to define each other, since to be at the western city limit (on Gage Boulevard, running north and south on the west side of town) was to be on the edge of town—beyond which lay uncultivated fields. Once *there*, whether on my bike or by driving the family car, I was at both limit and edge alike. The city limit is contrived as something that has been designated as such by the city administration at some particular moment in its earlier history. The considerations of the city council were doubtless economic, demographic, and historical; all three parameters are "cultural." But when I came myself to the edge of town, I found myself entering into the zone of the natural; homes and roads suddenly became scarce at this westernmost point of the city. Pausing at this edge as I did as an adolescent, I looked out upon pastures and fields, trees and small ravines, flocks of birds and prairie dog holes. At such moments, I felt welcomed and affirmed by the naturalness of the scene in contrast with the intensity of my family and the demands of school life in the city. Standing at the opening of the countryside, I was also standing at the city limit. In this way, the artificiality of the city limit and the naturalness of the vista seen from its edge of entry arose in my experience together and formed a seamless whole.

Similarly, the city limit of Las Vegas also combines the two parameters in intimate union. In contrast with the situation in Topeka, here I only glimpsed the local circumstance in passing. I was with friends, driving out of Las Vegas to reach Red Rock Park on the western edge of town. I was struck by how the last housing development on this western end of the city came to a sudden end, abruptly announced by a pink stucco wall that seemed to hold in the still unfinished development and, through it, the whole teeming city to the east. At the foot of this wall was a stream of water, and on its other side lay an open field contiguous with the park. Arrayed before me were two dimensions of one experience: one utterly artificial, defined by the limit of a housing development, the other starkly natural, a wilderness area that contained the dramatically vertical mountains of Red Rock Park.[12] Once again, the two dimensions were distinguishable but not separable. They not only belonged together, they *were together* as two integral parts of one world—where "parts" signifies holistic "moments" rather than detachable "pieces." In strictly spatial terms, wall and stream and park were contiguous, one abutting the other. But as my glance swept over this scene, I did not see them as apart but as conterminous elements of the same situation. I was confronted with the coordinated convergence of artificially contrived limits and naturally proffered edges.

Far from being exceptional, such convergences happen all the time in our experience of the place-world. We find the same situation, for instance, in Manhattan, where the East River and the Hudson River provide edges that are at once natural and constructed: these rivers have been features of the natural landscape for a very long time. The earliest settlers took them to be firm but unofficial limits to the growing city, and thanks to this they have since become outfitted with walls, piers, and docks, as if to reinforce these limits. The fact that the official city limit of Manhattan has changed over time—whether positioned at water's edge or in the middle of the two rivers, as measured by the river's breadth at any given point—does not alter the basic bidimensionality of the circumstance, artificial and natural at once. The reasons for such changes are themselves sometimes conventional and historical (in keeping with vicissitudes of city politics, relations with surrounding boroughs, routes of ocean liners, and the like) and sometimes natural (since the width of rivers changes seasonally, and along with it the location of the median point in any given stretch of water).

In Banaras, where the Ganges is the de facto city limit on the eastern side of this ancient, sacred city, we find something comparable. This holiest of holy rivers in Hindu life encloses Banaras (also called Varanasi) so completely that there is no "east Banaras"—nothing but mud flats and marshlands to the east, leaving the city to expand without limit in the other three directions.[13] I say "without limit" in the literal sense that any determinate statutory limits to the city are far from evident. When I searched for signs of such legally determined limits in a recent visit to Banaras, I could not locate them: even if they did exist at an earlier moment in time (and even if they are designated in certain historical documents), the city's multitudinous population has surged over and beyond them as if they had never existed.[14]

In each of these various instances of city limit and/or edge—in Topeka, Las Vegas, Manhattan, and Banaras—we come across something that is at once artifactual and natural, both together and simultaneously. In their bivalence, they resemble a ball that is "green and red all over," to recall an example that was much discussed by American philosophers in the 1960s.[15] How are we to understand the circumstance in which edges are both natural and artificial—that is, at once intrinsic parts of the natural environment and yet also cultural and conventional, constructed and historical?

## IV

There are four models by which we can think of the interaction between the natural and the artifactual regarded as distinguishable traits of edges. Except for the first, each model offers a plausible schema for thinking about the relationship between these traits; but I consider the fourth, that of interfusion, to be the most productive.

*Dialectical.* In this model, there is a dynamic interaction of traits, each affecting the other while both retain their own location and identity. On a Hegelian rendition, the interacting terms at first oppose each other, and then sublate into a synthesis that includes and affirms both. As the ancient roots of *dialectic* imply, each operates *through* the other (hence the *dia-*), much as interlocutors' words (thus the *lektos*, "word") play off against one another in an intense conversation. As the conversation progresses, earlier positions survive in later phases of the talk, even after they have been negated or extensively qualified. The result is a dialectical synthesis at the level of language and thought, diagrammatically depicted here:

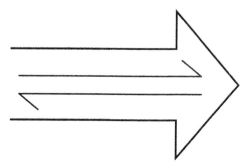

FIGURE 10. Schema of dialectical synthesis.

The limitation of this model is that it applies best to situations of interlocution in which the primary units are words rather than edges; and it implies a certain degree of progress or at least resolution that is not normally an issue for the interaction of natural and constructed edges.

*Dovetailing.* In this case, the interacting terms have no separately maintained bases, as is the case for dialectical phenomena in their initial appearance. (Hegel insists that the separation is only apparent, since the eventual truth of synthesis is already present in germ.) In the case of dovetailing, the action *is* the interaction. There is an increase in intimacy compared with the dialectical model, since the structures of each trait here run parallel to those of the other trait and exist in close proximity instead of being opposed as separate. But the two terms still maintain a certain independence in the process of relating to each other, as seen below.

FIGURE 11. Schema of dovetailing.

This diagram makes it clear that the two traits (in our case, artificial and natural edges) relate closely, yet do not merge into each other. The interaction is intense but stops short of a fusion of terms. In contrast with the dialectical model, no final stage of resolution is reached or even sought. The interaction itself is what matters most and is the aim of the process. This qualifies many instances of the artifactual-natural edge relation, for example, when my body with its natural edges slips into a car with its highly artificial steel edges: my body dovetails into the awaiting structure of the car, the organic fitting into the fabricated in a functional partnership.

*Intertanglement.* In this case there are no longer any distinct terms or forces to be identified separately; instead, skeins crisscross in a complex pattern of interinvolvement, as we can see in this image:

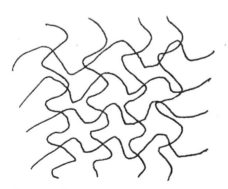

FIGURE 12. Schema of intertanglement.

I take the word *intertanglement* from the poet Robert Bly in an effort to convey the complex character of the interplay, which is at once more dense and convoluted than any of the two previous patterns. The original terms are not only not distinct but *there are no original terms*—none that exist in isolation from each other, not even provisionally; they present themselves as interconnected from the very beginning. This model characterizes those instances in which artifactual and natural edges, while remaining separable upon analysis, have become interthreaded in various ways, as in the construction of a building where the bodily movements of the workers (each with its own arc and profile) come to form a dense palimpsest of relations with the construction materials day after day until the construction is complete: the bodily motions of the workers and the emerging gestalt of the building are deeply intertangled. More than fitting together (as in entering a car) is at stake here; a productive collaboration is underway.

*Interfusion.* Still more radical is the circumstance in which the terms not only dovetail or intertangle—or are dialectically related—but are now so profoundly linked as to realize a certain kind of identity with each other throughout. They are intimately bonded to the point of being fused: not just mixed for the moment or tangled over time, but so continuous with one another that they can for various purposes be considered one interfused entity. Despite the extent of the interfusion, this is not a situation of simple identity, A = B, much less A = A. The interfusion of terms allows for distinctions to be made in the very midst of deep confluence, realizing a certain kind of complex identity in which the terms remain distinguishable even as they are inseparable in their being and becoming.

This is the model that best fits certain close combinations between artifactual and natural edges: combinations that are frequently found in the course of everyday experience. These combinations can be variously conceived, each with a certain philosophical forebear: of sameness with difference (Plato), as different attributes and modes of one supreme Substance (Spinoza), or as the fusion of horizons (Gadamer). Of these, I consider the last named as the most helpful for understanding the relationship between natural and artifactual edges. In *Truth and Method*, Gadamer writes of *Horizontsverschmelzung* as the circumstance in which one entire interpretive system—such as a given verbal language—intersects with another interpretive system in a way that allows the first to be a vehicle for *understanding* the second.[16] While each such system is initially distinct (and in this respect resembles the dialectical or dovetailing models), each already reaches out beyond itself and is fused with the other. This is more than making contact or touching at the edges. It is *reaching into* the other interpretive system, situating itself within it, feeling and thinking it from inside—to the extent of *becoming it* in some significant measure: not just like it but *as* it, sensing as it senses, thinking as it thinks, feeling as it feels, not entirely or perfectly so, but for the most part. And the converse is also true: the other interpretive system (person, culture, language) being understood can understand back, so to speak: she or it can understand my understanding. This kind of understanding across cultural or historical difference is two-way both in fact and in principle. In this way a deep co-understanding occurs. I call the resulting state that of *interfusion*.

The merging of horizons in interfusion resists visual representation, and so I offer no linear model of it. The merging is so intense that it results in a single mass that has no differentiated structure, thus cannot be drawn or otherwise depicted. Interfusion means that two (or more) otherwise different terms are both spread throughout a given thing or place, being there all over and all at once. Despite their inseparability in this commixture, the terms remain distinguishable in principle—or else we could not designate them coherently as one interpretive system in distinction from another, as "artifactual" vs. "natural" edges. Such distinctions are possible only if each member of these pairs of terms characterizes an interpretive system, a thing, a place, or an edge *in a different respect*—each pointing to a distinguishable trait of what it qualifies so thoroughly.

The Hudson River was once a scene of commerce among Native Americans, was explored by Henry Hudson, was party to armed conflict in revolutionary times, was the basis of distinction between individual states soon after; in more halcyon days, it has been the scene of pleasurable travel, was a subject of artistic representation in the period of the Hudson River School, was a venue for ocean liners and barges later on, and more. One and the same entity, a river, bears all these alternative descriptions and destinies. The same river also invites characterization as both natural and artifactual. This is not to say that it is these two things in exactly the same respect. Rather, it differs in how its naturality and artifactuality are merged at different historical moments. But at every moment in his history, it has been a dynamic commixture of both parameters, each coexisting with the other in a state of deep imbrication: the river interfusing with all that has occurred on and in it since human beings began to interact with it.

The Hudson River also exhibits a radical interfusion of artifactual and natural edges, the former reflecting origins in culture and history (the edges depicted in maps of the Hudson, for example, or in historical accounts of settlements alongside it); the latter stemming from its natural states (the ever-altering edge of the Hudson, an edge determined by natural forces such as hydraulics, the movement of tides, fish populations, changing seasons, and so on). Despite these descriptive differences, any portion of this river we might wish to sample exhibits edges that are both artifactual and natural, aspects that are intimately interfused. These aspects interact as descriptors of one and the same phenomenon: the flowing and

ever-altering Hudson River, considered as a body of water both naturally constituted and historically shaped and reshaped.[17]

Natural and artifactual are dyadically related traits of the edge-world; the
terms of this dyad interfuse in actual instances like that of a city limit which is also
the edge of a surrounding countryside or that of a historically overdetermined
river, such as the Hudson. In these examples and others like them, the members
of the dyad compenetrate each other yet remain distinguishable, thanks to the fact
that each member presents a different aspect of the edges of a given entity like a
river or a city limit. In fact, it is just this close conjunction of the natural and the
artifactual (and vice versa) that allows this pair of terms to intersect so intimately
and to form such subtle edge alliances. The edges of a city limit and of a flowing
river are *both* and *at once* artificial and natural: these terms naming distinct features
of complex imbroglios. The two terms are coextensive aspects of deeply interfused
phenomena, whether these be the city limit of Topeka, Kansas, or the Hudson
River as it passes by New York City.

## V

I shall now briefly address the relationship between borders and boundaries—the
subject matter of chapter 1—and the dyad at stake in this chapter, that of the natural
and the artifactual. Themselves kinds of edge—major kinds as we have seen—
borders and boundaries can also be considered alternative fates or functions of
edges in general: roles that edges come to play, as when we speak of a margin as
"bordering" a page. Artifactuality and naturality refer to the provenance of edges of
any kind, where they come from, including what they are made of: in the one case,
fabricated by human intervention, in the other generated by physical or organic processes. In this light, borders can be regarded as predominantly artifactual—created
for delimited human purposes, mainly historical and political—whereas boundaries
are more often intimately related to the natural world, indeed sometimes part of it.

Despite differences in their primary usages, relations between all four terms
are manifold. The Río Grande del Norte is at once a natural phenomenon *and*
marks the United States–Mexico border from Brownsville to El Paso; as such, it
is both border and boundary, artifactual and natural. Given such a complex collusion, one begins to suspect that however precisely the four terms in question
may be defined and described, in the actuality of lived experience they are more
often conjoined than disjoined, being closely paired and actively merged rather
than existing separately. In fact, there are special affinities among the four terms,
given that a border is prototypically artificial in origin—being created by a treaty
or other institutional arrangement—while the paradigmatic instances of boundaries are found in the natural world.

This is not to say that the distinction between artifactual and natural is
perfectly parallel to that between border and boundary. The most important

divergence is this: while there are many ways of being an edge beyond being a border or a boundary, whether the basic makeup is natural or artifactual is always at stake for any given edge. Sometimes it is one, sometimes the other—and often, as we have just seen, both together. No edge escapes such determination, even if a given edge may not be either a border or a boundary.

The complicity of these two dyads, their complex liaison as same and different, suggests the figure of the *chiasm*, Merleau-Ponty's term for the dense imbrication of things usually held apart. We see such imbrication at work in this thinker's later philosophy, notably in the statement that forms the epigraph to this chapter: "The distinction between the two planes (natural and cultural) is abstract: everything is cultural in us (our *Lebenswelt* is 'subjective') (our perception is cultural-historical) and everything is natural in us (even our perception rests on the polymorphism of the wild Being)."[18] This formulation is of particular pertinence to the present discussion. Not only are the natural and the artifactual (the latter here in the guise of "the cultural") merged in the manner I have been calling "interfused," but two further nuances are here proposed by Merleau-Ponty. First, the *Lebenswelt* or life-world is not something objective and indifferent to which we are strictly subservient, but it is itself "subjective," that is to say, experiential, though not confined to the experience of an isolated ego. Second, even "the wild being" of the natural world (*l'être sauvage*, alternately translatable as "brute being") is not formless or chaotic. It has an intrinsic polymorphism, where the *-morph* root signifies form or shape; it is substantial enough for perception to "rest on" it. Putting these two qualifications together, we can say that what we would have thought to be trans-subjective—the natural world— is subjectively structured in "cultural-historical" terms, and what we might have considered densely and defiantly "wild" is not amorphous but comes to us with its own shapes. It has its own regularities, much in the manner of the "morphological concepts" to which Husserl pointed, which are operative in the informal geometries that investigate the inexact shapes at stake in topologies of the indefinite.

In short, the interaction of the artificial with the natural and vice versa—and of borders with boundaries—is subject to ever-changing complications of a chiasmatic sort, in which crossing-over and interfusion are more operative than is containment and separation. All is here ongoing and outgoing; everything elaborates and expands. But all is also involuted and implicated. This is a world where edges effervesce outward even as they intermesh within this same world. Taken together, these two actions help to constitute a world on edge.

## VI

Despite their characteristic slenderness, edges accomplish a considerable amount. They do so in a strikingly two-sided way: as forward tending as well as inwardly receptive. In the first case, they are very often the *leading part* of a given thing or region, person or event; if not the literal "cutting edge," then the part that gets somewhere, as if guiding that of which it is the edge and putting it into inter-action with other things. They are often the portion of a thing or place one first notices or confronts. The outer edge of the computer with which I am now writ-ing serves to profile it against the table on which it is set, while this table's outer edges define the surface that supports my machine. The edge of my coffee cup goes into my mouth, itself a bodily edge, as I sip my favorite liquid substance in yet another collusion of artifactual with natural edges. All of these edges in this mundane situation, acting in concert, enable the fringes of my emerging thought to be realized in apposite words that put a verbal edge on the nebulous intuition I have of where I wish to go in my thinking, rendering it articulate and allowing me to write it down.[19] All such edges enable me to enter the interstices of a work-world that is also a world of thoughts; they escort me into the intimacy and depth of these thoughts, helping me to extend this world in new directions.

At the same time, edges are also the basis of many forms of *receptivity*—that is, of being open to other things, other people, other events, enabling me to gain access to those things of which they are the edge. Formally considered, this recep-tivity is based on their being turned toward the world in which they are located. In this capacity, they allow us to take in much that the world has to offer. The table on which I am writing establishes itself in local space by its outer edges, but it also invites the employment of my machine on its upper surface. In their receptive ca-pacity, edges create an ambiance in which diverse pursuits become possible; they open up the environing world to these pursuits, forging a space in which things can happen and with which I can ally myself in diverse ways.

Edges of my body and my thought usher us into various kinds of situation by way of our own forward movement, but they also welcome us into their midst on their own terms. Moreover, they often do *both* things in the same setting—as we have seen from the ongoing example of the worktable in a café. Here it is a matter of *bidirectionality*: edges *take us out* (extend us in space as well as time) as much as they also *take us in* (incorporate us into their midst). They move (us) forward and they draw (us) back, and they do the same for things, places, and events.

Edges thus exhibit a certain basic bidirectionality. In the enactment and expres-sion of this dual movement, the fact that edges can be natural or artifactual—and sometimes the two fused together—serves to broaden the range of their opera-tion and effect. There are places that metal and plastic edges can go, for example, that cannot be reached by edges made of wood or flesh. The absolute artificiality of my computer, its manufactured wires and circuits, trace out edges that, guided by the design of the computer program I use, allow my thought to move into ever-new channels. But there also remains a valid place for such pretechnological activities as note-taking and stone sculpting: here the touching edges of my hands take me into the physical realm in direct and formative ways that have their own validity. The natural edges of my hands link up with the materiality of paper and stone via the artifice of writing and sculpting.

When natural edges interact with artifactual edges, the activity of each kind of edge is often enhanced; so is their receptivity. This happens, for example, in the interaction between my hands and the computer keyboard on which I am now composing this book: organic flesh and metal-cum-plastic here form a nexus that is "cultural-historical" and yet also participates in the purely sensory or "wild being." This nexus itself is chiasmatic, each member crossing over into the domain of the other. At the same time, hands have histories—they are not dumbly physical entities, but act from habitual patterns acquired across a life history—while the metal and plastic from which a computer is made have been shaped in such a way as to facilitate the inscription and retention of thoughts that express themselves through hands active at the keyboard.[20] If writing "accomplishes thought" (Merleau-Ponty), this is largely due to the fact that "intelligence is in the hands" (Heidegger).[21] But hands in turn require instruments (pencils, typewriters, computers) with which to write down thoughts, thereby leaving traces of these thoughts to which I and others can attend subsequently.

This double-edged situation emerges whenever the artifactual and the natural conjoin in human experience—not only when employing current technology but in many other activities and domains as well (taking a walk, participating in a political protest). The conjunction itself is engendered and supported by the active and receptive virtues of edges as they move out and take in. This same conjunction becomes a scene in which edges of very different origins and types join forces, engendering an edge-world populated by disparate denizens and offering diverse directions. Some of these edges are humanly generated, others originate in the nonhuman realm, and many constitute collusions between the artifactual and the natural.

The edge is the Archimedean point of the spatial world—and, when implicated in events, of the temporal world as well. From *just here*, from this edge, much can be moved—whole worlds. As with the glance, the slender opens onto the dense. From a very narrow base, much ensues—on an edge, at an edge, or through an edge, thanks to its modest but highly effective means.

Otherwise put, an edge is *where nearing happens*. It brings events and places, sentient beings and things into each other's proximity—sometimes all at once in a single happening, sometimes in succession or by deferred action. In accomplishing all this, the role of edges is often discrete—yet no less important for not being obvious or even noticed. What Heidegger says of nearness can be said of edges that actualize nearness itself: "Nearing is the presencing of nearness. Nearness brings near—draws nigh to one another—the far and, indeed, *as* the far. Nearness preserves farness. Preserving farness, nearness presences nearness in nearing that farness."[22] The nearing action of edges is a form of "gathering"—to borrow another, closely related term from Heidegger's later vocabulary.[23] It generates a close community of entities or events that are drawn near to each other, from out of their initial farness, by an action of assembling that preserves their farness in the nearness thereby accomplished.

Extending this thought, we can say that the nearing of edges respects the farness of things and sentient beings, places and events, incorporating the farness of each in the very action of nearing, of bringing them close. Boldly or gently delving into its immediate surround, a given edge enters into—is literally an "entering edge" into—a common space shared, albeit momentarily, by other things or places, events or responsive beings. As a result, that to which the edge relates is no longer located indifferently in a separate far space or distant time but brings the farness itself into the nearness of the edge, incorporating it into its own receptive realm. Both actions of the edge—its outreach as it moves out toward its companions-to-be and its inreach (its nearing/gathering in alliance with its receiving/internalizing)—help to realize a mutual approximation and appropriation between the edge and that to which it relates.

Reciprocal but not symmetrical, the basic edge actions of going out and gathering back, far and near, are all the more effective for happening in natural as well as artifactual modalities. These modalities diversify even as they intensify the outgoing and incoming vectors of the edge. They contribute to the causal efficacy of edges as constructed by humans or as encountered in the natural realm. The effect of the continual conjunction and disjunction of artificial and natural edges is a world on edge: a world at risk even as it seeks stability.

## Notes

1. For the most part, I shall employ the term "artifactual" in lieu of "artificial." The former term alludes directly to the notion of "artifact" as something concrete that is made by human devising; it lacks the connotations of "stilted" and "superficial" that sometimes accrue to the latter term. But I shall not hesitate to employ "artificial" when the context calls for it.

2. In response to a question posed by Donald Landes, let me make it clear that the monochromatic plane is not itself an edge but the space for the visible edges of the mountain, which constitute its profile as seen while driving south on Highway 80, heading toward San Francisco. It is as if the mountain had been reduced to a plane or single surface and set perpendicular to the earth, leaving visible only its summit and higher ridges (e-mail exchange with Don Landes, February 14–16, 2012).

3. This last formulation recalls one of the primary senses of the invisible as discussed by Merleau-Ponty in *The Visible and the Invisible*, trans. A. Lingis (Evanston, IL: Northwestern University Press, 1968), especially on p. 215: "the visible itself has an invisible inner framework, and the in-visible is the secret counterpart of the visible, it appears only within it, it is the *Nichturpräsentierbar* [the not primally presentable] which is presented to me as such within the world."

4. These phrases are those of Descartes and are found in his *Principles of Philosophy*, part 1, section 51. They constitute the definition of a substance of any kind, mental or physical.

5. I say "almost altogether independent" in the case of rocks and minerals since their core can be altered by human mining techniques and other processes of extraction. One of my readers suggests that this independent core, in its intrinsic invisibility, is itself what makes possible the visibility of the outer surface of a material thing (with its own set of manifest edges): "Are counterfactual [i.e., concealed] edges such because they are the in principle invisible *by which* we are in a world of visibility? . . . If they are invisible epistemically, as counterfactual, could we say that they are present phenomenologically as that 'by which' we see, touch, etc.?" (Donald Landes, e-mail communication of October 15, 2012.) I would agree, adding only that what Landes designates as "in principle" and "by which" is a matter of a *material* condition of possibility—this indeed, yet nothing more.

6. This is the map I discussed earlier in chapter 1. I here exclude maps that are frankly fantastic—that make no pretense to convey the gist of any actual region of the earth. For a discussion of fantastic maps, see "Epilogue" in Edward S. Casey, *Representing Place in Landscape Painting and Maps* (Minneapolis: University of Minnesota Press. 2002). My focus here is strictly on cartographic maps—i.e., those that purport to give an accurate and complete representation of their subject matter (see ibid., glossary of terms).

7. As for maps that do not refer to any historical event, there are rare exceptions: those of an entire imaginary country (for example, the land of "Prester John"), areas marked "terra incognita," and images of untracked wilderness. Notice that in each of these cases, however, there is still an intervention of the human, whether as imagining an unknown country or land or wilderness or as speculating on its limits.

8. This is not to say that all natural beings lack intentionality: certainly dolphins and chimpanzees do things with a conscious purpose in mind, as doubtless is the case with many members of other species. My point here is only that human intentionality is a major component in the creation of artifactual edges. This is not to deny that humans also produce many things unintentionally (such as waste, which in turn can harm other animals).

9. Precisely because of their distinctive semiotic status, there has been long-standing concern about the defacement of stone markers. See note 51 in chapter 2 of Patricia Price, *Dry Place* (Minneapolis: University of Minnesota Press, 2004), citing Paula Rebert, *La Gran Línea: Mapping the U.S.–Mexico Boundary 1849–1857* (Austin: University of Texas Press, 2001).

10. Patricia Price, *Dry Place*, p. 174.

11. For an account of the harsh conditions and severe limits at Ellis Island, see http://www.shmoop.com/ellis-island-immigration. (I thank Lissa McCullough for this reference.)

12. This park, like that of Mount Tamalpais mentioned earlier, had its own official perimeter, as determined by city and federal statues; but my description above refers to the content of my spontaneous perception of Red Rock Park as seen from the city limit.

13. For a sense of the overall configuration of Banaras, see the map of the city in Diana L. Eck, *Banaras: City of Light* (New York: Columbia University Press, 1999), p. 121.

14. My use of *limit* in the foregoing pages—both as "city limit" and as the recognized "limit" of Manhattan in its two flanking rivers—deliberately relaxes the sense of limit on which I focused in chapter 2, where the term was taken mainly to signify something formally established, such as a limit in mathematics. In the above discussion, *city limit* is distinguished from *edge* only insofar as it is something statutory, that is, decreed by a city council. It is a close cousin of *border*, which is also typically mandated; both are historically constituted. But as we *experience* it, a city limit signifies the outermost, extreme edge of a municipality. There it is marked as such by indicator signs that clearly designate "City Limit" (or "United States–Mexico border"). When I stand at such a sign, I am at once on the (legal, statutory) limit of the city and at its (outermost perceived) edge. Here edge and limit converge—as they do so often in ordinary talk—even if, strictly speaking, there is a distinction to be drawn when we are seeking philosophical clarity. On this point, see also Edward S. Casey and Mary Watkins, *Up Against the Wall: Re-Imagining the U.S.–Mexico Border Wall* (Austin: University of Texas Press, 2014), pp. 13–26.

15. For discussion of this celebrated conundrum, see Morton White, *Toward Reunion in Philosophy* (New York: Atheneum, 1963).

16. See Hans-Georg Gadamer, *Truth and Method* (New York: Crossroad, 1984), p. 273.

17. New York earth artist Sandy Gellis has systematically taken samples of the Hudson River over a period of many years. She places these samples of water—taken in different seasons and at different times of day—in glass bottles labeled with the time and place of the sample taking. In this ingenious way, she contains river water—itself a composite of the artificial and the natural—within a delimited border of glass, in sharp contrast with the ever-changing edges of the river itself. For further discussion of Gellis's ingenious and suggestive work, see chapter 3 of my *Earth-Mapping: Artists Reshaping Landscape* (Minneapolis: University of Minnesota Press, 2005).

18. Maurice Merleau-Ponty, *The Visible and the Invisible*, p. 253.

19. To articulate thought in words is to establish determinate verbal edges at the joints of that thought. "Meaning," says Merleau-Ponty, "arises at the edges of signs." M. Merleau-Ponty, "Indirect Language and the Voices of Silence," *Signs*, trans. Richard C. McCleary (Evanston, IL: Northwestern University Press, 1964), p. 41. Merleau-Ponty is here discussing linguistic signs—i.e., words, phrases, and sentences—but the point can be extended to other kinds of sign as well as to images.

20. See Julia Upham, "Being in the World of Hands: The Phenomenology of Writing," dissertation, Pacifica Graduate Institute, 2015.

21. See Merleau-Ponty, *Phenomenology of Perception*, trans. Donald A. Landes (New York: Routledge, 2014), pp. 182–85, esp. p. 183: "Speech does not translate a ready-made thought; rather, speech accomplishes thought." What Merleau-Ponty says of speech is true of writing as well. The Heidegger citation is from *What Is Called Thinking?*, trans. Fred D. Weick

and J. Glenn Gray (New York: Harper & Row, 1968), p. 16. On p. 23 he writes, "We have called thinking the handicraft *par excellence* . . ."

22. Martin Heidegger, "The Thing," in *Poetry, Language, Thought*, pp. 177–78. See also p. 181: "The nearing of nearness is the true and sole dimension of the mirror-play of the world." Regarding "gathering" (*Versammlung*), see p. 177.

23. See especially Heidegger's *Country Path Conversations*, trans. Bret W. Davis (Bloomington: Indiana University Press, 2010), p. 74.

# FIVE

# Wild Edges

Outside of town, on a walk in coastal mountains, I experience a pattern that changes every few feet and that reflects the character of the immediately environing world: the incline of the hill on which the trail is located, the vegetation on this hill (varying with the season), the number and kind of trees (mainly live oaks in late summer), and the weather (had it been raining in the last few days, the edges of the trail would be still less distinct). As I continue to walk, I spot the fleeting forms of several animal species, among them rabbits, blue jays, and a distant hawk. I also note the top of the hill toward which I am wending an increasingly winding way: a modest summit whose external edge is ragged, fitting no standard geometric shape. The same is true when I glance at other hills that stretch toward the east: their uneven edges form a dense and ever-changing tangle. The ocean opening to the west has a comparatively stable horizon, interrupted only by a group of islands that rise from this same horizon and punctuate it. As my walk continues, I experience an ever-expanding series of unfolding edges, almost none of which are cultivated, much less constructed.

Edges in the natural domain are not only more disparate and diverse than those in the human world—think only of the differences between the edges of the branches of one species of tree versus those of another—but it is also clear that there is no process of deliberate design and fabrication that guides their generation. If there is any plan or purpose here, no given group of intelligent beings is responsible for it. Humans do intervene in the history of plants and animals, altering particular features to suit their ends (seeking better nutrition, more efficient production, genetic modification, clearing land for a building site, and so on), but this is a comparatively recent chapter in the earth's history, dating back about fifteen thousand years or so. For the most part, living beings and the inanimate world alike possess edges that are endemic to each species or kind of thing, with the most consistent determination occurring from within, as directed by genomic pattern (in the case of living beings) or crystalline formation (in the case of geodes) or volcanic activity (in the case of recently formed mountains). Notably absent are the direct intervention, concerted imposition, and outright manipulation that are so characteristic of edges that form part of human life-worlds. Instead, there is a largely autogenous emergence of edges that occurs in terms of the "species-being" of living organisms or the fracture patterns and strength of resistance found in inanimate objects. Environmental factors are important, indeed often crucial, but their influence is largely a function of natural entities' composition and internal structuration, which determine those factors that are consequential and those that are not.[1]

Wild edges, then, are predetermined in a strikingly different way from the edges that reflect human activity and intervention. Where edges stemming from human praxis are guided by consciously or preconsciously chosen designs that act as schematic projections of their finally realized states, wild edges subserve finalities (however we may wish to define these) that are inscribed in the very nature of matter, whether this latter is organic or inanimate in status. Indeed, wild edges are so deeply rooted in matter that the impact of forces from without often seems to be contingent or secondary. But even when these forces are required for precipitating a given natural process (as, for example, the fertilization of an ovum in the reproduction of the human species), their impingement proceeds in accordance with preexisting material determinations. If there is a factor of purpose present, it belongs intrinsically to the physicality of matter and not to any act of decision taken by a reflective mind that could have decided differently.[2]

In human life-worlds, the role of technology as *techné* (craft, skill) is always at play to some significant degree, whether in an idea or sketch that foresees a possible new kind of edge or in the actual production of this edge itself. Apart from humans and certain mammals, no such presence of projective ideation or technological praxis exists in the natural world, whose shape and character arise from inherent traits of matter that are always already there, even if evolving; they are given with matter itself, part of its internal constitution. Nature, as Spinoza claimed, is *causa sui*, self-caused. It does not call for humans, much less their technology, for its emergence. It preceded the appearance of the human species and will outlast the demise of this species.

These preliminary reflections—which carry forward those that opened the last chapter—underline the drastic differences that we should expect to find when it comes to the place of edges in the natural world, in contrast with those that characterize consciously planned and constructed human worlds. My own approach to these differences remains resolutely descriptive and peri-phenomenological. Nevertheless, descriptive differences are finally indissociable from causal factors that make these differences themselves possible. Even if peri-phenomenological description is not mandated to give an explanatory account of the phenomena it describes, it cannot afford to ignore the relevance of these factors at another level of consideration that attempts to understand how the generation and proliferation of edges can be so divergent in the case of the two great kinds of edge-world: the human and the wild.

A caveat: the word "wild" itself covers a very broad range of meaning and is far from unambiguous. I intend it here in the straightforward sense of whatever the nonhuman environment delivers on its own, unassisted by human influence or interaction. Of course, human beings are themselves natural or wild in significant ways, in their bone and body structure, their physiology, and their own genetic makeup. As Gary Snyder puts it, "the body is, so to speak, in the mind. They are both wild."[3]

Another caveat: this chapter focuses not on wilderness but on wildness. Wilderness is a condition that holds for a given territory that has been shielded from cultivation and the inroads of human civilization. Wildness, by contrast, is a state of becoming that is not located in any particular place or region; it is to be found everywhere, in every place or region, including modern cities and many parts of civilized states. It is not only all around us but also directly underfoot; indeed it is *in us*, in our stray thoughts, as well as in our unconscious mental life and repressed emotions.

A basis in natural givenness is subject to manipulation and reconfiguration by human beings, and the same naturalness is put to specifically technological use when our bodies manufacture and implement tools that, in turn, alter the course of the nonhuman wild world.[4] It cannot be denied that human beings draw upon, indeed count upon, natural reserves of several sorts, above all those that energize their own lived bodies and those located in the natural settings in which they live; but for the most part they are devoted to the marshalling and reshaping of these reserves. This reshaping (as the very word implies) involves the transmutation of edges in the surrounding environment as well as in humans themselves. But when we set aside such reshaping, we find ourselves standing starkly before wild edges that do not invite our participation, indeed that may resist it. This chapter is dedicated to the description of such edges.

## I

Nature, then, is an open set of worlds, each of which is on edge in its own distinctive way. Nature is not reducible to the placid or bucolic scenes some landscape painters convey to us, nor is it something purely sublime as certain nature mystics would have us believe. Instead, it is an edgy place in both senses of the term "edgy": it exists in a tension of conflicting forces and it is filled with myriad edges of indescribable variety. Directly reflecting such environmental edginess is the extraordinary alertness of earth creatures, their sensory systems attuned to the least noticeable change in their immediate environment—whatever might catch them by surprise, whether a predator or the animals they themselves seek to consume. Little escapes the acute glances of bats and eagles, hawks and owls, who track their prey from afar before attacking it directly; but slower-moving animals, such as seemingly torpid snakes and frogs—and even the three-toed sloth—can spring into action quite quickly when their survival demands it. Animals are literally on edge in their distinctive bio-niches, and this means that they are responsive to the least discrepancies in the microworlds they inhabit. These discrepancies themselves appear in the form of edges—for example, as a sudden discontinuity in the coloration of the immediate visual world, as an unexpected gap in what is seen. Alterations in the configuration of edges bring with them an attentional alertness that is most aptly described as "edgy."

The second sense of "edgy" in natural settings is closely related to the first. If the life-world of any given creature is filled with innumerable edges that continue to proliferate, it is no wonder that the nervous system of this creature will be geared to dealing with the greatest possible diversity of edges within its primary world. I have argued elsewhere that the power of the glance is due to this very circumstance: glancing allows us to be ever alert to the untoward as it arises unbidden in the visual realm. Integral to this alertness is an ability to respond quickly to the sensible manifold in the sheer multiplicity of what is presented there. The manifold itself is composed of edges of many kinds, and the glance (as well as its equivalent, the quick touch) must be capable of discerning all such edges as they bear upon the safe passage of the organism. As the diversity of edges is in no small measure due to the diversity of life itself as engendered within the natural environment, so the response to this edge-diversity will be differentially realized in various life forms as each such form copes with its own environing world—a world that is structured by its own characteristic set of edges. But this set is never settled in character—its contents continually change, as does the aging organism—so that in the wild edge-world we find *diversity rediversified*. Think only of the way in which changing tidal patterns minutely alter and erode the edges of coasts and marshlands with every passing moment. The diversity of edges in the natural world is a direct reflection of the physical conditions to which such edges are subject—conditions that may themselves mutate in the course of time, either in a more or less regular pattern (as with tides and seasons) or more drastically, as with hurricanes or tsunamis. (As remarked earlier, not even tides are perfectly predictable, since they are influenced in turn by other contextual factors, such as the position of the moon and seasonal conditions.)

The edginess of wild place-worlds is due to the radical becoming of nature itself. I borrow the term "becoming" from Bergson and Deleuze—ultimately, from Heraclitus—to designate that respect in which edges belong to the ceaseless and restless vitality of nature, its élan vital (in Bergson's celebrated phrase). No wonder that wild edges are so various and proliferate so greatly. For they are the liminal aspects of all wild things—from rocks to stars, animals to plants, viruses to bacteria—which are themselves always becoming: ever "mutating," as we say of viruses, but as is true of all entities in nature. Given this dynamic becoming of wild things, their edges cannot help but alter: not just because the entities are continually assuming different volumes and shapes but also because they are changing in their modes of activity, generating ever different edges with which to realize these modes in altering environments. More aggressive such modes call for sharper and tougher edges; more passive ones, for softer and more porous ones. At the same time, the interaction of wild things themselves also changes with time and circumstance, thereby calling for differing edge-relations: edges that worked well in one situation no longer serve in another if the character of the interaction has changed significantly. The denizens of the wild worlds of nature are ineluctably on edge during every phase of their trajectory on earth.

## II

From the continual becoming of natural processes of every imaginable kind there emerges the pack and welter of edges that are manifest in the wild world—edges that are as requisite as they are confusing. In order to reduce the confusion, I will focus on four exemplary but very different cases in point: leaves, mountains, rivers, and coastlines. I shall elicit certain general traits that hold true across the differences, proceeding as a deliberate amateur rather than as a natural scientist. My concern is not with scientific accuracy but descriptive fidelity to the experience of wild edges.

*Leaves.* Recently, in mid-August, I came upon a group of leaves on the ground in a park near where I live. These were not leaves from exotic species but those from the characteristic elms and oaks and maples that populate the park. Although some of the leaves had already turned yellow, the serration of the edges remained intact, and at first glance I noticed that there is no strict correlation between the size of a leaf and the shape of a given unit of serration. A small leaf can possess a more dramatic edge than its larger counterpart and vice versa. By observing the trees from which these leaves had fallen, it is also evident that leaf sizes proliferate independently of such variables as the overall stature of the tree that features them; some of the smaller leaves came from very large trees as well as the converse. But the pattern of serration is the same for each leaf—and by extrapolation for all the leaves—of the same tree, indeed for each kind of tree, so that the indentational pattern of leaves from different species of trees varies considerably. So much so that I am tempted to claim that this pattern is a distinctive mark of a given type of tree. In the case of the photograph I took on the spot, there are several basic edge forms, each noticeably different from the others, as seen below.

In one of the edge patterns evident in this photograph, there are three major parts of a leaf—a literal "trifoil" edge design—while in another there are five (two

FIGURE 13.   Leaves, Central Park. Author's photo.

on each side, one in the middle). In still another, there is only one basic format, roughly ovoid with no sharp indentations as in the two prior cases. The photograph also makes clear that the patterns of light and shadow in which the leaves participate differ markedly: these patterns have their own edges and patterns. So do the fallen branches that also appear in this image: they exhibit a continuous and connected linearity that contrasts with the self-enclosed designs of individual leaves. The result is a virtual bouquet of variously serrated leaves set within a complex nexus of sunny and shadowed areas and delineated from within by the structure of branches.

When we perceive the general shape of a leaf at a distance, it precludes seeing the exact form of the edge—a form that emerges only when we stand close to a group of leaves, as I did while taking the photograph that you see just above. Clearly, the *shape* of the edge is what counts in such near-space. I refer to the exact outline of the leaf as a whole, whether this be in three or five parts or in a single oval, or is damaged, or curled up. Each such shape is formative for a given leaf, being characteristic of it. Other factors, such as the veinage and stem type, are less conspicuous and require a scrutiny that is not called for by the overall shape. The latter is intrinsic to the basic gestalt of a leaf, part of its self-presentation; it is integral to what we see outright on first perception and what we recognize on subsequent perceptions.

When leaves are seen still attached to a tree, en masse, we rarely attend to their individual shapes, much less to their serrated edges They merge into the overall shape of the tree, becoming more or less indistinct in-lines rather than something with distinctive outlines. This amassing occurs as clusterings that have their own distinctive patterns and that act as intermediary entities situated between individual leaves and the tree as a whole. These clusterings eclipse the isolated leaf, merging into the tree's full presentation. They provide aegis for discrete edges within the tree's final outer shape: they fill up that shape from within as it were. There is thus a sequence of increasingly inclusive edge-shapes that accrue first to leaves, then to branches (or boughs), and finally to the whole tree. The delicacy and fragility of individual leaves should not mislead us: their edges are not merely of aesthetic interest, but also contribute to the creation of an entire serrated world of trees, regarded as primary denizens of wild worlds.

These considerations point to the fact that a wild edge is not a formal reality with a unique contour but depends on its manner of givenness for our seeing it as a certain kind of edge: a givenness that depends on the time of day (afternoon versus dusk) and the situation of the leaves (still on a tree versus fallen to the ground) as well as our distance from them. Grasping a purely geometric edge, by contrast, does not depend on its mode of presentation, since its definition, rather than its perception, is what gives it shape. That shape, including its edge, belongs to just one kind of figure.[5] In the case of leaves, we find no such pristine one-of-a-kind pattern but a congeries of edges variously displayed that come as a matrix of edge-forms that refer us back to the tree from which they stem.

*Mountains.* Most leaves are transient, emerging and passing with each seasonal cycle, lasting only a few months, whereas mountains are among the most ancient things on earth, many of them being hundreds of millions of years old. They have come to stay. They are the epitome of what perdures on earth, outlasting almost every other known feature of the planet, including major rivers and icecaps. Nevertheless, despite the manifest differences in size, age, materiality, and origin, leaf and mountain alike possess characteristic edges that we can compare. While leaves exhibit a pattern of repetitive edges for a given species of tree, mountains only rarely show themselves to possess edges in a single format; with rare exceptions, they are far less regular in the gestalt of their edgework. Where leaves show a certain symmetry and balance (the two sides of a given leaf normally displaying matching edges), the edges of mountains only very rarely convey such equipoise. Most often, they are deeply asymmetrical in their edge patterns: hiking up on one side of a mountain in no way guarantees that walking down the other side will lead to the same kind of experience of external edges. Vis-à-vis the massive gravity that mountains possess (thanks to their sheer density and weight), their edges might seem not to count for much. Yet mountains do have distinctive edges or, more exactly, kinds of edges. Let us consider two such kinds: their basic profile and their subsidiary edges.

(1) *Basic profile.* When we see a mountain in the distance we behold a characteristic silhouette, a profile from afar that is unique to that mountain, and the same applies to an entire mountain range. This silhouette "looms," we say, meaning that it thrusts itself outward and upward in such a way as to take the whole mountain with it. Every mountain sets forth its own outer edge. This is the edge we see from afar; it stays remarkably constant despite our own shifting points of view. For a mountain dominates a landscape, and in that capacity it stands out as just *this* mountain—as does Mount Tamalpais, seen from many places in the Bay Area of San Francisco. This mountain, first encountered in the last chapter, has a distinctive basic profile that allows it to be identified as this very mountain, whether I spot it from Berkeley or San Rafael. The precise configuration of the mountain alters subtly as it is seen from these different places, but its inherent gestalt remains recognizable despite the variations in its viewings. The edge of this mountain, profiled against the pellucid California sky, is a primary identifying mark. I count on it for orientation when I am in the Bay Area, and I retain it in mind when I remember having been there later on.[6] This circumstance is more extraordinary than it may appear at first. Other edges, including those of individual leaves, play no such deeply situating role. A mountain's profile surmounts the immediate visual world I inhabit, towering over that world, commanding my attention even from afar. This prepossessing presence is based on its outermost edge, which traces out its dramatic ascent from the land at its base. Here is a very different role for edge than we have so far found: *edge as perceptual dominant.*

   It is this same role that accounts for the importance of what we can call *signature mountains.* I refer to legendary mountains like Mount Everest (Jambalaya), Mount Kailash, Mount St. Helens, Mount Rushmore, Mont Ventoux, and Mont Blanc. Each of these is known as a singular mountain that is recognized by its distinctive profile, whether this latter is conveyed by photography or painting or in memory or even by a certain practice—as when Mount Kailash in Tibet is circumambulated

in rituals of walking meditation. So powerful is the factor
of singular profile that an otherwise indifferent or modest
mountain can gain recognition and even fame for its profile.
Mont Sainte-Victoire would have been of merely local curiosity
had Cézanne not painted it so tellingly. A small promontory
in North Dakota would never have been noted beyond its
immediate region had not the heads of several American
Presidents been sculpted out of it. A natural disaster can render
a mountain's outer edge famous, as in the case of Mount St.
Helens or Vesuvius. My point is not about the exact means by
which a given mountain is elevated to fame; rather, it is that the
fame itself often relies on its outer edge as identifying mark.

It is a curious fact that this same edge is also normally an
*upper* edge, suggesting that part of the power of the mountain's
signature silhouette resides in the factor of height as such. We
have here a metonymic relationship, specifically that of *pars
pro toto*. The telling profile is often that of the summit (or at
least the upper peak of the mountain) insofar as this particular
part comes to stand for the mountain as a whole. (Something
comparable occurs in the case of tall buildings: the standard icon
of the Empire State Building features its upper tower and spire,
with its lower parts overlooked.) Just as a caricature is most
effectively conveyed by a line drawing, so the singular profile
of a mountain consists mainly in a literal outline that traces its
upper outer edge. It is as if the mountain itself had drawn its
own profile before us and said, "Here I am, this is my distinctive
mark."[7] We are reminded of Merleau-Ponty's formula for things
outside us: the "in-itself for-us."[8]

(2) *Subsidiary edges.* However significant the outermost edge of a
mountain (or group of mountains) may be, it also possesses
subsidiary edges, those that structure it from within as it
were. I do not refer to the edges that are concealed inside the
mountain—the edges of the inner strata and masses from which
it is composed—but to the perceptible edges located between
the base and the summit. These can be considered intermediary
in the literal sense that they exist between the earth on which
a mountain stands and its peak. I have in mind the crevices
and cliffs and other structural features that make up most of
a mountain in its outer layer. *Anything that can serve as a ledge
counts as an edge*: anything that offers a toehold for humans and

other mammals, or a nest-hold for birds, counts as a subsidiary edge. Included here are minor fissures as well as dramatic promontories. Anything short of a summit and other than level ground forms part of this composite category. We can think of its members as the creases and wrinkles of a mountain, the places where it folds back in upon itself or comes out of itself in some noticeable manner.

Strikingly, subsidiary edges are rarely intrinsic to the public memory of a given mountain; for this, the basic profile usually suffices. Subsidiary edges are more likely to be remembered by individuals who have engaged somehow with the mountain—for instance, who have attempted to scale that mountain, as in my memory of climbing a certain mountain in Cottonwood Canyon in the Crazy Mountains in Montana. This was a demanding ascent on a trail that was barely marked. It was with relief that I came upon intermediary edges where I could catch my breath and take stock. A sudden thunderstorm drove me and David Strong, my climbing companion, to the protection of a small grove of trees that occupied their own ledge. From there we could see agile mountain goats undeterred by the storm, leaping between rocks—each of which constituted a momentary foothold for these animals. Observing them brought home the fact that what constitutes a significant edge for one species does not necessarily suffice for a different species. Subsidiary edges are thus selectively useful for various kinds of animals, and the same obtains for forms of vegetation: trees, bushes, flowers, mosses.

The close-up surface of a mountain amounts to an edge-work of far greater complexity than the same mountain's basic profile. Where the latter is uncomplicated to the point that it can be represented by a single line—enhancing its recognizability from afar—the former is typically considerably complex: its creases are many and highly variegated. These subsidiary edges reflect the multiplicity of activities that take place there—activities of growth, traversal, inhabitation, and so on—and are mainly accessible in the perceptual near-sphere, whereas the outer edge is mainly a matter for the eye at a distance.

In the end, a mountain is a mass of edges. These edges may not be as incisive as those that encircle a single leaf, but in their internal and external avatars they are constituent features of entire mountains and sometimes whole ranges of mountains. They are certainly much more so than are the edges of a flat plain, in which we have to search scrupulously to find any comparable salience. With rare exceptions (such as scorched earth), edges do not stand out in such a flatland: that is just what makes the plain count as a *plain* (a word whose origin reflects this very fact: *planus* means "level" or "flat").

We can conclude that a mountain presents itself as *all edge*, given that few parts of a mountain do not figure as either a basic profile or a subsidiary edge. This fits with the fact that every mountain has emerged from the underlying earth. A mountain is in effect an edge of earth, a place where the planet has given itself visually and tangibly conspicuous edges. In this spirit, we could say that a mountain is a fold upon the earth's surface: a fold outward from this surface, a *folding out*, a literal *unfolding*.[9] Mountains in effect unfold the earth from within; they are convex creases in its outer surface, its literal disimplication. A mountain is *a being in depth*; it comes from the depths of the earth as these have been thrust upward and outward beyond the earth's otherwise flat surface. Walt Whitman's words, intended for a very different purpose, here apply: "All goes onward and outward . . . and nothing collapses."[10]

A leaf is in contrast *mostly surface*, with little depth and none that is linked directly to the earth. No wonder that leaves thematize their outer edges in such comparatively regular and lucid ways: these edges terminate a surface that makes up most of the leaf itself. A leaf's flat surface offers no basis for anything comparable to the distinctive subsidiary edges of a mountain; it is the leaf's outer edges that contribute to its recognizability as belonging to a certain kind of plant on the part of expert botanists and knowledgeable amateurs. It is these serrated edges that are comparable to a mountain's external profile, by which it is often widely known: in both cases, the external edges are crucial for easy identification at a glance, whether from a distance or close up.

Unlike the edges of a leaf, a mountain's edges are more fully resident in and ramified throughout its entire surface, being found both at the outer contour and within its intermediate surfaces. In this respect, subsidiary edges can be said to be part of a given mountain's full material being: what it proffers if life and movement are to happen in its midst (or not, as in certain barren reaches). Nothing here suggests mere decoration or anything like symmetry, as with so many leaves; these qualities appear luxuries when everything bespeaks the unrelenting force of gravity and the stern demands of endurance in high places.

*Rivers.* Rivers can be considered intermediate between leaves and mountains— not only in comparative size but in regard to the way in which each sustains life. As sources of water, rivers are essential to the life of leaves, supplying ground waters to trees that are fed by rivers, while rivers themselves may flow out of mountains and over their surfaces in the form of streams and waterfalls.

Like leaves, rivers are subject to seasonal variations, whereas mountains stand remarkably independent of seasons, persisting through the most extreme changes of weather and other atmospheric conditions. In other respects, however, rivers are very different from both leaves and mountains. They are characterized by a sheer flowingness that has no counterpart in these other two phenomena of wild nature. The flow of rivers entails a definite directionality, a downstream vector that is rare in the botanical and lithic worlds, where the primary movement (if there is any) tends to be upward, for example, toward the sun in the case of heliotropic plants. Rivers cling to the earth's surface; indeed, they are integral parts of this surface, being major ways in which it is differentiated regionally. But in contrast with soil, rivers continually change their content, bringing along whatever floats with or on them: they are notably indiscriminate in what they bear forward.

Thanks to their flowing and changing content, rivers rarely retain the same width or height. Unlike leaves, they have no predetermined shape to assume and exhibit—no standard form in the manner of the leaves of a given species of tree. Nor do they reach a particular size or shape and keep it indefinitely as mountains tend to do. Rivers are always changing: with rivers, *panta rhei*, "everything flows,"[11] and the flow itself is continually changing. Rivers change not just in extent and composition but in course and direction as well. When the Romans (who had little sympathy for Heraclitus's dictum just cited) spoke of *stabilitas loci*, "stability of place," they certainly did not have rivers in mind; they were thinking of land-bound things, whether buildings or cities, mountains or trees. On these things one can count for purposes of identification and location. So mutable are rivers, on the other hand, that it is futile to expect from them anything stable or stabilizing; they are always flowing on, so much so that Heraclitus also said that you cannot step into the same river twice (even in the moment of immersion, the contents will be changing).[12]

It is not surprising, then, that the edges of rivers differ significantly from those of other natural things. To start with, they are not crisply repetitive in the manner of the edges of leaves; only as constrained by *something else* do they take on a determinate or fixed shape: say, by a concrete flood wall put up by the Army Corps of Engineers. This very thing happened at Mud Creek in Abilene, Kansas, when this meandering stream, tame for most of the year but raging in heavy spring rains, was redirected by a concrete embankment that prevented flooding. The edge of the creek at this embankment became perfectly straight; it obeyed the embankment's unyielding surface. It is only in such a circumstance—when the density of water comes upon a still denser material such as concrete—that its own shape becomes regular. Left to its own devices, it assumes no such shape: it bleeds into its own soft banks, disappearing in their midst. If anything, it shapes them more than they shape it. Usually, however, there is an uneasy truce established between the two, a coming and a going in which the edges of a river and its banks intermingle—a situation of mutual copenetration of edges.

This is an extraordinary situation and differs from anything we have encountered so far. Edges of mountains are largely indifferent to that with which they are in contact: the earth below, the air above, even the clouds they may touch. Their hard-and-fast edges act as if indifferent to their surrounding conditions; they assert themselves as such, starkly and uncompromisingly. Leaf edges, in contrast, reflect their immediate surroundings (other leaves, the branches on which they hang, the immediate weather), and unlike mountains, they do not thrust themselves brashly into their immediate surrounding, instead joining up with it in gentle and subtle ways. A river's edges, in contrast with the edges of leaves and mountains alike, directly affects the edge of the land up against which it flows. Not only is there a traceable causal interaction between rivers and its bed and banks, but all three alter their edges as a result of their impingement upon one another. Yet it is the river that possesses the primary formative power. Let us consider this power in more detail.

This power resides in the forceful movement of the river itself. Its edges make this power evident, *state* it as it were. Any part of the river can emerge as an edge, coming up against the banks and weighing down upon the bed. The paradox here is that water, seemingly an edgeless element (it certainly has no intrinsic edges), specifies itself as edge in myriad ways—that is, in any place where it becomes contiguous with its container (banks and beds, flood walls, and even beaver dams). Thanks to the continually changing character and content of rivers, their edges are far from futile or impotent: they can reconfigure an entire landscape, as we see in the flooding of the Mississippi in and around east St. Louis. In such a circumstance, subsidiary edges count for little; only one kind of edge matters and that is the outer edge of the river itself, the fulcrum of its full power. What overflows or breaks the levees of a river—notably, further down the same river in New Orleans—is the edge of the swollen river itself, the "dark brown god . . . intractable."[13] The intractability, as well as the force, is found in the river as it meets land—meets it at the edge, the ever-changing, conjointly configured edge that finally belongs as much to the land as to the river.

This is not to claim that destructive force is the primary predicate of rivers as they interact with their immediate surrounds. The edges created therefrom also invite exploration and inhabitation. "[River] banks are where so much information is stored," says Margot McLean, and thus "the edges are very important. . . . We love to build along the edges of the river."[14] We are drawn to a river's edge, especially when its scale is neither too daunting, as when a river backs up to a high cliff, nor too diminutive, as would be a tiny stream trickling at our feet. We are also drawn to it because of the pleasure we take in looking out onto water—seeing or imagining various episodes and movements viewed from the safe perch of land.

Here the directionality of the river's flow, bringing with it a continual parade of debris as well as floating vessels of several descriptions, conspires with the fascination of the unexpected. We love to be "down by the riverside," as the celebrated song puts it, because this puts us at an interelemental crossroads: where water, in one of its primary formats, meets earth as underlying matter. Being there, we have the sense of being at a point of transition between two basic ways of being in the world: being on land and being on or in or near water. This is as refreshing as it is challenging—inspiriting in and from the edge. Neither man nor beast is limited to one side alone, moreover, as we can get to the other side with sufficient skill. As McLean adds, "we come to the river from both sides."[15]

The mud that so frequently figures on the banks of rivers may be said to concretize the significance of the water/earth conjunction. Not only do these two cosmic regions meet on these banks, they commingle in the material medium itself. It is a striking fact that in many cosmogonic narratives, including those of Native Americans, the factor of mud is especially prominent: "Magically the mud spread out in the four directions and became this island we are living on—this earth."[16] Mud is invoked in these narratives not just because of its malleability—symbolically important as a basis for the genesis of new creaturely shapes—but also because it is the literal compounding of water and earth. The porosity of mud, its absorptiveness, supports the abundant plant life that so often occurs on the edges of a river—and that becomes dominant in marshlands in the form of spartina grass, cattails, and other flora. These latter are rooted in a muddy base that may not be visible on the surface of a marsh but that subtends their very survival.

Plants and mud, along with bushes and trees, various water birds and fish and other animals, together make the river's edge into a bank that is in effect a highly mediated band of disparate edges. Rather than a separate strip, this bank itself is a naturally generated margin that is constituted by the merging of river and land, their creative combination in a single interplace that has no determinate or exactly measurable dimensions. The bank sinks back from the river, holding it in and holding it back despite its many porous edges. It absorbs the potential violence of the river in times of flooding even as it promotes new plant and animal life that cannot survive on dry land.

*Coastlines and Shores.* These are literally unilateral, "one-sided," phenomena, since we experience them as situated on *this* side of an ocean or a sea. Sometimes one can spot another coastline over an intervening body of water—say, the coastline of Sweden as seen from the small island of Botorp across the northern Baltic Sea—but this distant land mass is in retreat before our very eyes. Even on the Mississippi with springtime flooding, Huck Finn could reach the other bank on his homemade raft. In stark contrast, the "farther shore" of an ocean or sea is an elusive entity, more the stuff of dreams and myth than of practical access or use.[17] Standing on the shore on Botorp, everything reminds me of my implacement just *here*—over against which the *there* of the other coast seems forbiddingly far away. There is little else to do but to look out toward it, much as Nick Carraway in *The Great Gatsby* looked longingly at the Connecticut shoreline from northern Long Island.

Coastlines are places where water meets land, sharing this basic fact with the edges of rivers, lakes, and ponds. But coastlines differ from these latter in two ways. First, if the two edges of a river are symmetrical in relation to each other, no such symmetry obtains in the case of a coastline, which attracts attention and energy by its unilateral status as the only edge that matters. The two banks of a river are democratically disposed, inviting us to go back and forth between them. But the edge where land and water meet in coastlines or shores is privileged: it is the only pertinent edge in this situation. For this reason, in the presence of a coastline, a difference of directionality is distinctly felt: our body or thought moves either from land to sea or sea to land, one way or the other in a pronounced pattern: we go "out to sea" from the shore, or we return to it after a long voyage. This valorizes and singularizes the coastline or shore as such.

Second, there is a difference in comparative saliency between coastal and riverine edges. Rivers' edges are characteristically muted in their appearance. As we have seen, they are often populated by grasses and reeds that "line" their banks—only rarely, however, forming anything like a perfect linear pattern. Their density and proliferation are such as to obscure any such quasigeometric regularity. Moreover, riverbanks tend to merge with the land behind them as one sort of vegetation gives way to another in a more or less continuous pattern of intercalated edges of closely neighboring plants. By way of contrast, coastlines *stand out*, being conspicuous features of the local landscape. They are easily identified as such, at a glance and even at a great distance, like ribs of land that emerge from one side of the sea ("rib" is in fact the primary root of "coast": *costa* in Latin means "rib" or "side"). Coastlines and shores are often constituted of rock formations and sandy beaches, which can be easily imagined as rib cages of the earth's body.

The saliency of coastlines (from here on, I shall employ this term generically to include both "shores" and "coasts") is based in significant measure on the fact that they are formed from constituents that, unlike the soil of riverbanks, act to discourage vegetation. A coastline allows the inanimate world to have its day, chasing out all but a few plants and allowing only intermittent visitors from the sea world such as the kelp and plankton, mollusks and crustaceans that wash in with tides—and just as often wash out again. It is as if these "gifts of the sea" (in Anne Morrow Lindburgh's phrase) are restricted to a limited appearance that reflects the rhythms of tides (and sometimes storms and hurricanes).[18]

Coasts are as indifferent as mountains in their upper reaches to the complications that life of any kind brings with it. Their receptivity to various vicissitudes reflects ongoing unsheltered exposure to weather and other atmospheric conditions. And in both situations, the primary constituent is rock of some sort (sand is itself granulated rock). Only material of this consistency and rigor can withstand violent weather or violent seas—which wash them smooth, forming a lasting substrate. The rock on a coast is at all times exposed to forces of water and air that pick them clean, leaving a lithic skeleton, an exposed rib, as residue.

Coastlines, like mountains, are special places where the earth's enduring elementarity emerges in striking ways. In each, the earth shows itself in a manner that is both reduced and prominent—reduced to bare rock, prominent in human (and other animal) perception. Thanks to these shared features, both coastlines and mountains are deeply orienting phenomena. A single mountain such as Pike's Peak in Colorado can help me know where I am, approximately, in a vast area of that state, and if I am lost at sea in a storm the sight of a recognizable coast can make all the difference between life and death. No wonder we speak of a coast-*line* and consider the basic profile of a mountain to be line-like in its definiteness: both can be construed as lines standing out on the land. No wonder, either, that many early navigational maps in the Mediterranean world were called *costeggiare*, that is, coastal charts that depicted all known ports on a given coast in serial order, one above the other and designated by toponyms inscribed perpendicular to the line of the coast itself.[19]

FIGURE 14. Sand Beach, Stonington, Maine, 2015. Photo courtesy of Parviz Mohassel.

Close up, coastlines are constituted by unkempt edges that are only rarely crisp in their perceived outline (and then only under special conditions, e.g., that of high tide on a shore composed of cliffs). Coastal edges are not formally geometric but informally "morphological," again using Husserl's term for shapes that elude Euclidean geometry. Moreover, even if they are fractal in comparison with other parts of the same coast—as Mandelbrot has claimed of the British coast—they do not appear in actual perception to instantiate any spatial regularities *in a given place*.[20] Instead, in that place they present themselves as frayed, porous, and ever changing, as is suggested in the photographic image of the coastline at Sand Beach in Stonington, Maine, as seen in figure 14.

Notice that there is no altogether distinct line between water and coast in the above image: we would be hard put to say exactly where the water of the cove runs out as it sinks into the sand. If there is such a spot, it has become imperceptible. What we perceive instead is a mixture of rocks, water, and sand—all juxtaposed unevenly in a conflux of things and elements that is nevertheless visually coherent.

Where, then, is the coastline in a situation such as this? I would suggest that the "line" of the coastline has been replaced by a *fold* regarded as a special sort of wild edge. A fold always has two contributing slopes or sides; every fold is twofold—or perhaps we should say threefold.[21] The leading fold, whether in the top or bottom position (e.g., in the case of folded paper) or situated on the side, laterally, as in the case of water currents (e.g., the ripples that gather close to the shore), is surrounded by curved shapes that are folds in their own right: they fold away from the leading fold in a continuous undulation. The leading fold counts as an edge in the technical sense examined earlier: it is a convex dihedral angle. But unlike edges in rectilinear patterns (especially as these emerge in architectural designs[22]), the edges constituted by folds are soft and yielding, so much so that they are not experienced as linear—even if they can be *represented* by lines, as in drawings of the circumstance I here discuss. At play is something that folds and refolds, that belongs to the tidal water itself as a natural element.

Foldings of water are especially pliable and multiple, given that they are the direct expression of that water's movements – movements that are themselves curved or rounded rather than perfectly straight. The swirling folds at Sand Beach are contained by sand and stone, but they manifest a free movement of their own devising: they fold over and under as they see fit, as if they had a mind of their own. The result is a coastal configuration with a deep coherence despite the complexity of its folded form. In Merleau-Ponty's words, "The flesh (of the world or my own) is not contingency, chaos, but a texture that returns to itself."[23] It returns to itself in the folds of its elementary substances—here in the form of seawater that washes onto a very particular coastline in the state of Maine.[24]

## III

Each of these four exemplary kinds of wild edge—those that accrue to leaves, mountains, rivers, and coastlines—has proved to be distinctive in character and structure, with telling differences that allow them to stand apart from one another. In treating these examples, I have certainly not presumed to give anything like a comprehensive account of wild edges. There are many more such edges that we could discuss, each of special interest and of divergent structure. They would include edges of grasses and bushes, forests, individual rocks and stones, ponds and lakes, though each of these is at least indirectly related to the four I have taken up so far. In addition, there are edges of various animals and insects that inhabit these natural settings. In all these various cases, we would need to go further afield to very different edges that call for separate study. The edges of animal teeth, for instance, have their own traceable evolutionary history, given the employment of these teeth both for attack and for mastication. The same is true for the edges of animal and human bodies. Darwin found in the exact shapes taken by animal faces, including the lines and profiles of these faces, an entire realm of emotional expressivity—a realm further explored by Adolf Portmann in his classical studies of "display" by means of the face. I mention these various studies in order to indicate the considerable interest in wild edges found in fields as different as comparative evolution and animal expressivity.[25]

Wild edges, despite their great diversity, constitute a genus of their own. A sign of this is the significant fact that nowhere in my discussion of such edges have I been tempted to invoke other kinds of edges such as "borders" or "rims." These latter terms were often invoked in my discussions of the various phenomena treated in earlier chapters, whether I was alluding to border situations such as at La Frontera or contrasting artifactual with natural edges. There we were continually confronted with the question, how much is an edge the specific work of human beings and how much is it due to other factors? These other factors certainly included those of an environmental or natural character, but we were not driven to consider these other factors for their own sake; rather, they were regarded as impinging upon human praxis, undergirding it or shaping it or opposing it—and sometimes fusing with it—as a reflection of the particular context in which this praxis occurs.

This chapter has concentrated on edges of natural entities and processes sui generis, in the absence of human intervention and construction. My effort has been to allow the natural to come to the fore: to make its own case, as it were. Wild edges call out to be recognized as having their own life, unconfined by artificial constraints. These constraints include the causal explanatory language of science. Generally, when we are engaged in the direct description of the natural world itself, we should employ as few formal terms as possible: hence my preference for the informal descriptions of the kind I offer here. Inspired by the spectacle of a wild world that sets its own terms, I have described edges with minimal recourse to technical vocabularies. My aim has been to let wild edges speak in their own voices and on their own terms so as to respect their sheer phenomenal presence. If nature likes to be specific, as Kant held, then it should be allowed to specify itself by speaking for itself.

*Chóra* is wild nature in Plato's *Timaeus*. *Ananké* (goddess of Necessity) is closely associated with *chóra (Space)*: Space is what is necessary. *Chóra* is not nature in general in its law-like aspect, that is to say, *physis* as subject to *logos* (rational account)—this conception leads quickly to physics as first set forth systematically by Aristotle. Plato's concern in the *Timaeus* is cosmogonic; he is speculating on the Becoming of things, their generation, not the logic of their ultimate physical Being. The "likely tale" (in Plato's own phrase) that is told in the *Timaeus* is parallel to Husserl's effort to trace the genesis of line and other limit-shapes in his "Origin of Geometry."[26] The difference is that Plato presumes that the Forms of things already exist—they constitute the realm of Being—and the cosmogonic challenge is to tease these Forms into a communion with Matter or Space.

Cosmogenesis construed in this fashion occurs by the violent shaking motion of the Receptacle, the choric vehicle that contains all that is becoming. Before the Forms can ingress into matter, *chóra* must achieve a minimal ordering by means of its shaking motions; this primal order takes the form of four great regions in which the material elements (fire, air, earth, water) coinhere despite their differences.

FIGURE 15. Jackson Pollock, *Untitled (Green Silver)*, circa 1949, enamel and aluminum
paint on paper. Guggenheim Museum, New York. © 2016 The Pollock-Krasner
Foundation/Artists Rights Society (ARS), New York.

Once this happens, Forms can ingress into these regions and material things can
be fashioned: bodies of water, regions of earth, stretches of air, fiery substances.

*Chóra* qua receptacle has no outer edge; it is finite but without limits. It is
something "boundless" (*apeiron*) in Anaximander's term. As Jackson Pollock said
of his action paintings—which are suggestively cosmogonic—they have to do with
a situation in which there are "no limits, just edges."[27] Pollock's paintings from
1948 onward consist of a flurry of edges within swirling masses of line and color.
These masses have no definite limit, no distinct terminus; but their proliferating
edges extend boundlessly outward.

If we imagine Pollock's powerful image above to fall into four regions, roughly
situated in relation to the four corners of the work, we have before us a painterly
analogue of cosmogenesis in Plato's *Timaeus*. The outer edge of the painting, its
nonexistent frame, is quite arbitrary: it is there where the volatile masses of color
end; the painting frames itself from within rather than being framed from without.
Our main attention is drawn to the image as a whole, and especially to its many
edges as they interact with enormous energy yet still exhibiting a deeply coherent
pattern. It is in some such manner that we can imagine the scene of creation in
the choric receptacle, in which the four elements intermesh in seeming chaos but

in truth realize an emergent order: a "chaosmos," in James Joyce's term. The only edges that matter are those between the regions, and these are truly wild—just as wild as are Pollock's painterly edges. In both cases, the edges constitute a scene of disarray, from which glimpses of cosmic order flash out intermittently. Disintegrative at first glance, they are in fact formative in their shape-shifting power.

If we may take such edges as Plato suggests and Pollock paints as paradigmatic of the natural world in its heterogeneous becoming, we can say that its wildness consists in a violent motion that is at once immeasurable and unlocatable, unforeseeable and untraversible. Aspects of such wildness are evident in the edges I have analyzed in this chapter, especially if we imagine them in motion: leaves flying wildly in the wind, mountains emerging suddenly from cloud cover, rivers overflowing their banks and wreaking havoc on the surrounding lands, coastlines awash in winter storms. And if we were to further imagine these four kinds of wild edges suddenly cast together in tumultuous interchange, we would come still closer to what Plato and Pollock see as obtaining at the cosmogonic level. The effect would be a wildness that is, in Thoreau's words, tantamount to "the preservation of the World."[28]

In their continual upsurge, edges reassert themselves as primary—as unreducible to the pure lines and sheer surfaces that are an epistemic ideal for so much of Western thought. Their being perceived as straight or regularly curving edges is no longer of critical importance (as it is when the generation of formal linear structures is at stake); we are not here on the path to geometric perfection in the guise of limits. Wild edges are edges that arise spontaneously in natural settings, including untraversed wilderness areas but also the neglected vacant lot next door or the unkempt fields at the city limit. The geometry of such edges is decidedly nonformal. We need not have recourse to cosmogony or painting to experience edges of this primitive sort. The fact is that we are surrounded by them at all times—in cityscapes as in landscapes, among human beings and with other animals, at sea and on land and at their outermost reaches. Their rebarbative shapes are felt and sensed directly by our lived bodies as we move between different place-worlds. These edges are as ordinary—as directly experienceable by sentient creatures—as they are extraordinary; they are at once quite accessible but also as elusive as only something appearing or vanishing abruptly can be.

To come into the presence of wild edges is to come back to where we and they have always been: we in the places and regions familiar to us as well as unfamiliar, they in front of and around us, attracting us and luring us into ever-new, yet also sometimes old, place-worlds. Their wildness, which we keep forgetting in the urge to sophisticate our concepts or to refine our life practices, shakes us up when we notice such edges anew. It is as if we are somehow still inhabiting the choric Space stipulated in the *Timaeus*. Which we are! *Chóra* takes on anticipatable guises.

Our experiential and philosophical task, accordingly, is to allow ourselves to be astounded by the edges we encounter everywhere, and a good place to begin is with the wild being of the natural world as it impinges on us every day and every night. Wild edges are the vehicles of this astonishment; they convey "the sting of the real" in William James's phrase. They are at once the sign and the symptom, the trial and the trace of the Nature and the Space that surrounds us.

## Notes

1. I say *"largely* a function of natural entities' composition and internal structuration" because the destructive mark of human presence is being felt increasingly in this Anthropocene era—including by nonhuman beings.

2. In this light, the very idea of "intelligent design" is untenable, however tempting it may be to posit it. It was in recognition of this temptation, yet in philosophical skepticism of its validity, that Kant wrote the *Critique of Teleological Judgment*, a book whose strictures regarding "final causes" still remain relevant today. It is theoretically possible that a creator god is responsible for the form of natural things, including their edges; the idea is neither incoherent nor preposterous; but we have no way of knowing if it is true or not. The very idea exceeds what humans can know; at most, we can regard it *as if* it were true.

3. Gary Snyder, *The Practice of the Wild* (San Francisco: Shoemaker and Hoard, 1990), p. 18.

4. I am not denying that numerous animals, especially certain higher primates such as chimpanzees, gorillas, etc., also create and use tools; but my focus here is upon the contrast between the human and the nonhuman.

5. Note that here what I am calling "edge" is in effect a "limit" in the strict sense discussed in chapter 2.

6. For an extended discussion of orientation, see Casey, *The World at a Glance*, chapter 3, "Being/Becoming Oriented by the Glance."

7. Of course, nothing of the sort occurs. The mountain is supremely indifferent to human perception: that is part of its transcendent status.

8. Maurice Merleau-Ponty, *Phenomenology of Perception*, trans. Landes, pp. 74, 336.

9. *Entfaltung* signifies "development" in the German language. It derives from *Falte*, "fold," "crease," "wrinkle"; the verb *entfalten* means "to unfold." This coherent complex of words points to the same kind of circumstance with which I am here concerned.

10. Walt Whitman, "Song of Myself."

11. Heraclitus, fragment 20, in Philip Wheelwright's translation: Philip Wheelwright, *Heraclitus* (New York: Atheneum, 1968), p. 29. The full fragment is, "Everything flows and nothing abides; everything gives way and nothing stays fixed."

12. "You cannot step twice into the same river, for other waters are continually flowing on" (fragment 21 in Wheelwright, *Heraclitus*, p. 29).

13. "A river is a dark brown god . . ." (T. S. Eliot, *Four Quartets*). For further discussion of the destructive potential of rivers, see my dialogue with James Hillman, "Rivers: A Conversation," in Margot McLean and Sandy Gellis, *Catching Light, Migrations, Water Flow, Extinctions . . .* (Florence, Italy: Museo di Storia Naturale, 2004).

14. McLean and Gellis, *Catching Light*, pp. 22, 25.

15. Ibid., p. 25.

16. This is from the Cherokee myth "Earth Making." See also the Crow legend, "Old Man Coyote Makes the World." These, and others that invoke mud, are to be found in R. Erdoes and A. Ortiz, eds. *American Indian Myths and Legends* (New York: Pantheon, 1984), p. 106 for the above citation and pp. 88–90 for the Crow Legend, which describes how Old Man Coyote creates the world and its contents from lumps of mud.

17. When an effort to span an entire sea is made, as with the Oresund Bridge that links Denmark and Sweden, it is regarded as a feat of engineering, something to marvel at precisely because it is something of an *opus contra naturam*. An intermediate case is provided by a major strait or inlet whereby an ocean is extended into a bay, as in San Francisco: part of the allure of the Golden Gate Bridge lies in its being suspended over a body of water that is more than a river but less than an ocean.

18. Further analysis of water in relation to edges is treated in my unpublished essay "At Water's Edge" (given at a SEED conference in New Mexico in 2008). Anne Morrow Lindburgh's book is titled *Gifts from the Sea* (New York: Pantheon Books, 2003).

19. For further discussion of *costeggiare*, see Edward S. Casey, *Representing Place* (Minneapolis: University of Minnesota Press, 2002), chapter 9, "Discursive and Presentational Symbolism in Maps," p. 181.

20. See the earlier discussion of fractal formations in chapter 2, "Edges and Surfaces, Edges and Limits."

21. As Deleuze remarks, every fold is in effect "a fold between the two folds" (Gilles Deleuze, *The Fold*, trans. Tom Conley [Minneapolis: University of Minnesota Press, 1993], p. 4).

22. With the notable exceptions of certain buildings, such as San Carlo alle Quattro Fontane in Rome and the Disney Concert Hall in Los Angeles.

23. Merleau-Ponty, *The Visible and the Invisible*, trans. Alphonso Lingis (Evanston, IL: Northwestern University Press, 1968), p. 146.

24. Merleau-Ponty adds that the world's flesh serves "as an element, as the concrete emblem of a general manner of being" (ibid., p. 147).

25. The studies I refer to include Charles Darwin, *The Expression of Emotion in Animals and Men* (New York: Appleton & Company, 1873), and Adolf Portmann, *Animals as Social Beings* (New York: Harper & Row, 1961). On the edges of forests, see Chris Anderson, *Edge Effects: Notes from an Oregon Forest* (Iowa City: University of Iowa Press, 1993). I owe this last reference to Gabrielle Milanich.

26. Edmund Husserl, "The Origin of Geometry," in *The Crisis of European Sciences and Transcendental Phenomenology*, trans. David Carr (Evanston, IL: Northwestern University Press, 1970), pp. 353–78.

27. Jackson Pollock, remark in an interview that became the title of a show at the Guggenheim Museum, New York City, summer, 2006. Spoken spontaneously and by a painter and not a philosopher, this remark serves to confirm the basic difference between edges and limits as I discuss it in chapter 2.

28. Henry David Thoreau, "Walking," in *Nature and Walking*, Ralph Waldo Emerson and H. D. Thoreau, ed. John Elder (Boston: Beacon, 1991), p. 95: "In Wildness is the preservation of the world."

# Listening to Edges in Music

> The edges [in music] are where things happen.
> —John Luther Adams[1]

> To be listening is always to be on the edge of meaning, or in an edgy
> meaning of extremity . . . as if the sound were precisely nothing else than
> this edge, this fringe, this margin—at least the sound that is musically
> listened to.
> —Jean-Luc Nancy, *Listening*

The very idea of *listening to edges* is doubly puzzling. For one thing, we tend to
think of edges as something we *see* or, more rarely, something we can touch or
handle—but not something we *hear*. For another, we are not accustomed to think
of sounds of any kind as having *edges*; the very idea of "edge" does not fit well
with our basic sense of the acoustic world, which we often take to be so smoothly
flowing as to be virtually edgeless. These two points are closely related: it is just
because the world of sound tends to be so self-enclosed and well-rounded that
it would seem to lack the kind of angular and definite edges that invite seeing
or touching. This world seems to be almost autonomous, as if coming from we
know not where: Merleau-Ponty describes sounds in music as "swirls of being."[2]
Yet, whatever their origin and their mode of presentation, sounds do have acoustic mass and force, and as such they possess shapes and contours. If clouds, which
billow and swirl, have edges (as I argue in chapter 10), then perhaps sounds do too.

## I

Stopping short of humanly created music for the moment, notice that we do speak
of certain *noises* as "jarring" or "sharp." John Cage, who sought to valorize street
noises as at least protomusical, urged readers of his book *Noise* to listen intently to
the shape of noise. If they do, they are likely to discover a whole world of formful
sounds that occur for the most part without repetitive rhythmic structure or ordered sequence: "a-periodic sounds," as the contemporary composer John Luther
Adams puts it.[3] At least some of these sounds have quite distinct shapes—not only
because they are associated with certain things (a chainsaw cutting through wood)
or events (rain falling on the roof)—but because *as sounds* they possess distinctive

profiles. We take a drilling sound to have its own contour, and so too a deep thumping: these arrive as *sui generis* acoustic entities with their own characteristic profiles, difficult as these may be to name or to discuss. Sometimes ordinary sounds are so elusive that we borrow a term from music to identify or clarify them: for instance, a "staccato" noise. Or else we immediately try to pin down the noise as having a familiar source: the heaving *of the ocean*, the bark *of a dog*, the shout *of a man*. Or, in another sidestep, we reduce the noise to its decibel level, something reassuringly quantitative. It is almost as if we cannot tolerate the idea that a mere noise, a sheer sound, has any standing of its own—any intrinsic *raison d'être*. For this reason, we tend to dismiss it as either commonplace or trivial. Regarding it as "just noise" and not deserving of our attention, we let it go, either to expire or to sink into the mass of other noises with which we are always surrounded.

Cage defined music as "sounds heard." He made a deliberate effort to bring music back to earth, back down to the ground of everyday experience: an admirable effort in the face of centuries of "high culture" in the West, in which music played a quite central role. Still, it is difficult to sustain interest in garden-variety sounds—car horns honking, subway brakes screeching—for very long. The restless listener asks for more—more complication, more structure, more intense and involving rhythms, some wisp of a melody if at all possible. The "sounds heard" call to be heard not just as noise but also as music. Without having to endorse Leonard Bernstein's thesis that we are genetically hardwired to appreciate certain basic harmonic structures, we can say that human beings (as well as birds and whales) seek something more than unadorned sounds alone can deliver. We seek a certain satisfying edge structure that is only rarely to be found in the world of ordinary noise. This is no less true of a rock concert—with its jarring edges, fiercely insistent beat, and fast rhythms—than it is of a classically played Haydn symphony. We hear sounds as music when their edges become satisfying to our listening ear.[4]

This satisfying edge structure is not single in kind and character—there is no one satisfying pattern of musical edges—but many. It is this very manyness that allows composers to proliferate their compositions: to write several quite different symphonies, various string quartets, or else many jazz compositions, and still other works of a certain recognizable structure yet quite diverse, as they sound from work to work and even from performance to performance. These works invite the listener to enter whole worlds of *unheard of* sounds: sounds never heard in the course of daily life, sounds that belong to alternate sound worlds.

These worlds are structured by their own distinct edges: edges after edges, edges upon edges, and edges beside edges. Edges are everywhere, even if we do not have many names for them other than conventional terms (often classical in origin) like *glissando*, which calls for merging discrete edges into one smooth glide whose edge is that of the whole assimilated mass. A term such as this attempts to suggest one kind of edge we hear in listening to music, but it rarely captures the minute infrastructure of a given heard edge. We listen to and hear the exact edge structure (in this case, one sustained swoosh), yet language fails us in the end. It also fails us elsewhere, in other edge-worlds—notably when it comes to wild edges, as we have just seen, or with bodily or psychical edges, both of which are especially elusive. But in the case of music the failure is acute. In listening to the rendition of a given musical composition, we are often left speechless when we ask ourselves, what precise kind of acoustic edges did I just hear? Wider intervals between notes or groups of notes (such as chords) may create a certain sense of sonic spread. A tritone or some other distinct and striking interval can make us aware of the tonal distance between individual notes. In such cases, whatever edges we can make out will dissolve with the next set of intervals, making it difficult to remember precisely which edges we have heard.

The difficulty of identifying distinct edges in music is part of a larger problematic: the discrepancy between hearing whole congeries of continuously evolving sounds and adequate nomenclature for the edges of these sounds as we take them in. I am not here referring to individual differences in hearing one and the same piece of music—these may be considerable in their own right—but to the character of the sounds heard, their phenomenal shape and structure. How are we to describe these? This book is attempting to supply a more discerning and extensive vocabulary for phenomenally felt or perceived edges than Western languages often possess, and the experience of music is no exception. But the problem goes deeper still; it goes into the very heart of time itself—or more exactly, of *temporality*, the immanent experience of time's flowing onward.

## II

The edges of sounds in music are those of *sounds temporalized*. Not only do these edges act to define the distinctive acoustic shapes of individual notes or single chords, but they accrue to entire acoustic clusters, whole stretches of a musical composition, and finally the full piece. At each level and throughout, musical edges exist in temporal terms. The widely held view that edges properly belong to static physical things in space is countermanded by the incontestable experience of edges of music as it unfolds in time. The relationship between time and music is close, and it goes both ways. Bergson and Husserl, who together provided some of the most penetrating descriptions ever of time-consciousness, both likened the flow of time to *melody*, and this was not an idle metaphor for them.[5]

Music not only occurs *in time*—that is, takes a certain amount of time to unfold—it is *of time*: it belongs to it and is made from it. This is why music is experienced *as temporal*, where "temporal" signifies the way time is experienced by the listener as constituting a flow with continually unfolding phases. Each of these phases possesses its own specifically temporal edges: a starting edge, an ending edge, and a series of intermediate edges (often in the form of ridges and hollows of time: temporal folds as it were).[6] Each such edge is itself subject to variation of several sorts, for example, that stretching between higher and lower pitch.[7]

Given how thoroughly music is at one with time and is heard in time, its edges will reflect those of temporal flow itself. To put it otherwise, if there can be edges in temporal flow, then there will be edges in music, in view of its being coeval and at one with that flow. More strongly put, there *must be* such edges. At the very least, the three generic kinds of temporal edges just mentioned (starting, ending, intermediate) are found as immanent structures in any music to which we listen—however disparately they are presented in a given instance. There could be no more dramatic contrast than that between the three distinct thumps that mark the end of Bartok's String Quartet no. 2 (1915–17) and the prolonged fading out of the finale of his String Quartet no. 6 (1939), in which the sounds diminish to the point of inaudibility. Yet both remain *modes of musical closure*: they are species of the generic structure of coming to an end in music. In listening to the two Bartok string quartets, one recognizes the two endings as variations of the basic edge-structure of coming to a close. Their differential modes of closure amount to a differentiated disclosure—a disclosure of two ways that temporal intervals come to an end. This structure holds for any given temporal experience as well as for what we hear in listening to a given musical performance.

## III

Edges in music are what stand out by their sonic shapes as such—by which I mean their inherent sound profiles, the audible configurations created by single notes or clusters of notes. These configurations are not heard in isolation but in relation to sounds that coexist with them (say, in a second and then a third motif that is added to an already stated primary motif, as in a Bach cantata) or that precede and succeed them. Whatever exact forms such configurations may take, they are heard as groups of edges that are, as it were, flying in formation.

Sounds of any kind, including musical sounds, not only *have* edges; they *are* edges. There is not some underlying sonic substance comparable to a physical thing—the usual model in the West for substance—but rather in the world of sound *the edge is the thing itself*. The very sounding of a sound brings with it its own edge: it could not be *a* sound, or *that* sound, or *those* sounds, were edges absent. Each of these instances, and still other variations, are not just composed of edges that are added onto an underlying sonic substrate; they are edges through and through, without remainder. Although a particular sound is usually surrounded by other sounds, often a multitude of them, there is nothing beneath it (acting as an acoustic substrate) or beyond it (such as its "meaning"). This is not to deny that sounds may gain meaning in relation to each other: most obviously so in the case of strings of spoken words, but also in music, whose concatenated sounds are more expressive than indicative. A series of notes taken as a single mass of sounds possesses relational meaning; this meaning is inherent in the sequence of the notes and is not beyond it: it is inherent *in their edges*. Just as there is no substance underneath sonic edges, so there is nothing over them like the sheen of a sheer signification, an epiphenomenon that lies *on* it (*epi*- signifies "upon"). If a C-sharp major chord is sounding, its presence is unmistakably what it is: just as there is nothing under it, there is nothing hanging over it. As heard, it cannot be confused with another chord, and for someone with perfect pitch its identity is unmistakable. This holds for their very edges: edges in sound *are what they are as they are*. Their being is their appearance, and this being exists as an edge or set of edges.

Out of the myriad possible instances of musical edges, I here single out the following few, ranging from conspicuous to muted.

*Drumming edges.* Drums provide abundant examples of distinct edges: crisp and unmissable when within hearing range. Each drum stroke has an integrity of its own, a separate standing; precisely as distinct, it can enter into rhythmic sequence with other drum strokes (as in a "drum roll") and with other drums and different percussive instruments, such as cymbals. Two sets of edges emerge here: those of the individual drum strokes and those of the series formed from such strokes. Either way, drummed edges readily assume a role of commencing or concluding a given event. Their acute edges convey an aura of authority, as we witness in military parades. In jazz, the drummer characteristically "sets the beat." Since the very distinctness and separateness of drumming edges can be experienced as reductive or too obvious, experienced drummers have devised ways to complicate the patterns of their sounding, for example, softening the abrupt edges of their basic strokes by employing whisks rather than drum sticks. Whisks give the sense of a continuous sound as opposed to a crisp and distinct striking, and this effect is similar to a drum roll in that many sounds converge to give the illusion of a single, longer, albeit complex, sound.

*Single voice or nonpercussion instruments.* Flute solos such as those in Boulez's Sonatine for Flute and Piano (1946) trace out a quasilinear edge by their smoothly shifting course. Such solos are in effect moving edges with a clean trajectory that leaves little ambiguity as to the direction or delivery of sounded edges produced by this instrument. Much the same is true for instruments that speak with a monovalent tonality: trumpets, oboes, French horns, clarinets. Something similar holds for the human singing voice. Leaving aside its semantic dimensions (which modulate it and allow it to appeal to other capacities of the listener, both cognitive and affective), a sustained singing voice creates an *edge-arc*: crisp and clear. Even when complemented by other sounds, including percussion instruments, it retains an integrity of its own. It often inaugurates and maintains a position as a *leading edge* in the circumstance; but between the voice-edge and those of pianos, drums, and other instruments, there can be echoing effects that effect an entanglement of diverse edges. In a successful composition for voice and other instruments, there is mutual enhancement and intensification of diverse edges. In Ravel's *Trois Poèmes de Stéphane Mallarmé* (1913), for example, the mezzosoprano takes the lead throughout by singing the Mallarmé poems in a decisive and dramatic way that is supported, literally subtended, by a group of six percussionists and a piano player. Even if one doesn't follow the French, the singer's voice establishes a decisive edge, or rather *it is that edge itself*. It is the effective edge of the musical work, neither simply at its periphery nor at its tonal center. The moving edge of the singing voice deconstructs the binary of center/periphery as well as the dyads of substance/accident and being/appearance. It is an edge sui generis; as its own edge, it makes its own way.

*Small groups of players*. We confront a very different situation when listening to a musical work in which the players take the lead at different times in roughly equal measure and are commensurate in the emphatic presence of the sounds they produce. For instance, in Bartok's String Quartet no. 5 (1934) we are treated to an extraordinarily condensed and intense series of sounds, often in strict unison but sometimes with one of the two violins or the viola or the cello taking the lead—soon to be joined by the others. The result is a rich medley of edges, no one of which is dominant. We have here—we *hear* here—a confection of *shared edges* in concert (taking "con-cert" literally as coming to harmony out of a potential for conflict and dispute). These edges interarticulate with each other subtly yet forcefully, producing a complex mass of sounds that seem at once long and short—long as intensely delivered and heard, short as coming to a swift close, sometimes seemingly in a race toward a place to pause (between movements, and then finally at the end). But there can be other moments, for example in the second movement of Bartok's Second String Quartet, when the whole movement constitutes a diversion from the main directionality—a pause of another sort in which a series of sharp, piquant notes are literally plucked by the players' fingers in keeping with the composer's instruction for this movement: *allegro molto capriccioso*, producing a seemingly freeform set of sounds that strikes the listener as intriguingly subversive of the general movement of the piece.

*Whole orchestras*. When we reach the level of an entire orchestra, a decisive difference occurs. Instead of the sounds of individual instruments (drums, the human voice) or a discretely delimited set of sounds (as with many string quartets), there are groups of sound-edges that are often determined by the clustering of instruments with each other in different locations—violins and other stringed instruments at the front of the stage, brass in a middle region of the stage, percussion usually at the back rim of the scene. These groupings not only allow for greater coherence and emphasis, they also generate an effect we can call *shifting edges*. These emerge in the moving of heard edges from one part of the orchestra to another, circling back, and then taking other complex directions. When such diversely gathered edges sound together, the effect is quite literally *symphonic*, ("sounded together") in massive harmony, given that "harmony is heard sounds together," in Cage's formula.[8]

## IV

As if adding the next chapter in the evolution of musical edges from origins in drumming and voice to small groups of closely concatenated players to whole orchestral groupings, we find John Luther Adams's recent works to bring in new dimensions of sounded edges. I refer especially to the works that Adams situates in public parks and other common spaces rather than in concert halls. This is done not just to include an element of deinstitutionalized, casual listening—a literally democratic move—but also so as to embrace the ambient sounds of animals, the city, the wind in the trees. In *Sila: The Breath of the World* (2014), as performed at the Ojai Music Festival of 2015, the musicians were grouped into six or seven areas of a city park composed of trees, grass, and sidewalks, with these areas being in fairly close contiguity but with no attempt at formal symmetry. Not only was there multiple sounding—and resounding—but multiple modes of listening. Adams puts it this way: "As the music of the performance gradually dissolves into the larger sonic landscape, the musicians join the audience in listening to the continuing music of the place."[9] This is just what happened in Ojai on June 10, 2015: the sounds of the park, including those of children playing nearby, birds chirping, traffic going down Main Street, and planes overhead, were accepted as integral to the musical work itself. These formed the predominant acoustic background as people informally gathered in the mid-afternoon. At a moment difficult to clock exactly, those who had come to hear *Sila* began to fall silent gradually and without a formal prompt as a very dimly discernible swelling of extremely low-pitched sounds began to arise from one of the performance areas: these sounds stemming from tubas, trombones, and human voices singing through paper megaphones. From there, various complications ensued as other instruments joined in (strings, wind, and drums), though never with a decisive, much less jarring, edge; throughout, the effect was that of one very long act of breathing on the part of the musicians. At the end, *as* the end, the breathing ceased just as subtly as it had begun but still more slowly. The drums moved to barely discernible sounds made by hands lightly passing over drum surfaces; the violins created gently spiraling curlicues of sound; until finally there was nothing sounding but the breath of a number of musicians as emitted through their megaphones—and the rest was silence. Just then, the circumambient sounds of the park and city returned to the notice of those listening, assuming their proper place as it were, as if to remind everyone, musicians and listeners alike, that they were in an actual place that had its own sounds and sound patterns.

Adams comments, "Listening to music indoors, we usually try to ignore the outside world, listening to a limited range of sounds. Listening outdoors, instead of limiting our attention to [the performance as such], we're challenged to *expand* our attention to encompass a multiplicity of sounds. We're invited to receive messages not only from the composer and the performers, but also from the larger world around us."[10] The contrast between the random and sometimes raucous sounds of "the larger world" and the performed sounds of *Sila* could not be greater: it is between "the discordant noise" of the actual surroundings and "a fragile skein of stacked harmonies."[11] What emerges is a set of literally *composed musical edges*—random noise and performed music joining forces across their very differences. The result is a deeply coherent tapestry of sounds that emerge directly from the entire situation. More remarkably still, the effect is that of sounds constituting, *indeed being*, the very breath of the underlying earth. We are here at a very different acoustic place from that generated by the distinct and strident edges of concerted drumming. We have entered into a space supported by a broadband edge that somehow conveys "the breath of the world." We seem to sense that we are hearing the world, the very earth, breathing—for the first time, or perhaps for the last time in dark premonition.[12]

Not only in *Sila* but also in countless other musical works by other composers, the edges are indeed "where things happen," as Adams observes in the epigraph to this chapter. They happen there in multifarious ways: far more than I have been able to indicate in the brief conspectus of types presented in the previous section. In the end, the five clusterings I have picked out are themselves arbitrary; there are many more types of musical edges, even within a single musical work, than these groups can contain or specify. I have merely tried to bring a minimal order into what is in fact an immensely complex circumstance—made all the more complex by Adams's extraordinary compositions. For music is a uniquely configured edge-world whose types and subtypes do not fit easily into the genera and species of other such worlds. It is a world replete with familiar and unfamiliar edges of sounds—of edges upon edges in successive waves that unfold with the tides of time. These edges need not come to any final or formal unison but can retain much diversity even as they interact with each other in subtle and sinuous ways.

## V

This is not to say that edges in music always unfold smoothly and mellifluously. Sometimes these edges are abrupt and are valued as such. Thelonious Monk was especially notable for his jagged and jolting but still swinging style of playing and composing. He was a creator of sharply dissonant musical edges that jarred (and still jar) their listener's expectations. This listener is often confronted with a series of disparate, strikingly angular chords and notes that cascade into (and sometimes interrupt) each other almost to the point of cacophony, yet always concatenating just enough to be acoustically coherent. A good example of this is Monk's composition *Ba-Lue Boliver Ba-Lues Are* (1957), which presents an empire of edges within the space of a single song.[13]

The musical edges created by a jazz genius such as Monk open up and open out, proffering odd edges whose incongruity is matched by a quirky beat in a disruptive stop-and-start time. Although rooted in earlier stride piano and other styles, Monk transforms this temporality into something far less focused, departing from earlier repetitive, more predictable rhythmic structures. The edges we hear in *Ba-Lue Boliver Ba-Lues Are* realize a decided chromatic and harmonic freedom even as they stay within the basic lines of the melody of the song Monk is playing. Rather than restricting himself to regular rhythmic movements—as in boogie-woogie—the edges of a Monk tune exfoliate in time, edging out endlessly. In such music we hear how edges can be *played* in creative and innovative ways. Monk's fingers in touch with piano keys bring about an immensely playful but also intensely demanding edge-work in sound. The fact that these edges are experienced as discordant and discontinuous only makes them more compelling. The withholding of familiar harmonies and rhythms becomes an integral part of what we hear, drawing our rapt attention and keeping it engaged throughout a given composition. Monk's composing and playing alike create music on the edge—on the edge of our expectations and of music history up to that point—while putting us on edge as we listen to it.

## VI

Music is an essentially social art. It is composed and performed for people to hear—and to hear together in groups, ranging from a handful (as when Monk played for his friends on a grand piano placed in his kitchen) to a concert hall, a public park, or a vast outdoor theater. I relate here a recent experience in which this social dimension of music was especially prominent.

It was Sunday evening and I was walking along Eighth Avenue in Harlem when suddenly I heard some extraordinarily intense music—a jazz group playing inside a newly opened restaurant. I could not resist entering and listening to what was being played. I was especially struck by the way the music brought edges of sound to bear on each other—not only by the pitch and timbre and tonality of these sounds but thanks to their rapidly altering rhythms as well. The performance by a quartet of musicians was creating an ever-changing edge-work as one person seized the lead, only to be rapidly replaced by another, and then by the convergence of all members of this small ensemble. The edges of the sounds of particular instruments were particularly prominent: the trumpet often adding a sharply echoing line that contrasted with the more straight-out playing of the saxophone. I marveled at the way these shifting instrumental edges, diverging and converging, were continually surprising and difficult to anticipate, yet intermeshed in ways that made melodic and rhythmic sense. They were *working their edges*, intricately and intensely, in and by playing them together. When two vocalists joined the band seemingly from nowhere, the edges of human voices joined the increasingly dense medley, adding not only different sounds but sounds that, by adding lyrics to songs, made instantaneous sense. The female singer sang of the dilemma in which she didn't love the man she was with yet could not part from him. This elicited shouts of approval—"yeah, sister!"—from members of the audience, who lent their enthusiastic if nonmusical voices to the occasion.

It was a truly heteroglossic situation, a "multivoiced body" in Fred Evan's apt term[14]—a veritable chorus of voices that joined up with the instruments (which also included a drummer and two keyboardists) in a complicated webwork of musical edges: a work that was ever changing course, as edges proliferated upon edges. The result was a moving feast of sounds whose intercalated edges were neither as interruptive as Monk's nor as smooth as classical music yet were quite forceful and moving in their own right. Edges were everywhere to be heard: not only in each discernible stretch of sound but also at the very front end of a given composition as it moved forward, as well as in the last phases of its dying down. The musicians, who have played together for a number of years, were alive to each other's contributions and deftly anticipated one another while laying down new edges to which their colleagues could respond spontaneously and aptly. These edges of sound, these *sounding edges*, cut in and out of each other—tracing, *being*, edges at every turn. They were at once improvised and (as they came across to myself, listening) ineluctably *right*: fitting with each other perfectly each time they intersected, each time they met. This was music that was working at the edge and with the edge, both at once. The resulting amalgam of sonically specific edges spread throughout the restaurant and spilled onto the street outside, where it attracted considerable attention from people walking by. The sociality of the occasion spread from the restaurant to the street and back again. Animating it was the music, whose dense fabric of edges was virtually irresistible.

The musical edges I have here singled out—in the Harlem restaurant and in Monk's music, as earlier with Bartok's and Adams's compositions—are those of *sounds in time, sounds of time*. They define their distinctive acoustic shapes, not just note by note, or chord by chord, but in the gestalt of entire acoustic masses—various stretches of a piece, and finally the piece as a whole. At each level and throughout, the edges are at once indefinite and definitive. Indefinite in that we don't even have terms for most of these contours of sound, being limited to terms such as "sweeping" or "sliding" or "disjunct." But definitive in that these edges *belong* to the same sounds; or rather they *are* these sounds, being our point of access to them. They are intrinsic to their identity and to their movement in and with time.[15]

## Notes

1. John Luther Adams, "Music in the Anthropocene," a lecture at University of California, Santa Barbara, sponsored by the Interdisciplinary Humanities Center, Santa Barbara, June 4, 2015.

2. Maurice Merleau-Ponty, "Eye and Mind," in Johnson, ed., *The Merleau-Ponty Aesthetics Reader*, p. 123.

3. John Luther Adams, remark in his lecture at UCSB, as cited above.

4. Judith Lochhead comments, "Acoustically defined noise (having a plethora of simultaneous wave forms vibrating) can be heard as music when its 'edges' (as you're using the term—I think) become satisfying" (e-mail communication of March 14, 2016). On the concept of noise, especially its social and political dimensions (whereby what counts as noise may vary from one class of listeners to another), see Jacques Attali, *Noise: The Political Economy of Music*, trans. Brian Massumi (Minneapolis: University of Minnesota Press, 1985).

5. In his early lectures on time-consciousness, Husserl hinted at the existence of edges in and of time by his idea that the retentional phases of time-consciousness have "haloes" and "horizons," both of which are edge terms imported from spatial experience. But the notion that temporal phenomena have *their own distinctive edges* was not yet in his purview.

6. Judith Lochhead remarks, "the composer-critic Edward Cone wrote about the beginnings and endings of pieces in terms of frames, specifically frames around pictures. He was evoking the beginning and ending as edges" (e-mail communication of March 14, 2016). See Edward Cone, *Musical Form and Musical Performance* (New York: Norton, 1968). My remarks about picture frames in interlude III connect with the framing that occurs in music: both cases have to do with a special kind of edge that acts to surround, to present, and above all to give shape to what it surrounds. The paradoxes of picture frames, to which I have pointed, have analogues in the framing of musical works.

7. Technically, pitch and frequency can be described as follows: "The pitch depends on how often a particle vibrates when a wave passes through, otherwise known as the frequency of the wave. . . . The higher the frequency (more vibrations), then the higher the pitch will be; the lower the frequency (less vibrations), the lower the pitch will be. Since frequency is the reciprocal of the pitch, the higher the frequency the more peaks and valleys within a given amount of time. Because sound waves in air travel at about the same speed regardless of their frequency, high frequency also means more peaks and valleys in a spatial picture of the sound wave. In other words, the wavelength of the high-frequency waves is shorter than of low-frequency waves" (https://van.physics.illinois.edu/qa/listing.php?id=2053; retrieved July 20, 2015).

8. Cited by John Luther Adams in his UCSB lecture of June 4, 2015.

9. John Luther Adams, in the printed program for *Sila: The Breath of the World* (2014), 69th Ojai Music Festival (June 2015), p. 35. Note that the Latin verb *sileo* means "to be noiseless, still, or silent."

10. Adams, *Sila*, p. 33 (his italics).

11. Steven Schick, "Steven Schick on *Sila*," in *Sila* program, p. 35.

12. "As John [Adams] says, it is the breath of the world. And, God help us, sometimes it feels like the last healthy breath the planet will draw" (Schick, *Sila* program, p. 35).

13. *Ba-Lue Boliver Ba-Lues Are* is included in the album titled *Brilliant Corners*. Eric Casey adds this comment: "Monk also has a *song* called *Brilliant Corners* that is very challenging for any group to play. There is a famous recording of it with Sonny Rollins on the saxophone. The song has a very odd rhythmical feel, almost loping and creeping around a tempo" (personal communication of July 15, 2015).

14. See Fred Evans, *The Multivoiced Body: Society and Communication in the Age of Diversity* (New York: Columbia University Press, 2008).

15. I wish to thank Eric Casey for his careful reading of this interlude and his apposite suggestions for its improvement. I am likewise grateful to Judith Lochhead for her discerning scrutiny of an earlier draft and for indicating places where clarification was needed.

# SIX

# Landscape Edges

Where does a landscape begin—and where does it end? This is to ask, where is its edge? We are tempted to think that landscapes go on and on indefinitely—one vista giving way to another, one stretch of land blending into the next. And to the extent that this is the case, is not any attempt to determine or even imagine an edge for them an act of unjustified intervention if not of hubris? Does a given landscape have any edge other than an arbitrary, humanly imposed one? Think of a seascape opening up before your outgoing look; regaled before you, it offers a more or less coherent and continuous outward view composed of masses of water merging and diverging. The perception of one particular patch of water in this vista is like a willful cut into the blue deep: it is what my glance happens to catch hold of, only to lose it again in the next instant, releasing it into a neighboring patch, into which it seems to tuck itself effortlessly. Is there any definitive edge here? Certainly there are many interim edges, but just as certainly there is no lasting edge. Other questions arise: Does a landscape or a seascape lend itself to quantification? How is its extent to be measured? Does it have a proper unit? Most pertinent for our purposes, how are we to think of the edge of a given landscape or seascape? Assuming that such an edge exists—something we cannot take for granted—is it a perimeter, a periphery, a rim? What is it, and how are we to think of it?

What follows is a description of the natural edges of landscapes. While recognizing that there are other valid "-scapes"—such as seascapes (which I shall mostly designate as "waterscapes"), skyscapes, and cityscapes—landscapes will form the focus in this brief chapter. Landscape itself I take to be the appearing of the earth in one of its major guises. It involves a factor of ground or soil, and almost always certain forms of vegetation, from plants to bushes to trees; it also often includes streams, ponds, and lakes. It is situated somewhere between earth as a material fundament, a chthonic resource, and the ethereal sky above; it tends to cling to the earth even as it opens into the sky. I say that it is situated "somewhere" between earth and sky because landscape is not a determinate entity that can be precisely located or measured. It spreads out on the earth as what we take in at any given moment of the earth's surface, an integral part of its extent. The land lays itself out before us so as to be seen and felt at large: such is the root connotation of the suffix *-scape*, which connotes that which has sufficient scope to be scanned from near or far.

Landscape requires our lived body as the counterpart to earth and as its essential witness. This body is actively engaged with landscape, not only viewing it but also walking through it, touching and smelling and hearing it. Throughout the first two chapters of this part of the book, landscape has been a largely latent yet distinctly formative presence, subtending and supporting much of what was said earlier about natural and wild edges. The time has come to address landscape as such.

## I

In thinking of edges of any kind, there are two extremes to consider: the *salient edge* and the *subtle edge*. The salient edge is perceptually obvious; it stands out, is unambiguous in its presentation, and often marked as such. It is the kind of edge that announces itself *as an edge*. Examples would include the shape of a gate, the edges of a table, the pleats of close-fitting clothing. Such edges are undeniably present in ongoing perceptual experience: not only do we notice them easily, we cannot deal with them without some physical negotiation (walking around the table, entering the gate, viewing the pleats from a different angle). A subtle edge is something else. It is not only ambiguous but also faint in its appearance. We may find ourselves asking, is it even an edge? It is so integral to its bearer as to be barely, if at all, distinguishable from the bearer itself, and it is rarely remarked as such. Instances include slight crinkles in the piece of paper on which I am writing, different areas of the same green lawn at which I am looking, or various stretches of a bright and cloudless sky. The subtlety is such that I cannot tell for sure whether or where the edge begins or ends: what distinguishes one patch of this smooth lawn from another? This is difficult to determine—not just at first glance but even with many subsequent glances. Leibniz, standing at a seashore, posited *petites perceptions* whose subtle infrastructure underlay the edges of the waves at which he was looking: just as we cannot tell precisely where one wave begins and another ends, so we cannot know for sure where our apperception of it starts or stops. In both cases, the subtlety of the difference means that we cannot track, much less name or count, the transitions from one wave to another, or from one apperception to the next.

Important and interesting as are these extremes, in the actual experience of landscape (or seascape in Leibniz's case) we find ourselves almost always witnessing something in between salient and subtle edges. In their intermediacy, many edges are neither starkly etched nor subdued to the point of indiscernibility. The exceptions stand out by their rarity: the forest that comes to an abrupt halt for no apparent reason, or the fog that swallows up every last edge of land. For the most part, our experience of landscape is such that we do make out particular objects or singular events, singly or in clusters, and we do so by noticing discernible edges. Moreover, we rely on such edges for orientation in the perceptual world: without them, we would be quite lost. On the other hand, if everything in the surrounding landscape were perfectly distinct—if each were itself only in stark contrast with every other thing—we would be just as disoriented, for there would be no fading into the distance, thus no depth and no horizons. It would be as if we were in a brightly illuminated artificial studio, filled with plastic objects that have nothing to do with each other. Such a world would be as inhospitable and confusing as a world that obscured all its singularities—like "the night," in Hegel's celebrated words, "in which all the cows are black." Both of these extremes—sheer dissolution and glaring distinctness—produce a situation in which individual things are perceived as indifferent to each other's presence.

Fortunately (and doubtless for basic evolutionary reasons), we only rarely have to cope with such extremes. For the most part, we find ourselves in a middle realm of partially differentiated objects and events—differentiated enough to allow us to recognize and identify them, yet not so clear and distinct as to rule out depth and horizons and other essentially indeterminate phenomena. Here we are addressing a medley of vague phenomena—which exhibit morphological rather than exact essences—along with other, much more definite entities and events.[1]

The world we perceive comes, then, as a mixed picture replete with subtle and salient edges, but for the most part edges that are situated between these extremes. Far from being a defect or a shortcoming, this is as it should be—indeed, as it *has* to be. Integral to the being of the perceived world is the sheer range of its composition, including both indeterminate and determinate features of things. This is true a fortiori of the specific landscapes, waterscapes of several sorts, and cityscapes that populate this world—which constitute its most primal regions at the level of vision and action. For these basic kinds of -scape are in effect *clusters of places*, which hold the main contents of the perceived world, putting this world on display with all that there is to see (as well as hear, feel, and touch). We sense these contents, we come to know them, as composing the place-worlds of ordinary (and sometimes extraordinary) perception. In such worlds, edges always figure. The question before us now is, how do they figure in the presentation of landscapes in particular?

## II

Edges accrue to landscapes in certain basic ways, including gaps (as in a deforested area) and verges (when one part of a field verges on another). Such edges and others are inherent in naturally given landscapes rather than being imposed on them by human activity.[2] Among all these kinds of edge the most pervasive and significant are boundaries, which abound in landscape worlds.

A boundary, as we know from earlier discussions, is porous by its very nature—filled with apertures and thus hospitable to the transmission of liquids, people, animals, and other substances. If borders act to close off and exclude free passage, boundaries facilitate movement of many kinds. This is so both at a molecular level, where differences of air or water pressure determine the flow across a given boundary, and at a larger scale, where the passage of whole bodies is at stake. Although plants can grow over borders, they actively migrate across boundaries by dispersed pollination—as do animals in the "animal corridors" that extend across natural boundaries (rivers, changing grasslands, mountain crests, and similar). Human beings also move across boundaries, not just as migrants but also as immigrants, where this latter term implies moving *into* another region or nation that attracts their ingression. The key idea is that the openings inherent in boundaries are built into them from the start—thus part of their very being or constitution rather than something forced on them from without.

A burned-out part of a forest introduces a "dead zone" that is, however, quickly reinhabited by plants and animals that come to populate it in the wake of a fire. The edges of the burned-out area not only mark the gap left by the fire but are also boundaries where reforestation begins almost immediately. Indeed, every edge of a forest that is not the result of clear-cutting is a boundary. On that edge and throughout it are found multiple plant populations: species mixed together in apparent disarray (but in fact following an integral natural order). Across this edge move equally diverse animal and insect and bird species—no respecters of border lines—who thrive in open-ended boundary situations. Humans also come and go across open boundaries: hunters and walkers, lovers and naturalists, and even an occasional philosopher like Rousseau or Thoreau.

Boundaries *bound*, and in this capacity they not only enclose, they also ground. In the instance of landscape, they provide something quite formative: a *double bound* for these special stretches of place-worlds. Here we move from boundaries as configurative—in competition with borders, rims, and gaps—to boundaries as the material condition of whole places and regions. The effect is that of a double framing of a given landscape—from without and from within, from above and from below as upper and lower bound.[3]

The *upper bound* of a given landscape is double in turn: *horizon* and *sky*. If I look into a long field, for example, I find the field effectively ending as it vanishes into a circumambient horizon. This horizon, far from being reducible to a horizon *line*, is an untraceable edge of the land itself: untraceable because it is not solid and continuous—as would be a rim set suddenly upon the outer edge of a landscape (say, a conspicuous hedge row or a retaining wall). A landscape's horizon is more of a *band* than a line: it is part of a place-world that insistently refuses to be a determinate object (such as a strict container). It encircles objects set in the perceived landscape itself, acting as their ground of appearing: there are no objects for perception here except within the horizon-band that embraces them even as they disappear into its embrace.[4] At the same time, the sky, looming just above the horizon, serves as a further circumambient upper bound—now in an even more expansive format than the horizon itself provides. For the sky is more of a *zone* than a band: it is found not just above the end of land, as is the horizon, but stretches out over it in an arc of cerulean space. It is still a boundary, but one that is not just occasionally or selectively permeable (as is the case with most finite boundaries, such as the skin on our bodies): the sky presents itself as infinitely porous. In this capacity and in its overarching display, it is a boundary for all the more finite boundaries that make up a given landscape. It is their encompassing upper bound.[5]

The *lower bound* of a landscape is provided by the *earth*. Under the same field at which I find myself looking lies a vast layer of materiality composed of soil and stone and vegetation that is, in its own way, as capacious as the sky. But where the sky is eminently visible, and the horizon is demi-visible in a recessive mode, the earth radically withdraws from sight: only the outer surface as rock or soil gives itself to me as a manifest presence.[6] Only rare glimpses of its upturned depths—excavated earth, cliffs striated with sedimentary deposits—reveal what lies below the surface. Even if largely hidden, the earth nevertheless acts as a lower bound of the perception of landscape. It is a boundary that lies at our feet and under our living body at all times; it is felt, tacitly, even when striding on city streets. As a material condition for sitting and standing, walking and moving in every way, indeed for life itself, it is an indispensable presence. As a kinesthetically felt lower bound, it acts as a telluric a priori for the perception of landscape.

Waterscapes offer much the same double boundedness. There, too, horizon and sky frame from afar our vision of a water world that undergirds them while calling for them to fill out its full presence. In the case of waterscapes, however, earth retreats into murky depths that are still farther removed from ordinary sight than when we perceive landscape. Earth goes under water, which becomes the dominant medium of our ongoing perceptual engagement with a waterscape: water replaces earth in a basic experience of elemental substitution. No wonder the early navigators feared dropping off the edge of the known world: believing that neither ocean nor earth would be there to support them!

Taken as the primary constituents of waterscapes and landscapes respectively, earth and water alike call for bounding from above and from below; without this dual enclosure, they would be all over the place, their contents unplaced, thereby losing the regional specificity that is essential to every landscape and every waterscape.

## III

Two other kinds of basic boundary operate in the landscape world: external and internal boundaries. The former refers to the kind of boundary that rings *around* a landscape, the latter to those that go *through* it. An *external* boundary in this context is a perimeter of a natural scene. In contrast with borders or rims—which may also surround such a scene but in ways that are arbitrary, constructed, and imposed to some significant degree—an external boundary as I here construe it is one that *belongs to* the scene itself and has evolved with it, even if at a differential rate of growth. Imagine still another forest, one that abuts a savanna: at the edge of the forest, populated by pines and certain hardwood trees, is found a dense ring of bushes that encircle it. They are located at its outer edge; in part at least, they *are* its external edge. They mark it for an observer, and they are felt bodily by any animal that must make its way across them to get into the forest. The bushes are penetrable in many places, and it is up to the ingenuity of the animal (including the human animal) to find its way through. Although perceived as a single coherent group of plants that is perceivable in its own right, they carry the forest they ring to its own edge, establishing its periphery. Thereby they give to this forest its characteristic outer shape, that by which it can be easily identified and located and eventually mapped.

In contrast, *internal* boundaries are edges that form an equally characteristic, even if often less conspicuous, inner shape. Such boundaries include inner pathways in the forest that are used by animals or humans and that configure it from within. Such pathways lack the precision of borders and with time they change in width and viability, but they are crucial to the constitution of the forest by furnishing spaces for moving within it. They bring parts of the forest together by linking them; still more importantly, they give direction to all those who move over them. They are often the basis of orientation within the forest; one might get lost without their guiding presence. Such pathways contrast with another kind of internal boundary, that of the canopy of the forest as experienced from underneath. This canopy is a special kind of internal boundary that allows light and sound to be constellated *from above*—under which an animal or human being feels sheltered and surrounded in a special way. The Kaluli people of Papua New Guinea speak of "up over sounding" to express this peculiar experience of being bounded from the top of a rain forest: not only by the nexus of trees but also by the birds who sing so fervently in the midst of this nexus.[7] Something like this situation is experienced by anyone walking in a forest that is crowned by treetops that touch each other as they sway high above the forest floor.

Taken together, the internal and external boundaries of a forest regarded as a landscape—and their analogues in a seascape (the shoreline and the concourse of diverse currents in its midst)—create a particular complexity that is integral to the material essence of being a land- or seascape. Neither kind of -scape comes as a simple block of space; each comes bounded from without and from within, both at once and in ever varying combinations. A significant part of what renders a particular landscape or seascape unique is precisely its singular combination of external and internal boundaries. These latter resist reduction to being border lines that demarcate sites in sheer space.

## IV

A promising model for understanding the fate of landscape edges is found in the *ecotone*, defined as "the boundary between two natural communities where elements of both as well as transitional species intermingle in heightened richness."[8] The result of such intermingling is a transitional zone and, more particularly, what is technically called an "edge effect" whereby an interpotentiation arises as the resources of one region cause those of the other to take a course of increased intensity not otherwise possible (the *tonus* root in ecotone signifies "tension"). In particular, when two different ecosystems (such as bioregions and econiches) meet, things happen that could never have emerged in the two regions taken separately. Instead of a mere summation of forces, there is an augmentation of the ecotone beyond its known and measurable constituents: rather than $1 + 1 = 2$, we have a circumstance of $1 + 1 = 2 + n$. The edge effect thus characterizes how, when two ecosystems are close at hand, the transition zone shows a tendency to greater variety and density of plant and animal life. As an environmentalist who lives on the edge of a forest observes: "For me the 'edge effect' has meant a greater variety and density of experience, a multiplying of perspectives. Life is fuller here on the edge, and harder. There's more beauty and more tension, greater solitude and greater obligation."[9]

Thanks to the ecotonal effect, the edge is "where most of the action is"—*not* the surface, as has been claimed by J. J. Gibson.[10] For the edge is where the most concerted activity in landscapes and waterscapes is to be found. Energies collect at the edges of place-worlds generally, and especially in ecotonal areas. Florence Krall Shepard describes it thus: "In the natural world, edges where differences come together are the richest of habitats. Animals often choose these ecotones, where contrasting plant communities meet, to raise their young where the greatest variety of cover and food can be found. A doe will give birth to a fawn on the edge of a forest, where she can find shelter as well as food in the open area beyond the trees."[11] Animal and plant life here collude in the buildup of edge energies. In such a buildup we again witness a form of *Seinszuwachs*, "augmentation of being."[12] Or rather, we should say, the augmentation of *becoming*. This is not a matter of simple addition but of exponentially increasing energies that seek and stay at the edge of things and that intensify in each other's presence.

It is not surprising, then, that the human eye and hand, indeed the entire organism, are attracted to these energies and try to bring them into their ken— not only in order to master them but also to savor them and, if possible, to draw

upon them directly. The human eye tends to move to the edge of things, seeking out the peripheries after the central phenomenon has been identified—and
sometimes even before. This obtains notably in the perception of landscape
and seascape vistas, which tempt the eye ever outward, farther and farther from
the near-space in which it is currently located. The same edge focus holds for the
hand, which looks for the basic shape of what it handles precisely at, and as, the
edge. Such lateral movements complicate, and sometimes contest, centrist paradigms of perception—which concern themselves with issues of precise identification and recognition and as a result concentrate on front-and-center features
rather than their edges.

The question of the evolutionary origins of this edgewise looking (and touching) is something as intriguing as it is highly speculative: Was it a matter of learning
to detect predators lurking in hideouts where they could attack more effectively?
The orbiting of the eyes and of the whole human head are well suited for alert
attending to the edges of potentially dangerous situations in ancient forests and
savannas. Even apart from this hypothesis—which also helps to explain the importance of glancing in the human repertoire of looking[13]—the eye has good reason
to gravitate to the edge of the visual field. For this is where such factors as the
width and depth of that field are easiest to access, as well as where basic tenden-
cies of several kinds prosper, for example, in the flourishing of phototropic plants.
It is also where creatively adaptive change is most likely to happen, given the combination of open access and partial shelter.

The edge as a source of energy and change is not limited to the edge of the
visual field. In *The Origin of Species* Darwin claims that many of the most significant
evolutionary advances occur among members of animal species living at the edge
of their colonies or communities. Instead of sinking into isolation or stagnation on
the margins, those who live in this edge circumstance are in a position to undertake forms of innovative adaptation which the more staid and settled members of
their species are less likely to pursue. Whereas these latter tend to remain in lives
of complacency and repetition—thanks to the reinforcement of habitual tenden-
cies in the context of a supportive community with fewer challenges—those on the
edge are exposed to more risk and are thus literally unsettled. If they can sustain
the uncertainty, they are more likely to seek out and find unprecedented modes
of adaptation and selection than are discovered or favored in the staid center. In
short, being located at the edge results in advances in the evolution of the species
as a whole—benefits that are passed on through genetic mutations.

Also apposite here are Darwin's observations on the differing tortoise populations on the Galapagos Islands—observations that focused on how each island
supported a variant tortoise population: "the tortoises differed on the different
islands . . . several of the islands possess their own species of the tortoise."[14] The

islands formed an archipelago directly west of Ecuador in which each island was in effect a *world at the edge*. It is precisely in such a circumstance that the evolution of the tortoises—as well as bird and plant species—could evolve in comparative independence of the main lines that reproduced themselves with little detectable change on the mainland. Darwin does not hesitate to exclaim that "one is astonished at the amount of creative force, if such an expression may be used, displayed on these small, barren, and rocky islands."[15] The same holds true, he believes, for human beings who choose to live on the margins of a settlement: they are much more likely to innovate in ways that benefit their fellow human beings in the long run as these new modes of adaptation are culturally transmitted.

## V

Landscape still matters in contemporary national and global culture—in fact, all the more so in view of the exponentially increasing site-ification of space: that is, the conversion of space into mere sites for building or land acquisition as capital investment. On television, cell phones, video, and DVD we are presented with an unremitting stream of images of *displacement*: both in the sense dramatized by the vast numbers of forced migrations happening on the earth today (it is estimated that fully 40 percent of all human beings will soon be engaged in such migration) and in the felt experience of an active loss of place. Such loss can be termed *dysplacement* in analogy with dysphoria: the diminution and dissolution of the primacy of place, its effective interment under the site-centered consciousness exemplified in big-box shopping malls and internet catalogs.[16]

With the loss of place comes the subsiding of landscape as an integral part of human experience. It is pushed ever further outside of cities and becomes just a place to visit, an escape, rather than a place to inhabit. Nevertheless, landscape, along with seascape, is difficult to leave behind: its haunting power is considerable. It is not in direct competition with global capital—though it can be devastated through its commodification by capital interests for purposes of investment and oil and mineral excavation as well as for the construction of tract homes and other forms of building for profit. But even if extensive areas of land have been lost to commercial development, extraction of natural resources, and foreign investment, vestiges of landscape do survive—just as vistas of seascape are accessible despite deep water oil rigs and the gentrification of choice coastal properties. Landscape and seascape remain basic parameters of human (and other animal and plant) lives, providing an abiding sense of what an intact and integral place-world consists in—a world not undermined by the depredations of dysplacement. To experience such a world is to gain, or regain, a vision of what being in the world construed as a nexus of living places with open boundaries can be like. It is to be reminded of what a difference a place-world can make in the very face of the massive site-ifying of space we encounter everywhere in contemporary existence. It is increasingly common to speak of "manufacturing landscape"; however, I would maintain that, as a deeply immanent dimension of human and animal experience, *landscape cannot be built*, much less manufactured: it can only be experienced, undergone—or ruined.[17]

The fact is that land- and waterscapes of many varieties not only provide the kind of place-worlds we need to affirm in an era of increasingly exhausted natural resources and environmental devastation; in addition, they are *indispensable to life of any kind on the planet*. Quite apart from the fact that the many species who thrive upon them would perish without them—as when certain animals are deprived of ecotones—human beings themselves, for all their pretensions to autonomy, cannot do without them: not only at the level of physical survival but also by way of experience and thought. The exemplary presence of open landscape and untamed seascape is essential to being on earth in a human way. Without this presence we would be confined to an inferno of artificial passages and airless corridors from which there is no escape: a disastrous environmental *huis clos*. Unexploited land and sea provide both *outlook* and *breathing space*, each of which is required for living on earth with the range and scope human life (and much other-than-human life) calls for, quite beyond issues of physical flourishing and survival. Outlook is needed not only for literal views of a pristine world but also for the experience of ampliative space—of outreach that inculcates and sustains an active sense of vitality and freedom: not so as to own or use it but to engender a sense of leeway, that underlies open walking and viewing and imagining. By the same token, the breathing space that landscape and seascape afford is requisite to a fully embodied implacement on earth. Not just the eyes but also the lungs, indeed the whole living body, are here at stake—a body that feels itself able to move through the open-ended spaces that land and water furnish so irreplaceably in and beyond their boundaries.

Indispensable to such expansive experiences are the edges of land- and sea-scapes themselves. There would be no such -scape effect without the enlivening edges through which we know the earth and its waters. We cannot look at or move in these latter without dealing with their edges. Edges are pivotal for visual and kinetic life on this planet. Not only do they affect all that we see and feel, not only are they collectors of their own unique forms of energy, they structure the very place-worlds in which we live, giving to them an inherent directionality and a distinctive delimitation.

Edges may not be limits in a strict sense, but they do serve to *delimit* things, events, and places. This is certainly so in the case of ecotonal areas and of such elemental boundary phenomena as earth, horizon, and sky regarded as lower and upper bounds of what we experience on a daily basis. But it is also true for many lesser phenomena of the place-world, including all the discrete edges we encounter in the undertakings of everyday life. There is no such life, no vision or movement, without the dynamics that edges infuse into that life, vision, and movement. The very freedom of outlook and outreach that matters so much to human beings and other species would not itself be possible without the amplification provided by the edges of landscape and seascape.

Just as we cannot eliminate such edges from particular land- and waterscapes if they are to retain the vitalizing force they afford, so they are sine qua non as well for the integral place-worlds that are more and more at risk on the earth today.[18] If these worlds are not to become wholly regimented—reduced to a mere collection of site-specific locations—they have to be experienceable in their edgewiseness. For edges and more especially boundaries are essential to constituting places in their uniqueness, their idiolocality, much as the shapes of our bodies are intrinsic to establishing our personal identities.

When places are concatenated into regions, they participate in—indeed, they help to create—a *smooth* space (in Deleuze and Guattari's term) that is the basis of every enlivened place-world.[19] In such space, edges figure more as folds than as anything strictly linear, as boundaries rather than borders. The very word *boundary* reflects its origin in "bound," and bound in turn is closely affine with fold: both entail enclosure by means of closely fitting enclosures. The bond between *boundary*, *bound*, and *fold* is tight, and all three give shape to the smooth space of new or renascent place-worlds. In the end, we can discern a chain of nested indispensabilities in the concatenation of edge, landscape, and place-world:

edges > landscape / waterscape > configured place-worlds

Just as edges are indispensable for landscapes and waterscapes and their perception, so these two modes of -scape are in turn indispensable to the constitution and experience of the place-worlds that are the effective modules of being-in-place. The triadic chain just posited is to be contrasted with another:

lines > striated sites > abstract / homogeneous / infinite space

As lines (qua perimeters and delineated limits,) are required for the very conception and construction of sites (in blueprints and building plans and laying foundations), so sites provide the basic units of abstract space. Together, they represent restricted artifactual modes of building and inhabitation: modes that contribute to the superfetation of sites. Propelled by the relentless forces of late capitalism, the effect is the predominance of striated and sited spaces amid an increasing dearth of robust and lasting place-worlds.

If place-worlds are to regain priority in human experience, landscape in all its dry and wet varieties must be appreciated and revalorized. For this to happen, the edges of landscape have to be recognized in all their shapeful vitality. Such recognition requires its own unforced evidence; but this will emerge only if we can find our way back to the very place where such evidence becomes once again accessible.[20]

## Notes

1. I return to the discussion of subtle versus salient edges, along with a more detailed consideration of indeterminate phenomena, in "A Last Lesson."

2. This is not to deny that certain gaps are manmade—for example, the celebrated "ha-ha" of British country estates, ditches that were meant to keep cattle contained within certain spaces; these structured gaps were notable for the fact that they were disguised, so that views of the estate from afar would not be compromised. See R. H. Gombrich, *Art and Illusion* (Princeton: Princeton University Press, 1969), 310–11.

3. By "bound" I mean a boundary that serves to contain from a spatial (or temporal) extremity. It is the functional equivalent of a limit insofar as it is the *non plus ultra* of a given place or region: that which cannot be exceeded or undercut. But unlike a limit as an ideal entity, it is not posited but perceptually given.

4. The same is true for events, which never happen without a temporal context acting as their historical horizon. This context gives to the boundaries of events a banded status. Compare my discussion of places in chapter 3 of this book.

5. For more on sky, see chapter 10.

6. A telling description of the earth as *refusing* our gaze is given by David Abram, *The Spell of the Sensuous: Perception and Language in a More-Than-Human World* (New York: Pantheon, 1996), pp. 213–14.

7. For a remarkable account of "up over sounding" in Papua New Guinea, see Steven Feld, *Sound and Sentiment: Birds, Weeping, Poetics, and Song in Kaluli Expression* (Philadelphia: University of Pennsylvania Press, 1990).

8. Definition cited on the cover of Florence R. Krall [Shepard], *Ecotone: Wayfaring on the Margins* (Albany: State University of New York Press, 1994).

9. Chris Anderson, *Edge Effects: Notes from an Oregon Forest* (Iowa City: University of Iowa Press, 1993), p. xiv.

10. See J. J. Gibson, *The Ecological Approach to Visual Perception* (Hillsdale, NJ: Erlbaum, 1986), p. 23.

11. Shepard, *Ecotone*, p. 4.

12. See Hans-Georg Gadamer, *Truth and Method*, trans. Garrett Barden and John Cumming (New York: Seabury Press, 1975), pp. 124–25, 132, 134–35.

13. See Casey, *The World at a Glance*, especially "Concluding Thoughts."

14. Darwin adds that the same is true of "the mocking thrush, finches, and numerous plants" (Charles Darwin, *The Origin of Species by Means of Natural Selection*, ed. J. Carroll [Peterborough, Ontario: Broadview Press, 2003], p. 458).

15. Ibid, p. 459.

16. For a penetrating study of these various displacements, see Mary Watkins and Helene Lorenz, *Toward Psychologies of Liberation* (New York: Palgrave Macmillan, 2008), especially chapter 11, "Communities of Resistance." One of the cruel ironies in all this is that most of those who are forced to migrate—for political or economic reasons—come to live at the edges of the great urban centers: in the *colonias* or bidonvilles (shantytowns) that have sprung up in the very shadow of these centers. This is the dark side of edge, as marking places of last resort in situations of desperation and misfortune.

17. I refer to the recent documentary film *Manufactured Landscapes*, directed by Jennifer Baichwal (2007); drawing on the work of artist Edward Burtynsky, it traces the effort to restructure whole landscapes in China and elsewhere.

18. I here adopt a position that draws close to that of Jeff Malpas in his *Place and Experience: A Philosophical Topography* (Cambridge: Cambridge University Press, 2007); although he does not discuss edges as such, were he to do so he would argue for their transcendental status as part of a larger commitment to the same status for places themselves.

19. For the distinction between "striated" and "smooth" space, see Gilles Deleuze and Felix Guattari, *A Thousand Plateaus*, trans. B. Massumi (Minneapolis: University of Minnesota Press, 1987), chapters 12 and 15. For my own conception of these terms, see "Smooth Spaces and Rough-Edged Places: The Hidden History of Place," Epilogue to *Getting Back into Place: Toward a Renewed Understanding of the Place-World* (Bloomington: Indiana University Press, 2009; 2nd ed.), pp. 349–66.

20. This chapter is a considerably altered adaptation of my essay "The Edge(s) of Landscape: A Study in Limonology," in Jeff Malpas, ed., *The Place of Landscape: Concepts, Contexts, Studies* (Cambridge: MIT, 2011), pp. 91–110.

# SEVEN

# Intermediate Edges: Parks, Gardens, Neighborhoods, Streets

My earlier walk on 110th Street was a stroll amid intensely urban edge-structures at various scales, ranging from the twenty-story building in which I live to the much smaller scale of local stores, curbs, corners, and sidewalks. Standing in contrast with this matrix of utilitarian structures were the two parks I glimpsed to the west and to the east—Morningside Park and Central Park—both designed by Olmstead and Vaux 150 years ago to provide space for leisurely activities, Sunday promenades, the playing of sports, ice skating in winter, swimming in summer. In contrast with enclosed and intensely cultivated gardens, such parks are open spaces, giving access at all times of day and night and allowing for free circulation once within: inviting perambulation on prescribed paths or straying across fields at one's whim. If there are edges here, they are inviting rather than foreclosing, and they belong mostly to plant and tree life, to bodies of water, and to the rocks that are prominent presences at the north end of Central Park and on the west side of Morningside Park. With the exception of the rocks and lakes, these edges reflect the character and demands of organic life. Their geometry is not Euclidean but biomorphic.

Such parks are hybrids of wild and artifactual edges: wild edges in flourishing flora (and whatever animal life lives there), artifactual edges in the planned pathways, low outer walls, surrounding sidewalks and streets (both mostly dictated by the city's stern grid plan). Public parks of this kind may not only contain landscape vistas but can even be considered to also be *urban landscapes*. (These stand in contrast with rural landscapes, which blend cultivated fields, typically agricultural in character, with untamed areas such as woods and rivers.) The spaces of virtually all public parks—with the exception of those that are paved over—are amalgams of both kinds of edges, artifactual as well as wild; they stand in contrast with stretches of undisturbed wilderness that contain only wild edges.[1] Both parks and wilderness contrast with densely built areas such as midtown Manhattan, a couple of miles to the south, where the edges are almost entirely artifactual. Both also contrast with carefully cultivated gardens, where natural edges are under the continual control of human supervision, resulting in a hybrid mix of artifactual with natural edges.

My concern at this point is with what I call *intermediate edges*: these belong especially to "green spaces" within or at the edge of urban settings. Such spaces include gardens and parks, each of which provides an amalgam of wild and cultivated edges—along with a minimum of strictly artifactual edges. Certain constructed things—streets, sidewalks, walls—are characteristically *kept at the outer edges* of gardens or parks in a telling gesture that expresses an effort to minimize and marginalize their presence.[2] The result is the creation of an opening in the very midst of intensely built and overbuilt structures: an elastic space in an otherwise breathless world of employment, acceleration, and pressure, all happening in what Whitehead calls the "immediate rush of transition."

The case of Central Park is especially instructive: its edges mix the wild with the cultivated and artifactual, while serving to mediate between different parts of a city in a creatively connective manner. This open public space is spatially distributed in a variety of inviting ways (paths, trails, bodies of water, fields, lawns, and so on), each with its own set of differentially determined edges; yet this same space is bounded on the outside by the fierce regularity of city streets. It is in effect an *opening in an overdetermined urban site*, allowing that site to breathe—and acting overall as if it were effectively the lungs for the island of Manhattan. No greater contrast can be imagined than that between the closed containment of the thousands of apartments that ring the park—each a cubicle of living space, some spacious but many (including my own) "cabined, cribbed, and confined" (in Macbeth's words)—and the open meadows and small fields of which Central Park is largely composed. The juxtaposition of these two kinds of space, each with its own characteristic kinds of edges, is striking to say the least. But they work together in remarkably effective ways. Within the embrace of a city, gardens are within parks, parks within parts of a city; both are surrounded by streets, which in turn form an endoskeletal structure of the city—an urban space that is located within city limits and eventually gives onto larger landscapes.

## I

Gardens and parks are not just places for leisure or escape—they are necessities much more so than one might imagine. They may not be required for physical health or mental stability—though they are certainly salutary in both respects—but they are requisite as liminal zones where human beings experience the surrounding world in a very different way than happens on city streets or in the interiors of buildings. They allow for deep play as well as frivolous cavorting. In and through their variegated edges, the natural and the cultivated meet in novel and unsuspected ways.

At their earliest known appearance in ancient Middle Eastern civilization, gardens were walled compounds that were set outside cities. They were quite literally "spaces apart" (in this respect they were *heterotopias* in Foucault's sense: "other/places" outside the orbit of centrated power). In the beginning, they were designed

FIGURE 16. *Akhairaj with Courtiers and Musicians in a Garden* (India, Rajasthan, Marwar, Rathore dynasty); opaque watercolor and gold on paper; Freer Gallery of Art, Smithsonian Institution.

as places of retreat for the ruling classes. Of Mesopotamian origin, they were almost always walled, or at least fenced, and became of special significance in Persian civilization, extending as far as India.

The figure above, for example, shows a painting of a garden in which a Rajput nobleman is sniffing flowers.

Notice the quasi-grid pattern of the garden, divided as it is into a series of quadrants that avoid perfect rectilinearity by the inclusion of blossoming flowers. Overall, the garden is viewed from above, though the flowers and trees at the left are presented as seen from the right side of the garden, while the nobleman Akhairaj and his attendants (and also the blue holy man) are viewed from a position below and to the left. It is as if the openness of the represented space of this miniature allows for these diverse contents to be seen from different perspectives with equal, and virtually indifferent, ease—whereas in three-dimensional reality no such compresence of perspectives can obtain at a single moment of time. The bold insistence of the painted border seems designed to contain and support this diversity of perspectives as well as the burgeoning plant life. It can also be regarded as an abstracted icon of the actual wall that must have surrounded Akhairaj's garden.

In the Christian Middle Ages, gardens took on a more practical function as places for the growing of herbs and vegetables that were essential to the sustenance of monasteries and nunneries; but they were also symbolic spaces that signified a special kind of bucolic bliss—as in the gardens featured in the celebrated "unicorn" tapestries of the Cluny Museum in Paris, wherein animals, plants, and humans conjoin in a paradisiacal community. (The word *paradise* means "walled enclosure" in ancient Iranian: *pardis* were walled orchards or fenced-in areas that contained domestic animals.) In this later phase of their evolution, gardens were still spaces reserved for privileged groups—if not royal families, then monks and nuns and other clerics. At the Grande Chartreuse in southeastern France, for example, only brothers of the Carthusian Order and assorted livestock (plus a few stray cats) were allowed in this peripheral space, which, though not formal or manicured—being a small field around the monastery—was surrounded by a low wall that separates the monastery from the city below. Only various service people and occasional visitors were permitted to enter through the gates in this wall. It was meant exclusively for use by certain brothers (especially for those who serve as cooks and gardeners), as we learn from the documentary film *Into Great Silence* (2007), which documents life today in the Grande Chartreuse: a life that continues much the same as in medieval times.

All this changes with the advent of public parks in western Europe and the United States in the modern era: Hyde Park in London, the Bois de Boulogne in Paris, Central Park in New York City. Park spaces were declared open to all comers—to all classes, all races, all ethnicities. Such parks embodied, in exemplary fashion, what Walt Whitman called "democratic vistas." Their extent was sufficient to incorporate gardens into their midst—and much else as well. This transition is emblematic of a more general shift of paradigm from the restricted access and concentrated space that are characteristic of cultivated gardens to a circumstance in which what matters is public accessibility and the intermingling of all who come there. The move is from a paradigm of the garden as an enclosed space to a public park that offers open spaces. With this comes a move from emphasizing edges that enclose and close off—whether by walls or trellises or dense vegetation—to porous edges that offer access to all.

In such spaces human and animal bodies move freely. If gardens encourage slowing down and sitting in meditation, public parks call for motion over a larger area. Walking is prized: not as a means to get to destinations but for its own intrinsic interest and virtue. In Gary Snyder's telling words, "Walking is the great adventure, the first meditation, a practice of heartiness and soul primary to human kind. Walking is the exact balance of spirit and humility."[3]

Just as gardens slow down our pace, they also encourage us to focus on what is immediately around us: this aromatic hedge, that cluster of flowers. Such a focus finds ready visual representation in two dimensions, as we can see in the works of Bonnard and Monet, both masters of representing intimate garden spaces. It is as if the pausing called for by such gardens—the meditating and admiring—finds its effective analogue in paintings that encourage us to pause to look at them in turn. Such pausing in a garden or before a painting facilitates attention to the surfaces of growing things, their colors and textures, rather than to the determination of depth—which is much more at stake in public parks, where we take account of the full sweep of the space as we stroll through it. In such active walking, we experience sensibilia that are not only visual and olfactory (favored in gardens) but also auditory (as in the spontaneous echolocation the walker habitually practices) and kinesthetic (how our feet feel in contact with the ground). To walk between points in a park of any size is to take ourselves into the depths of that park; it is to be unbound by artificially created obstacles like walls or precisely delineated paths so that we can ramble at our leisure.

In the actual experience of traversing parks, we are brought into a world of amassed things and receding vistas.[4] If we thereby lose the intimacy of enclosed spaces, we gain the expansiveness of a diversely sensed three-dimensional space. Where horticulture is the favored activity of gardens (*hortus* = garden + *cultura*, from *colere*, to care for or cultivate), perambulation (literally "to walk through") is doubtless the most characteristic bodily action associated with parks. We care for gardens by attending to their details, but we *move through* park spaces, our feet alternating in a comparatively rapid rhythm that matches our darting glances cast outward and ahead toward open views.

As we walk across such a space, we do so with others who are out for a ramble of their own. The great city parks possess a communal and collective dimension that is often lacking in the experience of gardens, which favor private delectation. In entering these parks we join with others, whether walking or reclining on lawns for a picnic lunch. We need not talk with these others to cohabitate with them as fellow denizens of the city, *citizens*, and to form together a living community.

For such walking to be present and for such community to be possible, the edges of public parks must be such as to allow for free movement and open sociality. They must allow for abundant air and light, and above all for the mobility of moving bodies. This also means that edges must serve not as obstacles to movement but as facilitators of it. Even when climbing the high rocks in the north part of Central Park there remain paths to follow that have been created by earlier climbers. Almost all edges in this park, as in their counterparts elsewhere, are *edges on the ground*—edges of walkways, of groups of trees and bushes, and of enclosed gardens. These are to be contrasted with the edges in the buildings just across from the park. Many of these latter edges are vertically arranged, whether as walls within individual apartments or between apartment units, or in the form of elevator shafts and downstairs hallways. All these upward-pressing edges have the effect of containing and limiting bodily movement and spontaneous sociability on the part of those who enter the building. No wonder nearby apartment dwellers so often seek out the park, if only to escape the constructed edges that so closely confine them!

## II

Central Park is a classical park space that, though exhibiting the primary features I have just been enumerating (open vistas, views in depth, relaxed sociality, and the presence of permeable boundaries, all of which encourage free striding, much glancing around, and the like), is also a space of borders and geometric delimitations. It is a complex amalgam of these otherwise contrary traits, which manage here to mix together in amicable equipoise.[5] This massive park is composed of walking paths and trails, lakes, ponds, streams, playing fields, meadows, rock formations, and hills of modest elevation. It can be entered in any of several ways: through major gates at the four corners and at a number of lesser gateways in between. Several streets cross it from east to west (though there are no north-south avenues)—sometimes open to traffic, sometimes not. Except for these openings, its outer perimeter is marked by a low wall that is easily scalable; this wall is more symbolic than protective or inhibitive: it is not designed to keep anyone out. (In fact, one of the gates on the west side is called "Stranger's Gate" and was designed to welcome newly arrived immigrants.)

More significant than the wall itself are the major streets that border the park on its outer edges: on the east and west, Fifth Avenue and Central Park West, on the north and south, 110th Street and 57th Street. These four thoroughfares constitute a rectangle that tightly encompasses the park on its four sides. Heavy traffic flows on them, regulated by traffic lights and concrete sidewalks. Taken together, these same streets fashion a frame around the park. This frame helps to define the park as a sanctuary: inside is the prospect of leisurely walking, outside is Manhattan's intensely pursued and very rapid pace of life.

Central Park is nothing if not paradox. It is neither a strictly walled space nor an entirely open landscape space. Instead, it is a *mostly open space with pockets of closure*: it affords far-reaching views across its whole breadth and into the rest of the city, but these views are differentially accessible because of the buildings around the park that occlude a more complete vision. At the same time, the park offers myriad intimate places: anything from a turn in the path to a bridge over a stream. It manages to combine far-sphere prospects with near-sphere locales. These locales include gardens, ranging from a sizeable formal flower garden on the upper east side to the small but poignant memorial garden on the west side dedicated to John Lennon, opposite the Dakotas residence where he lived. Scattered throughout are countless garden moments, beds of flowers on gentle slopes, semicultivated shrubs and miniature trees. Indeed, there is a considerable variety of vegetation in every part of this expansive public space—matched only by a diverse animal and bird population.

Central Park is a vast heterogeneous multiplicity whose constituent elements exist at many scales: human, more-than-human, other-than-human. It would count as "a plane of consistency," Deleuze and Guattari's term for a region whose considerable diversity is coherent despite all the differences in kind, level, and number.[6] It is a multitudinous scene that resists quantification, much less any simple summation. Built in the immediate post–Civil War period (1858–73), it takes the very idea of a public park to a new level, combining the seemingly incompossible: human and nonhuman, the diminutive (the many nooks) and the enormous (the large meadows and its overall extent), city and country, public and private, nature and geometry. It is an ongoing experiment that is at once social and cultural, raw and natural, horticultural and artistic.

One thing Central Park is not: it is not a garden writ large. It is a *park*, a term given new meaning by this very venture as the winning design in an open competition and as constructed by the city of New York over several decades of diligent labor, most of it manual. It was conceived and built on a large scale— where this term signifies not merely considerable size but also bold imagination. What the Greeks called "greatness of soul" (*megalopsychia*) is evident in the scope of this sweeping space, just as there is also manifest a special sensitivity to the delicacy of small spaces: *les lieux intimes*. Everywhere in the park there is *room enough*—room for many things, expectable as well as unexpected. There is room for companionship (including making love in remote corners as well as sizeable family reunions) and also for hatred and violence (in the form of "wilding," acts of violence that took place there twenty years ago), peacemaking (as in the Dalai Lama's 2003 appearance, preceded by massive demonstrations against the war in Iraq), athletics (tennis courts, baseball fields, a lake for canoeing), and commercial activity (the Tavern in the Park, taxis, horse and buggy conveyances).

There is also ample room for the elements with their wild edges. These elements are, in fundamental ways, the very basis for the qualitative diversity of Central Park. Intrinsic to its expansiveness is its provision of a space for the circulation of elemental presences—presences that are not to be found on the streets or within the surrounding buildings. Just as the cosmogonic *chóra* in Plato's *Timaeus* is characterized by the shaking of the four material elements, so the various physical elements of this park sort themselves out by their intense interactions. In order to mix as thoroughly as they do, they must relate to each other at edges that allow for the compenetration of air with water, water with earth, and (much more rarely) fire with the other three elements: "Fire lives in the death of earth, air in the death of fire, water in the death of air, and earth in the death of water" (Heraclitus).[7]

The commixture is of all with all—so much so that there is no settling into definitive regions as happens in the *Timaeus*: in the park we witness a loose confederation of factors, often overlapping, as when wind sends ripples through the northern lake (the "Meer") and these same ripples finger their way into the earthbound and rock-edge perimeter of this lake. Interlacing prevails; separation is rare. The scene is not tumultuous, except in times of high storm, but neither is it perfectly ordered. Despite initial and continuing landscaping efforts, it has come to assume its own order after more than 150 years of cultivation. This order is comparatively indifferent to the incursion of asphalt and concrete, plaster and metal. The park is receptive to all that is put into place in its omnivorous space.

In the midst of the *vita activa* of late modern metropolitan life, the presence of such a space is as salutary as it is significant. A park like Central Park offers—for free, and for all comers—an Other Space that contrasts with the confinement of office spaces and the constraints of living in apartment complexes. Basic to this alterity is the way in which freely circulating air—in collusion with the soil and the growing things of the Park—commingles in complex and ever-changing patterns rather than being controlled by the windows and heating systems and air conditioning devices of high-rise buildings: open air that is felt in its very absence in stifling subway stations deep underground.

What a park proffers at the most primal level is the chance to put one's feet on the ground—on the solid earth. One can walk on its grounds for hours—for whole days—not just staying on the cleared or paved paths but also cutting across spacious lawns or climbing rock faces in relatively remote regions. The opportunities for walking and sitting and running are endless, and they can begin anywhere one enters the Park—anywhere that one chooses to "set foot," in the revealing expression that picks out the organ that is the basis for perambulation as well as that part of the body that is in most direct contact with the ground. Not unlike Anteaus in the Greek myth, by touching earth in the Park one gains energy and direction not otherwise available—in short, new life, *vita nuova*.[8] To "the pleasures of merely circulating" (Wallace Stevens) is added the reinvigoration that walking in an open park brings with it.[9] For this renewal, one does not have to go to full-fledged wilderness: one can just step into the Park along with countless others.

The park into which we step need not be Central Park. Any sufficiently open expanse will do: it could be the city park called "Mecca" in Enterprise, Kansas, a park that also affords opportunities for free strolling in a community of fewer than 800 souls. Almost as old as Central Park, it also sports a swimming pool in its midst. Nevertheless, Manhattan's prize park space sets a standard for public parks in North America by its ability to support a truly remarkable diversity. In terms of water alone, for example, it offers lakes and ponds, streams and pools and waterfalls as well as underground sewers; some of these are natural features and have

FIGURE 17. Christo and Jeanne-Claude, *The Gates* (2005), Central Park.

been there from before the Park's construction (for example, the Meer, which goes back to Dutch times), some were scooped out during the Park's initial and later landscaping, and yet others are entirely artificial (the swimming pool; the zoo; the reservoir in the center).

A park like Central Park is a highly variegated composition whose complexity is integral to its very identity—and to its allure. Its hybridity is allied with open-edged spaces, which facilitate the coexistence of its many kinds of denizens, permanent as well as passing. These edges consist in a congeries of open-ended boundaries with borders only at its outer edges. In February and March 2005, Cristo and Jeanne-Claude created a memorable event that reinforced the boundaried character of the Park in a very striking way. Over many walkways, arches were put up—some singly and in isolation, others in groups of ten or twelve—from which curtains of saffron-colored material hung like veils. The effect was that of a continuously unfolding threshold to be crossed in a spirit of informal but powerful ritual. Tens of thousands of people—not only from New York but also from around the world—came to this much-publicized event. I was present myself and was deeply moved by the masses of people walking through the arches in a show of spontaneous solidarity. It was as if visitors to the Park were trying out a new form of sociality—even in bitterly cold weather and at a time of bitter division over the invasion of Iraq. In their considerable ethnic and racial and national diversity, and despite being unknown to each other, they walked through corridors of saffron curtains together, often arm in arm.

The slender but striking structures designed by Cristo and Jeanne-Claude took the boundaried character of the park to another level, one that was explicitly communal and confraternal. The edges of the curtains through which people walked were iconic of the way that the park offers open boundaries for visitors in all seasons. The transiency of this event rendered the presence of the curtained edges all the more poignant and pronounced. They embodied the park's inherent hospitality, a welcoming that emerges from its many open-ended spaces.

Thanks to its multifariousness, Central Park can be known in and through many parameters: historical and sociological, geomorphic and botanical. But it can also be experienced as a hugely bountiful edge-world. It manages to combine all of the major edge types I have discussed so far in this book: margins (of the lakes), thresholds (in the botanical gardens), rims (around the racing track on Round Hill), brinks (on the high rocks), borders (the sidewalks and streets on all four sides), boundaries (everywhere), and much else. Despite this sheer edge heterogeneity, to be in the park and to move around in it is to witness at every turn a remarkably coherent pattern of edges, creating a plane of consistency that renders this extraordinary space at once familiar and always surprising.

## III

To exit from Central Park through one of its many open gates is to enter a massive cityscape filled with unrelenting traffic and populated by preoccupied people. From a consideration of gardens and parks we now move to cities and their streets. This is not just a transition from pools of tranquility to scenes of frenetic activity in a crowded world of human beings obsessed with profit and pleasure. It *is* all this, but it is also a change of spatial configuration—from a life-world that is conspicuously open and inviting to a very different world in which issues of competition and class predominate. And this means in turn a move between two ways in which human bodies engage with the edges that configure these worlds as well as the way these edges appear and are experienced. We need to attend to this transition and this difference, which city dwellers often take for granted—yet which serves to subtly structure their daily lives from within and from without.

As cities are vastly complex entities, I here single out only two features that I consider especially revealing when it comes to the disposition of edges in their midst: interfaces between neighborhoods (discussed just below) and a special dimension of city streets that has little to do with ordinary traffic (examined in section IV).

*Neighborhoods* are the primary demographic and experiential units of city living. There, edges are not just formal demarcations but powerful presences in their own right. Their delineation on city maps—where they are represented by imaginary lines if they figure at all—fails to capture their inherent force and multiple effects. This force and these effects can be deployed for destructive purposes as well as for creative ends.

In Santa Barbara, California, State Street is the effective edge that separates the west side of town from whatever surrounds it. Recently, the west side in Santa Barbara has been the scene of gang violence—not as much as the police claim is the case but enough to lead to a pitched controversy over "gang injunctions" issued by the police. (We can imagine this as a contemporary version of "the west side story" made famous by Leonard Bernstein's musical of this title.) Putting yourself on the west side of State Street—especially if you are adolescent and of Mexican descent—is to place yourself at risk. Not just in Santa Barbara but also in many American cities, "turf wars" are waged, sometimes within a given class or race and sometimes between members of different ethnic or racial groups (in Los Angeles it is likely to be between Mexicans and African Americans). The edges of the disputed turf are often quite precise: just this street, and even this street corner and not another. Here the acuity of urban edges provide occasions for provocation and violence, as if to illustrate once more the wisdom in the Northwest Coast Indian saying that "the world is as sharp as the edge of a knife."[10] It is as if the edges between neighborhoods are sharp enough to allow simmering conflicts to come to a boil; they provide focus and shape to animosities that otherwise would be without a locus of enactment. They lay out a scene in which anger and resentment can be acted out and in a given location. Or to be *imagined as happening*: a judge in Santa Barbara recently ruled that the police had exaggerated the actual dangers on the west side, undercutting the case for issuing gang injunctions that were undermining the life of those of Mexican descent dwelling there, causing them to live in continual fear of arrest, followed by detention and deportation to Mexico if proper documentation is not shown.

It is another story when it comes to the edges of parts of cities that foster community by providing a locus for common understanding, collective discussion, and the convergence of inhabitants across and despite their manifest differences, racial and otherwise. In this case, city edges actively contribute to sense of genuine *Gemeinschaft*, where the *Gemein-* root of this German word signifies activities in *common*, leading to the real possibility of a "commons" in which human beings (and other species as well) can share a significant part of their time, their concerns, and their interests: in short, their lives.

I think of the small square in Barcelona where I once happened upon an informal concert of local singers and dancers, animated amateurs around whom gathered local residents, standing, laughing, and talking in a form of spontaneous community that had everything to do with their being bodily together in a *plaza*, literally a "place." The very sounds of this concert had drawn people out of their separate apartments and into the plaza: young and old came streaming into it from corners and streets that configured it as an open place where people could congregate informally on the spur of the moment. The space defined by these edges was attractive not just because of the musical event but also because of the intimate scale of scene in which everyone could see and even for the most part hear everyone else. Here the plaza's edges served as benevolent boundaries that contributed directly to creating an instantaneous community, holding it in place comfortably without constricting it unduly.

In other cases, a more lasting community is at stake. I am here thinking of identifiable neighborhoods. As the *neigh-* of "neighborhood" suggests, it is a matter of what Husserl called a "near-sphere" (*die Näh-Sphäre*) and Heidegger "nearness" (*die Nähe*): terms I have employed earlier in this book. Elsewhere, I have detailed the character and structure of the near in relation to place.[11] Here, I want to underline the critical importance of the edges of such spaces of nearness. These edges are highly porous and invite movement across them in both directions. Christopher Alexander, the visionary Berkeley architectural theorist, put it this way: "The fact is that every successful neighborhood is identifiable because it has some kind of gateways which mark its boundaries: the boundary comes alive in peoples' minds because they recognize the gateways."[12] Here porosity is associated with boundaries construed as "gateways"—openings, *poria*, in contrast with the closed aporetic gates of the gated communities that now plague the American suburban landscape. The gates of Central Park would count as gateways in Alexander's usage, and this is so even if they don't lead to neighborhoods inside the Park. On the contrary, the park is where people from various nearby neighborhoods come, singly or together, along with visitors to the city, to share in a common space that is a loosely knit version of a *commons* in the historically positive sense of the term.[13]

Of critical importance in Alexander's statement is his claim—which I here repeat—that "the boundary [of a neighborhood] comes alive in peoples' minds *because they recognize the gateways.*" In other words, the neighborhood doesn't prosper from the mere literal fact of being bounded by the edges provided by streets in a chockablock fashion (for Alexander, the fewer streets that converge on a given neighborhood the better) but rather from the residents' own recognition of the edges of their neighborhood as signaling open passage. This recognition *animates* these edges, endowing them with an extra half-life so to speak. It follows that edges need not be stolid markers of the physical limits of a neighborhood, but are boundaries that are enlivened by their being perceived and appreciated as giving access to human beings in motion. Rather than being just lines on a map or streets on a city grid (that is, species of borders), they "come alive *in peoples' minds*"; coming

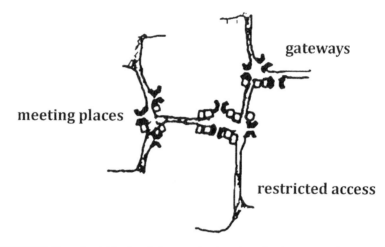

FIGURE 18. Plan of neighborhoods intersecting; based on the diagram in Christopher Alexander et al., *A Pattern Language* (New York: Oxford University Press, 1977). Courtesy of Christopher Alexander and the Center for Environmental Structure.

alive in this way, *en mentis*, they are able to gain an energized aura that translates into various forms of bodily activity.

Such edges are not only alive for those who are direct neighbors of each other—forming a coherent community within such boundaries—but in another way as well: as giving rise to spaces in which several neighborhoods conjoin. Alexander writes, "In case the idea of gateways seems too closed, we remark at once that the boundary zone—and especially those parts of it around the gateways—must also form a kind of public meeting ground, where neighborhoods come together. . . . [It is a question] of the land *between* the neighborhoods—the boundary land. . . . In this sense the boundaries not only serve to protect individual neighborhoods, but simultaneously function to unite them in their larger processes."[14] This statement testifies to the interanimation of edges, but this time those that connect neighborhoods at their boundaries—thereby creating common interplaces that are especially suitable for public meetings, shops, churches, and so on. Above is Alexander's own diagram of this situation.

In short, neighborhoods can enliven each other by being conjoined in common spaces at shared boundaries. These boundaries are remarkably effective in encouraging community-wide activities by creating common spaces for several neighborhoods at once. As Alexander adds, the patterns thus generated all "require a common space area at the heart of a [given social group], placed in such a way that people's natural paths pass tangent to this common area, every time that they move in and out of the place."[15]

The boundaries of both individual neighborhoods and those of collocations of neighborhoods—where all the associated edges work closely together—create the urban equivalent of what I have called (pace Deleuze and Guattari) "smooth space," a space that is heterogeneous in content yet intimately bound together by its many interstices (that is, contiguous edges). This space stands in contrast with the "striated space" that is so often predominant in malls and shopping centers, located as they are at the literal conjunction of major streets and highways—themselves characteristically arranged according to a grid pattern in which the rectangle is the dominant geometric unit. By contrast, the "living patterns" advocated by Alexander are qualitative in character rather than formally imposed; they are shaped by a life in common rather than by the commercial and efficiency values that prevail among isolated individuals and controlling corporations.

Life in American cities today is rarely endowed with more than a few such patterns, and in the postmodern era space is much more likely to be striated than smooth. Sheer striation encourages isolation and segregation at every level, and it is often extended to the design of buildings themselves—buildings conceived as boxes of incarcerated human beings, as in the numerous "projects" that were put up with such fanfare in the 1950s. Many of these mass housing units had to be destroyed several decades later—most famously, at Pruitt-Igoe in St. Louis—once the deleterious effects of their hasty construction became evident. Before that, "urban renewal" destroyed and emptied whole neighborhoods in inner cities in the name of "progress." Mindy Fullilove's book, *Root Shock: How Tearing Up City Neighborhoods Hurts America, and What We Can Do About It*, details the disruption wreaked by the mindless construction of projects and highways in the very places where preexisting neighborhoods had long been situated.[16] The animating and animated boundaries of these common places were violently removed by the literal bulldozing of whole neighborhoods.

The kind of spaces where people live and meet in the embrace of living patterns of communication constitutes a "multi-voiced body" in Fred Evans's apt phrase.[17] This body is that of the neighborhood, or cluster of contiguous neighborhoods. Thanks to its own self-defining history, this social body was alive in major American cities before urban renewal imposed geometric patterns born in a city planner's office and adopted by municipal governments in close collusion with private business interests.

It is a sad but highly instructive tale: remove the open boundaries and shared spaces and you destroy the neighborhood—and ultimately the constellation of neighborhoods that make up a whole sector of a city. The forcible removal of such boundaries brought on urban blight as described by Jane Jacobs in *The Death and Life of Great American Cities*. The death was first of all that of the neighborhoods that made up the critical core of these cities. Just such a death happened, for

instance, in the district called "the Hill" in Pittsburgh, Pennsylvania. In the case of
the Hill, there were few meaningful boundaries and open spaces left after urban
renewal had razed many buildings to the ground, replacing them with block apartments that permitted very little sense of community: such high-risers contrasted
with the on-the-ground horizontality of the previously existing neighborhoods.
In those neighborhoods, the edges that mattered most were *on or near the ground*
rather than high up between towering structures that in effect *left the ground behind*.

When the floors of such buildings are stacked on top of each other, there is
little direct contact with other residents besides those living on your own floor.
The slabs of concrete with a few hard benches parading as "parks" at the base of
these structures could not compensate for the loss of community that these bleak
monoliths brought in their wake. In a more horizontally valorized urban space,
residents encounter each other more frequently and in more diversified spaces.
In such spaces, people interact daily—hourly—on sidewalks and in the streets.
An older resident of the Hill district remarked, "Yeah, we was on the streets, selling papers. And we used to have little jam sessions on the corners. And someone
would come around [who] done got a new step or something. 'Hey, look, man,
here's a step I got!' And we would show each other steps, and we were actually
teaching each other that way."[18] Fullilove remarks, "Everyone was in the streets,
the fundamental place where the magic was created."[19] Basic to this magic is the
fact that even a formally striated space—say, a grid plan of streets such as we find in
Harlem—can be converted into a smooth space of close-up interactions, showing
that the distinction between striated and smooth space is by no means absolute.[20]
The people themselves brought about this transformation of space, and they did
so thanks to their proximity to each other in buildings that gave direct access to
the streets, as in the front door stoops that were so prominent in Harlem a century ago, and which functioned as friendly gateways between houses and the sidewalks in front of them.

"Sorting out," as the term is used by Thomas Hanchett in his book *Sorting
Out the New South City*, means a still more radical loss of community. It signifies
the division of a city along disparate class and racial (and sometimes religious)
lines, so that formerly open and mixed neighborhoods become de facto segregated
into separate sectors, as happened dramatically in Charlotte, North Carolina, after
1950. Between the sorted-out parts of such cities—and they are many in the United
States today—there are no longer porous boundaries but only impermeable borders. As Fullilove comments in her recent book *Urban Alchemy*, "In the sorted-out
city, we are divided by race and class and our separation is reinforced by spaces that
lie between neighborhoods . . . In addition to the difference between urban and
suburban places, there is a landscape of separation, of borders that make crossing
from one sector to another a scary and difficult act . . . As some neighborhoods

are going up and others are going down [in terms of relative prosperity], there are borders that develop between these increasingly divergent places."[21]

In urban renewal as practiced in the United States since the 1950s, rigid lines between populations emerge: "The fracture lines, whether inscribed with walls or with highways or simply understood as a matter of local usage, define passage in the city according to the rules of apartheid."[22] Fullilove draws here on the literal core sense of "apartheid": standing apart. When the blending of boundaries in and between neighborhoods is undermined, a dead zone arises between formerly ani-mated proximate spaces. This zone is a de facto border, even if it is not declared so as such. As Fullilove puts it, "I became convinced that our cities [are] mired in a profound contradiction. Human beings create cities so that they will have a site for social and cultural interaction and development. Cities fulfill this function be-cause people connect with each other and exchange goods and ideas. The sorted-out American city cannot do what it is meant to do, as division is antithetical to connection."[23] Such division amounts to a substitution of the hard edges of the high-rise buildings of housing projects for the soft edges of historically generated and spontaneously occurring communal life. It is reflected in the drawing of lines of strict separation on city maps instead of respecting the nonlinear, open-edged boundaries that are actively ingredient in neighborhoods that share communal suf-ferings and joys in their common spaces.

## IV

In the course of this chapter we have considered several kinds of intermediate edge. As cultivated special spaces, gardens are intermediate between domiciles and open landscapes; city parks are located between the living areas that flank them on several sides; and viable neighborhoods connect through permeable edges ("gate-ways" that are effective urban boundaries) which act as interim links between one neighborhood and another. The mode of intermediacy differs across these various sorts of places, but in each instance the characteristic edges possess an in-betweenness that exhibits formative force and significance: to be between things is not to be consigned to compromise but can embody a power of its own.

Fullilove's observation that the streets of the Hill in Pittsburgh were the "fun-damental place where the magic was created" leads us to a final and fourth form of intermediate edge: that of *city streets*. Streets exemplify a distinctive form of inter-mediate edge, for streets serve to connect whole parts of cities. They facilitate the movement of traffic—mostly automobile and bus traffic in the current era, elec-tric trams and street cars in earlier times. But their connective power, their distinc-tive intermediacy, has other dimensions, other powers. Among them is serving as a place for political protest and resistance. I here take inspiration from the Occupy Wall Street movement in New York City. My working premise is that streets—in concert with urban parks and accommodating plazas—are not neutral spaces that belong to a city's infrastructure; they are always already political in character. In Henri Lefebvre's words, "there is a politics of space [precisely] because *space is political*."[24] And it is most intensely and effectively political in public spaces, such as certain parks and plazas—and many streets.

It is surely striking that the Occupy Wall Street movement began with the occupation of Zuccotti Park in lower Manhattan, a modest oblong piece of land with benches and sidewalks and a few trees—a quiet place before the original occupation occurred in September 2011. Unlike the creation of People's Park in Berkeley decades earlier, however, the choice of the original location of the Occupy Wall Street movement (this was its first manifestation in the United States) was not about reclaiming this park for diverse uses by the general public. It was to contest corporate control over too many aspects of contemporary life in the United States and abroad, resulting in inequitable differentials in salary between 99 percent of Americans and the very wealthy 1 percent.[25] What, then, was the point of occupying this modest park? It supplied more space than did sidewalks, but this was not the primary reason for its occupation.

David Harvey offers a clue in his book *Rebel Cities*: "Spreading from city to city, the tactics of Occupy Wall Street [were] to take a central public space, a park or a square, close to where many of the levers of power are centered, and, by putting human bodies in that place, to convert public space into a political commons."[26] What can a *"political* commons" mean? The most pertinent sense is that of a common space in which discussions concerning the life of a community or a city can take place in a genuinely horizontal way: that is, by face-to-face discussions that at once resist and undermine vertical hierarchies of power and leadership. The concept of *horizontalidad*, as it emerged in Argentina in the 1990s, is of direct pertinence to the formation of the kind of political commons created by Occupy Wall Street, that is, a shared space that encourages open discussion with others—in short, a genuinely democratic *polis* that fosters the direct presentation of ideas and the unreserved sharing of experiences.[27] For this to happen, interlocutors need to be in the same place, facing each other as they speak, able to see and hear each other talk in proximity.

Such a scene can flourish in a place whose spatial parameters are neither too vast, as with Central Park, nor enclosed within walls, as in the office cubicles that populate the financial headquarters directly bordering on Zuccotti Park. The common space of a genuinely political commons such as emerged in September 2011, and then elsewhere, needs to be small enough to foster a coherent sense of community yet large enough for a diversity of active participants to come together as a single group, for instance, in a "General Assembly" such as Occupiers instituted from the very beginning. Such a commons can be considered a transitional space between casual encounters of individuals and whole neighborhood spaces in the sense discussed in the last section.[28]

Literally undergirding this situation is the land of the place where people gather, serving as a terra firma that lends its support *from below* to the expressive activities, the gestures and the talking, flowing freely over its surface.[29] The ensuing horizontalist community transformed the idle public space of Zuccotti Park into an active political commons: a scene of a very different kind from that found in the nested hierarchies of nearby Wall Street, just two short blocks away. The difference is that between the smooth space of heteroglossic discourse in the direct presence of others and a closed striated space of managerial direction in which the bodies of managers and employees are positioned in separate spaces. In the one case, intensely pitched dialogue is an intrinsic feature of the circumstance; in the other, it is a comparative rarity.

It is surely significant that the settings for revolutionary activity have been, with very few exceptions, urban. Cities offer opportunities for political protest more effectively than do rural scenes: city streets, squares, parks, and other public spaces lend themselves to political protests, subtending and enframing them. Among these several spaces, streets are especially significant: if it is true that "you have to *take back the streets* if you don't have the kind of money it takes to do effective political action,"[30] the streets one takes back are almost always *city* streets, for these are spaces that facilitate rapid movements (brisk marching, running if necessary) while also holding the potential for disrupting traffic when this is part of the overall strategy. If these streets are in the close proximity of corporate headquarters and the US Stock Exchange, as at Zuccotti Park, they are all the more meaningful as public settings for the collective expression of outrage at the concentration of power in the hands of the super-wealthy. Indeed, bands of Occupiers flowed out of Zuccotti Park itself and into the surrounding streets that provided locations for centers of corporate capitalism. The link between street life and the history of a city is profound, given that streets are the avenues of urban life and carry with them a special geohistorical valence. Broadway was originally a road that went from New York City to Albany, and was thus from early times a central axis of political power in the state of New York: it was not accidental that one of the major demonstrations of the early Occupy movement was on Broadway in the Times Square area.

City streets are composed of the edges of paved roadways, curbs, and sidewalks. Edges are always at stake, directly or indirectly, in the use of public spaces as places of protest. Outside Lincoln Center late one evening in fall 2012, a crowd of some sixty-five people was contesting the private financial backing of opera and other musical events by the likes of Charles Koch and Mayor Bloomberg. When I arrived, the police were just setting up the aluminum barricades that established a hard metallic edge between the space of the plaza above and the Occupiers below at the bottom of the stairs leading down to Broadway. Those of us on the protesting side of this aluminum barricade vehemently voiced our objections across this artificial edge, appealing to the theatergoers—some of whom joined us as they streamed out of *Satyagraha*, staged by Robert Wilson, with music by Philip Glass. These sympathetic souls boldly strode down the steps and climbed over the barriers. Throughout, the police stood impassively at the top of the stairs, above and on the other side of the barricades' edges. It was a literal standoff, and continued in this confrontational manner until the wee hours, with members of the protesting crowd speaking up one after another—including Philip Glass, who had himself joined the crowd.

This action manifested as a deliberate, sometimes defiant, standing at the line, being *right there*, there and nowhere else.[31] Edges, especially in urban settings, tend to be markedly linear in character: think of the edges of steps and stairways and the corners and curbs of streets. Such sheer linearity induces a circumstance of direct confrontation between those located on the two sides of a single *linea divisoria*. Unlike a wall, another linear structure, confrontation over a linear edge that is on the ground and at one's feet engenders face-to-face encounters between those situated on opposite sides. Such an edge is at once absolute (at least in the eyes and minds of those hired to protect public or private space: hired, quite literally, to "draw the line") and yet relative—relative to the actions of whoever or whatever is present in such a situation. In the case of a line set up by police, those on either side can *look right across* the line at those on the other side, eye to eye and body to body. There is an entire political history of "holding the line" and of "crossing the line."[32]

Just as one can look across such a dividing line, one can also *step over it*—as happened when the concertgoers at *Satyagraha* joined the Occupy crowd at the base of the steps—and step over it in two directions, though with markedly differential effects. The concert crowd who joined us crossed the line with impunity, whereas those few who attempted to cross in the opposite direction and lunge toward the plaza were immediately arrested.

Occupy Wall Street was an edge phenomenon at every level, happening within certain established edges (such as those of the privately owned but public space of Zuccotti Park, in which it first arose) even as it contested other edges (many of which were institutional). In one form or another, such edges are always acutely at stake in political occupations and other protests, including riots inside prisons. They contrast with permeable edges that not only allow for but also actively encourage the crossing of what would otherwise be preestablished and preoccupied borders—as happens when public demonstrations succeed in undermining preexisting barriers. There is confrontation across a line of separation, an edge of stark difference across which there is no easy passage.

City streets are composed of linearities of many kinds: not just their delineation by curb structures and street signs but also the literal lines that are painted on them to indicate traffic lanes and directions in which to drive, as well as the lines that represent these streets on city maps. Precisely as multilinear, streets are edge bearing and edge producing: bordered by sidewalks and crosswalks, they constitute the literal edges of neighborhoods and other urban districts. At the same time, streets support various distinctive activities: walking, driving, buying, and selling—as well as public protests, "taking to the streets." Street action can suspend the regularities of urban existence and allow for the expression of concerted views on charged issues. During the Occupy movement, this happened a number of times with the deliberate disruption of traffic across the Brooklyn Bridge: the normal flow of automobiles was replaced by a band of bodies moving across the entirety of the bridge in protest.

Confrontation must be perceived and felt across edges for the sparks of dissensus to fly forth. Edges of the sort I have been discussing, especially those that structure city streets, literally configure political actions; they provide both location and traction. Such edges not only give shape—definition, profile, contour—but they also give grip, impact, point, force. They are, in Derrida's term, "levers of intervention," the very points, the actual lines, where political demonstrations can be staged with the most forceful effect. In all such ways, and in numerous others, streets are powerful presences in urban life quite beyond their utility as trafficways—furnishing many of the most definitive edges as bases for action and interaction in the city.

Streets are connectors that circle around gardens and parks, and traverse whole neighborhoods. They serve to link nearly all aspects of life in the city. They mark the edges of neighborhoods, and often of whole cities (as with East River Drive and West Side Drive in New York City). A city limit is frequently identified with a certain street, such as Gage Boulevard at the western edge of Topeka, Kansas. Whether as connective conduits or as indicators of spatial limits, or as avenues for political protest, streets are definitive edges of public spaces.

In this way street edges complement and reinforce the edges of parks and gardens and neighborhoods, thereby contributing substantially to the formation of the full fabric of a city. They subserve tranquility in spaces of leisurely walking and restful contemplation—supplying embracing outer bounds—even as they also support tumult in the case of intense traffic and political demonstrations. Each of the major forms of urban edges discussed in this chapter is intermediary in its own manner: parks between parts of a city, gardens within parks, neighborhoods as situated between whole swaths of a city's total space, and streets throughout this space. Each edge is transitional, none is ultimate. But taken together, all such edges constitute a city as anything but static—as an ever-evolving interplay of edges. In cities, the edge is where the action is. Cities thrive as well as suffer from the edges of which they are composed. Every city is first and last—and at many points in between—an edge city.

## Notes

1. The fact that fully wild areas are extremely rare on the earth today, though reflecting a mercilessly aggressive world economy as well as climate change, does not alter the fact that wherever such areas are found, they contain genuinely wild edges. The photographer Sebastião Salgado has tried to document some of these last remaining reserves of wildness in his recent show, "Genesis" (International Center for Photography, 1133 Avenue of the Americas, New York City, September 14, 2014—January 11, 2015).

2. In the case of landscapes, roads and highways are all too often built right through them and not around them. This is a literal incursion of edges of convenience and utility into sanctuaries composed of wild edges.

3. Gary Snyder, "The Etiquette of Freedom," in *The Practice of the Wild* (San Francisco: North Point Press, 1990), p. 19. See also Rebecca Solnit, *Wanderlust: A History of Walking* (New York: Penguin, 2000).

4. This is not to deny the existence of hybrid cases: gardens whose extent is such that they verge on parks, and closely configured parks that are in effect extended gardens. The "gardens" at Versailles are so extensive that they could just as well be designated as "parks" in the sense I here adopt; only parts of the vast Versailles horticultural complex qualify as gardens in the more delimited sense. In this chapter, I am treating only paradigmatic or ideal cases—which is in no way to exclude mixed instances.

5. I discuss Central Park further in my essay "Borders and Boundaries: Edging into the Environment," in *Merleau-Ponty and Environmental Philosophy: Dwelling on the Landscapes of Thought*, ed. Suzanne L. Cataldi and William S. Hamrick (Albany: State University of New York Press, 2007).

6. On the plane of consistency, see Gilles Deleuze and Félix Guattari, *A Thousand Plateaus*, trans. B. Massumi (Minneapolis: University of Minnesota Press, 1987), esp. chapter 10.

7. Heraclitus, fragment 34, in Philip Wheelwright's translation; Philip Wheelwright, *Heraclitus* (New York: Atheneum, 1968), p. 37.

8. On *vita nuova*, see the book of this title by Dante, *Vita Nuova*, trans. Ralph Waldo Emerson (Turin: Aragno, 2012).

9. "The Pleasures of Merely Circulating" is the title of a poem of Wallace Stevens found in *The Collected Poems of Wallace Stevens* (New York: Vintage, 1990), pp. 149–50.

10. Cited by Gary Snyder, *The Practice of the Wild*, p. 19.

11. See *Getting Back into Place*, chapter 3.

12. Christopher Alexander, Sara Ishikawa, and Murray Silverstein, with writing credits to Max Jacobson, Ingrid Fiksdahl-King, and Shlomo Angel, *A Pattern Language: Towns, Buildings, Construction* (Oxford: Oxford University Press, 1977), p. 89.

13. On the commons, see Lewis Hyde, *Common as Air: Revolution, Art, and Ownership* (New York: Farrar, Straus, and Giroux, 2010), especially chapters 1–4; Gary Snyder, "The Place, the Region, and the Commons," in *The Practice of the Wild*, pp. 27–51.

14. Ibid., p. 89.

15. Christopher Alexander, *The Timeless Way* (Oxford: Oxford University Press, 1979), p. 330; I have changed past tense to present in the quote.

16. Mindy Fullilove, *Root Shock: How Tearing Up City Neighborhoods Hurts America, and What We Can Do About It* (New York: Ballantine, 2005).

17. See Fred Evans, *The Multi-Voiced Body: Society and Communication in the Age of Diversity* (New York: Columbia University Press, 2008).

18. Henry Belcher, quoted in Fullilove, *Root Shock*, p. 31.

19. Fullilove, *Root Shock*, p. 30.

20. This is just what Deleuze and Guattari emphasize in their discussion of smooth versus striated spaces; see especially chapter 12 of *A Thousand Plateaus*.

21. Mindy Fullilove, *Urban Alchemy: Restoring Joy in American's Sorted-Out Cities* (New York: New Village Press, 2013), pp. 104–5. The second use of "borders" is in italics in Fullilove's text.

22. Ibid., p. 106.

23. Ibid, p. 33. Fullilove adds, "It is this deep contradiction that rumbles in the guts of our cities: we feel the unease, suffer from the dysfunction, and act out the madness."

24. "Il y a politique de l'espace, parce que l'espace est politique." Henri Lefebvre, "Reflections on the Politics of Space," in his *State, Space, World: Selected Essays*, ed. N. Brenner and S. Elden (Minneapolis: University of Minnesota Press, 2009), p. 174; my translation and my italics. See also the statement that "space is political and ideological" (p. 171).

25. It follows that if the most effective revolutions occur as reclamations of public *space*, then the spatial dynamics of the urban settings in which occupation takes place will be of special significance. This point applies to Zuccotti Park: despite its status as a privately owned public park (it is controlled by a private board of directors), its manifest purpose was not to make money like a business but to serve as an open park for public use.

26. David Harvey, *Rebel Cities: From the Right to the City to the Urban Revolution* (London: Verso, 2012), p. 161.

27. As Marina Sitrin testifies from her experiences during the economic crisis of 2001 in Argentina, "The Occupy movements globally have all begun with the same two features, which must be explored in depth and taken seriously: the creation of horizontal spaces and the opening of new territories in which to create new social relationships" ("*Horizontalidad* and Territory in the Occupy Movements," in *Tikkun* [Spring 2012], p. 63).

28. The practice of the "human microphone" takes advantage of this situation by locating what is being said in successive waves that pass from one group of listeners to another, all in the oral mode and all within a certain proximity. Fred Evans observes that the issue is how to create the equivalent of such an amplified set of voices on a much larger scale than any single scene can provide (Fred Evans, e-mail communication of September 15, 2012). For a close description of the Occupy Portland movement, see Jim Seger, "The Occupy Movement: Signs of Cultural Shifts in Group Processes Shaped by Place" (PhD dissertation, Pacifica Graduate Institute, 2017).

29. Lissa McCullough observes that "Occupy gatherings were more about physical presence together as a political act first, and the talk was patently second in importance. Valuable, or even invaluable, yes, but second. This was a place and time when *body* was the *word*. Being a corporate body together said it all: citizens of one body, no word needed to be uttered" (e-mail communication of August 4, 2015).

30. David Harvey, interview with Amy Goodman on *Democracy Now* (www.democracynow.org), April 30, 2012. Harvey adds that today, in a period of plutocracy, "We have only one action—on the streets." He spells this out further in this statement: "Since all other channels of expression are closed to us by money power, we have no other option except to occupy the parks, squares and streets of our cities until our opinions are heard and our needs attended to" (Harvey, *Rebel Cities*, p. 162).

31. There were many such cases. For example, see the article on incidents involving Occupy Los Angeles: "Chalk Protests Draw a Defiant New Line," *Los Angeles Times*, July 14, 2012, p. A1. Note also "As 'Occupy' Turns 1, Some Who March Are Arrested," *New York Times*, September 16, 2012, p. A22: "By 9:00 p.m., almost all of the remaining protesters left the area as a line of officers advanced toward a group standing on the corner of Liberty Street and Broadway while a captain announced through a megaphone that the group was blocking pedestrian traffic."

32. "Crossing the line" reminds us that this phenomenon is not associated exclusively with progressive or radical causes; to cut across a labor line, as when scabs attempt to take the jobs whose low pay unions have contested by setting up lines of protest, goes in just the opposite political direction.

# PART 3

# Edges of Body and Psyche, Earth and Sky

# Preface to Part Three

In this penultimate part, I turn to two groups of edges so far largely ignored in an increasingly thickening plot. These are given by the human dimension of the edge-world on the one hand, and by the earth and larger cosmos on the other. In the first case, it is a matter of edges that are located *on our side*, belonging to us as human subjects. These subjects are not merely the passive witnesses of edges encountered in the surrounding world—edge-undergoers, as it were—but beings who actively contribute edges of their own to the full constitution of entire edge-worlds. Such edges are of two main sorts: those belonging to the lived body of the human subject (chapter 8) and those found in various psychical states, especially those in which falling apart is an issue (chapter 9). Each kind of edge is distinctive in its formation and effects, and calls for its own treatment.

Beyond these two edge situations, we shall look to the far-out edges of the earth as well as to the still further out edges of the sky and beyond (chapter 10). We shall not take these up from the standpoint of geology or physics or astronomy any more than we will rely on somatic medicine or psychiatry for the first two types of edge. Instead, our interest lies in such outermost edges insofar as they are perceived (and sometimes imagined) by the human subject who is on earth and looking into the horizon or up at the sky. Our concern will be with how this subject experiences these edges at the extremities and how she takes them to be configured, quite separately from what they are in objective fact. Accordingly, we shall engage in what Don Ihde calls "experimental phenomenology" in an effort to regard them as full-fledged members of the spectrum of edges that compose the complex life-worlds that human beings (and other animate beings) undergo.[1]

This is a part of the book that is redoubled at every turn, as we travel in two diametrically opposite directions. The first is in and toward ourselves as human agents whose bodies have their own edges and whose minds are edged and often split in their own specific manner. In this way, we will be discussing *our edges*— the edges that we bear as embodied subjects with a psychical dimension: both at once. But second, we will also move resolutely beyond our bodily and psychical being into the earth beneath our feet and to the sky above our heads. Both of these extrasubjective directions are fundamental to human being in the world. The four dimensions I shall address—body, psyche, earth, and sky—constitute a special fourfold that is integral to a full account of the edge-worlds that humans and other animate beings inhabit.

Omitted here (for reasons of length) is an explicit discussion of the edges at stake in the social worlds to which human beings always also belong; but these have already emerged in my discussion of urban edges, and they will also figure at various points in the next three chapters, most notably in the discussion of how bodily edges convey meaning to others in particular social settings as well as in the consideration of the interpersonal bearing of the severely split psyche.

### Notes

1. See Don Ihde, *Experimental Phenomenology: An Introduction* (Albany: State University of New York Press, 1977).

# EIGHT

# At the Edges of My Body

The body is not a "being," but a variable boundary.
—Judith Butler, *Gender Trouble: Feminism and the Subversion of Identity*

All the edges we have so far considered have been edges of things or events, parks or streets, landscapes or waterscapes—that is to say, of parts of our experience that do not belong to us, the human subjects who encounter such edges. They are the edges of the Allon, that is, the *other* beings that surround us at all times and places. It has been *their* edges that have preoccupied us up to this point—and rightly so, as they confront us first of all in the daily life-world. But this raises the question, what about *our own edges*? By which I mean the edges of our own bodies—yours and mine and those of any human being, as well as those of other animal beings. What is distinctive about these edges? How do they figure in the ever-increasing spectrum of edges I have discussed so far in this book?

It is striking that I did not think to mention such edges in my opening forays into the main types of edges. This was not mere oversight. It reflected a first important fact about bodily edges: in each case, they are *mine*, so much so that I did not think to describe them separately. They belong to my body, they are part of my flesh, thus they are something I do not ordinarily focus on unless I am injured in a particular place on or inside my body or concerned with decorating it with tattoos. For the most part, I am oblivious of the edges of my own body, which I live from within—from the central visceral mass with which I tend to identify my physical being. The center of my corporeal self seems somehow to be located in this bodily core, somewhere between my hips and my shoulders and sometimes including my head as well. These bodily regions are felt as where I exist most intensively and massively. To the extent that this is true, it is not surprising that we do not attend to the outer edges of our lived bodies unless we are directly stimulated there. For the same set of reasons, these same edges of the lived body have been largely overlooked in phenomenology and in other disciplines.

And yet it is by these very edges that we are most fully in touch with the world around us—the very world whose own edges figure so prominently in ongoing experience. These latter are the edges with which we have to cope in everyday life, sometimes struggling with them and sometimes enjoying them outright. It is not

surprising, then, that so many of my previous descriptions have been of these surrounding edges. They make up the majority of what I earlier called salient edges,
whereas our own bodies' edges tend to be much more subdued in contrast—that
is to say, woven into our experience, tucked into it—so much so that we come to
take them for granted.

Still, if we are to keep with Heidegger's axiom in *Being and Time* that "our existence is ours to be, one way or another,"[1] we must pay special attention to the particular ways in which the edges of our own bodies are configured and how they are
actively ingredient in our experience. Unusual as this undertaking may seem to be,
we need to enter into the rarely explored domain of just how and where our bodies end: where they come to be felt and perceived as giving out, including where
and how they interact with other edges. In this perspective, the primary issues become, from what basis in bodily edges do we approach the world around us? And
what is the nature of our own edge-armature such that our bodies connect in so
many ramified ways with the edges of all that is not us?

In what follows, I explore the character of proprioceptively experienced
edges, that is, those edges I feel or sense to be mine, to belong to my own body.
Some of these edges are experienced as located on the surface of my body—say,
the creases where my forearms are linked to my upper arms, or the folds of flesh
in my less-than-svelte stomach. These surface edges are important, as they outline the body's felt mass and its own presence to itself. Still more instructive, however, are the outer edges whereby my body is in commerce with its immediately
surrounding life-world. Such edges are my body's advance agents, as it were, picking up signals from the environs while transmitting to that same environs my responses to its challenges, and sometimes taking new initiatives within it. They are,
in Merleau-Ponty's expression, "silent sentinels" that stand guard over the course
and fate of my body in the life-world to which it belongs.[2]

## I

The edges of my body? The phrase rings awkwardly. It is less awkward to speak
of the body as having its own "contour" or "shape." These latter terms make
perfect sense in such concrete contexts as health or cosmetics, where issues of
precise body outline are specifically at stake—especially when we find ourselves
guided by certain cultural and gender norms. These norms, taken as something
to which we should aspire, are an instance of what are more properly called "limits," given that they are absorbed or imposed rather than chosen and are subject to metric determination (for example, "the perfect waistline"). I may adopt
one of these norms by my own volition, but the norm itself is a cultural ideal
that I take over from others (peers, cultural stereotypes, film stars, body build-
ers, and so on). I can attempt to approximate to this ideal, but I cannot create it

myself; at most, I can attempt to "shape" my body to fit what the ideal or norm dictates. This I do with diet, exercise, close-fitting clothes, and the like. Nevertheless, my bodily shape is not a perfectly pliable thing that I can sculpt at will. Short of radical cosmetic surgery, I find that my body clings stubbornly to its usual form—give or take a few pounds. Nowhere near as mercurial as my mind, my body is not subject to reconfiguration in the manner of an ordinary physical object that I can create or manipulate for instrumental or aesthetic ends. Still, with enough time and effort I can reshape my body: my muscles begin to bulge, my stomach flattens out.

In contrast with its shape or contour, my body's edges are not merely recalcitrant to reshaping but also remain much the same even as the exact form of certain of my body parts (my biceps, my stomach) may change. For these are *my edges*, those of the outermost parts of my body—inalienably so, in a way that cannot be altered, much less determined, by a cultural ideal or norm. The latter may dictate my diet and my exercise, and these in turn can alter the precise measurements of certain body parts. But the various outer edges of my body form a pattern that belongs to me and that is one of the major ways by which I know myself. This is not to say that they never change, especially as I grow up and age. But at each stage of my life, these edges cling to me as indisputably *mine*, whatever may be the influences to which I am subject and despite the changing shape and weight of my body as I get older. In addition to being able to claim these edges as uniquely *mine* and as slow to change, how are bodily edges to be described?

If we cannot answer this last question readily, this is not just because the phrase "the edges of my body" is an awkward locution in English: this linguistic fact points to a basic aspect of such description. This is the *elusiveness* of these edges. Whenever we attempt to spell out what these edges consist in, we find ourselves stalled: not only do we not know *what* they are, we do not even know exactly *where* they are. As for the first perplexity ("what they are"), they do not seem to fit any of the common categories of edge: they are neither verges nor margins, nor are they borders or boundaries in any usual sense—nor any of the other kinds of edge with which we are by now familiar. They seem farthest from being rims, which are fixed and often rigid edges *around* a physical object or place, and closest to being thresholds, given that it is *through* my body's edges that I gain access to much of my surrounding world.

Concerning the second perplexity, that of their proper location ("where they are"), a moment's reflection indicates that my body's outer edges are not found in any precise corner or part of space. Although I can point to some of them— the edges of my knee and my right hand; but we cannot say *just where* they are located. For their locus is not only a matter of their position in objective space; it belongs primarily to my lived body, which is no object at all but an animated mass

of flesh that is indefinite in its exact extent. My bodily edges are not simply *there*—
not in any customary sense of physical being-there. Indeed, they are not some-
*thing* to which I can simply point. All we can say is that they *are there*—there at
the periphery of my body. Here as elsewhere (but especially here), the paradigm
of "simple location" (in Whitehead's term) misleads us: this paradigm, stemming
from early modern models of space and time, requires that location be determined
at a definite point in a homogeneous spatial or temporal field—as with a location
on earth that is designated by so many degrees of latitude and longitude or is represented on a global positioning system (GPS).

Does this mean that my body's outer edges are to be grouped with such other
nebulous phenomena as auras or silhouettes, profiles or figures? It is tempting to
assimilate bodily edges with one or more of these phenomena, each of which
conveys an aspect or sense of bodily edges. To realize how this temptation must
be resisted, let us consider each of these "exemplars" in brief succession: each is
exemplary of how bodily edges can be projected in an image that, however suggestive, fails to capture what is essential about such edges.

*Aura.* As the term has been employed in the last century in the West, *aura*
refers to a discharge of energy rays or vibrations emitted by the human body that
is not visible to the naked eye yet can be detected in certain photographic images.
It is a hybrid term—partly spiritual, partly scientific—in which the authority of
the latter is invoked to demonstrate the existence of the former. As its very existence is highly controversial, it cannot be regarded as a definitive display of the
edges of my body but only as an indirect and tenuous method of trying to detect
the presence of these edges.

*Silhouette.* A silhouette is a flat image of a body with no figuration of its volume or internal features. Despite its reductive status, a silhouette can be very
telling: it is a genuine image of a human body and is accurate within certain limitations (for instance, it cannot convey bodily volume). It is capable of conveying
things about myself I may not realize without this image: for instance, my overall
bodily bearing and posture.[3] If an aura conveys the energy of my lived body beyond its anatomical limits, a silhouette is a black-and-white representation of this
same body presented within these same limits.

*Profile.* A profile has at least two distinct senses: one is the outline of a person's
face, usually from the side; the other refers to a person's professional persona or
public standing. The latter kind of profile belongs more to others than to myself
(or to myself regarded as an other), though its roots lie in my own activities and
accomplishments. In relation to it, my overall bodily edges are more or less indifferent. A third, expanded sense of profile is darker in its connotation: "racial profil-
ing," in which case I am singled out by others on the basis of my race or ethnicity
or, more exactly, my appearing to look (and act) like those of a presumed racial or

ethnic origin. Of these three senses of profile, only the first is concerned with my body's own characteristic edges.

*Figure.* Taken in a literal sense, figure is virtually synonymous with bodily outline or shape. This quite physical sense is at stake when we say that someone "has a good figure," even if the parameters of this figure are socially determined by extant norms of beauty: the admired female figure of Rubens's art is quite different from the anorexic extremes of contemporary Western culture. But we also speak of "cutting a good figure"—where this means being admired in certain social or political settings. Like persona, this usage trades on a very public sense of the self: myself as noticed by others. In a further extension, we speak of figure vis-à-vis ground, where figure is no longer a separate and freestanding shape but has meaning only in relation to the perceived ground from which it arises and is inseparable from it. This second sense of figure is neither strictly private nor wholly public: neither one nor the other exclusively but possessing aspects of both in the act of perception. Something like this is true of the edges of my body: I can see many of them, but others can see them all—a point to which we shall return. To this extent, we can say that bodily edges manifest a figure whose perception is shared by myself and others, albeit differentially: my edges as *seen*—as constituting a seen figure—are not equivalent to my edges as felt to be mine from within.

The attempt to assimilate my bodily edges to an aura or a silhouette, a profile or a figure is subject to two severe limitations. First, these edges cannot be fully captured in any single form of bodily presentation, including those at play in the four instances I have just examined. My bodily edges evade the kind of definitive representation that is at stake when I refer to *my* silhouette or *my* profile, or to *my* figure or *my* aura. Second, my *experience* of my own edges evades these same exemplars, which in various ways (some direct, some indirect) bear on my corporeal edges viewed from without—from the standpoint of another self who regards me, or of myself looking onto myself. But in fact I bear and undergo my bodily edges *from within*—from within the nonobjectifiable and nontransferable experiencing of my own lived body.

## II

Two fundamental points need to be made here. First, my bodily edges are always plural: they are both felt and perceived as *several*. This means that my body as experienced does not possess a single, definitive, or final edge. Second, even if my bodily edges can be projected in various ways—in the four ways just considered and in still other ways (for example, in a film I might make of myself)—they belong to me in a quite singular way: they form *part of me*, an intrinsic part of my lived body. They are not detachable in the manner of these various kinds of projection, which are all external expressions of my bodily edges. In order to exist

as I do, I do not depend on any of these expressions, but I do require the possession of my own bodily edges as a basis for experiencing them as mine. Given their
deep immanence in my body, it follows that these edges cannot ever be displayed
as such in public space. Only their facsimiles or other forms of projection or representation can be so displayed. My own bodily edges are so much mine, so much
a part of what I alone can experience, that they do not lend themselves to public
consumption, whether this takes the form of commercial or sexual exploitation,
professional self-promotion, or even bare recognizability by others. We might say
that external projections of my bodily being entail my being *turned out* from myself toward others—whereas my own bodily edges are ineluctably *turned back in*
toward myself, folded into my own body. These edges accrue to me as an integral
part of me. It is as if they have always already sunk into me—even if their outer
surface, their skin or nails, is exposed to the surrounding world, being open to the
gaze of others, whether to be appreciated or reviled or treated with indifference.

Concretely considered, this felt immanence of the edges of my body is experienced as a burden when I am physically tired or as ecstatically suspended in
certain extraordinary experiences, such as sexual orgasm or transport by the sublime. Most of the time, however, I feel these edges as just being *here*: not over
there, somewhere else, but here, nearby: "here-by," *here by myself*, as belonging to
the fleshly outer surface of my personal self, as part of the covering of the core of
this self. The covering itself is sensed as "thick," by which I mean felt as stemming
*from me* as its source and subject, while at the same time situated *in me* as part of
myself. This from/me and in/me double dyad is another expression of the bivalent being of bodily edges, contrasting with other dyads such as private/public,
felt/perceived, inner/outer. This new bivalency is constituent of who I am, being
one with myself; it is not situated outside or alongside me, but belongs to my
unique bodily identity.

Bodily edges are primarily experienced by me *from up close*. This happens
continually during the waking day as well as through the night. At times, I catch
glimpses of the outer edges of my body, as when I stare at them in a mirror or
apply a salve to a part of my skin that is experiencing pain. In these cases, it is as
if my own immanent bodily edges are turned outward momentarily, just long
enough to be seen or touched. In each instance, instead of my whole body, I see
this forearm, that elbow, that foot. I see body parts and thus their distinctive edges.
It is as if I were witnessing a "fragmented body" (*corps morcellé*) in Lacan's term for
the circumstance of the infant in the period before the mirror stage in which the
infant identifies with its own image in the mirror. But I never see *all* of my body;
not even in the mirror, which offers me only one view of my body at a time.

Despite the partiality of the up-close perception of my bodily state, it is definitive in its own way. I can trust it. I am, after all, grasping *my own bodily self*

through its turned-out and turned-in edges, however discontinuously or partially. The edges I apperceive are certainly my own. They are not someone else's: of this I am certain.[4] I am as sure of this as knowing that my thoughts are mine. Which is not to say that I know my body in its entirety, any more than I know all of my mind: parts of both remain concealed. But the body parts I do see, and the parts of my mind of which I am conscious, *I know to be mine.* Such knowledge is definitive within the bounds of its own limitation.

Concrete bodily edges realize a paradigm of definitive but partial self-knowledge in a very particular way: namely, by the fact that such edges are *parts of parts.* They are distinctive ending parts of such major body parts as head and arms, legs and chest. Every such body part has its own characteristic edges, ranging from the comparatively angular edges of my elbows and shoulder blades to the smooth and bulbous edges of my thighs and buttocks. Such edges, even if perceptible from without, I know from within as inhering in my own body parts, integral parts of these parts ("integral" because accruing to the body parts themselves, not imposed upon them as an exterior layer).

## III

At stake here is a special tension that can be stated as the Antinomy of Corporeal Edges; it takes the form of a thesis and an antithesis.

*Thesis:* Physical edges of any kind, including those belonging to my body, are parts in their own right. They are parts of things, precisely those parts where that thing comes to an end. They are also parts of parts of a thing but with the special proviso that such edges are to be found precisely where a given part undoes itself, vanishes as that part. The edge of any given particular body part is that portion or phase of the part where it comes to a more or less abrupt termination: where it literally nihilates.

*Antithesis:* Yet, for all this, an integral part of something belongs to that same something, precisely as *its* edge: my elbow, part of my arm, is also an edge of that same arm. Both the elbow and the arm remain integral components of the whole lived body. They do so as felt and perceived, for they are demonstrably here *by* my body, where "by" does not mean alongside (which would imply that it is detachable) but *right at,* just there, on that arm or elbow. As the edge of that body part, it is itself a part that belongs to that body part, even if it is at the same time just where that part vanishes from view or withdraws from touch.

In this antinomy, which combines discontinuity with coherence, we witness another expression of the bivalence of bodily edges. On the one hand, such edges are where my skin comes to an end—and thus the whole flesh of the body part to which this skin adheres. Bodily edges are where parts of my body (most notably, the skin) depart from a continuous or uninterrupted state. On the other hand, such edges belong to that same skin—and in this capacity, they count as continuing parts of that skin: parts of that part of my whole lived body.[5]

Although we here confront two very different aspects of the edges of my body's parts, aspects that seem to look, like Janus, in opposite directions (discontinuous as ending, continuous as belonging), they prove to be compatible with each other—just as are space and time, freedom and causality in Kant's First and Second Antinomies, that is, once the antinomial terms are adequately understood. The presumed opposites complement each other, one being or having what the other lacks. Just as an edge has to give out somewhere as a diminishing part *of* something—though not of something infinite in extent, which could have no definitive edge—so it also has to inhere *in* some whole, organic or artificial, to which that same edge belongs. To say that a bodily edge is a part of a part is to say just this. Yet such a part is not subordinate to the whole to which it belongs, as if it were a mere portion of it. As Aristotle says, "We should take that which applies to the part and apply it to the living body as a whole" (*De Anima* 412b).[6] But the part/whole relation also works the other way around: from the whole to the part. As Rilke observes of a sculpted hand by Rodin, this hand "has the power to give any part of [its] vibrating surface the independence of the whole."[7] Body parts and their edges allow us to move both from their differential status to the whole to which they belong (Aristotle's preferred direction), and also back again from that whole to themselves as such parts having such edges (as in Rilke's remark).

## IV

Most of the bodily edges on which I have focused so far are *outer edges*: edges that give the distinctive configuration of something. In particular, they are edges where a body part comes to a shape by which we commonly identify it: the shape of my elbow, the shape of my nose, the shape of my left foot. At the same time, however, bodily parts also possess *inner edges* in the form of creases and folds—"in-lines" rather than "out-lines," as it were. I have in mind such things as wrinkles, scars, birthmarks, and similar things. Even if less useful for purposes of identification (though we should recall Odysseus's scar, by which his childhood tutor recognized him), these edges are subject to the same kind of analysis I have given of the outer edges of body parts. For they, too, are places where skin, emerging from flesh, comes to a particular edge. The difference is that such edges are the involutions of a body part, occurring where the body part turns in upon itself. They inhere—literally—in a body part even as they are parts of their own. Although they are not as graphically limned as are the body's external edges, they, too, count as parts of parts: inner parts of the body's surface.

The inner and outer edges of bodily parts are not only glimpsed in the course of ongoing experience—seen as visual markings—but they also provide a *grip* for our hands: we can touch them and sometimes grasp them in such a way as to hold onto them. Just as the lacing on a football furnishes an edge for holding the ball as we prepare to throw it, so we take hold of such naturally given bodily edges as wrists, elbows, knees, and ankles furnish—for example, in assuming certain postures in yoga. These fleshly edges give visible and tangible purchase to our efforts to move our bodies in certain contexts. They are analogous to the way that instruments and tools present features like handles for varied uses. Again invoking Heidegger's apt term, they are "ready-to-hand" for use in practical contexts. Thanks to its organically configured edges, each person's own body is ready-to-hand for his or her own activities. Not only *are* we our own bodies—as Merleau-Ponty insists, "I am not in front of my body, I am in my body, or rather I am my body"[8]—but we also deploy our bodies in certain specific ways, regarding them as instruments for the realization of diverse purposes: skillful movements, physical exercise of various sorts, and many other maneuvers.

It is useful to compare bodily edges in their instrumental being with two other kinds of edge: rims and psychical edges. Rims, as I have insisted, are comparatively rigid edges; they tend to be fixed in size and shape, being the rims of material things that are themselves comparatively unchanging, whether these be tin cans or the Grand Canyon. As if to underline their rigidity, artificially produced rims are often reinforced in various ways, for example, by being constructed of extra layers of metal or being raised up. In the case of natural rims, they are composed of relatively dense or compacted matter—whether earth or stones—or else they would erode and waste away. In these respects, rims contrast starkly with bodily edges, which are comparatively soft and pliable. Fleshly edges are also notably animated, changing in contour in keeping with bodily movement such as walking or flexing one's biceps; only in deep sleep or a coma—finally, in death—do they lose their animation.

Psychical edges, on the other hand, are even more flexible than bodily edges. They are remarkably fluent, as is signified by the strong temptation to regard them as belonging to streams or flows. Such edges flow into each other so subtly that making distinctions between them is often difficult: it is not always possible to tell where one memory or thought starts and another ends. It is as if their whole being were consumed in continual connection making (memories giving rise to other memories; new ideas interconnecting with older ones). Rims, however, by their very nature set things apart and isolate them: sometimes physical substances (the kernels of corn preserved in a metal can), sometimes one part of a landscape from another (again, the North Rim as viewed from the Rio Grande Valley below). Bodily edges are less separative than rims, but they do serve to distinguish one part of the body from another, as when the edges of my neck establish it as situated between my head and torso. Whereas the neck both distinguishes

and links, and the rim on the can of corn strictly separates, psychical edges are connective through and through: their being is that of *xunos,* Heraclitus's word for
"linkage" or "tie." If they are closer to bodily edges in this respect, this is not surprising, given the intimate bond between Psyche and Soma.[9]

Despite their affinity with psychical edges, somatic edges constitute a class of
their own. They are not a mere subclass of another edge-type but possess structures and functions rendering them unique in the realm of edges. This is so even
if we tend to pass them over—to take them for granted and to bypass their significance in favor of more salient edge types, like brinks or peripheries or margins.
Also, bodily edges tend to be subordinated to the actions of the mobile body. It
is as if the edges of my body dissolve in the drama of such actions—even though
they are indispensable to the enactment of the drama itself.

## V

Let us now take up two situations so far neglected in my treatment of bodily edges:
the interaction of these edges with one another in the case of my own body, and
the interaction of my bodily edges with those of other bodies. Since both situations are quite complex, I shall restrict my discussion to one particular instance of
each: touching myself and touching others.

*Touching myself.* By this basic action, I mean not only touching myself with my
hands but the touching that occurs between any two or more of my own bodily
parts when they are contiguous, as when one leg crosses over the other. Either
way, we are concerned with an event in which my flesh is in contact with my own
flesh: thus a flesh-on-flesh, skin-to-skin relation. Although we rarely attend to this
phenomenon as such, it belongs to having the kind of multiply jointed and limbed
bodies that human beings (and other vertebrates) possess. For the most part this
happens spontaneously, without premeditation, indeed, every time we change our
bodily position, whether we are seated or walking.

A question arises immediately: in such self-touching do we create or discover
a *common edge*? Not so, if this means a third edge beyond those of the (at least)
two body parts that are touching. The idea of a third edge induces the specter of
an indefinite positing of edges (positing an edge that subtends the two edges that
do touch, then having to posit a new edge for the intersection of the first posited edge and the original two edges, and so on). In short, this leads to a version
of Aristotle's "third man" critique of Platonic Forms. We are here reminded of
Ockham's rule of the razor: "Do not multiply entities beyond necessity." The fact
is that we merely have to address a conjoining of coexisting and conterminous
edges. This is complex enough in its own right, but it does not require the ad hoc
positing of an extra edge. The challenge is that of understanding what is happening when one body part touches another.

To begin with, there is a *felt reciprocity* of self-touching. The hand or leg or arm that touches another part of the same body is *touched in turn*: touched back, as it were. The touching and the touching back occur in the same moment: *im selben Augenblick*, to employ a phrase of Husserl's that was meant to apply to the instant in which intended meaning is at once expressed and understood by way of signs.[10] But the moment of self-touching, unlike that of the passing instant, is notably thick—as thick as flesh itself. Instead of happening in an instant, touching oneself requires a certain density of duration, as the event has to do with an internally generated circumstance of self<touching>self that takes time to happen. Unlike Plato's indefinite dyad, this binary is quite definite in character, for it consists in two (or more) body parts that enter into carnal reciprocity simultaneously.

Merleau-Ponty adds to this analysis the fact that even if touching and being touched are the "reverse" of each other—that is, if one can be considered the counterpart of the other, and their roles can be reversed—they never merge entirely. As Merleau-Ponty puts it, "They do not coincide in the body: the touching is never exactly the touched."[11] This essential noncoincidence is what allows for the act of touching to take the initiative and for the touched to be receptive—all this within a "spread" or "hiatus" that amounts not only to a durational moment but also to a nonnegotiable felt difference.[12] This difference, however, is not equivalent to the distinction between pure (voluntary) activity and abject (involuntary) passivity. Rather than any such sheer oppositional difference, there is a drawing together of two sides of the same situation in and through a difference of modality within one and the same flesh (where "active" and "passive" are regarded as modalities of the lived body).

When one hand touches another that is, in turn, touching a thing alongside the body, we have a circumstance in which the touched hand has to assume one of two roles: either to continue to touch the outside object or to relinquish its primary function of doing this in order to become the touched hand of one's own body: "My left hand is always on the verge of touching my right hand touching the things, but I never reach coincidence; the coincidence eclipses at the moment of realization, and one of two things always occurs: either my right hand really passes over to the rank of touched, but then its hold on the world is interrupted; or it retains its hold on the world, but then I do not really touch *it*."[13] There is a curious asymmetry at the heart of the touched/touching dyad—an exemplary instance of their noncoincidence. Merleau-Ponty adds that if my two hands can be said to form a "circle," it is a circle differently centered in each case.[14]

Touching oneself is thus a complex and subtle process in which simplistic models of subjects in contact with objects fail to capture what is happening. What does happen is a process in which one and the same whole body manages to complicate its immediate life by turning upon and touching its own flesh—in active and passive modalities—rather than merely reaching out to objects around it. When the latter does occur, my effort to touch myself is distracted: my bodily intentionality overflows my own body and moves toward the thing touched. But when I touch *myself*, I effect a momentary suspension of the environing world in order to concentrate on a part of my own body—a part that is being touched by another part, one set of edges brought up against another set of edges. This is not a circumstance of *partes extra partes* (in the Cartesian phrase that applies to relations between objects in the external world) but of *partes intra partes*: parts of one body feeling other parts of the same body—my own body, animated by a continuously self-generated intentionality that is directed to itself.

*Touching another's body.* Just as in touching myself there is no simple opposition between activity and passivity—but instead an "indivision" between these two modalities[15]—so when I touch you, neither of us need be the sheer agent or the simple patient of the interaction. Apart from situations in which I thrust myself upon you, we are interinvolved in such a way as to draw each of us into a special self/other bonding that has no exact equivalence in the rest of human experience. Nor are we exactly equal partners; the matter is more complex than any model of sheer cooperation allows. If the interaction is not altogether one-way (from active to passive, myself to yourself), it is also not strictly two-way (as if we were paired equals). Instead, things happen with an asymmetrical reciprocity that involves a certain overlap of bodily intentionalities: an overlap that is another expression of the noncoincidence emphasized by Merleau-Ponty—except that this time I cannot claim that I know what I touch from within: I know it as other, as *your* flesh. I touch it. It is flesh. Yet it is not *my* flesh; it is the flesh of another bodily being.[16]

Let us consider two cases in point.

(1) *Erotic intertouching.* In an erotic experience of freely consenting, mutually attracted adults, a touched-touching dyad is generated that is like two raised to the second power: two concurrent pleasures, each intensifying and intensified by the other.[17] Let us take the caress as emblematic of this experience. Whether I or someone else initiates it, in caressing I derive pleasure from touching my partner and in being touched back by this same partner. I enter into an interplay of engaged reciprocities between myself as toucher-and-touched and the other as touched-and-toucher in turn. But this interaction, no matter how intense, is rarely strictly symmetrical. It is a dialectical process of shared enlivenment in which erotically enmeshed bodies play a game of continual catch-up: if I lead with a certain

caress, the other is invited to follow up in some fashion. Yet that other can decline to follow in my footsteps (more likely, "handsteps") and may initiate a new round of quite different caresses. Both the leading and the catching up (which are interpersonal avatars of the active/passive modalization) involve an immersion of my body with another's body and vice versa, the two bodies intertwining at their fleshly edges. For it is through the outer edges of flesh that the caress is accomplished, whether these edges belong to the hand or breast, the lips or the leg, the forearm or the penis. These need not be the edges of the same bodily organ or part. Distinctively different edges of diverse body parts often conspire in the caress: say, those of the hand with those of the vagina. In each case, erotic contact is realized through the edges of living flesh—edges that vary in felt consistency and texture, indeed in their basic identity as determined by their location in a given body part.

These intercalated edges complicate the fleshly experience of erotic partners—sometimes to their mutual delight, sometimes to the frustration of one party or the other. Despite their differing thrust and their difference in exact bodily location, they are synchronized through bodily movements that bring them into felt proximity. These are movements of my body and of the other that can be so closely coordinated that they can seem at times to become one movement of one body. Synchronization does not mean strict simultaneity. It should be considered instead as a temporal convergence, an overlap in time, in which any divergence of bodily motions reconverges soon after. Although very close convergence can certainly be achieved—in mimetic stroking or in "mutual orgasm"—strict coincidence is by no means necessary to the enjoyment of erotic experience with another person. This is because there are many ways for the erotic intertouching of bodies to occur, some of which are quite familiar to the participants, but others of which are exploratory and invented on the spot. An interbraiding of known with unprecedented touchings ensues—with many variations in between. Subtending the diversity of touchings is a shared erotic interest, which need not be the same in each party for intense bonding to occur: same does not here mean *identical*. (The same dialectic of same-with-different obtains at other levels of the encounter, such as occur when affection or love between

the primary parties is at stake: levels that complicate and
intensify the sensual excitement of intercalated edges.)[18]

(2)  *Nonerotic interaction.* Less intensely intimate are the many ways
by which bodily edges mingle among friends and members of
a family or a group of friends. Very often, these take the form
of momentary mutual touching. In a handshake, for example,
two people reach out to each other in a gesture of greeting.
The surfaces of their hands interact in ways that are at once
physically contiguous—each person literally grips the other—
and yet that are tempered by being customary and transitory.
Discontinuous surfaces of each person's hand, palm and fingers,
are in touch with comparable surfaces of the other's hand—
and it is the same hand for both: my right hand shakes your
right hand in a kind of mirror effect. (This indicates that the
handshake is in principle reversible, for in it "I can feel myself
touched as well and at the same time as touching."[19]) If the
aim of many erotic gestures is to intensify and maximize skin
contact, this is no longer the case with nonerotic touching: only
selected surfaces and their edges are now at stake. Much the
same is true of the parting hug, except that now the edges of
entire arms and upper backs and cheeks come into contact.[20]

Many gestures of touching among familiars are less mutual
and less ritualized than handshakes or embraces: touching on
the shoulder, patting on the back, stroking the other's hair.
Belonging here are many expressions of affection or emotion,
some of which are frequently repeated and others of which arise
rarely and in the moment. Still others are enacted only within
the bounds of a certain particular family or circle of friends:
these are comparable to closed rituals, in contrast to the open
rituals of the handshake or mutual embrace in public space.
If the overall purpose of erotic gestures is to arouse the other
and to facilitate full sexual engagement with that other, the
primary aim of gestures of touching among one's family and
friends is to give recognition to others and to reassure them of
our continuing affection and trust; in other words, to reinforce a
shared historicity and often to indicate a certain special personal
connection.

We may infer from these brief remarks that in both erotic and nonerotic
relationships with others, *it is bodily edges that interact*—and through them, bodily

*surfaces.* Across such surfaces in turn, *whole persons* are in touch with each other—persons with multiple psychical, characterological, and social dimensions. This is an instance of active *pars pro toto* relations; the parts that are touching convey and express intentions that belong to the whole person from which the touching proceeds. Experiences of touching bring people to bear on each other through interactive bodily gestures, and this mutual bearing—the fulcrum of interpersonal connection, as it were—is effected first of all through the corporeal edges that convey greetings and partings, as well as affectionate (and sometimes aggressive) feelings. Thanks to their interarticulated forms of crossing and tracing, such edges serve as effective vehicles of communication among people. Their more or less continuous and subtle structure (a structure that reflects the disposition of body parts and organs) enables them to convey messages between people at a subvocal and prelinguistic level. For this reason, bodily edges are a privileged medium of "body language," capable of bringing about a deep level of empathic understanding between people—without a word of verbal language having to be exchanged.[21]

In addition to the special sensitivity of those bodily edges that lend themselves to communicative and expressive connections with others—most notably, the edges of my hands or my tongue—my other bodily edges are capable of meaningful interaction with others and with the edges of other bodies. None of the many edges of my lived body is altogether insensitive vis-à-vis myself or others. Compared to many other edges, bodily edges of every sort possess a unique vibrancy and responsivity that express themselves in a decisive malleability of modes, shapes, and contours. For all their pliability, however, they realize in my own body a familiar and consistent pattern, a configuration that I take to be the gestalt of my bodily being as I feel it from the inside.[22]

## VI

Edges of a bodily sort come double-edged. On the one hand, some come shaped in ways that facilitate the path to communication, as with tongues that speak and hand gestures that are highly expressive. At the limit, the body itself seems to speak—or, almost, to write, as connoted in the phrase "written in the flesh." (Tattoos literalize this potentiality by inscribing words or pictograms on the physical skin.)[23] On the other hand, other such edges are fully organic, fleshly, and smooth; these are not communicative in themselves. In one respect, edges are angular and disjointed (like consonants); in another, they are bulbous and rounded-off, not unlike vowels.

Such two-sidedness is also found elsewhere in the edge-world—for instance, in the doublet of border and boundary: these, too, are bivalent in comparable ways. They share with the two aspects of bodily edges just identified the fact that the same edge can be characterized by one descriptive term in certain contexts (say, as a delineated "border," or as a distinct body sign) and by another in other contexts (as a porous "boundary" or as the phasing out of rounded flesh). This parallel is all the more remarkable in that borders and boundaries are most characteristically found in the larger worlds of which we are a part—in city and landscape worlds—while quasi-graphic and smooth bodily edges obtain mainly for our own flesh. Yet they can be paired in the ways I have just suggested.

These paired ways of being an edge suggest a more comprehensive bipolar model of edges in which one pole favors precision of form (thus favoring edges like borders and crisp bodily edges) while the other gives preference to what is intrinsically indeterminate (boundaries and rounded bodily surfaces). With such a model, we have a new level of bivalency, no longer limited to a given sort of edge but one that is capable of sweeping under its aegis a wide variety of edges—rims and margins, thresholds and brinks, and doubtless many more. We have in effect a bipolar model for edges of many kinds; one of the poles favors determinacy of form and structure, the other the amorphous.

Bodily edges exhibit one especially pronounced binarism: that by which such edges figure as characteristically *between* pairs of basic terms. Such edges come between myself and yourself, serving to differentiate us by the way each of us possesses a particular bodily type. If I am lean and you are chubby, we will each possess a distinctively different set of outer edges. But bodily edges also come between me and myself. On one side, I am in and with myself, contained by the edges in which my body is ensconced; on the other, I exist as a set of edges that relates to other edges in the world, including those of other people. Thanks to my bodily edges, I am in the world as a bivalent being.

In play here is the body's "genius for ambiguity," in Merleau-Ponty's telling phrase. This ambiguity is both intensive (possessed from deep within the resources of the body itself) and extensive (able, with such resources, to range broadly over many experiences and situations). Moreover, acting to order the many edge variations to which the lived body gives rise are certain paired structures such as inside and outside, paired limbs (arms, legs), the fact of having two eyes, the complementarity of touch and sight (themselves related to the inside/outside distinction).

## VII

One last binarism of bodily edges is worthy of special mention. This is the conjoining of certain semiotic capacities and organismic substructures. This pairing is especially prominent in higher primates—above all in human beings, who have developed it most fully. In the case of creatures such as ourselves who are capable of emitting signals coded broadly enough to include hand gestures, meaningful vocalizations, and written signs, the role of bodily edges is powerfully instrumental, indeed indispensable. These edges act as the hinges or pivots of communicative and expressive utterances—as the junctures where certain parts of the lived body are able to articulate and convey messages and thoughts that are meant for other human beings, not just for oneself. These semiotically charged edges are the critical purveyors of messages that are intended to influence other members of the species by letting them know what we think or want, particularly as it bears upon our relationship with them. The edges of these parts constitute a virtual cat's cradle of communication, outlining the direction of intended actions and the content of closely held thoughts. They act to specify these actions and thoughts—literally to *express* them—so as to bring them effectively into a shared public domain.[24]

The binarism of the organic and the semiotic is nothing strictly metaphysical (in contrast, say, with Spinozist attributes of thought and extension), nor is it exclusively epistemological (as with Kant's distinction between intuitions and concepts). Rather, this binarism is at one with my lived body, which possesses it as a dual potentiality; it is experienced by the speaker or actor herself rather than being abstractly posited for reasons of metaphysical system or theory of knowledge.

Further, the meaning at stake in communication or expression is itself bivalent. For *my body as I live it can go both ways*: it can live meaning from its own resources but can also express this meaning to others. These alternatives are not exclusive, nor need they be sequential: they often occur at once, coenacted. I live out my bodily life even as I send signs to others through the expressively toned edges of my lived body regarded as the messengers of my feelings and thoughts: starting with my lips and fingers but also by way of other body parts. Indeed, the edges of certain body parts have a unique potential to become meaningful in basic acts of communication with others: the flickering of my eyelids, the disposition of your hands, the shrug of her shoulders—all such edges constitute the crossroads of communication where I and other semiotically capable beings (including many animal species) meet in meaningful ways.

This is not to claim that understanding the meaning set forth by my bodily edges is transparent or straightforward. Any meaning conveyed by the corporeal semiosis of bodily edges is inherently ambiguous and uncertain. Interpretation is required at every stage. Nor is meaning expressed or understood once and for all; we find ourselves in a circumstance of continually changing and compounding semiotic meaning making and meaning construal. Still, for all the complications and convolutions to which it is subject in corporeal expressivity, meaning comes to be transmitted and to be understood for the most part by those for whom I intend it.

Far from being self-contained, then, my bodily edges enter into an *arc of articulation* that extends from myself to others, and back again. In certain circumstances— when I am bottled up within myself, or when others refuse to listen to me—the arc is interrupted: the avenue between myself and others becomes a gauntlet. That the transmission occurs at all is remarkable; but whether the context of such transmission is affectionate feeling or the conveyance of thought, it certainly does occur. Without it, we would be abjectly self-isolated, caught up within our own internal drama, stewing in our own semiotic juices. Even when we are thus caught up, however, we never altogether lose the capacity to signal to others our intentions and thoughts through the expressive edges of our lived bodies.[25]

In keeping with this last line of thought, we see how bodily edges, even though experienced in uniquely intimate ways by those who possess them in the first person, enter the domain of intersubjectively shared life at a meaningful level. They manifest one's own experience to others, who are called upon to interpret them, and they solicit concrete bodily actions on the part of these same others—who in turn express to us their own subjectively sensed interests and needs through the expressive edges of their own bodies. The circle of the touching and the touched here expands to include the more capacious circle of the emitter of signs and their receivers; but this happens only insofar as the bodily edges of myself and those of others act as indispensable intermediaries, as partners in an always imperfect but necessary communicative matrix, a conjoint semiosis.

Throughout this excursion into being at the edges of our bodies, we have found ourselves engaged with mereology, the study of parts, whether those of physical substances or geometrical figures or the parts of the corporeal transmission of meaning. Peculiar to bodily parts is not just their coinherence in our lived body but also their capacity for allowing this body to connect with other bodies in physical interaction. These parts reach out in social situations to connect with interlocutors by way of the implicit or explicit message they express and seek to impart to others. This last direction of our discussion demonstrates that the very idea of parts, like that of the edges that delimit them, cannot be confined to the isolated, single bodies they help to compose. The choice is no longer restricted to that between inner and outer parts. Now we must add a third option: that of *partes inter partes*, "parts between parts."[26] Thanks to the intertwining of their respective edges, the parts of my body interlace with yours, both literally (in the circumstance of intercorporeal touching) and by way of making meaning together in conversation and other forms of communication.

In addition to mereology, we have also been in effect practicing eschatology, given that bodily edges can be considered the endpoints, the last stages of all parts of our body (*eschata* signifies "last"). Edges are where things end, where they run out. More generally, how the edges of things—whether bodies or landscapes, parks or streets—relate to the parts of which they are composed (as well as to the wholes that include them) reflects the intersection of the mereological with the eschatological. This intersection is a veritable threshold, a *limen* or lintel. More generally, limenology as the study of thresholds provides the concrete context in which mereology and eschatology find common cause. In and through edges, parts and ends of parts meet, and they often do so thanks to intermediary edges acting as their lintel, their threshold. In the case of the human body, flesh is the most effective single such threshold, that *through which* bodily edges connect, whether these edges are those of my own body or those of others. Flesh is the medium for the interaction between all such bodily edges.

Looking ahead to the next two chapters, bodily edges are to be compared with the edges of the earth and with the edges that structure the human psyche from within. In all three cases, the edges are deeply ingredient in that of which they are the edges; they figure as structural parameters of these phenomena. We cannot perceive or imagine the earth except as ending in a single vast edge (like the far horizon at sea, where the water meets the sky), and the human psyche is especially prone to splitting into the edges of various kinds of dissociation. In terms of scale and scope, bodily edges are located between these two extremes, one enormous in extent and the other intangible in its being. The edges of our lived bodies act to mediate between these outermost and innermost edges. Despite significant differences in structure and function, bodily edges serve as their go-between: we cannot connect with either except by means of our own bodily movements. In this respect, such edges constitute the *tertium quid* between the earth as an ultimate "basis-body" (Husserl) and inner psychic space; they connect what would otherwise be radically disconnected if we concentrate only on the overt differences between an outsize physical body like the earth and an invisible agency like the psyche.

The fact of being diversely edged aids the lived body in its ongoing role as the indispensable middle term between earth and psyche. Bodily edges act as the mediatrix between the edges of the earth as perceived under and around us and those of the psyche as felt inwardly. Thanks to their intermediation, bodily edges link these two extremities of edge: in and by our flesh *les extrêmes se touchent*. The edges of my body—and yours—are where what is outwardly located in lived space and what is most inward in felt mind interdigitate, just as in their midst parts of our bodies link up with other parts and with the ends of these same parts. Bodily edges provide the connective tissue for many things in experienced life-worlds: for the earth around us, for our indwelling psyches, and for much else besides.[27]

### Notes

1. Martin Heidegger, *Being and Time*, trans. J. Macquarrie and E. Robinson (New York: Harper, 1962), p. 68; translation modified.

2. The phrase "silent sentinels" is my translation of the phrase *la sentinelle qui se tient silencieusement*. This phrase occurs in Merleau-Ponty, "Eye and Mind," in *The Merleau-Ponty*

*Aesthetics Reader: Philosophy and Painting*, ed. Galen A. Johnson (Evanston, IL: Northwestern University Press, 1993), p. 122, where it is translated as "this sentinel standing quietly."

3. A body silhouette is employed by Jean-Luc Nancy in his discerning descriptions of our being-with-others, of whom we more often catch glimpses rather than steady percep-tions. The contents of such glimpses are silhouette-like in that they give us a brief but tell-ing sense of others who have come into our ambience: "People are silhouettes that are both imprecise and singularized, faint outlines of voices, patterns of comportments, sketches of affects" (Jean-Luc Nancy, *Being Singular Plural*, trans. R. D. Richardson and A. E. O'Byrne [Stanford: Stanford University Press, 2000], p. 7). See also Nancy, *The Muses*, trans. P. Kamuf (Stanford: Stanford University Press, 1997), p. 53. But in both of these instances "silhou-ette" is being used metaphorically—that is, by extension—and not in the stricter sense I invoke above.

4. If I am not thus sure of myself, I am likely to be in a troubled psychological state. For more on not being one's own bodily self, see chapter 9, "Being on Edge and Falling Apart."

5. I am here taking skin to be the cover or integument for "flesh," which is the term for felt body mass, as composed of adipose and muscle, ligaments and sinews. The edges of body parts are most directly attached to skin; but given that skin is contiguous with flesh, such edges are at the same time outer parts of this same subtending flesh. All three—flesh, skin, and edge—together compose the body part, which also, at a deeper level, contains bone and cartilage. I return to flesh briefly in the conclusion to this chapter.

6. Aristotle, *De Anima*, trans. H. Lawson-Tancred (London: Penguin, 1986).

7. Rainer Maria Rilke, *Rodin and Other Prose Pieces*, trans. G. Craig Houston (Salem, MO: Salem House, 1986), pp. 17–18. Aristotle also anticipates the two-way relation between part and whole: "the part in the whole" versus "the whole [as] in the parts" (Aristotle, *Phys-ics: Books III & IV*, trans. E. Hussey [Oxford: Clarendon,], 210a 16–17). Gary Snyder puts the part/whole relation in this intriguing way: "To know the spirit of a place is to realize that you are a part of a part and that the whole is made of parts, each of which is whole. You start with the part you are whole in" (Snyder, *The Practice of the Wild* [Washington, DC: Shoemaker and Hoard, 1990], p. 41).

8. Merleau-Ponty, *Phenomenology of Perception*, trans. Landes, p. 151.

9. For more on psychical edges, see chapter 9.

10. See Husserl, "Expressions in Solitary Life," in *Logical Investigations*, trans. J. Findlay, vol. 1 (New York: Routledge, 2008), pp. 190–91. See also the commentary of Jacques Der-rida, *Voice and Phenomenon*, trans. Leonard Lawlor (Evanston, IL: Northwestern University Press, 2010).

11. Merleau-Ponty, *The Visible and the Invisible*, trans. Alphonso Lingis (Evanston, IL: Northwestern University Press, 1968), p. 254. On "the reverse" as "the other side" or "the other dimensionality," see ibid. Merleau-Ponty adds, "This does not mean that they [i.e., touched and touching] coincide 'in the mind' or at the level of 'consciousness.'" If anything, there is an "untouchable" at stake here that has no exact bodily correlate—an untouchable that is the equivalent of the "invisible" in the visual sphere (ibid., pp. 254–56).

12. "There is always a 'shift,' a 'spread,' between them . . . this hiatus between my right hand touched and my right hand touching." What guarantees that this "hinge" stays open

and operative is "the total being of my body . . . the massive flesh" (Merleau-Ponty, *The Visible and the Invisible*, p. 148).

13. Merleau-Ponty, *The Visible and the Invisible*, pp. 147–48; his italics. See also this statement: "When my right hand touches my left hand while it is palpating the things. . . The 'touching subject' passes over to the rank of the touched, descends into the things, such that the touch is formed in the midst of the world and as it were in the things" (pp. 133–34).

14. "There is a circle of the touched and the touching, the touched takes hold of the touching" (Merleau-Ponty, *The Visible and the Invisible*, p. 143).

15. "The flesh of the world (the 'quale') is indivision of this sensible Being that I am and all the rest which feels itself (*se sent*) in me, pleasure-reality indivision" (Merleau-Ponty, *The Visible and the Invisible*, p. 255). What is true for the flesh of the world is also true for my bodily flesh.

16. Merleau-Ponty writes, "If my left hand can touch my right hand while it palpates the tangibles, can touch it touching, can turn its palpation back upon it, why, when touching the hand of another, would I not touch in it the same power to espouse the things that I have touched in my own?" (*The Visible and the Invisible*, p. 141). The short answer is that only in my own case do I touch from "within my landscape"; my two hands "open upon one sole world." My hands, after all, "are the hands of one same body" that has "to do with one sole tangible" (ibid.). I cannot assume the position of the other; I cannot approach the world through *her hands*, which open onto *her world*: a world that may overlap with mine but that is never strictly coincidental with it.

17. Recall Freud's observation that in sexual intercourse four adults are implicated, thanks to the remaining traces of the Oedipus complex.

18. For further discussion, see Luce Irigaray, "The Fecundity of the Caress: A Reading of Levinas, Totality and Infinity," and "Phenomenology of Eros," both in *An Ethics of Sexual Difference*, trans. Carolyn Burke and Gillian C. Gill (Ithaca, NY: Cornell University Press, 1993), pp. 185–217. See also the fundamental work on the caress by Jennifer Carter, "Luce Irigaray and the Fecundity of the Caress" (PhD dissertation, SUNY at Stony Brook, 2017).

19. Merleau-Ponty, *The Visible and the Invisible*, p. 142. In this passage Merleau-Ponty is discussing the handshake.

20. In this paragraph "surface" is more fully recognized than elsewhere in this chapter. In fact, surface is an indispensable substructure of edge, its tacit ally: surface provides the very plane of presentation whose terminations *are* its edges. This is especially the case with the lived body, whose surface (the "skin") is in effect a continuous edge of the body mass and, conversely, whose edges assume the form of surfaces. See chapter 2, "Edges and Surfaces, Edges and Limits," as well as the insightful discussion of the perception of surfaces in James J. Gibson, *The Ecological Approach to Visual Perception* (Hillsdale, NJ: Erlbaum, 1986), pp. 22–36 and 170–81, and my own treatment in *The World at a Glance*, pp. 47–48, 140–42, 274, 369–74.

21. Body language exemplifies the general affinity between edges and signs: an affinity at play in the fact that the visible structure of written letters is traced by inscribed edges. For more on this and related themes, see my unpublished essay "Making Meaning at the Edge of Bodily Gesture," presentation at a panel on the work of Eugene Gendlin, annual meeting of SPEP, New Orleans, 2014.

22. The other's body, if I know it well, also has a familiar pattern of edges as seen from without, but I cannot claim to know just how this pattern feels from within the other's sensibility, no matter how much she may attempt to describe this pattern to me.

23. On body writing and tattoos, see Karmen MacKendrick, *Word Made Skin: Figuring Language at the Surface of Flesh* (Albany: Fordham University Press, 2004).

24. I concentrate here on human expressive powers, but I do not wish to deny the extraordinary communicative and semiotic capacities of other species.

25. Those disabled by stroke or in other extreme conditions still manage to convey to those who look after them what they have in mind. The potentiality of such extraordinary communication continues to exist, as portrayed in the film *The Diving Bell and the Butterfly* (2007), in which the protagonist manages to dictate an entire book solely with movements of his eyelids—yet another bodily edge that bears semiotic potentialities.

26. *Partes inter partes* thus contrasts both with *partes intra partes* (mentioned earlier) and *partes extra partes*, Descartes's expression for parts that are mutually exterior to one another.

27. This chapter is an extensively rewritten version of my essay "At the Edges of My Body," in Dan Zahavi, ed., *The Oxford Handbook of Contemporary Phenomenology* (Oxford: Oxford University Press, 2012).

# NINE

# Being on Edge and Falling Apart

Ich bin ein Zwiefaches in mir.
  —Hegel, *Anthropology, Encyclopedia*, par. 406, Addition

In the human soul there are only processes.
  —Henri Bergson, *Creative Evolution*

You could not discover the limits of soul, even if you traveled
every road to do so; such is the depth of its meaning.
  —Heraclitus, frag. 42 (trans. Wheelwright)

The previous chapter and this new one deal with edges that are radically singular—one of a kind, incomparable, unique. Such singularity certainly holds for my bodily edges, which can never be the same as the edges of *your* body or anyone else's body. Were they shared, we would in effect have the same body—my body could not be distinguished from yours. This is in keeping with Leibniz's principle of the identity of indiscernibles. For you and me to claim to be different bodies – and to *know* that we are different as bodies – each of us must be characterized by a set of bodily edges that are ultimately incommensurable, even if many of them display morphological similarities, for example, of gender, race, or age. The same holds true for the edge of the earth as well as for its more discrete edges: these, too, are altogether singular. They are the edges of *this* earth and this earth alone, and they help to constitute it as the unique planetary body we know it to be: science fiction aside, there will never be another earth even if there are heavenly bodies that sustain life of a comparable kind. Moreover, these two major avatars of singular edges are not unrelated to one another. It is the edges of my body that allow me to engage with the edges of the earth. I could not relate to the latter without the former. And the converse also holds true, given that being on earth is a material condition for being a body. Although my body contains millions of microbiota, it is the body of an earthling: evolved to be at home on earth, to be earth-bound in very intimate ways. My body is an earth body, and the earth is inhabited by living bodies, not only mine and not only human bodies but those of all other living beings as well. Between all these bodies and the earth there are very special bonds. My body is what it is because it is alive on earth, and the earth has become what it is thanks in considerable part to the various animate bodies that walk its lands, fly its skies, and ply its oceans, as well as live in the interstices of matter. Earth itself is a unique geological mass. For this reason, we can speak of bodily and earthly edges as *bisingular*: singular not just separately but *singular together*, unique as a pair. Body and earth are codependent and coessential variables of the world on edge.[1]

Psyche or soul is a third mode of singular being with its own distinctive edges—this time not physical, yet just as highly differentiated as those of animate and inanimate bodies and of the earth itself. Psychical edges are as singular as those of body or earth, even if they lack physical mass and force.[2] This means that we have a situation that is structurally *trisingular*. It can be represented in this way:

Each of the three terms possesses its own characteristic edges. Now that we have explored those belonging to body, and will soon examine those endemic to earth and beyond, we are at the right point to consider the edges of soul.

The comparative solidity and steadiness of bodies and earth alike contrast with the insubstantial and fleeting nature of soul.[3] Hobbes observed that "thought is quick"—where thinking was regarded as the primary activity of soul for early modern thinkers.[4] The ancient link between psyche and breath—*psychein* means "to breathe" in ancient Greek—points to the soul's weightlessness and transitoriness but also to the fact that breath is essential to life and bodily movement. Souls change direction and shape many times over in the course of a lifetime—indeed, many times every minute if Bergson is right. As Hegel insists, in extreme states we can have more than one soul even though we are given only one mortal body; and soul itself is twofold at any given time.[5]

Given the buoyancy of soul—in many traditions soul is the source of movement—how are we to discern its edges as well as the edges of its ever-changing states? Edges it must have if it is to possess a certain identifiability over time. Without the discretion introduced by edges, it would have no identity of its own. These edges are inherent structures—the soul's in-lines as it were—that give to it a certain self-sameness over time, enough at least to be able to refer to a given soul as "yours" versus "mine." In their uniqueness, these edges allow for the differentiation of discrete individual souls.

Our concern in this chapter is not with a general theory of soul, such as Aristotle offers in his treatise *Of Soul*, nor with a typology of souls, as set forth in Jung's *Psychological Types*. We shall focus instead on how human souls come to assume precarious positions: how they come to exist on edge and stay there for the most part. We shall also deal with how some souls decompose or fall apart: in particular, how they split off from themselves. In keeping with these two basic avatars of psychical edges, we shall proceed in two parts: first, being on edge, and second, falling apart.

On a terminological note, I use the terms *soul*, *psyche*, and *self* interchangeably in this chapter. I use the word "mind" gingerly so as to avoid assuming anything like "mental substance." Nuanced differences do exist between all these terms as they have evolved in English, but to spell them out would require an extensive exercise in semantic analysis beyond the scope of this book.

## I

*Being on Edge.* We often speak of "being on edge" and of "being edgy" but rarely reflect on what these expressions really mean. If asked to say what they signify to us, we are likely to respond with something like "being nervous" or "being upset." But these casual phrasings do not tell us why the language of edge is so often employed by speakers of English, much less what kind of edge is at stake. Clearly, these two expressions—and others such as "you're driving me over the edge"—have to do with psychological states that are engendered by demanding or dangerous circumstances.[6] The fact is that we frequently respond to such circumstances by reverting to locutions that employ the language of "edge."

This is not to deny that there are other ways of feeling ourselves on the edge that are not psychological in any usual sense of the term. Certain bodily states—for instance, when we feel, after heavy physical labor, that we are reaching the limit of our available energy—are likely to be described as pushing us over our edge. Here it is more a matter of exhausting our physical energy than of a particular subjective psychological state: our mind can be daydreaming even as our body is straining our endurance at the level of muscle and sinew. In gymnastic exercise, a rule of thumb is that one can push one's body very far—farther than one might first imagine—but should regard any acutely felt pain as an edge not to be tolerated: one must back down from that edge. As in yoga, one is encouraged to go up to one's edge but not to exceed it.[7]

In all such instances of body-at-the-edge states, we are dealing with a sense of edge that is something not to be surpassed, or to be surpassed only at risk. Despite its variability over time, at a given moment such a sense has enough structure and force to allow us to say that we are *at our edge* or nearing it—nearing the point where ease of movement is no longer available to us. Whatever the physical determinants of the experience, being on edge in such situations is something we experience psychically: we *feel how it feels* to get to such edges.

Another way in which we come to feel on edge is found in circumstances of pointed social pressure, as when I am asked by others to perform something in a certain highly skilled way: "Recite the Gettysburg address," my friend might taunt, knowing that I could do this once—but that was twenty-five years ago. Very often, the kind of social urgency that leads us to an uncomfortable edge is found in expectations of high-level activity, as when I am asked to "outdo" myself, which means in effect to go beyond previous levels of achievement, each of which carries its own edge with it. Closely related to this is the sense of being pushed to the breaking point, "forced to the wall," or else, more mildly, "put on the spot" by what others ask of us.

Whatever its somatic or social basis, being on edge usually brings with it a psychical dimension. Take, for example, voter registration practices in several southern states of the United States. Heightened requirements for registration—showing a driver's license, having to answer trick questions—and limiting the hours for voting to times when voters are likely to be working establish a barrier to efficient and easy registration and voting. The barrier is at once physical (poll doors that are locked early), social (reflecting a regional culture of resistance to African-American enfranchisement in the South), and political (since the requirements frequently stem from legislative decisions that are determined by party politics). But taken together, they are likely to engender sharp edges of anger and frustration and of an intense sense of injustice on the part of citizens who are caught up in the vortex of such overtly prejudicial practices. These edges are experienced by those who are disadvantaged or discriminated against as acutely painful; they are primarily psychical edges.

But wait! "Psychical edges": what can these be? Are not all edges *physical*, or modeled on physical ones? Or at the very least external to the self, if we include the edges inherent in social practices (as with voting registration procedures). We reach here a crux in our examination of edges. The question becomes whether there *are* specifically psychical edges—edges of states of mind, of moods, of feelings, of thoughts. Do they really exist? I maintain that psychical edges are perfectly real and an integral part of ongoing human (and doubtless animal) life. Indeed, a comprehensive study of edges cannot avoid a discussion of psychical edges, given that most of the existing rhetoric of being on edge bears on psychological states. I refer to these states as "psychological" insofar as they occur to human beings and other animal beings who have cognitive powers of anticipation and reflection as well as a range of feelings and emotions. These powers and affective states are implicated in the apprehension of edges of many things and places and events in our immediate environments. But they have their own edges:

specifically psychical ones. More generally, if we take "psyche" to connote such things as consciousness, memory, the emotional realm, and certain preconscious and unconscious states, *the psyche has edges.*

You may ask, but how can edges belong to something as seemingly amorphous and fluid as a psychological state? This book has often discussed the edges of physical objects—buildings, bodies, and landscapes—each having its own distinctive character and pattern of presentation. We have not paused to ask ourselves if this range of leading examples does not amount to an undue constriction of focus. Already in moving to edges of events, we expanded the range of edges in an importantly different direction. In the afterward/forward to this book, I discuss thinking on the edge—another departure from a physicalistic paradigm, and one that takes us squarely into the realm of psyche itself.

Ordinary language offers a crucial clue: in speaking so often, and so concertedly, about being "on edge" in a nonliteral sense, is not ordinary English indicating that edges indeed belong to the psyche in its conscious and also less-than-fully-conscious states? However tempting it is to regard exemplary cases of having an edge as physical, this does not preclude the possibility of genuinely psychical edges—that is, edges that belong to soul (thought, memory, emotion) in their own right. And more than just the possibility! Psychical edges are altogether actual insofar as they are *felt*—felt by us directly. When we are on edge psychically, we know this with special poignancy. We have come into this state and are stringently *in* it; it is not just one psychic reality among others, it is now *our* psychic reality. (This is so even if the state itself is so fleeting that we can snap out of it at any moment.) Just here we reach a first basic aspect of psychical edges: their actuality is such that we *know them from within*—from inside our own experience. They belong to that experience as integral parts of it: we are in touch with these edges, we know them, in a uniquely first-person way. They belong to our psyche as having its own edges and constitute this psyche as something singular; such edges harbor and present the many states of mind (emotions, feelings, memories, and thoughts) that makes this same psyche the unique being that it is.

This edge situation stands in contrast with that which obtains in the world around us: the edges of tables and chairs, cities and landscapes. All these latter display edges that are experienced as outside us, whether far distant from us (the horizon of a landscape), in the middle distance (that building over there), or just immediately beyond (say, the edges of our shoes or the glasses on our nose). We reach out to them with our vision and sometimes with our touch and hearing. With the interior edges of psychological states, however, there is no such reaching outward—nor even reaching inward, since they are always already part of our ongoing stream of experience.

In the rest of this first section, I explore the presence of psychical edges in everyday conscious states of being on edge, states that are perspicuous in their phenomenal appearance. These can be uneven and troubling, but they are not disabling or deeply disturbing. For the most part, we endure them as a matter of course. Sometimes we even expect them and prepare for them: "having that conversation with her is going to be very difficult," we say to ourselves as we prepare for a talk that bears on our future as a couple. In saying this, we feel apprehensive about a situation that we fear will set us both on edge. Indeed, we are *already on edge about becoming more intensely on edge*: being on edge can compound itself. But this need not immobilize us altogether. We sense that we are able to draw back from being on edge somehow, later if not sooner. (When we are implicated in psychical states from which there is no such easy retreat or no retreat at all, we encounter a quite different phenomenon: falling apart, when the psychical edges are split apart from each other. These are explored in the next section).

Let us consider four basic aspects of situations in which we find ourselves in the state of being on edge.

*Temporality.* If we regard psyche as reflective of its original sense as breath and life, it follows that its edges as well as its constituent states are radically temporal in character. They are part of lived duration, in Bergson's sense of the stream of ongoing becoming, animated by "the fluid mass of our whole psychical existence."[8] Within this mass are phases and processes that have their own edges as events inhering in that stream. The edges of things and places are primarily spatial, being situated *out there*, on the other side of our own body—which is itself spatially specified for the most part. This is so even though this body, along with things and places and events, also possesses temporal characteristics, with the result that any full description of these four items is spatiotemporal. This bivalence does not obtain, however, for internal states: this was Bergson's (as well as James's and Husserl's) point about the peculiarity of psychic being, which gives itself to us in intensively and exclusively temporal terms. It follows that any edges that appear there will be ineluctably temporal: none will persist indefinitely between states of consciousness, as they might were they spatial in character. Even if these states do overlap and permeate each other in patterns that recur (in repetitive thoughts or habitual trends of feeling or thinking), there is nothing in such states like the "object permanence" that Aristotle, Kant, and Piaget all ascribe to spatial objects.

It is important to realize that my very claim that edges are integral to both psyche and its experiential stream suggests that there is something in the psychical realm of sufficient consistency to yield structures that can meaningfully be called edges. And if this realm is indeed edge-specific, it further implies that there can be no altogether monocentric self wrapped up in itself to a point of being altogether private. If the self extends to its very edges—to the peripheries of its being—it will be exposed to whatever surrounds it and will be responsive to it. Even as internally cohesive and complex, it will be a self continually edging outside itself.

At the same time, the edge-extended psyche has experiences that are so radically transient that they continually alter their configuration: what is apperceived in one mental glance vanishes by the time we get to a second such glance—in contrast with the comparative stability of things and places and other human bodies in our local environment. We can keep looking and relooking at the latter, seeing ever new aspects of overt edge structures that we count on remaining largely the same over a given stretch of time. Psychic states and their edges, in contrast, are always altering, whether by becoming other to themselves or merging with other states and their edges in the same stream of consciousness. As Bergson phrases it, "The truth is that we change without ceasing, and that the state [of consciousness] itself is nothing but change."[9] Just as our psychical being is one of continual becoming, any edges it may possess are rarely consolidated into anything lastingly the same.[10] The edges of and in my temporal stream do not act to close off or to define, much less to terminate (except at death, when time and life cease simultaneously). Parallel to edges in music, they unfold continuously. As soon as I attempt to locate a single edge in my consciousness of time (say, by trying to synchronize it with a clock) this effort itself has already transitioned into another phase of my temporal stream, folding into that succeeding phase, indeed *becoming* that phase. All such phases "continue each other in an endless flow."[11] But these phases will have their own newly generated edges.

*Mineness.* Such deep temporality does not mean that psychical edges lack all identifying characteristics. They are experienced as *my* edges, the edges of my mental states, both cognitive and affective. Indeed, they are altogether mine, in the strong sense of *jemeinig* that Heidegger posits as essential to human *Dasein*: "Because Dasein has *in each case mineness [Jemeinigkeit]*, one must always use a *personal* pronoun when one addresses it: 'I am,' 'you are.'"[12] Such radical mineness inheres in all my conscious psychic states and is at one with their livingness. Its lack, as we shall see later on, is symptomatic of a deeply disturbed self. Yet, as Heidegger employs the term, mineness itself lacks its own distinct edges. It is not useful in distinguishing your stream of time from mine; it is an ongoing rider on this stream that is not reducible to a single characteristic of my personal self. I share it with you, since you also undergo your ongoing experience as what you also forcibly call "mine." Such pure mineness fails to capture what is peculiar to my own psychical experience. "Mine" in Heidegger's usage is a purely claimative word that assures me only that the stream of consciousness is my own, but it does not serve to tell me what such mineness feels like in my own case—that is, what its edges are.

The fact is that my psyche as I experience it consistently possesses its own unique edges. I know what it feels like to be this unique person I call "me" (and others call "Ed Casey") even if the descriptive adjectives are slow in coming: "nervous" (about too many things), "alert" (in a very particular way), "hopeful" and "curious" (regarding what is coming next), and so on. These adjectives help to define the very edges of my personal being, my idiosyncratic self; they are the discernible marks of my being-a-self who is always and only unique. Such edge-marks inhere in my own psychical being and are experienced from within—that is, from within my prereflective and reflective conscious states. They differ from the edges of whatever I experience by means of this same self: not only the edges of other human beings, and of chairs and trees, but also the evanescing edges of the very temporal stream in which I inhere.

*Beginning and ending.* An important class of internal psychical edges is found where my psychic states—affective as well as cognitive—emerge and then come to an end, whether abruptly or in a slow phasing out. Physical edges also begin and end, but they do so in more or less definitive ways, with rare exceptions, such as fog banks. The edges of my psychical states are never altogether definitive, since they are engaged in the process of becoming the edges of other psychical states, shape-shifting all the time: think of the way one mood gives way to another, say, the indeterminate edges of my melancholy shading into despair without any abrupt break in between. One already indeterminate mood shifts to another in a continuous development that is not easily divisible into anything like a punctuated "before" and "after." The scene of psychic being at this level is highly protean, and so are its edges as they melt and merge in the continual succession that is the most basic trait of what Husserl calls "absolute flux."[13] (Exceptions occur in cases of sudden surprise or trauma: we shall return to these below.)

*Outer vs. inner edges.* Despite the melting and merging, the edges of such shifting states remain discernible. Even if they do not have definitive parameters, they are experienced as such, being noticed if not named. Here we need to enter into a closer discernment, difficult as this is to do in a circumstance in which the vague prevails over the determinate, the uncertain over the certain, the less than definitely known over the precisely perceived. This very imbroglio is itself a major trait of psychical life, which rarely possesses the clarity and distinctness that Descartes considered an epistemic ideal for the ideas by which we think. But we can certainly distinguish between outer and inner edges of our psychical life, just as we did for the lived body, despite all the differences between the two cases. These are not the edges of psyche itself but rather the edges of what and how we experience psychically. The two kinds of psychical edges, outer and inner, are at once exclusive and exhaustive: independent of each other in principle, together they compose the inscape of psychical life.

(1) *Outer psychical edges* are experienced when we find this life
     to be extended, especially when stretched to the breaking
     point. A signal of such psychical extension is the experience
     of something like a ring around our current psychological life.

This ring may be sensed as tight or loose, with many variations in between. When such an outer ring is drawn tight, we feel constrained: forced, set upon, subject to undue pressure, as when our patience is stretched to the limit. In that case we sense that we cannot continue as before: we have reached a felt limit of our psychological powers beyond which we cannot go—an edge that is literally *non plus ultra*. But outer psychical edges are also felt when I am cruising through life, taking in things casually and without effort. I then experience myself as a single ongoing receptive self. Any sense of a containing ring is dissolved as I sense myself moving easily between one situation and the next.

(2) *Inner psychical edges* are subtle structures that act to give to our inner being its own intrinsic contours. Instead of acting from the periphery of the psyche, these edges serve to structure psychic life from within. They are the filaments of this life, its infrastructures as these are felt to be present in ongoing experience. They present themselves as being always already part of this life—an *integral* part, with emphasis on the prefix *in-*. Not only do they belong *to* the psyche, they belong *in* it. They are the very structures of psychical interiority. Inner edges in this sense belong to the experiential stream I have discussed in terms of its ongoing temporal flow. They are immanent presences within that stream, self-inherent parts or moments of it and not detachable from it as disjointed pieces. They range from subtle changes of emotion to the characteristic ways in which I "face the world" every day—whether hopefully or with a despairing sense. These latter are usually considered mere "attitudes," but along with more nuanced affective shifts they are formative factors in my psychic life. They give to this life, otherwise a sheer flux of becoming, a singular shape, constituting it as specifically my own (and not just "mine" in the formal sense underlined by Heidegger).

Even short of the self-alienating states that I shall address in the next section, my psyche presents itself as diversified from within thanks to the presence of inner edges that both complicate and enrich my consciousness of an ongoing self-identity. This identity is not a permanent possession, nor is it analogous to a single trait we can know as such. What we blithely call *self-consciousness* does not entail anything like the sheer positing of a simple object of which we are conscious in a fully transparent way. Contrary to Descartes's claim that the *cogito* is the expression of one and the same thinking substance, my own consciousness is fissured from within by its own inner edges. My psychic being—my very mind or soul—consists in a congeries of inner edges that install difference in the very core of self-sameness. I may not yet be divided against myself in outright self-opposition, nor yet have fallen apart. But I am not the single unitary self that I like to think I am when I say that *I am I* or that *my psyche is mine*. Both the "I" and the psyche in these apparent tautologies are gently undone, self-sundered, by their own complex combinations of feeling and thinking, imagining and remembering, crisscrossed by the psychical equivalents of rills and creases in the physical world.

It is significant that there is no specific vocabulary for these subtle substructures in western European languages. But each of us is familiar with their internal topography: the contours and rhythms of changing psychical states. These states have their own edges. These are the edges of acts of feeling in a contrary mood, remembering something pleasant, imagining the possible, or thinking new thoughts. Each of these acts is further specified by its own mode of intentionality, whereby all acts of consciousness are distinguishable from their contents. I can feel from within the edge of the difference between any such act and what it is directed toward, its own psychical content.[14]

Every circumstance of self-differing brings edges with it, as is already the case with a tear in my shirt that leaves visible edges in its wake. In the case of psychic self-sundering the edges can be difficult to discern: transitory, often ambiguous, and even self-effacing. But they are no less formative of the sense of self that emerges from their delicate destiny: a psychical history whose closest analogue may be "writing on water," that is, the tracing of shapes that vanish almost as soon as they appear. But the inner edges etched in psychical life, however elusive and evanescent they may be, are essential to this life itself. The fabric of my inner life is woven from self-differentiating edges in continual concatenation. The traces of these edges constitute me as other to myself within myself: not divisively so but in intimate interweavings that defy any direct intuition of *who I am* or any claim that my mineness is a given property.

From this discussion of inner edges it becomes evident that my psyche or soul possesses its own distinctive edges. Rather than being a "sphere of pure immanence" (Husserl) in which edges have no place or point, edges of various sorts permeate psychical life from one end to the other—and from one moment to the next. The conscious psyche is not comparable to a perfect diamond in which there are no fracture lines, no internal flaws. Psychical life, yours as well as mine, comes always already differentiated into manifold edge-structures. These edges are felt internally even if they are not visible in ordinary perception or action (though their effects may well be evident in these). To be invisible is not the same as not to exist: to believe otherwise is to subscribe to an uncritical ocularcentrism.

It ensues that the psyche not only exhibits edges—inner as well as outer—but is composed from their complicated concurrence, in psychic states of many sorts, in feeling as well as in thought, indeed in consciousness itself. To exist psychically means being subject to all these edges and structured by them from within. It is not surprising that human beings are so rarely fully equanimous or lastingly tranquil. They are living in and from a psychical domain that is edge-ridden at every juncture. Despite their subtlety and sinuousness, psychical edges make up an edge-domain that is every bit as complex and demanding as the edge-world of things and places and events. If I started in this book with a description of the latter, this was only in recognition of the fact that this is where most thinking about edges begins—and ends. These literally outstanding edges belong to what Husserl called the "natural attitude," which favors the externalism of the fact-world (*die Tatsachenwelt*). But any complete account of edges must recognize and pursue the edges pertaining to our psychic being: those internal to its ongoing life as well as those at its periphery. The very idea of *being on edge* implies a psychical state that can take many specific forms and that always has both inner and outer edges. Unlike thinking on the edge—a reflective venture—being on edge is a matter of direct immersion in our psychical interiority with its plethora of edges of several sorts while managing to stay intact as an integral self. It is at all times a delicate balance.

When this balance is upset, the psyche can fall apart. We must now explore two of the most significant ways by which the human psyche is broken asunder into quite specific forms, often routinely classified as pathological, and which manifest deep proclivities of splitting on the psyche's part. These fragmentations of the self exhibit quite another dimension of psychical edges—a troubling but immensely revealing one.

## II

*Falling Apart.* Sometimes we can best grasp the edges of soul, paradoxically, by examining its very breakdown: its shaking and shattering, its falling apart and falling away from itself. In order to show how this is so, I here trace a trajectory that goes from acrophobic shaking at the edge of a high precipice to experiences of being shaken up and shattering. My analysis of this new direction will proceed from passing moments of psychical destabilization to entrenched conditions conventionally labeled "schizoid" and "schizophrenic."

Shaking at the edge offers a first glimpse into the experience of falling apart. Let me give a personal example. When I finally managed to climb to the top of a high ridge in the Crazy Mountains in Montana, I suddenly found myself staring into a vast abyss straight down before me at least a thousand feet below. Immediately upon taking in this unexpected vista, I started trembling outright, realizing how easily I could fall into the dizzying depth. Caught up in a state of vertigo, I was literally shaking on the edge. In a case like this, the split was between my petrified body and the space opening up below me so precipitously. I was in effect *divided from without*. My body, usually the agent of agile mobility, was set over against the deep space into which it could fall with a single misstep. I was riven apart by the fearful prospect at my feet: I found myself in an utterly alien situation, shaking at the edge of an abyss that threatened to engulf me. Even if the circumstances were manifestly physical (the prospect was starkly visual and it was my physical body that trembled), my acrophobic anxiety was a psychical state: both dimensions of my personal being were afflicted.

This archetypal circumstance of vertigo contrasts with circumstances in which I am split *from within*. These latter experiences have in turn two modalities: being split from within my body and being split within my mind. The first occurs when we experience intense internal pain in the form of nausea or heartburn. The pain separates my body from myself: it is as if it were a foreign object even as I know that it belongs to me. We seem never to be altogether prepared for the resulting distress. If we do not literally shake, as I did on that high ridge in Montana, we may experience an internal shudder that is the subjective equivalent of the overt trembling that occurred on that high ridge. While my physical shaking at the high ridge was observable by anyone standing near me, the inner shudder at my own bodily pain may not be visible to others even though it is felt intensely by myself, and felt as foreign to me. Some part of my body has become alien to me, split off from a coherent and unitary sense of self.

But my psyche can also become split from itself. I shall approach this in a series of three steps.

(1)   In psychical splitting, part of my psyche (my "mind" or "soul") becomes alien to other parts: set apart from them and experienced as alien, sometimes as an oppositional force. This is easiest to see in cases in which in a moment of indecision we find ourselves suspended between two equally attractive or repulsive possibilities. As we say revealingly, we are "of two minds" about what to do. Each alternative appears to be equally valid and there seems to be no greater reason to prefer one over the other. The question might be, should the assistant professors in one's department be encouraged to vote on a controversial matter? On the one hand, they should certainly be encouraged to express themselves; on the other hand, doing so

might endanger their chances of promotion if they vote against what the Dean is recommending and their identity becomes known. In this example the splitting is between two analytically isolatable directions, and familiar criteria of precedent, commonsensical judgment, and reasoning power are likely to help resolve the situation.

Something more difficult happens when I am *divided against myself* in ways from which no previous experience or sound judgment rescues me. I find one part of myself directly at odds with another. I am a split self. The most striking such circumstance is that of multiple personality, in which "I" am actively dissociated into several selves. These selves all count as *myself*, yet they are not in communication with each other; I am in communication with them only in sequential monologues.[15] In this case I am not conscious of the splitting of my self as such: each separate self is autonomous.

Different still is a situation in which I am suddenly subjected to an unanticipated psychical state; for instance, when I am overcome by uncontrollable grief upon learning of the death of someone close to me. I acutely feel the difference between my former untroubled state and the onset of grief upon learning of my friend's death. Yesterday, everything seemed to be going fine; today, learning of this death, things are very different. Between the two states there is a gulf, which is experienced as a poignantly felt edge of difference between two states of myself.

This circumstance is not the same as that of a mourning that has never been adequately expressed. In such a case as this, I experience inside myself a heavy zone that bogs me down—an internal, intangible gravitas—against which I find myself helpless. This psychical state has no proper name even if it was engendered by the demise of someone I loved. It is felt as a recalcitrant psychical mass that depresses me: literally "presses me down." Its presence is insistent yet does not emerge as a distinct object. For years I may bear this inner burden in melancholy moods, dark thoughts, and a general state of hopelessness. Only if it is "worked through" (in Freud's term) do I find myself relieved of its downward pull.[16] Before that, I am *beside myself* without always knowing why. I have been split off from my former untroubled self without noticing the process of splitting itself. Along with the example of multiple personality,

this situation illustrates that psychical splitting need not be
explicitly conscious for it to be potently present in psychical
life.[17]

(2)  The plot thickens when I am torn apart in circumstances where
I find myself caught up in obsessive-compulsive behavior whose
unremitting hold upon me puzzles me as much as those around
me. The object of my obsession may be fully conscious to me,
yet the grip of the obsession itself is beyond conscious control.
Typical instances include a cleaning compulsion or an idée fixe.
The obsession takes the form of being compelled to render a
house or room "squeaky clean" by active bodily movements,
accompanied by a strong belief that this is the right thing to
do. There is a strong commitment to purity that is at once
monothetic and unattainable in a complete state: "purity of
heart is to will *one* thing," wrote Kierkegaard.[18] In the case of
cleaning, the ideal is to bring about a dust-free and germ-free
local environment: a singularly clean room or house. The idée
fixe is likewise a singular thought—just *this* thought and no
other: "pure, never pure enough!"—as we also see in the case
of a fixated ideological commitment. Neither goal is strictly
attainable, as dust and germs continually accumulate and one's
commitment to a certain idea is subject to compromise by
the incursion of alternative ideas that act to complicate the
commitment one has made.

When in the grip of an obsessive frame of mind, I find
myself *compelled* to clean the house or to affirm a certain idea:
hence the common diagnostic term "obsessive-*compulsive*." My
conscious mind is taken up entirely with the content of the
obsession and engaging in whatever activities help to attain it.
Despite this intense absorption, there is splitting going on here.
My obsession with cleanliness or with an idée fixe tears me
asunder into two alien psychical states that possess different aims
and pleasures and styles of conduct. When I am not obsessing, I
can be a comparatively relaxed and satisfied person. But once the
obsession seizes hold of me, I am transformed: all my psychical
and physical energies go into acting out what I am convinced
I must do or must be even as I may be conscious that my
dedication to the task is excessive.

Each form of psychical splitting just discussed possesses
its own characteristic edges. If one has multiple personality

disorder, oneself is several selves, each with a discrete edge that bars meaningful intercourse between them. When I am overcome with a sudden grief, I am afflicted with a sharp edge of despair at the thought that my friend will never return. If my mourning for someone is delayed and drawn out, I will experience the blunt edge of an unacknowledged and undigested psychical mass that weighs me down until it is clarified by being worked through. When in the grip of an obsession, I enter into another way of being in the world in which demanding edges of devotion and duty require my absolute attention. All these edges, different as they are, accrue to psyches that have been split apart. Like Humpty Dumpty, my psychic being has been fragmented into pieces that cannot easily be put back together, for *the edges of these pieces do not mesh*; they do not cohere. I have been disassembled into a loose collection of ill-fitting parts, each with its own set of edges. My psyche has been riven apart, not just complicated as in being on edge. Just as those suffering from such splitting did not choose to enter into such unhappy states, so they cannot choose to be freed of them by an act of sheer will.

(3) Such self-splitting can be still more severe. It may take on a life of its own that resists change of any significant sort. Prominent among such psychical states are those conventionally designated as *schizoid* and *schizophrenic*—diagnostic terms whose common root in *schiz-* means "severed" or "split." I shall now discuss these two "abnormal" conditions in sequence, followed by a section on the true versus the false self. Throughout, I shall focus on the edge dimensions of falling apart in these particular ways rather than on the pathology as such.[19] It is as if the human psyche has a certain proclivity for falling apart and in particular for self-splitting in ways that come to be named and treated as pathological syndromes.

*The schizoid self.* George Eliot spoke of the "gusts and storms" of our inner life. She pointed out that "there is a great deal of unmapped country within us" that we have to account for in understanding extreme psychological states.[20] A major unmapped area is that of the split self. This form of diremptive self-being exhibits a stubbornly recurrent pattern of thought/emotion/behavior in which the human psyche has been torn apart, usually from early childhood. The split is so entrenched that intervention by others, including psychotherapists, is often futile. In this case the falling apart has become an entrenched feature of the life of the psyche and is not precipitated by a single event, such as the death of a family member.

Technically, we are talking of "the schizoid personality." Taking its initial inspiration from the work of Melanie Klein (who posited an early "schizoid position" in the life of the infant), the syndrome was refined in the hands of practitioner-theorists such as W. R. D. Fairbairn, D. W. Winnicott, and Harry Guntrip, all members of the British school of "object relations" that flourished in the wake of World War II. These figures shared the conviction that the primary base of a serious schizoid condition is a disturbance in a person's relationships with other humans (parents, siblings, close friends, and lovers) rather than a deviation or fixation in drive development, as Freud had speculated in earlier decades.[21] As Guntrip put it, "The schizoid condition consists in the first place in an attempt to cancel external object-relations and live in a detached and withdrawn way. . . . The more people cut themselves off from human relations in the outer world, the more they are driven back onto emotionally charged fantasied object-relations in their inner mental world. . . . The attitude to the outer world is the same: *non-involvement and observation at a distance without any feeling.*"[22]

In the schizoid state one assumes a stance of indifference toward others as if one were bored or did not care. But this nonchalance conceals another level of psychic being that is seething with emotions such as anxiety and anger. The schizoid posture covers over the fact that one is in fact intensely cathected with other persons, starting with the primary figures of one's early childhood. The affects thereby generated are felt to be intolerable and unsustainable, and to deal with this inferno of excessive emotions, their direct expression is suppressed. The result is that a person with this syndrome lives unhappily suspended between inner and outer realms: "When a schizoid state supervenes, the conscious ego appears to be in a state of suspended animation in between two worlds, internal and external, [with no] no [effective] relationship with either of them."[23] Because of the intensity of the feelings and emotions generated by others—first of all in early childhood—an interpersonal quarantine is in effect declared: early and later others are kept at a distance by a strategy of withdrawal and of refusal to manifest affect.

The basic dynamic is one that Guntrip calls the "in-out" dilemma, whereby I need others for their attention and support yet am unable to tolerate too much dependency on them, powerfully tempting me to retreat into my own inner world.[24] For the schizoid person, this inner world as established in childhood consists mostly of "bad internal objects." One gets caught up in a schizoid double bind by being dependent on these bad or hurtful figures for love and basic support, while also having to take distance from them in order to survive as an intact self.[25] These problematic others make up my "unconscious, inner, and purely psychic reality,"[26] to which the schizoid self remains deeply attached despite strong ambivalence toward it. In effect, the schizoid person continues to be immersed in this inner world, which is intensely cathected with introverted psychic energy, however much the conscious ego tries to strike a pose of independence from it.[27]

In the schizoid condition, one never wholly escapes from one's inner world, even when departing from it in occasional forays into relationship or when coaxed out in psychotherapy. No sooner does the schizoid self reach out to a new person or a therapist than he or she is likely to retreat to the inner sanctum of difficult but unavoidable figures from childhood. As one agoraphobic schizoid personality put it when she was in the midst of a crowd of shoppers, "I suddenly feel a lack of contact with everybody and everything around and I feel I'm disappearing in the midst of everything"[28]—thereby slipping into her readily available schizoid shell.[29]

In short, "however much the schizoid person tries to make contacts she is also always withdrawing."[30] Such maneuvers are not limited to those with disabling schizoid symptoms; diluted character traits of a schizoid sort are common in late modern society in experiences of anomie, intense social loneliness, and (especially prevalent among academics) intellectual aloofness.[31] In all these conditions we find a conspicuous inability to initiate or maintain satisfying relations with others, accompanied by a retreat into a world of self-absorbed inner edges. Whether occurring in debilitating extremity or in milder forms, the schizoid condition is a concrete manifestation of what Freud designated as "ego-splitting." In his *Outline of Psychoanalysis*, he wrote, "The weak and immature ego of the first phase of childhood is permanently damaged by the strain put upon it in the effort to ward off the dangers that are peculiar to that period of life. . . . The view which postulates that in all psychoses there is a *split in the ego* could not demand so much notice, if it were not for the fact that it turns out to apply also to other conditions more like the neuroses and finally, to the neuroses themselves."[32] Freud is here suggesting that the "permanently damaged" infantile ego, an ego that is split off from the mature self, underlies many neurotic as well as psychotic conditions.[33]

What can this key phrase, "a *split in the ego*" signify? What is the character of the self such that it can be disunited from itself to the point of becoming split? And in particular, what kind of edges are at stake in such splitting? Drawing on the foundational work of Freud, Fairbairn, and Guntrip,[34] we may infer that the internal figures of the schizoid's inner world possess edges sufficiently definite and lasting to allow them to persist inside the psyche as recognizable presences. These edges occur as the corrosive impingements that troublesome figures in childhood made upon the vulnerable infantile psyche. The same damaging edges of early impingement provide the basis for later relationships with external figures who resemble these figures (like "father figures," for example, where a *figure*, inner or outer, is defined by its characteristic edges). More generally, the adult schizoid person has considerable difficulty entering into the vicissitudes of involvement with others, thanks to the abiding presence of this person's deeply conflicted inner world. Hence the characteristic position of the schizoid as someone who vacillates between being attracted to the enticements of the outer world and beating a rapid retreat to a fixed world within.

One set of inner psychic edges begets another. Given the quasi-permanence of inner objects, it is not surprising that Guntrip can refer to "living in an internal world"[35] as in a domain with its own stability. More completely considered, edges in this domain belong not only to individual internal figures—structuring the edges of these figures—but also to the periphery of the whole inner world that these figures coconstitute. Both kinds of edge are examples of what I earlier designated as "inner psychical edges." In the case of the schizoid personality such edges have become part of an entrenched pathogenic process.

Abiding as such interior psychical edges may be, they are not fixed forever. They can change their configuration over time: most notably, in the course of a formative and healing relationship with a new person or with a skillful psychotherapist. Such a relationship may not be able to remove all the baleful effects of problematic childhood figures, but it can loosen their stranglehold upon the psychic state of the subject to whom they cling.

*The schizophrenic self.* Schizophrenia is another way by which the self (psyche or soul) falls apart and splits. Indeed, it is characteristic to claim it as a form of "intrapsychic splitting,"[36] yet one that is more entrenched and devastating than that occurring in the schizoid self. Hegel, whose sister was likely to have been schizophrenic, may have had such radical splitting in mind when he wrote (as in the epigraph to this chapter), "Ich bin ein Zwiefaches in mir" (I am twofold within myself).[37] Hegel here poses the question: What if I am split into two parts so radically different that they cannot easily be reconciled with one another, if ever?

The redoubling of the psyche in schizophrenia is complex and very difficult to endure; a "cure" for it has never been found. Interpreted in ancient times as demonic or divine possession, the splitting with which its very name is associated (*schizophrenia* means literally "split mind") drew increasing attention in nineteenth-century psychiatry in the West. Eugen Bleuler coined the term in 1908 to designate a special dynamic within the more general diagnosis of dementia praecox. Schizophrenia in Bleuler's view is "fundamentally nothing else than the splitting off of the unconscious; unconscious complexes can transform themselves into . . . secondary personalities by taking over so large a part of the original personality that they represent an entirely new personality."[38]

Since this inaugural moment of being named as such, schizophrenia has been generally interpreted as a "psychosis" or severe mental disease, and its etiology has been considered variously as genetically predetermined, as due to a "schizophrenogenic mother," or as resulting from an insufferable double bind in early communications. The fact is that schizophrenia has evaded any fully convincing explanation, leading some to question whether it is a single syndrome or instead a group of loosely associated symptomatologies. I shall not enter into this ongoing debate; instead, I will single out only those aspects that bear on psychical splitting and thus on psychical edges.

At the very least, schizophrenia can be considered as bringing together two paradoxes in the life of the psyche. The first paradox is easiest to grasp. On the one hand, it is interpreted as "loss of vital contact with reality" in Eugène Minkowski's formulation; that is to say, as a falling out of touch with the real world, implying a retreat or withdrawal into a devitalized region of the psyche. On the other hand, it is characterized by insistent hallucinatory presences—typically in the form of voices—that dictate what one should do or not do, sometimes including violent actions. One form of reality—consensual, shared, social—gives way to another that is radically closed and private, one that it is tempting to label as "unreal" (that is, which does not meet the criteria of spatiotemporal objectivity or interpersonal consensus). From the standpoint of the self here at stake it is difficult to explain why this loss of shared world should ever take place: are not the demands of ordinary perceptual and social reality sufficiently challenging and (when successful) satisfying to preoccupy us entirely? Why does the psyche abandon the "reality principle" (Freud) for overtly hallucinatory unreality, especially when this latter can be so threatening in its content, and all the more so when projected onto the very world from which retreat has been taken? Put differently, why does the psyche replace the reassuring edges of the real with the unsettled and unsettling edges of hallucinatory presences?

I am not implying that any of this is chosen or willed (a question to which we shall return below), but it does happen and it may well have a biogenetic and neurological basis. We can wonder *why* this happens, especially when it does not make sense: why tolerate, much less create, such self-destructive (and sometimes other-destructive) hallucinatory voices? But the schizophrenic herself does not have the liberty to ask such questions, given how caught up in her experience she is likely to be.

A second paradox arises from the combination of impenetrable with penetrable edges in the schizophrenic condition. At first glance, one would think that in view of the severity of this condition, the schizophrenic has withdrawn behind the very hard edges of what Bruno Bettelheim labelled "the inner fortress." His or her highly idiosyncratic behavior, often resulting in virtual unapproachability, certainly cuts the schizophrenic off from ongoing open communication with others, leading to extreme social isolation that lands the afflicted person in a mental institution or to becoming a homeless person on the street. But a closer look reveals another feature of schizophrenic experience: "interpenetration" (*Interpenetranz*), Wolfgang Blankenburg's term for a circumstance in which others (real or hallucinatory) are felt to invade one's personal space all too easily, or conversely a situation in which one considers oneself able to enter their space and to influence their lives in uninvited and untoward ways.

Blankenburg discusses interpenetration in a classical article titled "The Psychopathology of Schizophrenic Self-Experiences," in which he conceives of schizophrenia as primarily a disorder of one's *Meinhaftigkeit*—ability to act on one's own behalf. In those not afflicted by schizophrenia this ability allows for agency and passivity to come together so as to take effective action in relation to others. In schizophrenics, the sphere of one's ownness in relation to that of others is especially troubled. On the one hand, my *Eigensphere* (Husserl's term for the domain of my personal being) is invaded by something—a person or a voice—that is felt as forcefully *ausser mir* (outside me). For example, a person might believe that all of his own actions are being performed for him by an unfamiliar outside source— say, a woman whose voice he hallucinates. In this case, his ownness shows itself to be highly porous to captivation by a hallucinated other. On the other hand, the same person may thrust himself unduly into the personal sphere of others. He might be convinced he is reading the minds of others, or directing the drivers of automobiles, or changing the weather. Under extreme circumstances, a schizophrenic patient might even insist that the survival of the world depends on the actions he takes. Moreover, an incursion in one direction (being taken over by others) is often accompanied by an action in the other direction (intruding into others' personal sphere).[39]

Blankenburg designates the first situation as that of *Gemacht-bekommens* ("being beset" or literally "becoming made").[40] In the second situation one believes oneself able to penetrate into the sphere of (real or hallucinatory) others, making a difference in their lives that is not in their purview, much less intended or wished for. Uninvited, one inserts oneself into their experience of feeling or thought in an action of *Machen-Könnens*, that is, "being able to do or make" some difference in how or what they experience. In neither case is the schizophrenic authorized by those with whom he interacts. He is not invited to intervene in what they feel or think, but they are also not invited to enter his experiential stream: they are unwelcome there.

Especially suggestive from the standpoint of edges is the concept of a special border that is traversed in interpenetrability. Blankenburg thinks of the situation of the schizophrenic as a "transgression" (*Überschreitung*) across a border (*Grenze*) between you and me. The transgression takes place on the border between "mine" and "yours." At issue is not only this border but the ways and means by which it is transgressed.[41] As we know from earlier discussion, a border is, or purports to be, an *impermeable edge*. Yet in the case of schizophrenia the border in question is just what is traversed, often without any apparent difficulty. Whereas in ordinary social reality borders are distinct structures that are for the most part recognized and respected, the schizophrenic moves through them as if they did not exist. A schizophrenic woman believed not only that President Obama was present in her room but that she could dance with him whenever she wished. Many of the usual interpersonal borders melted away in this woman's belief system: dancing with a sitting president who appears in her room, but also (on other occasions) claiming that others were out to get her, even if the others and their threat were as imaginary as her fantasy of dancing with Obama. Hence the disconcerting character of schizophrenic behavior that amounts to continual border crossings. Unlike the crossings of international borders by desperate immigrants, however, these crossings are not intentional: the borders in question are not material or political realities but are traversed without design or plan but in accordance with what the schizophrenic fancies or projects in the moment.

The frequent recourse to the language of borders is especially striking in the literature on schizophrenia. K. P. Kisker, for example, has written an entire monograph on this subject in which he employs such terms as *Grenzveränderung* ("alteration of border"), *Grenzverschiebung* ("displacement of border"), *Grenzeinbruch* ("break-in border"), *Grenzrestitution* ("restoration of border"), and so on.[42] Kisker focuses on what he terms "*seelische Grenzen*," that is, psychical borders. It is just here that he and Blankenburg contribute in parallel ways to an edge analysis of schizophrenia. For every border is an edge, and this is so whether we are speaking of a materially massive border wall, such as that now found at La Frontera or in Berlin before 1989, or of social or psychical borders. Unlike the edge of a boundary—which opens onto surrounding spaces—that of a border is, or purports to be, definitive and unambiguous: to be just precisely *this* impassable edge. Such a strict edge is built or posited in order to stop passage over or through it. Yet it can be trespassed or transgressed in one way if not another. This is as true of a psychical as of a physical border.

Regarded in this light, the border-edge in schizophrenia is not that between a closely held inner self and a public self that feigns indifference, as in the schizoid condition. It is instead a special kind of edge, one that is at once absolute *and* trespassable. It is absolute in that the schizophrenic subject, however complex her or his psychical makeup may be, remains one subject—in contrast with multiple personality syndrome, in which one's very identity is literally confused, being shared out among several selves who coinhabit the same person. But it is trespassable as subject to the two-way interpenetration discussed by Blankenberg. It is both fiercely intact and quickly traversed or traversible.

Given all this, we must decisively ask, just where is the split in schizophrenia? Where is the critical pathogenic edge located? Clearly, this split is not anything so simple as that between inner and outer self, or self and other; each of these dyads becomes immensely complicated as they figure into schizophrenic syndromes and symptoms. The locus of the splitting at stake, I would propose, is a radical and intransigent split between voluntary and involuntary action. A nonschizophrenic person may well influence others: a teacher her pupils (by embodying exemplary attitudes toward learning), a therapist his patients (by adroit handling of transference), a politician her constituents (whether by truthful speech or by obfuscation and falsehoods), and so on. In these circumstances of social influence, there is a strong element of the voluntary: a wish to have a desired effect on others (students, patients, political constituents) and a willingness to be influenced in turn by these same others. These active and receptive modes of voluntarism are not merely occasional but are consistently enacted over time.

Starkly different is the experience of the schizophrenic subject, who finds himself suddenly invaded and overwhelmed by threatening forces and who also believes he can influence others' behavior at his whim, on his own schedule, thereby becoming what Victor Tausk called "an influencing machine."[43] In neither case is there a considered choice to render oneself highly vulnerable to influence or to be massively influential. These involuntary episodes supervene upon the subject, who is taken over by a spell of voices or disruptive thoughts, precipitating bizarre behavior. Hallucinations, delusions, and untoward bodily behaviors are outside of the schizophrenic subject's conscious control and come to dominate significant stretches of the subject's life. There is a split between what can still be done voluntarily (attending to daily matters like dressing, brushing one's teeth, for example) and various forms of hallucinatory domination or subjection that occur in unwilled ways.[44] Schizophrenics are split off from the domain of voluntary self-guidance and situated in the zone of the involuntary, where their presence to others can be very demanding and difficult to deal with. Indeed, their presence to themselves is often deeply disturbing as well.

Schizophrenic splitting is more radical than the splitting that characterizes obsessional episodes, from which the subject retains a capacity to draw back with some degree of volition. The edge for the obsessive subject—that between voluntary and involuntary—is found in that dimension of the psyche which concerns itself with behavior and ideation, including activities of intending and planning. These activities are debilitated by the schizophrenic's condition of being overwhelmed by what is not intended or chosen in any coherently identifiable manner. The schizophrenic is not able, by sheer acts of will, to suppress certain ideas, emotions, or behavior that occur during periods of intense affliction, or to redirect his conduct, ideation, or emotion in the accessible ways that those unafflicted with the condition possess. In effect, the schizophrenic subject is consigned, or consigns himself, to a life in which the involuntary plays a disproportionate role and dominates thought, emotion, and behavior in ways and at times over which this subject has little or no effective control.[45]

*True versus false self.* Despite the complexities we have addressed in the case of the schizoid and the schizophrenic self, we have not yet fully answered the very basic question, what is it to split up an otherwise unified self and what kind of edges result from this action? Rather than continuing to focus on highly pathologized schizoid and schizophrenic states, I will now explore a third case of splitting that will illuminate this fundamental question. I have in mind the distinction between "true" and "false" self.

According to D. W. Winnicott, the true self is the primary self that begins very early in life; it is closely affiliated with biological life and is built up from gratifying experiences of aliveness (feeling vital and energetic); it is expressed in spontaneous gestures that precede the acquisition of language, "the spontaneous gesture is the True Self in action."[46] Such a self is primary in two senses. It is associated with "primary process" in Freud's sense of the term and is, above all, the very basis of a human being's sense that it *exists*, that it really *is*: is its own "psyche-soma" as well as its many modes of expression. As such, it is not inside us, much less outside us, it *is us*.[47] Nevertheless, despite its existence at and as our core, the true self is vulnerable and is continually threatened in the course of everyday living. In particular, it is likely to be buried under a false self that is erected to protect it from the disappointments of early love and relationship.

The false self develops as a response to various familial and social demands placed upon a human being in his or her formative phases. In its more innocent forms, it consists in all the ways that we are "polite" toward others as belonging to civil society or able to act as our own "caretaker," directing our life in strategic ways that help us to be successful in certain contexts: for instance, by concerted flattery.[48] But the false self can come to be so compliant toward others that it overlooks its own interests—"compliance is then the main feature, with imitation as a specialty."[49] This may eventuate in the schizoid pathology described above: cutting oneself off from others in states of indifference and withdrawal. But this need not happen. The true versus false self distinction identifies another syndrome: the advent of inauthenticity.

Vis-à-vis the true self, the false self is decidedly ambivalent. On the one hand, it acts to *protect* the true self from undue incursions or compromises; on the other hand, it may act to *hide* the true self, concealing its very existence by its own tendency to live on loan to others.[50] Instead of living from its vital core, the false self lives in terms of what it thinks others expect of it; above all, it lives in accordance with *their* values and virtues rather than its own. Instead of affirming its own originality and vitality, it becomes other-directed, coming to be locked out from its own inner resources—with the result that a person "lives, but lives falsely."[51]

What is the purport of the true versus false self distinction for the inner edges of the psyche? To begin with, Winnicott reminds us that the psychical sphere is continuous with the domain of our bodily being. Thus we cannot divorce experiences of the psyche from their corporeal dimensions, especially experiences that bear on the sense of comparative liveliness that constitutes the original core of the true self. When the young child is deprived of adequate attention from its main caretaker, it can undergo an undue split between mind and body: the mind of the child tries to care for its own body and the roots of an inner schism, a psychical splitting, are generated, sowing the seeds of a false self.[52] The true self as the primal vital self is then eclipsed by the false self. This is to say that its own edges are not so much juxtaposed with those of the false self (as we might be tempted to think according to a more limited split-self model, with one part next to the other, *edge-to-edge*, or better *edge-against-edge*) as they are hidden under the domination of the edges of the false self, engendering a two-tiered edge hierarchy: *edge-under-edge*. The false self eclipses the true self, forcing the latter into retreat.

This analysis suggests the more general truth that psychical edges rarely occur in isolation but much more frequently emerge in groups of closely related terms. These terms are related not just as literally contiguous but also as enveloping each other in the manner of chevrons of intersecting edges: *edge-into-edge*. Alternately expressed, they envelope each other in dense "folds," Merleau-Ponty's preferred term for the structure of flesh in the body and in the world.[53] The Winnicottian model of true versus false self implies that an analogue of such folding occurs in the psychical sphere, as well as in the social domain. The defining edges of the psyche, its characteristic contours, are not autogenously generated but evolve in relation to primary caretakers in early life, so that the edges that matter most are inherently *relational* rather than isolated from the very start: if fortunately situated, the psychical and somatic edges of the early self are enfolded into a loving and supportive family matrix.

It is precisely when the early family matrix is disturbed that a false self is likely to result. The ensuing schismatic condition of true versus false self is thus a derivative formation, a response to an alienating circumstance. It is certainly not an ontological state, as in the Cartesian model of an independent self that is separate from others and separate from itself (in the mind/body split) from the very beginning. It is instead a departure from a vital primal state that is characterized by inclusive edges of acceptance and support: loving arms and affirmative words. In this state, the inner psychical edges of the child are felt as congruent with familial and social surroundings and complementary to them. Thanks to this congruency, there is an ongoing conjunctivity between inner and outer worlds.

But if this is so—if felt psychical edges act to enable confluence rather than disruption—how can the human self become so deeply split, split all the way through, whether into pleasure versus reality ego (Freud), or *I* versus *me* (in Sartre's preferred terms), or true versus false self (after Winnicott)?[54] The self clearly has to have some minimal unity to be considered as *split from* itself. But inherent in this minimal unity must be the seeds of subsequent splitting. What are these seeds and how are we to identify them?

This is not the place to give an adequate answer to this last question, which is in part epistemological (how can I find out the roots of self-splitting?) and in part metaphysical (is there *one* self that is split into two or more selves, or perhaps several altogether different selves from the start?). For us the issue is the more limited one of how do the edges of a split self relate to each other and to the edges of other human selves in our local ambience? For it is by edges—edges at once psychic and somatic—that we meet up with others and, indeed, with our own self.

If we take as a model for splitting the true versus false self model of Winnicott (also explored by Laing and Cooper in *The Divided Self*), we find that the false self is constituted from incorporating the hard edges of early caretakers who have been experienced as unyielding and resistant to the needs of the young child. Such edges, so formed, tend to be fixed and to become the basis of the schizoid personality; they are also definitive of the false self in Winnicott's sense. They are the edges of that in me which, being derived from the introjection of others with whom I have had difficult relations, does not belong to my true self, which is spontaneous and not liable to such internal stultification. In their very rigidity, these introjected others become the basis of a false self I come to present to others as my public persona across a screen of indifference.

A case in point is R. D. Laing's patient, David: "He had grown up taking entirely for granted that what he called his 'self' and his 'personality' were two quite separate things. . . . What the individual variously terms his 'own,' 'inner,' 'true,' 'real' self is experienced as divorced from all activity that is observable by another, what David called his 'personality.'"[55] Here we witness a division of a person's self that has him putting his "real" inner being on one side of a fixed line and his alienated public self or "personality" on the other side. The result is the emergence of a true and a false self—not as two separate substances but as two sides of the very edge that separates David from himself, and thereby from others.

The true self is animated by a spontaneous psyche that is not beleaguered by a legacy of inadequate care and early traumas but is a source of energy and growth from within. Its edges are comparable to those of the temporal stream discussed earlier: there is no determinate beginning or ending, no definitive temporal borders. There is instead an ongoing current of continual unfolding with interleaving edges between phases of the flow. In the true self, "everything flows and nothing abides; everything gives way and nothing stays fixed."[56] All edges are here fluid: they are forms of open boundary that act not to close off and close in (as do the fixed edges of introjected problematic figures) but rather to open outward. These open boundaries are generated from within the true self even as they interact intimately with the boundaries of other selves who coinhabit the subject's life-world.

Such boundaries, lively and permeable, are vehicles for realizing continuities between psyche and soma, as well as between self and others. The interplay of psychical and somatic edges, as well as those of self and other, shores up the fragile unity of the self—fragile insofar as the true self is subject to compromise by the emergence of a false self that undermines its spontaneity. In a split self, there is an uneasy mixture of rigid and flowing edges, those of the false with the true self—the two kinds of edges being in a disruptive relation. Such a riven self is *set on edge*: on the edge of falling apart at any time, in which case whatever delicate equilibrium between true and false selves has been accomplished disintegrates. The edges fly asunder and the precarious unity is lost.

Nevertheless, this disaggregation is not an end state. Winnicott maintained that the therapist should consider allowing the patient to fall "into bits and pieces" within the protective shell of therapy. This is done in the hope that the premature organization of the self that was forged in the absence of attentive early nurturance can give way to a new and more viable organization in the adult. In other words, the disaggregated edges of a split self can be coaxed into assuming a pattern that is more reflective of the full panoply of needs and desires experienced by the mature human subject. This pattern manifests an expressive unity that engenders a sense of self that is no longer undermined by its split condition. In this emergent self, the basic edge-against-edge and edge-under-edge structures that I have identified as the pivot of the split self can be transformed into a conjunctive rather than a disjunctive relationship: the edges of the false and the true self, no longer severely divisive, can begin to relate to each other in subtly cohesive and mutually supportive ways—in a pattern of edges-with-edges, edges-alongside-edges.

The dynamic reunification of the split self is by no means easy to achieve. Suffering from a split-self syndrome is not anything that can be easily resolved or overcome by the victim himself. I propose that any creative change for the better is likely to involve expressive gestures in words or by bodily motions. By their very example, such gestures suggest ways by which alienating dichotomies of several sorts can be transcended: not only the one between false and true self, but other oppositional dyads as well, such as body/mind, self/other, and inner/outer. Expressive gestures are exemplary connection makers that help to create bridges between all such otherwise divisive dyads.

Expressive gestures act as hermetic intermediaries—recalling that Hermes was the Greek god of crossroads, considered to be places where unexpected meetings occur. Such gestures act to link self and world in effective ways. They also act as animating forces that bring a self divided from itself back together with itself, allowing the self-alienated subject a measure of affirmative continuity with itself and a more responsive connection with others. In this way, the rebarbative inner edges of a self divided from itself—edges acting as separative borders between a true and a false self—are softened and transformed into something closer to porous and receptive boundaries, enabling more resilient interaction with oneself and with others.

Expressive gestures allow feelings and thoughts arising within the psyche to become perceptible to ourselves and others in the guise of manifest bodily movements and verbal expressions. Laing emphasizes how the schizoid self has in effect consigned his or her body to the status of a mere object. One's body is de-animated, pitting the intimate "I" over against its own body. "The basic split," writes Laing, is "a cleft that sever[s] the self from the body, as indicated in this formula: self/(body-world). Such a scission cleaves the individual's own being in two in such a way that the self is disembodied, with the body becoming the center of a false self-system."[57] In this circumstance of the divided self, spontaneous expression is at a minimum. Laing singles out not only alienation from a sense of lived body (this body being regarded as nothing but an "object among other objects"[58]) but also a failure to link oneself to the surrounding world in a vital way: "Such a divorce of self from body deprives the unembodied self from direct participation in any aspect of the life of the world, which is mediated exclusively through the body's perceptions, feelings, and movements (expressions, gestures, words, actions, etc.)."[59] It is telling that Laing here has recourse to the very class of activities that I discussed near the end of the last chapter under the heading of "expressive gestures." It is these same gestures that are lacking in the case of the divided self; that is, a self that is split into a disembodied false self and a fully embodied and socially interactive true self.

Through the entire later part of this chapter, I have been exploring the question: What is it to split up an otherwise unitary self and what kinds of edges precipitate this action and what sort of edges result from it? In effect, the schizoid and the schizophrenic selves represent two outcomes of such splitting—two painful and ill-adaptive responses to it. In the schizoid self we witness a divisive distinction between a privately held inner self, dominated by an early history of difficult relations with introjected "bad" others, and an indifferent exterior self that is the outcome of not coming to terms with this history. The splitting in schizophrenia involves the diremption between a voluntary self that chooses to have an effect on others and to be affected by them in turn, and an involuntary self that invades others' lives and is itself invaded by them in turn: an interpenetration that disempowers a self that has become its own involuntary victim.

The differentiation between the true self and the false self that we have just encountered in Winnicott and Laing suggests that pathogenic splitting may contain the seeds of its own overcoming. I have argued that this is best seen in the phenomenon of expressive gestures understood as healing actions that bring about a reunified self that supersedes the splitting; by their creative conjoining of the gap between psyche and soma, such gestures offer an avenue into a more vital relationship with oneself and with others. I do not pretend that this is anything that is easy to realize, much less a panacea for problems that issue from the splitting of the self. It remains exceptional and often requires the guidance of experienced psychotherapists or other healing figures. But when it happens, we can say that a self that has been split in various destructive ways—not only in schizoid and schizophrenic conditions but in "borderline" and other states as well—is given the opportunity of becoming a unitary self. Such a self is not a primal or original self that has been lost and then regained; it is a self that needs to be accomplished for the first time, every time. The movement is not from the unitary to the split self; just the reverse is the case. The unitary self is an achievement, not something given or presumed, even if its roots lie in the vitality of the childhood self. Attaining this more authentic new self is the key to the enigma of self-splitting.

In closing, I want to consider briefly what a unified, or reunified, psyche means. To begin with, we need to distinguish the *unitary*—in its psychical as well as other forms—from *formal unity*. Formal unity is fixed and static in character. In the context of the development of the self, such unity takes on concretion in the life of the self in the early mirror stage: in Lacan's account, the rudimentary ego, emerging from a state of bodily fragmentation, prematurely unifies itself in and as the fixed image it sees of itself in the mirror. The effect is a state of alienation of the self from itself, for the subject looking at itself in the mirror cannot be captured in any one image of itself. More generally, beyond the context of ego development, formal unity is the kind of unity that is imposed from without—as when one's racial or gender identity is thrust upon the human subject, or when "compulsory heterosexuality" is assumed in the upbringing of a child.

The unitary is something quite different from formal unity. In this case, becoming a self is accomplished in and by a loosely gathered set of elements—an assemblage, what Heidegger designates as a *Versammlung*, which actively unifies and reunifies itself from within, that is, on the basis of its own resources and its own actions. Such self-ordering is more organic than mechanical; it is "alive" and "animated," in Winnicott's terms. The elements of the unitary do not act separately, one by one, but in unison—that is, in a concerted and coordinated but diverse set of motions. Each such element is an integral part of the whole that they together compose: employing an earlier distinction, each is a genuine "moment" rather than a separate "piece." Each contributes to a coherent creative action of something emergent—whether this be the lived body, the spontaneous self, or the life-world to which body and self both contribute so significantly.

In the unitary thus understood we recognize the root of the "creative originality" identified by Winnicott as "the essential central element" in the early life of the human child who is fortunate enough to have attuned and sensitive caregivers.[60] When an adult self carries forward such originality into its psychic life, a stage of animated becoming is activated. It is such becoming, expressed in diverse ways, that is operative in the life of the psyche regarded as a creative force, as a concrete mode of élan vital. Such a vital life is expansive, spreading across whole fields of affects, emotions, ideas, and thoughts, permeating the lived body that is the close companion of such a soul, and extending itself to other human beings in active sociality.

When this happens, soul comes into its own; from being split in various ways, it becomes unitary. Such a unitary soul was already glimpsed by Heraclitus in words that provide one of the epigraphs to this chapter: "You could not discover the limits of soul, even if you traveled every road to do so; such is the depth of its meaning."[61] Heraclitus is saying that you cannot determine the depth of soul, its refulgent unitariness, by any known method of measurement. This depth cannot be exhausted by any established metric. Unlike formal unities, the psychically unitary cannot be quantified. But to be immeasurable is not to be without edges; among these edges are those diverse permeable boundaries and thresholds that allow human psyches to flourish.[62]

## Notes

1. Much the same is true of the relationship between my body and the sky and its constellations: between all of these there is a special bonding, since only from and with my lived body can I perceive heavenly bodies. On this relationship, see chapter 10.

2. In this respect, psychical edges resemble musical edges, which can be very soft and sometimes barely discernible, as in John Luther Adams's composition titled "Become Ocean." Maybe this resemblance is not surprising if we consider that the psyche is the seat of time-consciousness, the place where time's passing is apprehended by us most intimately (as treated in section I above). The comparative smoothness of unfolding temporal duration is deeply analogous to the flowing of heard sounds in music; yet there are also edges in and of music itself. See interlude IV, "Listening to Musical Edges," for further discussion.

3. In what follows I am limiting myself to the human psyche, leaving aside a discussion of other possible kinds of soul, e.g., plant, animal, mineral.

4. Hobbes, *Leviathan*, ed. C. B. Macpherson (London: Pelican, 1968), part 1, chapter 8.

5. See Hegel, "Philosophy of Subjective Spirit," Part 1: Anthropology (part of the *Encyclopedia of Philosophical Sciences* [1830]), pars. 405–8. In these sections, Hegel distinguishes between the split that obtains (a) for *every* soul as *zwiefaches* or twofold (as cited in the epigram for this chapter) and that reflects the difference between the conscious and the "feeling" (*fuehlende*) aspects of each soul, and (b) for the more disturbed states of having two separate souls in a state of *Zerrissenheit*, which is expressed by the alternative German term *zweifaches*. Hegel relates this latter condition to *Verrücktheit*, "derangement." I owe these precisions to my colleague Allegra de Laurentiis.

6. "Edgy" often refers to a risky situation: "Corporal Amaya was one of 40 female Marines training at Camp Pendleton, Calif., in an edgy experiment: sending full-time 'female engagement teams' to accompany all-male foot patrols in Helman Province in southern Afghanistan" ("Female Troops Form a Bond with Afghans," *New York Times* [May 30, 2010], p. 1) If this situation is as risky as it sounds, one would certainly expect Corporal Amaya to *feel* quite edgy about being part of such an "experiment."

7. The edge here in question is not so much to be avoided as *recognized*: in doing a certain exercise, it is good to press one's body up to the edge of comfort or tolerability—getting as close to an ideal pose or posture as possible—but not to try to surpass it. On this point, see my earlier discussion in chapter 2.

8. Henri Bergson, *Creative Evolution*, trans. Arthur Mitchell, edited and presented in *Henri Bergson: Key Writings*, eds. Keith Ansell Pearson and John Ó. Maoilearca (London: Bloomsbury, 2014), p. 210.

9. Ibid.

10. I here leave aside the role of the ego as described by Lacan and the persona on Jung's conception, each of which possesses a certain stability; but this same stability is not intrinsic to them as self-engendered *psychical* beings: it is rather a feature of an individual psyche's relationship *with others*, thus is interpersonal rather than personal—even if some of these others are mirrors in which one sees oneself. The ego lacks *mineness*: which I argue, just below, is only a formal feature of individuated psychical life. I discuss Lacan's "mirror stage" at the very end of this chapter.

11. Bergson, *Creative Evolution*, in *Key Writings*, p. 210. On edges in music, see interlude IV.

12. Martin Heidegger, *Being and Time*, trans. John Macquarrie and Edward Robinson (New York: Harper & Row, 1962), p. 68; author's italics.

13. On absolute flux, see John B. Brough, "The Emergence of an Absolute Consciousness in Husserl's Early Writings on Time-Consciousness," *Man and World* 5 (1972), pp. 198–326.

14. I here refer to Brentano's classical definition of intentionality as "directedness to an object . . . or immanent objectivity." See Franz Brentano, *Psychology from an Empirical Point of View*, ed. Oskar Kraus, trans. Antos C. Rancurello, Dailey Burnham Terrell, and Linda McAlister (London: Routledge and Kegan Paul, 1973), p. 88.

15. Mary Watkins, *Invisible Guests: The Development of Imaginal Dialogues*, 3rd ed. (Woodstock, CT: Spring, 2000), p. 107. Watkins adds that "the illness of multiple personality is problematic precisely because of its singleness of voice at any one moment, not because

of its multiplicity. Improvement starts when dialogue and reflection between the selves begins to happen" (ibid.).

16. On the process of "working through" (*durcharbeiten*), see Sigmund Freud, "Mourning and Melancholia," *Standard Edition of the Compete Psychological Works*, vol. 14, trans. James Strachey (London: Hogarth, 1963).

17. In multiple personality, the splitting is not conscious at all; in the case of deferred mourning, it is tacitly present but not known as such. In my own case, the death of my parents in my early twenties was not addressed until fifteen years later in intense psychotherapy, part of which consisted in the recognition that I was in a state of mourning that did not know its own name.

18. This is the title of a volume of religious writings by Søren Kierkegaard, *Purity of Heart Is to Will One Thing*, trans. Douglas V. Steere (New York: Harper, 1964).

19. In proceeding thus, I leave aside other suggestively named syndromes such as "borderline condition," whose very name incorporates edge both as "border"—a rigorously imposed and maintained barrier—and "line," which invites an action of crossing. Those diagnosed with this condition must be, in Kernberg's words, "considered to occupy a borderline area between neurosis and psychosis" (Otto Kernberg, *Borderline Conditions and Pathological Narcissism* [New York: Jason Aronson, 1975], p. 3).

20. The full statement is, "There is a great deal of unmapped country within us which would have to be taken into account in explanation of our gusts and storms" (George Eliot, *Daniel Deronda* [Auckland, NZ: Floating Press, 2009], p. 450).

21. "What is new in all this is the theory of internal objects as developed in more elaborate form by Melanie Klein and Ronald Fairbairn, and the fact that Fairbairn [in particular] makes object-relations, not instinctive impulses, the primary and important thing. It is the object [i.e., the other person] that is the real goal of the libidinal drive. We seek persons, not pleasures" (Harry Guntrip, *Schizoid Phenomena, Object-Relations, and the Self* [New York: International Universities Press, 1969; 3rd printing, 1976], p. 21). I draw on Guntrip's classic study of schizoid states extensively in what follows.

22. Guntrip, *Schizoid Phenomena*, pp. 19–20; the first sentence is in italics. The last sentence is from p. 18; his italics. Kriszta Sajber points out that this definition of the schizoid state is continuous with Eugene Minkowski's notion of "schizophrenic autism" (e-mail communication of June 7, 2015). We are forewarned here as to the provisional and sometimes arbitrary character of psychiatric nomenclature.

23. Guntrip, *Schizoid Phenomena*, p. 18 (I replace "real" with "effective"). Guntrip adds that the schizoid personality "has decreed an emotional and impulsive standstill, on the basis of keeping out of effective range and being unmoved" (ibid.).

24. On "the in-out programme," see Guntrip, *Schizoid Phenomena*, pp. 36, 291, and especially p. 48: "You are always *impelled into* a relationship by your needs and at once *driven out* again by the fear either of exhausting your love-object by the demands you want to make or else losing your own individuality by over-dependence and identification" (author's italics).

25. "An inner psychic world . . . has been set up duplicating an original frustrating situation, an unhappy world in which one is tied to bad objects and feeling therefore always frustrated, hungry, angry, and guilty, and profoundly anxious" (ibid., p. 22; all in italics).

26. Ibid., p. 23.

27. "The withdrawn libido is turned inwards, introverted" (ibid., p. 27).

28. As reported by Guntrip, in *Schizoid Phenomena*, p. 20.

29. Another patient reports, "With you [Guntrip, her therapist] I feel if I accept your help I'll be subjugated, lose my personality, be smothered. Now I feel withdrawn like a snail [so that] you can't swallow me up. I get a shutting-myself-off attitude which lessens my anxiety" (ibid., p. 34).

30. Ibid., p. 61; in italics. Otherwise expressed, "the schizoid [is] always being tantalized, made [emotionally] hungry, angry, and [as a result] driven into withdrawal. Whereas the depressed person turns his anger and aggression back against himself and feels guilty, the schizoid person seeks to withdraw from the intolerable situation and to feel nothing" (p. 25).

31. "Many practically useful types of personality are basically schizoid. Hard workers, compulsively unselfish folk, efficient organizers, highly intellectual people, may all accomplish valuable results, but it is often possible to detect an unfeeling callousness behind their good works, and a lack of sensitiveness to other people's feelings in the way they over-ride individuals in their devotion to causes" (ibid., p. 38; see also p. 46 on "common mild schizoid traits").

32. Sigmund Freud, *Outline of Psychoanalysis*, as cited by Guntrip, p. 76; author's italics.

33. As Guntrip puts it, "the process of withdrawal in successive stages through fear emerges as a major cause of what we have come to call 'ego-splitting,' the loss of unity of the self" (Guntrip, *Schizoid Phenomena*, p. 64; the entire quote is in italics). The "fear" at issue here is that occasioned by the thought that one's need for the other's affection and attention may put too great a demand upon them and that, as a result, they will not be willing to assist the self in times of urgency.

34. Guntrip and Fairbairn tend to complicate matters beyond what is useful for our purposes. Guntrip argues for a split between an "orally needy" libidinal ego and a "regressed" ego—where the exact sense of regression requires scores of pages to explicate (ibid., p. 77, and the long chapter on "The Regressed Ego, the Lost Heart of the Self, and the Inability to Love"). Fairbairn distinguishes between "object-splitting" and "ego-splitting," each of which has several subtypes. See Fairbairn, *An Object-Relations Theory of the Personality* (New York: Basic, 1952), and Guntrip's summary in *Schizoid Phenomena*, p. 71.

35. Guntrip, *Schizoid Phenomena*, p. 19. This is the title of an entire section of the opening chapter of Guntrip's classical text.

36. Dan Zahavi, "Schizophrenia and Self-Awareness," *Philosophy, Psychiatry, and Psychology* 8, no. 4 (2001): pp. 339–41. "The just-outlined difference between the self as subject and the self as object is obviously not peculiar to schizophrenia; it is just that the very relation between the two is so severely disturbed that it takes the form of an intrapsychic splitting."

37. G. W. F. Hegel, *Anthropology, Encyclopedia*, par. 406, Addition. Hegel is not speaking expressly of a psychopathic condition but of a splitting that will ultimately be overcome in a movement of *Aufhebung* or "sublation."

38. See Eugen Bleuler, *Dementia Praecox oder Gruppe der Schizophrenien* (Leipzig: Deuticke, 1911), where this concept is explicated at length, including the statement I here cite.

Putting it this way implies that the split is between an unconscious self and various conscious selves: an especially disruptive version of what would later be designated as multiple personality disorder in the sense discussed above.

39. Wolfgang Blankenburg, "Zur Psychopathologie des Ich-Erlebens Schizophrener," in *Psychopathology and Philosophy*, ed. Manfred Spitzer, Friedrich Uehlein, and Godehard Oepen (Berlin: Springer, 1988).

40. *Gemacht-bekommens* is close in meaning to what Giovanni Stanghellini calls "heteronomic vulnerability." For this latter term, see Giovanni Stanghellini, *Disembodied Spirits and Deanimated Bodies: The Psychopathology of Common Sense* (Oxford: Oxford University Press, 2004).

41. Blankenburg, "Zur Psychopathologie," p. 187.

42. See Klaus Peter Kisker, *Der Erlebniswandel des Schizophrenen: Ein Psychopathologischer Beitrag zur Psychonomie Schizophrener Grundsituationen* (Berlin: Springer, 1960).

43. Victor Tausk, "On the Origin of the 'Influencing Machine' in Schizophrenia" trans. Dorian Feigenbaum, in Tausk's *Sexuality, War, and Schizophrenia: Collected Psychoanalytic Papers*, ed. Paul Roazen (New Brunswick, NJ: Transaction, 1991).

44. This circumstance is compatible with a schizophrenic being convinced that he or she is acting from her own volition. A schizophrenic woman I know obsessively cleaned the rug in her room, picking up imaginary dust and dirt for hours on end. She considered this to be work that she had decided to do; but the sense of choice was illusory—since it took place in an assisted-living situation that did not call for her cleaning in the first place and her actions involved the active hallucinating of dust and dirt. This was not just a "cleaning compulsion" in the usual sense of being driven to keep one's home "squeaky clean," but entailed a delusional state of mind in which this afflicted woman believed that there was debris when there was none.

45. I am not here proposing a theory of the ontogenesis of schizophrenia; this would require discussing a complex causal matrix at once genetic and neurological. My proposal is restricted to a massive and striking *effect* of this matrix: that of a major restriction of actions or thoughts that are otherwise subject to conscious control.

46. D. W. Winnicott, "Ego Distortion in Terms of True and False Self," in his collection *The Maturational Processes and the Facilitating Environment: Studies in the Theory of Emotional Development* (New York: International Universities Press, 1965), p. 148.

47. For Winnicott, the sense of having an "inner reality" comes somewhat later and builds on the life and liveliness of the true self: "According to the theory being formulated here the concept of an individual inner reality of objects applies to a stage later than does the concept of what is being termed the True Self. The True Self appears as soon as there is any mental organization of the individual at all, and it means little more than the summation of sensori-motor aliveness" (ibid., p. 149).

48. On the false self's politeness, see Winnicott, "Ego Distortion in Terms of True and False Self,", p. 147; on its caretaker role, see p. 143.

49. Ibid., p. 147.

50. Speaking of the false self, Winnicott says that "its defensive function is to hide and protect the True Self" (ibid., p. 142). Winnicott adds, "In the extreme examples of False Self

development, the True Self is so well hidden that spontaneity is not a feature in the infant's living experiences" (ibid., p. 147). The same suppression is integral to the False Self syndrome.

51. Ibid., p. 146. Winnicott is here speaking of the infant, but his point is that a pattern that is set up early by a not "good enough" mother may eventuate in an entire life coming to be lived on false premises—i.e., by striving to comply with others rather than to express oneself spontaneously. One adult patient remarked that "over the years all the good work done with him [in analytic therapy with Winnicott] had been futile because it had been done on the basis that he existed, where he had only existed falsely. When I had said that I recognized his non-existence he felt that he had been communicated with for the first time" (ibid., p. 151). What Winnicott means in this latter remark is that his patient's true self never had a chance to exist fully after early childhood—so buried did it become under the unrelenting regime of the false self.

52. This formulation owes much to comments by Mary Watkins.

53. See Maurice Merleau-Ponty, *The Visible and the Invisible*, chapter 4, "The Chiasm."

54. For the distinction between the active I and the objective me, see Jean-Paul Sartre, *The Transcendence of the Ego: A Sketch for a Phenomenological Description*, trans. Sarah Richmond (New York: Routledge, 2004).

55. Laing, *The Divided Self* (1960; New York: Pantheon, 1969), p. 76. Laing adds, "One may conveniently call its 'personality' the individual's 'false self' or a 'false-self system'" (ibid.). Here Laing acknowledges his debt to Winnicott.

56. Heraclitus, fragment 20, in the translation of Philip Wheelwright, *Heraclitus* (New York: Atheneum, 1968), p. 29.

57. Laing, *The Divided Self*, p. 189.

58. "*The body is felt more as one object among other objects in the world than as the core of the individual's own being*. Instead of being the core of his true self, the body is felt as the core of a *false self*" (ibid., p. 71; author's italics).

59. Ibid., p. 71.

60. Winnicott, "Ego Distortion in Terms of True and False Self," p. 152.

61. Heraclitus, fragment 42, in the translation of Philip Wheelwright.

62. I want to acknowledge the very substantial contribution of Dr. Kriszta Sajber to the composition of this chapter, especially to the section on the schizophrenic self: she is in effect the coauthor of this section. I also thank Mary Watkins for insightful comments, particularly regarding my treatment of the schizoid self.

# TEN

# From Earth's Edge to the Sky and Beyond

Ancient Mediterranean sailors set out to discover the ends of the earth, traveling over the open ocean that stretched beyond the Pillars of Hercules (the Straits of Gibraltar). Tempering their enthusiasm was the fear that the earth, and more particularly the wide ocean itself, would suddenly drop off in a gigantic precipice, taking them and their ships into the abyss. Not long before the Age of Exploration, medieval theologians similarly pondered the conundrum of an imagined javelin thrower at the edge of the last circle of the heavens tossing his instrument into the void: that edge was the outer edge of the known universe, the *oikoumené* or "inhabited world."[1] In both instances, a fascination with a final cosmic edge was evident: the farthest edge of all edges.

In each case, the idea of the outermost edge reflected the experience and knowledge of the time. In our era, thanks to astrophysics, our sense of the last edge of the universe has been pushed beyond any reckoning in nautical miles or any analogy to an athlete poised in the outer circle of the universe. Nevertheless, we remain fascinated with the question as to how large—how long or wide—the universe is. Models of its very vast extent are irresistible to curious minds. At the same time, we have a much better idea of the actual extent and mass of the earth; we know for sure that it has no single falling-off point within its dense mass and that it possesses a definite diameter. We also know something about its evolution as a planet as well as its oncoming future as threatened by global warming.

However differently we may now think about the outer edges of the earth and the known universe, we are continually confronted, every day and every night, with the perceived edge of the earth as well as various edges found in the sky. Let us now explore these various edges in succession; they will prove more complex than they appear at first.

### I

The *edge of the earth* forms part of contemporary experience in at least two concrete ways: photographs taken from space that depict this edge, and earthly horizons.

*Photographs of Earth taken from space.* After the world-historical photograph of planet earth was taken from the Apollo 17 flight in December 1972, human beings saw the planet they inhabit from afar for the first time: a single globe in space, a "blue marble" as it came to be called. This is to say, they saw it as a circular disk with its own edge—an edge that rings around the spherical figure of the earth itself.[2] They witnessed the state of the earth at a single instant, allowing its outer edge to stand out against the empty space around it. Despite the accuracy of the image, the representation of earth's edge in this photograph (and other comparable photographs) is artificial in two respects: it fails to convey the motion of the earth as it spins on its axis and it shows us how the earth looks from a rarely assumed position in space 28,000 miles above its surface. In both respects, the photograph exhibits what Merleau-Ponty calls a "freezing of being."[3] For all its indisputable accuracy and historical uniqueness, the image itself comes across as strangely disincarnate and somewhat surreal. Whatever its limitations, this single photograph has become an icon of the modern age—an avatar of "the epoch of representation" (in Heidegger's phrase).[4]

*Earthly horizons*. Meanwhile, how does earth's outer edge present itself *on earth*? The most concrete and pervasive place in which we experience this edge is *the horizon*—where we may take this term in the sense discussed in chapter 6: namely, as what we see as the farthest feature of a given landscape or seascape, a thin band wherein the earth comes to an apparent end. At sea, especially when the vessel we are in comes into a deep trough, we observe the curvature of the horizon itself—the arc it makes. This is rarely the case with open landscape scenes, whose horizon most often manifests itself as linear and straight—as children and amateur painters demonstrate in their efforts to capture it in a single horizontal line. In perceptual fact, the horizon presents itself as a fading region in which the earth meets the sky: a place of conjuncture that is more of a bleeding boundary than a strict border. Construed as such, a horizon is always present in perceptual experience—if not explicitly as in the paradigm cases of open landscape or seascape, then by implication, as when we are in cities or forests and sense a horizon beyond what we can actually see, positing it as looming or lurking there, hovering on the far side the currently accessible scene.

At this early point we must ask, are the various edges that enclose land- and seascapes as well as the singular edge that surrounds the earth as viewed in the space photographs only *apparent*? A photographic image is admittedly an appearance—it shows things as they appear when observed by a photographic apparatus—but *that which* appears is nonetheless actual (and this is so even if the photograph is of an *image* of something: the image is actual enough to be captured on film). In the case of horizons, the appearing is of *a feature of the surrounding world itself*. This feature itself comes forward in being perceived: it *takes place* there as an event in the history of our and others' perception of things, including the perception of the earth itself. It is an intrinsic part of what we see of them—where "see" signifies open-eyed looking, ranging from the glance to the gaze, thus including all that we witness with our own eyes. This applies to images and percepts alike, even though images (sketched, painted, or photographic) represent what they show by way of an intervening medium (paper for paintings and traditional photographs, virtual space for digital images) in contrast with the directness of lived percepts. Each image or percept conveys its own respective content more or less unambiguously, depending on the actual conditions of its transmission, the medium of representation, the situation in which we attend to it, and so on. This content includes the edges of discrete things set within horizons, horizons themselves, and the edge of the earth itself as seen from space.

## II

The "edge of the earth itself"? What is this? Innocent and obvious as it may seem to be, such an edge is fraught with anomalies—or better, aporias (literally, "no opening," "no way out"). Let me take up just three of these here.

*Everywhere versus nowhere.* If we are talking about the earth as a whole, we soon realize that its edge is (virtually) everywhere in our immediate perception—everywhere where it impinges upon us, such as underfoot, or as seen at a certain distance (again, as in the case of the horizon)—yet it is literally *nowhere*: at no particular location, no one place. Every edge of earth that we might choose to explore, whether on foot or with our eye, recedes as we approach it, exceeding our reach. As we advance toward the horizon, it withdraws from our visual grasp with each step we take. As we begin to focus on the upper surface of the earth that lies just under us, we become aware that one edge (one ground swell, one ridge, one crest) gives way to another in seemingly endless progression, but none of these successive edges can count as *the* edge of the earth. However obstructive or prominent they may be—as with the Crazy Mountains in Montana—having arrived in their presence does not count as *reaching the earth's edge*. Even when in the midst of such edges (say, camping out in the Crazies) the earth's edge itself eludes us.

*Near versus far edge.* The earth's edge, however it may come to our attention (in aerial photographs, in/as the horizon, or underfoot), is anomalous in that it seems to be at once close and yet far away. It looms in the near-sphere—the experiential zone to which I have more or less immediate access—and yet it also emerges in a far-sphere. In the former, it presents itself as close to me: *in* the photograph I hold in my hands, *under* my feet, and *within* my vision. In the latter, it is experienced as *over there* rather than *in here*: in the distance, at the horizon, over the ocean swells. The earth's edge is somehow in both near and far spheres at once. In this double-sidedness, we encounter a decided ambivalence of experience: the same edge is situated in two spheres that, despite their considerable descriptive differences, somehow manage to hold or present this very edge. But *just where* is this edge? It is difficult to say. One thing is for sure: the earth's edge has no simple location, no determinate locus; in this regard, it is neither here nor there.

*The whole in the part.* However differently configured or presented it may be, the earth's edge is experienced as a distinguishable part of what we perceive, whether this is a given landscape or seascape, or even a cityscape set on earth. This suggests that the earth's edge is a portion of what we perceive, belonging to it as an integral part. But it is a decidedly odd part. Unlike many parts (such as the tires on my car, the interior components of my computer), it is not detachable from the full scene of which it is a part. We can talk about it as if it were—indeed, I have been doing just that—but as we *experience* it, it belongs to the earth as a whole and cannot be pried apart from it. The most striking case of this perceptual paradox is again found in the horizon, which is a distinct part of the experienced earth (a band or quasi-line) that also presentifies the entire earth of which it is the edge.[5] In this capacity, it is what Merleau-Ponty terms a "total part," that is, a part that is not just a piece of an additive or syncretic whole but in which the whole itself resides.[6] It resides there as if by adumbration as a compressed or condensed presence that radiates throughout the part. Much the same is true of the earth's edge as I feel it underfoot: despite its being just *this* part of the earth—this stretch of soil, this patch of lawn—it is also the earth itself that I sense beneath my feet (and even beneath the sidewalk on which I walk). This is why we could say that we are "on the earth" when answering the simple question "Where are you now?" *The* earth exists in the part I see or touch, a part that presentifies the whole—rather than being an independent, separable part, as on the reified logic of the natural attitude in which the whole is the simple summation of its parts. In the case of the earth, the whole is present in the part; it is there not as such but by adumbration or implication. Otherwise put, the part of the earth I am on just now is a *moment* of the earth as a whole, not a mere piece of it.[7] The earth's edge in any of the several senses just mentioned offers us a circumstance in which this edge implicates the very whole of which it is also a part. Part it is, but a *whole part*.

There is no definitive, much less easy, resolution to any of the above three aporias. But we can accommodate them by means of an inclusive logic of both/ and rather than relying on the exclusivist dichotomy of either/or. In the case of the first aporia, that of the earth's edge being everywhere and nowhere, we realize that this means that the earth has no final edge. Or rather, that the ultimate edge is all over, anywhere that you have an unobstructed view of the open land or sea, or feel its extent underfoot: it is out there, at the perimeter of the scope of our look or just beneath our body. Such an edge, whether appearing as a gentle ellipse or as

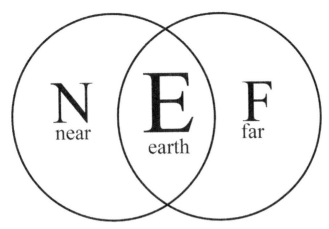

FIGURE 19. Near and far space intersecting in the earth.

a "brute being" (Merleau-Ponty: *l'être sauvage*), is not tied to any single locus: not, say, to just *these* hills or *that* island on the distant horizon, or *this* very place where I now stand or walk.[8] In experiential fact, the status of the earth's edge is captured in the medieval conundrum, often attributed to Nicholas of Cusa: like the universe, its center is everywhere (*ubique*) and its circumference nowhere (*nullibi*).[9] So, too, the terrestrial edge is everywhere to be seen or felt even if nowhere to be found as such: it is experienced *in* kinaesthesia or vision—it is given *in* them but not given *to* them as a determinate object.

As for the aporia of the near and the far, we can say similarly that one and the same edge of the earth figures as both of these in our experience of it. In other words, the near sphere and the far sphere are not just contiguous—for that would imply a certain differentiation between them—but also overlapping with the earth as the area of overlap. Near (N) and far (F) can be represented by a Venn diagram, with an overlapping common space designated as E, which signifies the earth.[10]

More radically still, the earth's edge is both near and far at once and together. They are coextensive, even if there is a difference in their qualitative feel. Like the celebrated object that is "green and red all over"—a conundrum discussed by philosophers in the 1950s in an effort to clarify the synthetic a priori—so the earth's edge gives itself out as both far and near, even if there are nuanced or graduated differences between the details of its appearings in a given land- or seascape. The near is what appears as belonging to the vicinity of the lived body, the far as comparatively distal to this same body. But each envelops the other so that when the earth's edge is felt as near—as when the earth is felt underfoot—the farness of the other parts of the earth is sensed as diminishing accordingly. As Heidegger might put it, the near is what "amounts to making the farness vanish"[11]—yet never altogether so, since shades or traces of the latter remain within the earth's edge sensed as near. The converse also holds: the farthest appearing such edge is felt as including near aspects, albeit in reduced presence, as if approaching our body without ever actually reaching it.

Regarding the earth's edge as part of the whole, the last of the three aporias, we can concede that thinking of the earth's edge as a whole or total part *abstractly*, we may find nothing but an oxymoron or, worse, an outright contradiction. But if we consider it concretely, we can understand what is at stake here. Take the horizon once again: this is both part of a larger landscape scene—though never the full extent of it—and yet somehow contains or reflects the whole scene, being the place where earth and sky merge and become one continuous phenomenon. The part here conveys the whole, or we can say conversely that the whole dwells in the part, without our being able to keep them strictly apart: they are inseparable even if still distinguishable.[12] One envelops the other, or still more radically one *is* the other, albeit with subtle differences of structure as well as history. It is not just that the whole is *in the part*, but the whole *has become* the part. And the same holds for the part, which contains the whole, by condensation as it were—so much so that we can say that the part has become the whole. The dynamic is two-way for both pairs of terms.

In all three aporias, then, we have an expanded form of identity in which terms that are normally averse or opposed have come into a oneness of kind— but a oneness that is not to be confused with formal unity or "*the one.*" *E pluribus unum!* But the *unum* is closer in spirit to the "unanimous" than to the number *1*, given that unanimity is a convergence of many around a single issue or conclusion. If we seek representation by natural numbers, we would say that this is a situation in which $1 + 1 = 2+$, though these numbers cannot have a determinate quantitative value as applied to the situation we are now discussing.

In short, the earth's edge possesses an active and plurivalent identity that encompasses predicates of part and whole, near and far, everywhere and nowhere. The initially contrasted terms of these several dyads achieve a oneness in which individual members are dissolved as separate terms and come together in an intermingling that allows and even welcomes differences of many sorts. The oneness (which we can also call "the sameness") cuts across the dyads by virtue of assembling them into one whole: one *unitary* whole (to invoke a term discussed at the end of the last chapter). This assemblage makes these differences themselves aspects of a common oneness in which all participate even as each plays a distinctively different role in the achievement of this very same oneness.

## III

We must now address the ways by which we are able to relate to the earth's edge. We do so, first, through three basic parameters that act as critical connectors to this edge: my body, others as coperceivers, and what I shall call "other others." After discussing these, I consider how the range of my previous experience and my present interests figure into the more complete picture.

*My body.* My bodily edges, as discussed in chapter 9, extend into the edge-world that surrounds them. In this capacity, they are frankly exterocentric. This outer-directedness is solicited with special intensity by the earth's edge in its various avatars. For it draws out my corporeal edges in quite specific ways, either by way of bodily motions of going-toward (things, the horizon) or by activations of my several sensoria, especially touch and sight, less often smell and taste. Sensorial capacities are especially effective in this respect, since they allow me to move out into the surrounding field of perception in seeking food, changing location, and so on. Operative here are various modes of corporeal intentionality, each of which represents an effective inroad into the outer ranges of my experiential arc. Without them, I would be radically self-enclosed, cut off from the larger landscape world that surrounds me at all times. By their means, I *reach out* into the edges of this world.

This outreach of my body is paired with an equally important inreach. For the edges of the circumambient earth reach back into my bodily mass. They are continually becoming immanent, intimate within me. Thanks to their informative action, what is around or beneath me comes to be *in me*—even that it *is me* finally. This transformation is due to the fact that the edges of my body are radically porous: they are boundaries. Heidegger is again pertinent: "A boundary is not that at which something stops but . . . that from which something *begins its presencing.*"[13] To this statement, Heidegger adds, "That is why the concept is that of *horismos,* that is, the horizon, the boundary."[14] As we know from earlier analysis, to be a boundary is to be permeable, to allow flow across its sides and surfaces. My body is a permeable entity, thanks not just to the openings in the surface of its skin (bodily orifices and minute pores) but especially to its sensorial openness as a lived body. These openings and this openness admit not just what immediately surrounds and stimulates my body but also that which is found further afield, thanks to what Merleau-Ponty calls *teleperception.*[15] My bodily self is open to the many edges of any given perceptual field, including those provided by the earth as the most encompassing such field. At the same time, the horizon itself, situated at the extremity of this field, has the being of a boundary: it possesses a porosity that allows it to incorporate such diverse phenomena as the sea (or rivers, lakes, and finally the ocean) as well as the sky in its diverse appearings, taking them in and compressing them into the band of its thin margin. Among body and horizon and landscape there is an active trialectic of influence—of influx and intake across diverse boundaries.

Considered as a nexus of inreach and outreach, my lived body has remarkable orientational powers that allow it to undertake the active exploration of the known and the unknown facets of the world. The explorations of the earth in fifteenth and sixteenth centuries that I have taken as exemplary of the impassioned search for the ultimate edge were not due to the navigational technology then available (such as dead reckoning) but instead owed everything to the orientational capacities of individual navigators: to the subtle synthesis of their cognitive and corporeal intentionalities, both of which can be considered modes of edge negotiation requiring considerable ingenuity in the deployment of bodily skills.[16] Thanks to these skills (and a good measure of courage and intuition), voyages were taken into the *apeiron*—the "boundless." We can think of these intrepid sailors as steering into the trackless oceans of the earth guided by a navigational know-how embedded in their lived bodies, bearing toward the horizon as the dominant edge in their perceptual field, all the while negotiating turbulent seas. They were sailing toward the edge of the earth they at once feared and sought: moving their bodies toward the horizon even as they were actively imagining the earth's acute drop-off. Each of us, in our customary day worlds, are doing little less if we consider that every foray into these worlds deals with edges by means of the moving body in its habitual modalities—edges figuring as the perceived perimeters of the sensory field, or as peripheries of what awaits us at the end of the foray.

*Others as coperceivers.* If I am on a ship, looking with other members of the crew at the horizon, I am not just seeing this visual edge for myself, I am sharing my perception with others. Something significant is happening here that we cannot afford to ignore. It is true that my experience is mine insofar as it is happening in and by means of my own bodily self. I am one sole being throughout: my identity is not siphoned off into that of others. *I* take in the horizon—undeniably so. But something else is now occurring when I do this alongside others, who are now taking in the same horizon *with me.*

To start with, the fleshy edges of my body are in touch with those of the others who share my vision—if not literally, then through a form of indirect coparticipation. *We* are looking at the horizon *together* in a species of coperception that is unique to this kind of situation. To begin with, I am aware of the fact that others are also looking at the horizon. Even if we do not exchange a single word with each other, and despite the fact that I am not now looking expressly at their bodies, I am conscious *of their very looking* as if by a kind of lateral side-sight. My visual intentionality is experienced as *accompanied* by that of my companions; we form a company of seers, each embodied and each engaged in gazing toward the horizon.

Second, I sense that the horizon itself at which we are looking is *cointended*: it is not just the exclusive focus of my personal looking but something seen together, witnessed in tandem. I and the others have momentarily transcended our individuated bodily bases, taking ourselves somewhere else. But this somewhere else is not just anywhere: it is just *there*, at and as the far edge presented by the horizon. As the continuous visible enclosure of the sea, this edge is one. It is seen separately by each of us, and yet it is shared between us, in such a way as to become the common perceptual content of several convergent gazes.

This content differs somewhat in each case in accordance with the exact perspective taken, but it is not literally divided or partitioned as so many pieces of the same thing. It, the horizon itself, *stays the same* even as it is seen differentially. It is thus a special instance of the one-in-the-many—of one entity *seen out* in the various lookings of those who are now perceiving it together. In Husserl's language, the noematic core of the horizon, its identity or "determinable X," comes to guide the directed attention of the several acts of perception here at play. These perceivings are coordinated twice over: in terms of the sameness of their perceptual content as well as their situatedness in the shared place of their apprehension. In this same place, that of the deck of the ship, the bodily edges of the onlookers converge, both laterally across bodies and contentfully (in terms of what is seen). In the first case, the edges are intercorporeal, being felt in the mingling of the outer extremities of the subjects who are coperceiving the same exterior edge; in the other case, the mingling is of the perceived content (here, the horizon as seen) as it is entertained simultaneously by those who witness this scene together.

*Other others.* Some, indeed most, others are not actually present at the kind of scene I here describe. They are elsewhere but are coingredient in my current experience. I refer to the way that other human beings in my life-world, past and present, effectively codetermine what I now see as well as how I see it. These others may have been directly formative of my earlier experiences as teachers, parents, friends. Or they may have been incorporated from what I have read or heard about: figures whose lives reach me by narrative accounts, say, Ahab in *Moby Dick*. Still different others I may know nothing about as individuals are coingredient as they have become present to me through acculturation of many kinds: ethical, political, or social. So, too, animal and plant and rock others—indeed, whole seascapes—have become sedimented into what I now perceive, shaping and reshaping my experience from within by way of memory. They, along with other human beings, are silent companions of my contemporary perceptual action of now looking out to sea. Taken together, they are hosts and I am their ongoing guest; they have shaped my current perceptual life in a profound interplay of influences that belong as much to class and society, history and geographical implacement as to my individuated body and mind.

The edges of all these indirect forms of presence meet in me as the perceiver in this circumstance, and they meet as well in my fellow perceivers—even though the exact configuration in their case may be significantly different than in my own. Each of these presences inculcates in me and others distinctive ways of looking and sensing, modes of attentiveness, and so on. The effects upon my current perceiving are rarely fully conscious, but they are no less determinative for being pre-conscious in their operation. I may not be able to identify them in myself, but I can often discern them in others—as in the case of imperious American staring or alert and cautious Japanese glancing, a dog's intent sniffing, a snake's attentive slithering, a flower's opening to the sun. These various styles of apperception may be very dissimilar, but any of them may play a part in the layered experience of the earth's edge, whether at sea or on land—an experience in which all human beings and animals and plants continuously engage, whatever the differences may be in their exact modes of taking in the earth to which they together belong.

## IV

I must here point out a curious anomaly about both the edge of the earth as such and the multifarious edges it supports, a distinction to be discussed in more detail in section VI below. Both kinds of edge have the peculiarity that results in our having little idea what is on the other side—at least not from merely looking at them. They are unilateral edges whose far side is essentially and not accidentally concealed. I cannot tell from scrutinizing what is to be found on the other side of the horizon, nor what is on the unrepresented side of the earth in a given Lunar Orbiter photograph. Eventually, I can determine what is on these other sides; but this requires a dedicated journey in the case of the horizon and another set of photographs in the case of the images made from outer space. Similarly, I cannot tell from a bare look what lies under a ridge or a rill in the earth's surface. It takes another action—such as excavation—to determine what lies on the concealed sides of these ordinary earthly edges.

It is true that many edges, not just those of the earth, do not reveal their other sides to me, but this does not normally pose any problem: the underside of the table on which I'm typing is likely to be constructed from the same material as its top side. For the most part, we take for granted such continuity of material or other means of construction, especially if the object in question is a familiar one. In the case of the horizon, the Orbiter photograph, and a rill or ridge, however, we are far from sure what lies on the other side, as with the ordinary perception of a distant horizon: what lies beyond may be quite unknown if I have never been there before.

This phenomenon reflects what Heidegger considers to be the "self-seclusion" of the earth, its powerful tendency to withdraw from overt display: the earth "is continually self-secluding and to that extent sheltering and concealing."[17] Such self-withdrawal stands in stark contrast to the manifestness of *world*: the Open that discloses itself in language, historical events, and overt political actions.[18] Earth itself lacks these modes of manifestation, tending toward self-concealment. Painters sometimes strive to capture the self-withdrawal itself, as in Van Gogh's early paintings of agricultural fields in Holland. I take this tendency toward self-seclusion to be the force that makes the other sides of the earth's many edges inaccessible on the face of it. *On the face of it*: that is, on the surface proffered to us by these same edges. That which faces us in the earth's overt surfaces contrasts with the contrary movement toward retreat and concealment that belongs to their obverse sides. These sides are not just veiled from view or partially seen; they are radically *out of view*. It follows that the earth's edges are insistently one-sided. They show me the accessible face of the earth insofar as I have access to it. But the other sides of these same edges are turned away from me as I look into what I can see before and around me. They are something else that is somewhere else.

## V

You may have noticed that most of the examples I have given of the earth's edges (and edges) have all been taken from what we experience on the broad surface of the earth: on land and at sea. Despite their considerable variety of presented aspects, they are all situated on a horizontal and mostly level expanse. What would happen were we to plunge *under* these immense expanses, drop down below them? What then?

A number of early civilizations (Mesopotamian, Egyptian, Hindu, Buddhist, Greek) imagined an entire underworld to lie under the exposed surfaces of the earth. It was as if they acknowledged the inaccessibility of what lies under the earth—its refusal to divulge itself fully or even in part—and decided in a compensatory move to actively *imagine* what is situated on the underside of the earth. Precisely because this underside is inaccessible it asks to be populated by deities, events, and forces that are literally invisible on the surface of the earth. Rilke emphasizes this invisibility in his ninth *Duino Elegy*:

> Earth, isn't this what you want: an invisible
> re-arising in us? Is it not your dream
> to be one day invisible? Earth! Invisible![19]

For the modern poet, what is under the earth is so radically unseeable that no excavation could find it—unlike the undersides of intermediate earthly edges such as sand dunes. All that is possible for the poet is to posit the invisible as a dimension or region out of our ken—and to bring this invisible into poetic discourse by naming it. Addressing this realm, Rilke adds, "What is your urgent command, if not transformation?"[20] The transformation is into poetry; but the underearth itself remains unavailable in its unseen depths. It is literally terra incognita.

Rilke is in effect telling us that there is a realm under the earth's surface which is inaccessible, and that we can only invoke its invisibility in poetry. Earlier civilizations were unwilling to stop there. Precisely because the underearth is inaccessible and invisible, it calls out to be populated—in myth and story if not in any other way. This was not a conscious strategy, of course, but the lively imagination of the underworld in legend and saga was a creative response to the phenomenological fact that the earth itself refuses to proffer its own depths: in its stark reserve, it keeps to itself. If Heidegger calls this refusal "self-seclusion" and if Rilke names it the "invisible," these are characteristic and revealing late modern views that contrast strikingly with the efforts of earlier cultures to fill up the tellurian emptiness with various beings and happenings brought forth by the collective imagination.

The ancient Greeks distinguished between the layer of *Ge*, "Earth" as the realm of fertile soil, ruled by Demeter, goddess of fertility and agriculture, and *chthon*, the lifeless icy level inhabited by shades—the realm of death, ruled by Hades and Hecate and populated by "the dead and the infernal gods."[21] The Egyptians had a comparably bifurcated conception, considering the underworld (Ba) to be the "reverse" of the upperworld: "people there walk with their feet against the ceiling."[22] However differently configured such models of the underworld may be, they share the basic structure of having distinguishable layers, being themselves radically *under* the day world of life and growth, and sometimes possessing their own further subdivisions, as with the nine Circles of Hell in Dante's *Inferno*. These literary and theological underworlds populate what is otherwise empty and unknown—and threatening as such.

All such lower worlds possess different *landscapes*—whole topographies that differ markedly from those of what is situated on the earth's upper surface: the deepest circle of Dante's Hell is composed entirely of an icescape. At other levels, rivers of fire and staggeringly precipitous mountains abound; we encounter fabulous and ferocious animals like Cerebus; sinister figures or gods live there (Satan, Hecate, Hades) along with numerous demons (the *di manes* or "underworld spirits"[23]). The differentiation of levels was not an arbitrary matter but reflected the basic belief that the House of Hades has many chambers, each filled with its own distinctively different contents. These contents are so diverse that they cannot all coexist on the same level. A proliferation of levels allows things to be sorted out by kind or type.

The same differentiation and proliferation undergirds manifold literary and religious representations of the underworld. The contents of these representations are not merely projected onto the various levels, nor do they serve merely to paper them over; instead, they fill them out and fill them in with a special zest that is evident in Dante's great epic (it is widely held that the *Inferno* is superior in literary merit to the *Paradiso* in *The Divine Comedy* as if the underworld had been a special spur to his imagination). Highly imaginative constructions endow otherwise amorphous shades and substances with distinctive identities, each with its own set of edges—edges that arise from verbal description rather than from being actually seen. Indeed, the very entrance to the underworld itself as recounted in ancient writings constitutes a singular edge of earth. This entrance had its own name in Latin epics: Avernus. Similarly, the Egyptian deity Aker protected "the entrance to the underworld at the edge of existence."[24] The fact that such an edge is a literary creation does not undermine its edge-likeness; it only puts it on another basis, one brought into being through evocative language. This edge may not "exist" in the usual sense of having a spatiotemporal location. But it *subsists* in and through its verbal articulations—that is to say, in the projections of myth and religion. In this way, it becomes fully imaginable even if not literally perceivable.

## VI

Returning to a main theme of this chapter, we must distinguish between the earth's edge itself and the many edges by which the earth brings itself into our awareness. Earlier I mentioned that the former kind of edge is to be conceived of as a "total part" in Merleau-Ponty's sense of the term. Part though it is, it is the earth's own edge, and is the place where the earth as a whole comes to be present in one of its parts. On the other hand, the earth presents a multitude of particular edges that are found on its variegated surface: mountains, hills, rivers, cliffs, and ditches. At one extreme is the razorback mountain I scaled in central Montana: it is a radically upturned edge. At another extreme are the gentle lamellae that cut across the dunes at the beach in Oceano on the California coast. The edge of the mountain in Montana is very longstanding, even if not immutable, whereas the dunes' edges alter their configuration with passing winds and in keeping with the season. Still more transitory are the crests on ocean waves, whose edges change with such speed as to be barely trackable with the naked eye.[25] In point of fact, there is a virtually infinite variety of edges that accrue to the land and sea surfaces of planet Earth, each of which reflects the material nature of that of which it is the edge—carrying that materiality (granite, sand, soil, water) into the edge, *becoming the edge*, which then, as it comes to its own terminus, abruptly closes off the very matter of which it is composed.

*The edge of the earth.* If we seek the edge of the earth itself, there are four plausible candidates.

(1) The edge that lies at *the far end of the known earth*, its terminal point: such an edge is not a literal terminus but is an object of belief based on the conviction that water and land must end *somewhere*—come to a halt there—and with them, the earth

that undergirds them. Such was the thought that dominated the imagination of many navigators who set out from the Pillars of Hercules before the earth had been circumnavigated by Magellan and was shown to be one continuous sphere—such that going around it far enough at the same latitude will bring you back to where you started.

(2)  The edge that leads into *the underworld* in many world cosmologies; not just the supposed entry point itself (such as Avernus) but the whole radical downward turn away from the earth's surface into a nether realm of multiple levels and mythical geographies. This realm shares with the far end of the known earth the fact that both are imaginary, as we would now say from the perspective of late modernity. This is not to say, however, that they are trivial constructions: after all, earth's projected drop-off inspired the very sea voyages that led to its very denial, and entrances to the underworld were articles of faith for many in ancient and indigenous worlds. They are both efforts to give meaningful configuration to the earth's self-withdrawn character: its unknowable dimension.

Neither (1) nor (2) can count as a *found* edge; each derives its standing from belief systems, geographic or religious, and does not exist outside the mythical or speculative positings of these systems. For this reason, they do not survive the kind of skeptical scrutiny that draws on independent criteria of verification. Each is a soft edge that melts away when rigorous empirical standards are applied to it. As Sartre has argued, an imagined object resists being scrutinized at the level of quantifiable detail: we cannot reliably count the number of columns on a purely imagined Greek temple.[26]

(3)  The edge that is on the far side of any perceived landscape scene: this is, once again, the *horizon*. This edge is not imagined or projected; it is *there* as a presence within the compass of our vision. Like the imagined underworld and the anticipated downturn of the ocean, there is just one of them. But unlike these latter, it is genuinely perceived, and thus its singular qualities and traits are actually apprehended. The horizon is a distinctive visual *phenomenon*, that is, something that shows itself and persists in showing itself as unique: no two horizons are exactly the same in their perceptual features. Horizons change character from one landscape to another, from one season to

another, and even from one moment of perception to another. But *some* horizon is always there in any open landscape and seascape scene in which our perception is not cut short; it is a constant feature of such a scene, however differently it may appear on different occasions.[27]

(4) Horizons share with *the ground under our feet* the distinction of being avatars of the earth's edge in a nonfictive and nonimaginal format: each is sensuously present in every instance of its encounter. Both horizon and ground, acting in concert, count fully as *the* earth's edge. Even if this edge is spread out and smooth and has none of the abruptness of most edges, it counts as an edge: an edge of presentation in which the whole (the earth) is immanent in a part (the ground on which I stand). Nothing else is so continually present in my ongoing experience as the stretch of earth on which I am now located and where I stand and move. Similarly, we are always able to find some vestige of a horizon by repositioning ourselves (it can be visible even in the dark, as when I see it traced by distant lights that outline a horizontal arc). But horizon and ground differ in that, while the extent of the earth underfoot is subject to at least casual reckoning, horizons resist measurement altogether; we cannot say that a given horizon is "seven miles long" or "twenty feet high." Even as early European mariners gave up their stance on terra firma when they went west into the Atlantic, they kept their eye on the horizon at sea. It was a cynosure of their vision because it was reliably there at the outer edge, indeed *as* this outer edge, even if the "there" itself could not be measured in meters or miles. It was there (there in vision) but not there (in measurable fact).

*Edges of the earth*: several of these we see directly, as determinate features of our environment. They are already there, awaiting our discovery and perception and measurement. Unlike the horizon or the ground, they are always multiple, belonging to this protuberance here or that rill over there. Whether they are sought out or not, they come forward into our experience as configuring the surface of the earth. By contrast, the edge of the earth is fugitive and recessive. It is neither a thing nor an event; it is fundamental yet intermittently experienced, sometimes confronting us but just as often eluding us, as if coming and going on its own, whether we are looking for it or not, and wherever we may be on earth itself at the time we take it in.

## VII

So far in this chapter we have been bidirectional in our description of the earth's own edge, looking *out* toward the horizon and *down* onto the earth. Similarly, in locating the earth's many discrete edges we have tended to search far and wide on the one hand and down deep on the other: outward on the plane of perception and downward at what lies beneath us. But what happens when we look in a third direction: when we look *up*? It remains to consider the edge-world with which we are presented high above us as witnessed from our position on earth.

When we glance into the sheer sky, we are not looking into a void. Despite the tendency to think of the sky as vacant, we see such things as flying birds, tree-tops, cloud formations, colors of the atmosphere, and the sun, moon, and stars. We also feel with our sensing body such other things as gusts of wind, a rain squall that falls from above, and sometimes snow. The fact is that the sky is filled with a medley of things and events, each with a characteristic set of edges. How are we to account for all this?

Take clouds to start with: although there are basic recognized types of clouds (the standard four being cirrus, stratus, nimbus, and cumulus, though sometimes ten are specified), in ordinary observation—unaided by Google Glass—we are concerned not with strict classification but only with whatever cloud shapes catch our eye. The transitoriness of these shapes invites our bare glance rather than any concerted scrutiny: we just "look up at the weather." When we do, passing cloud patterns often catch our eye. Only rarely do we fasten onto a particular cloud or group of clouds, as when there is a dark mass of clouds portending difficult weather, or else (still more rarely) a particular shape that resembles an animal or a human being:

> Hamlet: Do you see yonder cloud that's almost in shape of a camel?
> Polonius: By the mass, and 'tis like a camel, indeed.
> Hamlet: Methinks it is like a weasel.
> Polonius: It is backed like a weasel.
> Hamlet: Or like a whale?
> Polonius: Very like a whale. (*Hamlet* 3.2.38–44)

Apart from the humor of this scene, it illustrates a basic point about clouds: their highly ambiguous, rapidly changing shapes. These shapes are articulated mainly by their outer edges, sometimes perceived in the form of something familiar on earth that is projected onto them in the guise of something recognizably similar. Thus we seem to see a camel, a weasel, or a whale *in the sky*. Polonius's credulous-ness, falling prey to Hamlet's fanciful identifications, demonstrates two very basic characteristics of cloud edges beyond their sheer ambiguity: their mutability and their suggestibility. A mere word suffices to induce the Polonius in us to "see" such things as animal shapes. Just insofar as the edges of clouds are indefinite, fleeting, and passing, they lend themselves to what Bachelard calls "a need to animalize."[28]

We here add a new entry to our edge lexicon: that of *fleecy edges*. In striking contrast with the rigidity of rims, these edges are soft, indeterminate in shape, and continually changing. They could never count as borders—meant to keep a pre-determined form—but they are boundary-like, since they are altogether porous and permeable by many things (hot air balloons, airplanes, birds, other clouds). But they have their own unique being that sets them apart from all other kinds of edge. A sign of this is the fact that John Constable devoted many years to his "cloud studies," paintings of passing clouds over the fields he knew so well in his native England. Other painters have paid special attention to clouds—notably the American painters John Marin and Marsden Hartley, both of whom featured clouds as having a certain solidity and thing-likeness, as if to mock their very tran-sitoriness and thereby to remind us all the more of their intrinsic mutability.[29]

## VIII

Beyond clouds and their groupings (clouds almost always come in clusters, com-pounding the complexity of their perceived edges), as we look up into the sky we are presented with other edge phenomena. Notable among these is the special character of the light in the sky: its comparative *luminescence*. This is more notice-able during the day, but it is also perceptible at night, when the indirect light from the moon and stars creates a special sheen that is the nocturnal equivalent of day-time luminescence. In the latter, we experience a special translucency, *through which* sunlight plays in different degrees and qualities, with effects that are some-times sparkling and sometimes murky, with many phases in between—a diapha-nous scene that is both recessive and forthcoming, subtle and forthright. We often take this for granted, having experienced it during our entire lives, yet it is difficult to pin down and describe. Painters have tried to capture it over many centuries and in diverse cultures. In the West, the great painters of open skies include J. M. W. Turner and Georgia O'Keefe. O'Keefe showed what lucidly clear skies (emblem-atically those of New Mexico) look like when represented by pure colors such as cerulean blue at high intensity. Turner demonstrated how high-flying skies possess their own inner animation, especially as experienced on the open ocean. Employ-ing high-value yellows shading into white, he managed masterfully to combine effects of effervescence with the suggestion of the movement of air that sweeps over the sea.

But we don't need the assistance of painters to experience for ourselves the luminescence of skies: just go outside at any time of the day or night and you will experience this very quality hovering above us and around us. We do not so much look *at it* as see *through it*. It is at once a vast expanse and yet something through which our look moves freely. It is much more a medium or a field than it is an object or a thing. *On it* objects and things can appear, graphically profiled there: clouds, birds, flying leaves, balloons. Sky is the domain of air, which the ancient Greeks considered as a basic element of equal importance with water, earth, and fire. The air that holds and exhibits luminescence is not only up in the sky—that is where we are most likely to notice its presence—it is *everywhere*, all around us, indeed *in us* as we breathe it in and out. Anaximenes described it this way: "As our soul, being air, holds us together, so do breath and air surround the whole universe."[30]

Air is the basic constituent of the atmosphere (a word whose original root in *atmen* means "to breathe"), and the atmosphere constitutes a zone around and just above the earth. As essential to life, it is called the "biosphere," redesignated as Gaia by James Lovelock in an effort to capture its pervasive presence in human and animal life.[31] Whatever the specific scientific merit of Lovelock's "Gaia hypothesis," it points to the elemental necessity of air in the layer of atmosphere that encircles earth and enables life to flourish there. For flying creatures, the sky is an accommodating and supportive matrix on which they rely for their mobility. For earth-bound creatures and birds alike, it is the source of breath and life. All this—air and atmosphere together—we sense when we look into a luminous sky: we do not so much observe it as *inspire* it, literally "breathe it in."

For us the question becomes, where are the edges of this immense and diaphanous field of presence? The answer is that it has no intrinsic edges—no internal or external edges of its own, or none that belong to it exclusively. Nevertheless, it is often perceived as *edged*. I remarked on this in chapter 2 when I described the way the sky above New York appears when seen from the street. I noted that the sky's edges don't belong to it as such but are borrowed from the high edges of buildings. They are in effect grafted onto the sky's expanse, woven into it; the sky takes them in as if they were its own property; at the very least, I suggested, they are shared between sky and buildings. The same is true of more open vistas—of landscapes and seascapes. Wherever the sky is perceived as coming to an end, *there is its edge*. This edge is in effect a perimeter since it is always located *around* (as *peri-* signifies) the seen and sensed sky. A sunset fills out and thickens this edge in fading but striking ways. In more mundane moments, the sky ends for perception when it is interrupted by intervening masses—buildings, trees, mountains.

It will be noticed that the outer edge of the sky changes as I change the position from which I view it. As I walked west from 8th Avenue on 110th Street, the sky's presented profile altered in keeping with the way the edges of the tall buildings continually presented different patterns. The same is true, pari passu, whether I am on a vast heath in Scotland or sailing on the Atlantic Ocean. In these latter cases, the horizon provides the sky's effective edges—low down in the visual field instead of high up as in New York.[32]

And the sun? I have so far avoided mention of the single most powerful presence in the sky, as if mimicking the physiological fact that I cannot look directly into it without strain and discomfort. Beyond its being the source of heat and light (thus of the luminescence cited above), the sun has extraordinary edges of its own. Blazing and blinding, these are quite literally *unbearable*: we cannot bear to look at them for more than a few fleeting seconds. It is also highly evasive: it seems to flee from our look, which can only be a glance, not a lasting gaze. We observe here a unique form of collusion between the glance and its object—or rather *nonobject*. Only in photographs is the sun a steady presence; otherwise, it changes position continually during the day, shifting even as we try to look at it, never staying constant; it takes itself apart before our very eyes.

The sun is not so much a thing as a source of things: most notably, of light and life. Indeed, it is more an event than a thing: something that is continually happening, and differently so every microsecond, without ever entirely congealing—not even at sunset, when it appears poised just above the horizon, which is as close to stasis as it gets, with the exception of a solar eclipse. Otherwise, the sun's edges are dissolving and moving—both at once and one because of the other. At the end of day these fitful edges move under the horizon and under the earth only to reappear at the start of the next day in the auroral moment of sunrise. This combination of the daily regularity of its course with the irregularity of its glimpsed edges makes the sun something quite unique in the natural world of ordinary perception: no wonder the sun's rising and setting are associated with the creation of the world and with regeneration of many kinds.

What of the moon? In contrast with the sun, its edges can be quite distinct and lingering, not just when it forms a perfect circle at full moon but also at various phases. The French phrase *claire de lune* (meaning moonlight, but literally "clarity of the moon") refers to this distinctness of edges along with the light reflected from its surface—light borrowed from the sun but taking on a mellow cast that allows us to gaze at it for prolonged periods. Hence the phenomenon of the moon's seeming to hang in the sky as a steady presence. Even if the moon's edges can be obscured by clouds and fog and though it can generate rings that are quasi-supplemental edges, these variations do not undermine our sense that the moon itself possesses crisp edges. Hence our references to the moon as a "disk" or as having some other definite shape or quality (half-moon, new moon, autumn moon, sliver of a moon) whose external edges are distinct.[33] Any internal edges—invisible in the case of the sun ("sun spots" not being accessible to unaided vision)—are seized upon and anthropomorphized, as with "the man in the moon," as if to complement the pellucid character of the moon's outer edges.

Other major nighttime presences include the stars and the planets. These belong to the nocturnal sky above us, indeed far above and forming a "canopy" as if constituting a vast stellar tent. Star edges share with sun edges an evanescence of appearing, but they exude this in a much less insistent modality: they twinkle gently or compress themselves into a sheer point rather than burning intensely. Mainly for this reason, it is difficult to make out the edges of a given star; even when we focus on the star with our naked eye, the twinkling or (in more punctiform cases) the concentrated central mass dissolves anything like a definite edge. The same holds true for planets—such as Venus, whose early rising form is often jagged and lacks any easily traceable edge.

Moreover, unlike both sun and moon, each of which is an altogether singular presence, stars and planets tend to appear in groupings (including "constellations," literally, "stars-together"). When a single bright spot is visible in the nightime sky, it is exceptional enough for us to give it a name of its own: Mars or the North Star. Otherwise, as amateur stargazers we are content to let planets and stars remain nameless in their multitudinous appearings as they shift positions from night to night in ways that are difficult to foresee yet ultimately regular. Such patterns of appearing (some of which come to bear names of their own: "Andromeda," "Pegasus") act further to defeat efforts to determine the exact edges of stars and planets. Yet indefiniteness of precisely traceable shapes does not mean that these heavenly bodies are altogether edgeless.

The schematic descriptions I have just given of the sky's habitual residents allow us to compare their respective edges. First of all, it is striking that the moon alone presents us with a presence possessing reliably definite and distinct edges. The outer contours of all other inhabitants of the sky present themselves as unclear or transitory to the point of threatening to obscure any distinctly perceived edges, whether this happens because of the rapidly mutating fringes of clouds, or in the form of edges too bright to bear (the sun), or with the twinkling or pointilization of stars. It is as if being a denizen of the sky brings with it the risk of bearing self-dissolving edges that disappear as much as, if not more often than, they appear. This contrasts with the telluric edges taken up earlier, especially those belonging to the ground underfoot or to the horizon—each of which is an enduring presence on which the perceiver can count. Second, for this very reason earthly edges solicit our *gaze*—a steady look—whereas the denizens of the sky (with the notable exception of the moon) call for our mere *glance*. Between the gaze and perduring objects there is a special bond, just as there is between the glance and ephemeral things. In the former case, edges stare us in the face, being incontestable presences; in the latter, they elude our look as lacking the kind of consistent presence that favors protracted gazing. There are two significant subgroupings of the sky world: those of its occupants that figure into our perception as unique one-of-a-kind phenomena: the sun and the moon, and those others that normally occur in clusters, clouds and stars. Despite such groupings, only the moon presents edges that can be clearly seen, whereas the other residents of the sky have edges that are endemically and not just accidentally indistinct. It is as if the sky acts to obscure almost all edges of whatever appears there—with the notable exception of the moon, as well as those birds, airplanes, and other flying objects that are close enough to be seen clearly.

These findings should not surprise us. The sky, after all, belongs to the atmosphere and consists mostly of air, both diaphanous presences that are indefinite in extent and in felt material constitution. Both air and atmosphere lack proper edges of their own, having to borrow them from determinate presences such as buildings and horizons. Their most characteristic contents—clouds and stars, sun and moon—convey edges only across the translucent veiling that air and atmosphere themselves provide. This veiling acts to make their inhabitants characteristically indistinct in their presentation, including their edges.

"The sky [is] acutest at its vanishing," wrote Wallace Stevens.[34] Indeed, the whole sky vanishes—into thin air, into the atmosphere beyond. The sky is a vast vanishing act. Its denizens are subject to the effects of such vanishing—that is to say, the massive withdrawal that the sky brings with it even in its most luminous moments: a withdrawal that is the aerial counterpart to the insistent presence of the earth below. And the same retreat takes the edges of what belongs to the sky with it; these edges exhibit much the same obscuration that characterizes the sky as a whole. It is a situation of elemental *obscurum per obscurius*, being made "obscure by the more obscure": the edges of unclearly presented entities tend themselves to be unclear.

## IX

It is time to go to the furthest edge of all: to the outer edge of the sky itself, its sheer periphery—that which we witness, or think we witness, when we look straight up and out and search to the limit of our visual capacities. When we do this, however, it is not clear just *what* we see in our searching. I have insisted that we see *through* the air that makes up the atmosphere. But through to *what*? Just *where* does our look go? Certainly not to a determinate object, given that the main candidates for objects are those I have just discussed: clouds and sun, moon and planets and stars, along with transitory occupants such as birds and airplanes. Note that our searching look does not seem to go to a particular region, a set place, not even to "the heavens," a term that names an indeterminate zone with biblical and poetic overtones whose semantic range is very close to the sky and its various "heavenly bodies" as I have described them. It is apparent that there is no proper or privileged thing or place to be found as we look into the upper sky; there is only the indeterminate *whereto* of our gaze or glance as it directs itself up from the earth and out from our lived body into the "wild blue yonder."

The paradox is that the outermost edge of the sky is no edge at all, if by edge we mean something that has a definite structure (for example, that of a convex dihedral angle) or that terminates a thing or an event (the edge of the room in which I am located) or that opens onto a separate situation (as when a narrow defile in the mountains gives way to a vast upland pasture). And yet we find ourselves inclined to believe that some sort of edge *must* be there, if only as belonging to the outer surface of the atmosphere, where the sky gives out and gives way to interstellar space, which we now know is not empty but populated by meteorites, concealed galaxies, gamma rays, whole gravitational fields, and much more. Such space appears to have no finite terminus but to go outward endlessly, or else, on an Einsteinian paradigm, to bend back in time as well as space.

The mere invocation of Einstein—or later theorists of cosmic space—signals that we have moved far beyond a realm in which concrete perception is pertinent, as is still the case when we look into the sky with its differential properties of density (of felt texture) and direction (of air currents), luminosity, and color. All these qualities are experienced by animate bodies situated on earth or just above, or else, more rarely, suspended in the air itself above earth in a helium balloon or other flying machine. All such circumstances draw upon the sensory powers of lived bodies—powers that are especially adept at seeking out edges of many kinds, including the edge of the upper sky, despite the difficulty of its discernment. But in order to do this, by what means can we grasp what it is like to be in outer space?

We return here by a curious twist to the medieval conundrum of the javelin thrower: *into what* does he throw his spear, if he is himself situated on the outermost edge of the known universe? He cannot *know* into what his instrument is to be thrown or where it will land, since he is throwing it into precisely the radically unknown. It was repeated meditation on this thought experiment in the twelfth and thirteenth centuries that led, along with other developments, to the positing of infinite space several centuries later. This line of thinking was reinforced by speculation as to what space God himself occupies if he is ubiquitous and unlimited: his infinity was construed as tantamount to the infinity of space itself. By the time we reach the seventeenth century, we find that both Newton and Spinoza ally God with space, and vice versa, insofar as each possesses infinity of extension.[35]

The moral of this tale is clear. If our perceptual powers are not able to locate the edge of the physical universe with any specificity, we must take recourse to *thinking*—whether as metaphysical or theological speculation or as scientific theory—to deal with shortcomings at the level of sensory awareness. As Kant would have it, whatever we do not have in our perceptual grasp as an object of empirical intuition as subsumed under the understanding's categories, we must attempt to think though pure reason's Ideas. Both understanding and reason belong to the domain of thinking. But each is problematic when invoked in the context of considering the outermost edges of the universe. On Kant's paradigm, understanding must limit its reach to what is given through the forms of sensible intuition that condition human experience—whereas the edges we now seek are not so intuited. They can only be posited by a dialectical reason that proceeds by what Kant calls "the logic of illusion," which ignores the limits of possible experience by speculating about things we can *think* but cannot *know.*[36] This latter situation describes our own circumstance at this late point in the book; we seem limited to speculating what the edges of that which lies beyond the upper atmosphere *might* be like, what we *think* them to be, without any assurance of knowing what they are really like, and with no reliable way to gain such knowledge. At least we have no such assurance as amateur surveyors of the outer skies.

As Kant implies in "The Dialectic of Pure Reason," the last part of *The Critique of Pure Reason,* purely speculative thought can only lead to insoluble antinomies such as that space is both infinite and finite. Each of these claims can be shown separately to be plausible, yet the two taken together are incompatible. Let us agree with Kant on two basic counts: thought without content is empty, and speculative thinking on its own ends in impasse.[37] Recourse to pure thought is futile when it comes to discussing the outermost edges of all that is—tempting as this has been for many centuries and doubtless still is.[38]

## X

If ordinary perception and speculative thought fail us when it comes to the extreme edges of the physical universe, we do have one other recourse: the traces of such edges if not the edges themselves. Here I shall call upon suggestions contained in a recent film by Patrice Guzmán, *Nostalgia de la Luz* (Nostalgia for the Light).[39] From this film, we can take away the idea that what is very distant in space or time (so distant as not to be in the purview of human sensibilities), instead of disappearing altogether, can be shown to reveal its outermost, barest edges to us in certain traces of its existence. This holds true even of what is *most* distant in time, that is, the origin of the universe in the big bang, vestiges of which can still be detected in the lens of special telescopes located in the vast and ancient Atacama Desert in Chile. The images received by these telescopes are accessible to scientists and ourselves, yet they are in fact images of states of affairs dating from billions of years ago; they bring us the beginning moments of the universe or microseconds just after.

As is said at one point in *Nostalgia de la Luz,* we have here "remains of remains." Note that "remains" can be either temporal or spatial. Temporal remains are indicated on a sufficiently sophisticated clock; spatial remains, as literal *remnants*, are to be found in the reproducible images derived from powerful telescopes—or else, at a very different scale, from bone fragments left over from the *desaparecidos* of the Pinochet era, fragments left in the sands of the Atacama Desert. It is the relentless search for these latter that furnishes the dark counter-plot of the film: the frantic, unending search by the mothers, sisters, and children of those who perished under the regime of Augusto Pinochet that extended from 1973 to 1990. These bereaved relatives are shown looking desperately, most often without success and with little hope, for the remains of their loved ones in the vast and pitiless desert. (The Pinochet regime had a notorious concentration camp there where many were tortured and killed, their bodies thrown into the desert nearby or else into the ocean.) What are these obsessed relatives seeking? Any surviving part of the body of a departed member of their family. If found, such a part, however fragmentary, allows survivors to finally accept the death of the departed; but more than this, it represents the continuing *presence* of a son or sister, husband or mother. One woman featured in the film clung fiercely onto the recently discovered foot and sock of her son, clinging to them as if her son might somehow miraculously return by virtue of this forlorn gesture. Another mother had been given the jawbone of her son, but insisted that this was not enough; she could not rest, could not herself die, until his whole body was discovered—which was almost certain never to happen.

The plot thickens when the two primary narratives of the film—searching for the origins of the solar system in the wake of the big bang and digging for the bones of the disappeared—converge late in the story. A physicist points out that the calcium found in human bones has been in existence since shortly after the primal cosmic explosion. A striking image shows a driven and haunted woman walking gingerly over the desert with her tiny shovel, on the outlook for fragments as the light of day recedes and a very bright planet (presumably Venus) begins to glow above her; this planet is also a trace of the primal explosion, as is the earth itself.

A young mother whose parents were disappeared testifies that just thinking about the vast scope of cosmic time brings her consolation for her otherwise unbearable loss: within its undelimited extent, everything emerges and disappears in its own time. In a poignant image, a young physicist whose mother does physical therapy for those traumatized by the Pinochet terror is shown helping two of the women most intent on finding traces of their loved ones by allowing them to look into a telescope that brings the most distant parts/moments of the solar system into view. In this episode, a sentence from early in the film returns to haunt the viewer: "the secrets of the sky fell upon us." These secrets have to do with the fact that "the present does not exist," as the young physicist states in an interview. Only the past can tell us about primal origins—whether cosmic, familial, or personal. But this past is not accessible as such, on its own terms; it reaches us only through temporal traces and physical remnants. These traces and remnants were themselves emitted from a past event (in this respect like the light/energy sent out after the big bang) or else were a literal part of that event and have survived in a form that can be discovered at a later time (as with the literal bones of those who were killed under Pinochet).

To draw a parallel between that which remains of the origin of the universe and a politically motivated systematic massacre is not to deny the real differences between these two events. One has to do with creation—cosmic creation—and the other with violent destruction in the ultimate form of death. The traces of the former are accessible only in sophisticated telescopic views and photographs, whereas the remnants of the latter are discrete physical things (bone fragments, pieces of clothing). The time of the big bang is the beginning of time itself, while the era of the Pinochet killings is located in recent history. Moreover, the space of the first moment of creation is condensed into a hard core of protomatter that burst asunder; the physical remains of Pinochet's camp are late avatars of such matter. The primal cosmogonic event and the evidence for the Pinochet crimes are both viewed in and from the same place: the Atacama Desert in Chile, which brings together in one place the beginning of the universe and the forced extermination of innocent human lives—two irreversible events, however different they are in kind.

The residua of cosmic and tragic events alike exhibit a very special form of edge: that of *extreme states*. These extreme states can be as cataclysmic and distant as the big bang or as intimate and personal as the death of a loved one. In both cases, human beings find themselves on the receiving end: living in what they call "the present," their hands empty of anything like the full presence of a past that alternately intrigues and haunts them. "We have only bits and pieces," says Ernestine De Soto, a surviving member of a six-generation family of Chumash Indians first located in Santa Barbara; "the whole history is lost."[40] The truth is that, even in less dramatic or tragic circumstances, we do not have, and never will have, the past event itself, the past person herself, much less the entire lived history of a people. Nor do we have the past of the universe itself, forever receding from us—much less the ur-spatiality of cosmic creation or the full mass of bodies tortured by Pinochet. We have only the bare traces of the spatio-temporal edges of cosmic creation and of the fleshly edges of the bodies of the *desaparecidos*.[41]

## XI

Indicated here is a special class of edges, *ulterior edges*, which deserve their own description. Such edges have two dimensions: physical (visual, tangible, photographic) and semiotic (traces considered as human or cosmic signs). When the outermost edges of events and processes no longer directly accessible are regarded as physical, they amount to the material remains of their specific origins.

As semiotic, these same depositions signify beyond their own physical mass and configured surface: they allude, however indirectly, to what has happened long before. In this allusive signification, these personal and celestial origins show themselves to be immemorial: far beyond recollection (which requires a representational format) and as such not belonging to any mind or brain or text but to "an immense world-Memory."[42] They are also supra-spatial—not to be encompassed in any finite measure of spatial spread.

In their cosmic parameters, ulterior edges take us to the very extremities of the known universe, the astrophysical perimeter, no less surely so than did Aristotle's argument for the position of the First Mover in the outermost circle of the heavens. It was on this last circle that the javelin thrower posited by theologians of the Middle Ages was poised. Out there, at the last limit, there is sparse company—no humans, no animals, nothing alive and moving. The first edges following the big bang belonged to barely distinguishable nascent "things" and "events," whether these were molten masses, vast leaping flames, or tumultuous explosions. The astronomers of the Atacama Desert aim their telescopes at nothing less than the primal edges accruing to the first moments of the solar system and the galaxy to which the earth belongs: edges that reach us still today, in our own time and space, through traces that show up as images in one of the most powerful observatories on earth.[43]

As human, ultimate edges are found in the skeletal remains of dead bodies, in the bones of the deceased. The foot of one dead person, the jawbone of another: these suffice to prove that the human person to whom they belonged, once vibrantly living, is now dead—gone forever as alive, rejoining the unliving and inanimate materials and elements of the universe. We have only the surviving fragments of someone who once existed. These fragments are literally *partes extra partes*: detached parts of a person gone forever as a living person. They are signs of a life lived in extremis: a life brutally taken away from an innocent victim.

Ulterior edges, whether cosmic or human, are literally *extraordinary*: they fall outside the range of ordinary edges. In this far-ranging chapter we have moved from the earth and the underworld to the sky above and from there to images of the moment of cosmic creation considered in analogy to body parts left over from heinous murders. This is a move from naive innocence—what could be more childlike than looking up into the clouds in the day or at the moon at night?—to intense drama as well as tragedy: the creation of the universe and the massacre of innocents in the Atacama Desert. It is also a move from the physical edges directly underfoot as we stand on earth looking out to the horizon—perceived but intangible—and from there to the sky above the horizon, an open field of diverse presences: a sky whose own outer edges are unperceivable.

In making such a journey, we may find ourselves tempted to feel a certain nostalgia over ultimate origins, especially if we remind ourselves that the root meaning of *nostalgia* is literally "pain on returning home": more expansively, it signifies the pain of longing to come back home, back to first origins, whether of the cosmos or an individual life. But in making this journey, we can also allow ourselves to be inspired by the vistas we have glimpsed—vistas that take us beyond the personal, indeed beyond the human, into the larger reaches of the cosmos: reaches where edges no longer figure as only finite and close-fitting or as intermediate and transitional but as indefinitely expansive: so expansive that we can only discern them in the guise of the images they leave in telescopes. Even a glimpse into such a domain is as philosophically refreshing as it is humbling for mortal earthlings who are confined to the flatlands of two- and three-dimensional edge-worlds.

## Notes

1. The word *oikoumené* was first employed to designate the Greek world, including several non-Greek lands (Ethiopia, India, Scythia). It then came to designate the vast territories under Alexander the Great's control. In the first and second centuries AD it signified the Roman world. After Constantine's ascendance in the early fourth century AD, it referred to peoples united by adherence to Christianity. In each of these various usages, the term connoted those parts of the known earth that were inhabited by those who spoke a particular tongue (e.g., Greek, Latin). I owe these precisions to Wesley Mattingly and Eric Casey.

2. The earth's edge as a strictly self-enclosed entity is visible only as the earth is viewed all at once—in a single flat image of it, pre-eminently in a photograph taken from space of it. As I have maintained earlier, *as a three-dimensional sphere*, the earth has no effective single edge insofar as its surface is altogether continuous and as such has no outer edges.

3. This phrase is from Maurice Merleau-Ponty, *Phenomenology of Perception*, trans. Colin Smith (New York: Routledge, 2003), p. 63.

4. For a study of Heidegger's responses to the 1966 photos of the earth taken by the Lunar Orbiter, see Benjamin Lazier, "Earthrise, or the Globalization of the World-Picture," *American Historical Review* 116 (2011): 602–30.

5. I employ Husserl's term "presentify" (*vergegenwärtigen*) to indicate that the earth is not presented as if it were a sheer physical thing but rather as something absent in its very presence, as a case of *sterésis* in Aristotle's term. See Bryan Bannon, "Flesh and Nature: Understanding Merleau-Ponty's Relational Ontology," in *Research in Phenomenology* 41 (2011): pp. 327–57, especially 340.

6. See Merleau-Ponty, *The Visible and the Invisible* (Evanston, IL: Northwestern University Press, 1968), p. 134. Referring to the "double and crossed situating of the visible in the tangible and of the tangible in the visible," Merleau-Ponty writes, these "two parts are total parts." See also *Phenomenology of Perception*, trans. Landes, pp. 454–57, including "total being" on p. 482. See also his mention of "moments of my total being whose sense I could make explicit in different directions, without our ever being able to say if it is I who give them their sense or if I receive it from them" (ibid.).

7. I refer here to Husserl's distinction between parts that are integral components—i.e., "moments" (*Momente*)—rather than being separable "pieces" (*Stücke*): a distinction on which I draw elsewhere in this book.

8. Here "limit" is something purely posited, in keeping with the usage I proposed in chapter 1: that is, a theoretical entity that lends itself to geometric or mathematical description. But in the case before us it is entirely imagined.

9. For further treatment of this conundrum, with a history of its conception and evolution from a pseudo-Hermetic text of the twelfth century through Cusa to Pascal, see Casey, *The Fate of Place*, pp. 116–17. Bruno's version is telling: "Surely we can affirm that the universe is all center, or that the center of the universe is everywhere, and that the circumference is not in any part, although it is different from the center; or that the circumference is throughout all, but the center is not to be found inasmuch as it is different from that" (*The Fate of Place*, p. 117). "Circumference" is the name for a very particular geometric edge—that of a plane figure—and is here projected onto the outermost part of the universe.

10. Wesley Mattingly puts it this way: it is as if the Venn diagram "moves over a sense field as the common space grows or diminishes" (e-mail communication of June 15, 2015).

11. This phrase is from Martin Heidegger, *Being and Time*, trans. Edward Robinson and James Macquarrie (New York: Harper, 1962), p. 139: "'De-severing' [*Ent-fernung*] amounts to making the farness vanish—that is, making the remoteness of something disappear, bringing it close." Upon seeing the Lunar Orbiter photos of the earth referred to earlier, Heidegger remarked that they gave the earth a sense of nearness that obscured its farness (op. cit.). See also Joan Stambaugh's translation: Martin Heidegger, *Being and Time*, trans. Joan Stambaugh (Albany: State University of New York Press, 1996) p. 97, which uses "de-distancing" for *Ent-fernung*.

12. An analogue from another domain is the "local absolute" as this idea has been developed by Deleuze and Guattari in *A Thousand Plateaus*. What is in one respect absolute qua global comes to inhabit that which is a single place, a limited locality like a town or a shrine or a house. On the other hand, any of the latter can be said to ramify into the absolute-global so completely as to be at one with it. See especially *A Thousand Plateaus*, trans. Brian Massumi (Minneapolis: University of Minnesota Press, 1987), pp. 382–83. The "relative global" is a matter of positions in striated space, whereas the "local absolute" is "an absolute that is manifested locally, and engendered in a series of local operations of varying orientations: desert, steppe, ice, sea." The core of the latter is "making the absolute appear in a particular place" (p. 382).

13. Heidegger, "Building Dwelling Thinking," in *Poetry Language Thought*, trans. Albert Hofstadter (New York: Harper & Row, 1971), p. 154; his italics.

14. See also the next sentence: "Space is in essence that for which room has been made, that which is let into its bounds" (ibid.).

15. Maurice Merleau-Ponty, *The Visible and the Invisible*, trans. Alphonso Lingis (Evanston, IL: Northwestern University Press, 1968), p. 258: "The sensible, the visible must be defined not as that with which I have in fact a relation by effective vision—but also as that of which I can subsequently have a teleperception" (working note of May 1960). Nothing parapsychological is meant here: rather, it is a matter of *perception at a distance.*

16. For further on orientation, see Casey, *The World at a Glance*, chapter 3, "Being/Becoming Oriented by the Glance."

17. Martin Heidegger, "The Origin of the Work of Art," in Heidegger, *Poetry, Language, Thought*, p. 47.

18. "The work moves the earth itself into the Open of a world and keeps it there. *The work lets the earth be an earth*" (Heidegger, "The Origin of the Work of Art," in Heidegger, *Poetry, Language, Thought*, p. 45; author's italics).

19. Rainer Maria Rilke, *Duino Elegies*, trans. James Blair Leishman and Stephen Spender (New York: Norton, 1963), p. 77.

20. Rilke, *Duino Elegies*, p. 77. In a celebrated letter to his Polish translator of 1925, Rilke continues in prose: "Transformed? yes, for our task is to stamp this provisional, perishing earth into ourselves so deeply, so painfully and passionately, that its being may arise again, 'invisibly,' in us. . . . The earth has no other refuge except to become invisible: IN US." "In us" refers to human beings as language-capable and in particular to poets as the masters of language whose meanings are quite literally invisible.

21. On this distinction, see James Hillman, *The Dream and the Underworld* (New York: Harper, 1979), especially pp. 35–45. The phrase "the dead and the infernal gods" is cited on p. 39, from F. Cumont, *After Life in Roman Paganism* (New York: Dover, 1959), p. 80. Hillman distinguishes between soil as such (the proper place of Demeter) and *Ge* as the source of "the rituals and laws that guarantee fertility."

22. Cited by Hillman, p. 39, from J. Zandee, *Death as an Enemy According to Ancient Egyptian Conceptions* (Leiden: Brill, 1960), p. 73.

23. See Hillman, *The Dream and the Underworld*, p. 41. The *di manes* were "the Roman equivalent of the Greek *theoi chthonioi.*" As a term, *di manes* is a first cousin of *daimonia*, the demonic gods.

24. Hillman, *The Dream and the Underworld*, p. 38.

25. For this reason, Leibniz took them to be exemplary of the domain of *petites perceptions*, a level of apperception so subtle that we are rarely if ever conscious of it as such.

26. See Jean-Paul Sartre, *Psychology of Imagination* (London: Routledge, 1991) pp. 99–101. See also Sartre, *The Imaginary* (New York: Routledge, 2004), p. 87.

27. A horizon figures into every perceiving of an extended land- or seascape, being an integral part of such scenes. However elusive it may be at certain moments (as in a deep fog), it is always accessible in principle: I know that it will reemerge when the fog lifts.

28. See Gaston Bachelard: "A need to animalize . . . is at the origins of imagination. The first function of the imagination is to create animal forms" (*Lautréamont* [Dallas: Pegasus, 1986], p. 27).

29. For a thorough study of the importance of clouds in the history of painting, see Hubert Damisch, *A Theory of /Cloud/: Toward a Theory of Painting*, trans. Janet Lloyd (Palo Alto: Stanford University Press, 2002).

30. This is the sole surviving fragment we have of the Milesian thinker Anaximenes of Miletus. I here cite the translation of Kathleen Freeman, *Ancilla to the Pre-Socratic Philosophers: A Complete Translation of the Fragments in Diels, Fragmente der Vorsokratiker* (Cambridge: Harvard University Press, 1948), p. 19.

31. See James Lovelock, *Gaia: A New Look at Life on Earth* (Oxford: Oxford University Press, 2000). "The Gaia hypothesis" is Lovelock's term for his conception of the biosphere as one vast living super-organism.

32. The main internal edges in a given sky scene are provided by cloud formations, but these do not belong to the sky as such: they are impressed upon it, though as a very gentle presence that normally does not last for more than a few passing moments.

33. Even the curious effect of a phantom moon—whereby a sliver of the moon's edge is completed by a ring that is noticeably pale yet perfectly circular—retains the characteristic shape of the moon's outer edge.

34. This line is from Stevens's poem, "The Idea of Order at Key West": "It was her voice that made / The sky acutest at its vanishing."

35. More exactly, Newton considers infinite space to belong to God's sensorium inasmuch as God must be capable of taking in the "phenomenon of omnipresence" (*omnipraesentia phaenomenon*). For Spinoza, space is one of God's infinite attributes, thus characterizes him all the way through; so, too, does the infinite attribute of thought qualify him throughout. I trace out this story more completely in *The Fate of Place*, pp. 325–26 and 150.

36. My colleague Jeff Edwards suggests this formulation: "When we employ pure ideas (i.e., a priori concepts that can have no reference to objects of possible empirical intuition) in order to think of our experience as having the kind of unity that the understanding cannot provide, the human use of reason necessarily *becomes* dialectical on account of the unavoidability of transcendental illusion" (e-mail communication of May 21, 2015; his italics).

37. Immanuel Kant, *Critique of Pure Reason*, trans. Norman Kemp Smith (New York: St. Martin's Press, 1965), p. 93 (A51, B75): "Thoughts without contents are empty, intuitions without concepts are blind." Note that Husserl proposed a distinctive "categorical intuition" that does not limit intuition to the specific contents of space and time, as on Kant's model. See the sixth of his *Logical Investigations*, trans. J. Findlay, ed. D. Moran (New York: Routledge, 2001).

38. With the notable exception of advanced astronomy, where sophisticated mathematical thought has been able to uncover some of the structure of the outlying regions of the universe.

39. *Nostalgia de la Luz*, Atacama Productions (2010), shown at the Santa Barbara International Film Festival, Santa Barbara, California, January 30, 2011.

40. Ernestine De Soto, speaking in the film *Six Generations: A Chumash Family's History* (Santa Barbara Filmmakers, directed by Paul Goldsmith; shown at the Santa Barbara International Film Festival, January 31, 2011).

41. *Le reste* is a term that could be used in this context. It is Derrida's term for remnants that survive in the form of lingering traces. For this term, see Jacques Derrida, *Glas*, trans. Richard Rand (Lincoln: University of Nebraska Press, 1986) pp. 11–15.

42. Maurice Merleau-Ponty, *Phenomenology of Perception*, trans. Landes, p. 73. "World" here stands in for several things: earth, the universe, the history of humankind. See my chapter "Edges of Time, Edges of Memory," in David Morris and Kim Maclaren, *Time, Memory, Institution: Merleau-Ponty's New Ontology of Self* (Athens: Ohio University Press, 2015).

43. For suggestive images of the "infant universe," consult these NASA website photos: http://map.gsfc.nasa.gov/media/121238/ilc_9yr_moll4096BW.png; http://map.gsfc .nasa.gov/media/121238/index.html; http://map.gsfc.nasa.gov/resources/cmbimages .html; http://map.gsfc.nasa.gov/resources/imagetopics.html. I thank Julia Sushytska for bringing these images to my attention.

# PART 4

# Parting Thoughts

# A Last Lesson: Not to Put Too Fine an Edge on Things

There is a crack, a crack in everything—that's how the light gets in.
　—Leonard Cohen

[I]t is only by means of the crack and at its edges that thought occurs, that anything that is good and great in humanity enters and exists through it.
　—Gilles Deleuze, *Logic of Sense*

*The World on Edge* has moved through a series of three waves, as if in keeping with what Socrates proposed in the *Republic* when discussing how to set up an ideal state.[1] A first wave was taxonomic and typological. In part 1 of this volume, I distinguished various *kinds* of edges so as to bring some order into a situation where few pause to distinguish one sort of edge from another. I practiced what Plato called the "method of division" (*diairesis*), a process of separation that follows upon the "collection" (*synagogê*) of diverse species.[2] But where Plato attempted to bring the members of a given collection (for instance, candidates for being a sophist) under a single form (that of the Sophist), I have resisted this temptation by refusing to offer a generic definition that applies to any and every edge. (At the most, as we shall see a little later, I offer a small assembly of characteristic traits rather than a single definition.) I have engaged in my own activity of collection, in effect dividing edges into a number of distinctive species. I have accorded to borders and boundaries a special status in view of their wide applicability in numerous edge-worlds. I also discerned basic differences between edges and surfaces, which are close allies in ordinary perception, and between edges and limits, which I showed to be fundamentally divergent from each other despite their frequent confusion in ordinary discourse. In a series of three interludes, I delineated a number of distinct types of edges, ranging from brinks and folds to cusps and frames.

　　Equipped with these various distinctions, in a second wave I proceeded to describe how places and events bear their own edge-structures—structures rarely recognized as such. Entering thereby into the larger world of edges that are no longer constricted to being the armature of physical things, I explored how naturally given edges differ from those that are culturally constructed, even as these differential origins collude closely in many contexts. I singled out one concrete context, that of wild edges, considering these as edges that fall outside human intervention. In stark contrast stand the intermediate, mixed edges of parks and gardens, city streets, and neighborhoods. I also discussed how edges accrue to landscapes—a critically important but rarely fully acknowledged sector of human experience. The variety of situations treated in part 2 was meant to demonstrate how we live in entire zones and regions of edges, some of our own devising, but many given or presented to us by the other-than-human natural world of which we are a part.

In a final wave I examined how edges inhere in such different things as our lived bodies and sensitive psyches as well as in the earth below us and the sky overhead. Here I pursued the differences between *the* edge of the body—its outer surface as skin or flesh—and its many subordinate edges, inner as well as outer, in an effort to show that we could not exist as animated and sensuous organisms without possessing a virtual latticework of bodily edges, which alert us to our environment and serve as a basis for coping with the world and taking it into ourselves. Since psyche is a central component of our personal and interpersonal being, I next reflected on our psychical being with respect to its subtle edges insofar as they belong to time and to consciousness, which act to hold our lives together from within. I underlined the fact that the psychical dimension is continually at risk of falling apart and splitting into fragmentary selves (or parts of selves) in schizoid and schizophrenic states. So as not to be unduly anthropocentric, in the remainder of part 3, I went on to investigate what it means to say that the earth has its own edge as well as various particular edges, and how both kinds of edges articulate with the far-flung edges of the sky above and the stars beyond, concluding my descriptive project in the outermost reaches of the known universe.

## I

I call my way of proceeding in this book *peri-phenomenology*. Considered as phenomenology, this has been a descriptive undertaking, an effort to tease out and identify the major edges in human experience, and many kinds of minor ones as well. Unlike Husserl, however, I do not seek essences or even essential structures of edges (though I do speak of "edge-types") that can be presented in an unchanging format; my concern is rather to depict the ingredience of edges in various situations—how they figure and configure there rather than in isolation. In contrast with Merleau-Ponty and Sartre, I am not concerned mainly with pre-reflective experience but instead with any kind or level of experience, implicit or explicit, in which edges are operative, including those that belong to transhuman realms, as in wilderness or the sky. For edges confront us not just in our up-close lives, as we can easily concede, but often beyond them—elsewhere, indeed everywhere, given that we live in a congeries of overlapping edge-worlds. In distinction from Heidegger, my concern is not with the relationship between edges and Being or Event. I stop short of anything like an ontological enterprise and stay within the compass of what can be described as such; that is to say, the domain that is the proper subject matter of a genuine "radical empiricism" (in William James's phrase), which is reflected in the scope and style of my phenomenological descriptions.

Given that *peri-* signifies "around" or "about" and is associated with risk (as in "perilous"), the affinity between a distinctive peri-phenomenology and edge situations is apparent. Peri-phenomenology describes the outstanding parts of things and phases of events as these parts and phases are integral to all that we experience. Just as the glance seeks out the peripheries of what it discerns so quickly and so tellingly, so edges are basic constituents of these same peripheries. Not that all edges can be so considered. Some of them are internal to things and bodies, places and psyches. They are folded into them, as is most evident in the case of creases and rills but is also operative in psychical splitting. Even if it is true that the most prominent edges—which are literally epiphenomenal—are those that provide the outer shapes of things, we must embrace a more capacious vision that valorizes all the other edges that figure into our experience.

Peri-phenomenology is designed to attend to internal and external edge-structures in a detailed and dedicated way. Admittedly, this is easiest to witness in the case of the edges of physical things: the rims, thresholds, margins, and the like that I described early in this book. In their case, the edges are often conspicuous, making them matters of straightforward description. The rim on the coffee cup from which I am drinking is a prominent feature for my eye and hand alike, and my words of description follow forth as if tracing out this rim: "circular," "smooth," "claylike," and so on. But peri-phenomenology as I practice it is also prepared to offer descriptions of more diverse and subtle edges, such as those that adhere to events and places, bodies and psyches. Such edges inhere in that which they serve to define in complex ways, as with the edges of a park designed by British landscape architect Capability Brown: here the edges blend almost imperceptibly into its surrounding space, with no abrupt break, in contrast with a French formal garden created by Le Nôtre.[3] Peri-phenomenological description accommodates the very disparity that is evident among the bearers of a vast variety of edges, whether internal or external, somatic or psychical, wild or cultivated. It does so by a special form of attentiveness—*notitia* in the medieval term—to whatever presents itself as an edge in our perception or imagination or thought.

Peri-phenomenology focuses on the areas and phases of discontinuity in one's experience and thought: the interstices where things and events begin and end. These same areas and phases, taken together, constitute a special plateau from which we can connect with other plateaus in an ever-expanding nexus. Soon we find ourselves caught up in a virtual Indra's net of densely interwoven phenomena and peri-phenomena. I would like to think that this book has itself woven such a net from the multiple descriptions of edges I have given.

## II

The time has come to explore what it means that a certain kind of edge has been especially valorized in Western culture: this is the *fine edge*, the edge of exactitude and precision. The passion for esteeming fine edges is deeply held within the psyche of modernity—so much so that it has become tempting to take it as paradigmatic for all edges, as if every edge, once fully understood, is or should be a fine edge. But is this so? Here I argue not. But this is not to suggest that we should embrace the opposite extreme: imagining that edges are at base radically imprecise, that all edges are finally rough edges. How can we do justice to the many edges we encounter without erring toward either extreme—the Scylla of overprecision or the Charybdis of the unduly imprecise?

There are certainly circumstances when it is appropriate to put a fine edge on something; say, when we have to sharpen the knife with which a Thanksgiving turkey is to be cut. We also count on certain nonphysical edges to be quite fine; for example, when we are figuring up our monthly budget, anxious to find out if we can afford a new computer, we need to know the exact numbers. Or when we wish to "make ourselves clear" in a letter in which we are sending advice to the wife of a friend who is afflicted in certain major ways. Whether writing with a computer or penning a personal letter, we want our words to carry the precise import we intend, and for this purpose our words need to be carefully constructed: cursive handwriting as well as computer-generated text must both meet a certain minimal standard of intelligibility to convey what we want to say. If it is true that "meaning arises at the edge of signs," as Merleau-Ponty wrote,[4] then in certain contexts this edge should be as exact as we can make it. But do we always want to insist on such precision?

Fine edges, for all their utility in certain situations, need to be supplemented or replaced by edges that are inherently vague—indeterminate, blunt, blurred. The latter are of considerable value, indeed are in certain circumstances indispensable. More generally, as contemporary philosopher Timothy Williamson has put it, "our contact with the world is as direct in vague thought as it is in any thought."[5] The contact in question is between the edges of my thought and the world's edges, whether these latter are edges of meanings or words, physical things or temporally arrayed events, or bodily and psychical states. This contact can be quite direct—thus informative and valuable—even if the operative edges are vague.

This book has presented an extensive discussion of the differential deployment of edges. Yet nowhere have I analyzed edges with regard to the basic contrast between fineness and vagueness as such. In exploring this contrast now, I offer a critique of edges that are *too* fine—fine to a fault—in certain contexts. These contexts call for a recognition of less-than-precise edges without endorsing edges that are so amorphous as to lose their standing as edges. Whereas most edges must have sufficient structure to be intelligible or at least tractable—allowing them to close off things if not to give a grip on them—this is not to say that such edges are, or need be, altogether fine.

## III

As a young boy, Edmund Husserl was said to have sharpened the blade of his pen-knife so often and so conscientiously that one day the blade disappeared.[6] Let us take this as a cautionary tale. It indicates one extreme in the saga of fine edges: when made *too* fine, their very edginess is undermined. A too-fine edge risks becoming so subtle as to lose its effective presence in the contexts in which it figures. All edges come to an end, but an overly fine edge risks losing its effectiveness as an edge that intervenes in these same contexts and makes a difference there. At the other extreme, instruments as well as words can become so bluntly edged, so indeterminate as to lose any capacity to cut or fit or hold or refer; they have lost their edge. Think of dull knives, or old clothes that have become so shapeless that they no longer suit my body, or words so loosely chosen that they ramble and lose their point.

It remains that certain extremes of edge have their attractions and uses: sharp tools are prized in particular contexts, such as scalpels in surgery, pencils poised to write. We also value the soft edges of pillows and comfortable, "baggy" sweaters. We observe much the same polarity in philosophical writing. Rigorous precision is prized when a proof for God's existence is argued, such as the "ontological proof"; yet at the same time, some philosophers turn to literature for inspiration in philosophy—as Heidegger did to Hölderlin's poems, and Cavell to Shakespeare's tragedies—texts that are valued for nuances that are difficult if not impossible to pin down. Literature has its own precision, but its reliance on indirect modes of discourse, notably metaphor and other kinds of trope, entails a high tolerance for meaning that is less than exact. Indeed, in literary texts the inexactness itself may be a source of strength. These differing instances testify to a draw to divergent edge extremes in philosophical argumentation and discourse. Indeed, one and the same thinker may favor concepts and words exhibiting both extremes: Heidegger's close readings of other philosophers can be quite rigorous, while St. Anselm waxes poetic in his praise of God. No philosopher holds a patent on fineness of edges, and none seeks to be altogether lost in the miasma of the indeterminate.

Since comparative fineness of edge is at issue in such philosophical and nonphilosophical extremes—whether as valorized or as disdained—let me clarify that by *fine* I mean any of the following: exact, precise, clearly delineated, or (in certain cases) subject to calibration of some determinate sort. The "things" at stake in the phrase "not putting too fine an edge on things" are either topics of thought or discussion (*Sachen* in Gadamer's word) or material things (concrete, physically specified material objects that exist in space and time) or the very discourse that bears on the characteristic profiles of these things or topics. The converse instances of fine edges include all edges that resist definition or description in metric or quasi-metric terms, or that demand recognition in their very vagueness. The lower limit of the vague is the inchoate: here we find edges that are undone or undo themselves as effective edges and thus no longer function as edges at all. This is the zero point where an edge becomes a nonedge, as when the flesh of a drowning victim dissolves underwater after a certain length of time:

> Phlebas the Phoenician, a fortnight dead,
> Forgot the cry of gulls, and the deep sea swell
> > And the profit and loss.
> A current under sea
> Picked his bones in whispers.[7]

## IV

One kind of edge I have not taken up in any sustained manner in this book is the *conceptual* edge: the edge of discrete concepts as well as the edge at stake when concepts are strung together in certain patterns. We are here in the domain of sequential thinking and logical reasoning. In this domain, precision of edges is highly valorized, as is the discourse in which edges are embedded. The following are three circumstances in which fineness of conceptual edges is prized.

- Edges in which the symbolism (whether linguistic or mathematical or formal-logical) that exemplifies the fineness is itself both consistent and lucidly formulated, thanks to the rigorous definition of terms in accordance with the axioms and postulates of the symbolic system.

- Edges in which certain "laws of thought" are at stake as these have been conceived from Aristotle to Leibniz, with significant modifications by Hegel, Peirce, Husserl, Frege, Church, and many more recent figures; the symbolic medium (whether formal or verbal) is bound to reflect these laws, at the risk of incoherence: for example, the law of noncontradiction in Aristotle.

- Edges in which the phenomena dictate finely crafted descriptions by their very character: for example, the internal parts of a car's

motor, the arterial network in the human body, or the syntactic
structures of meaningful sentences. At stake here is just how these
parts, that network, or those structures are actually disposed in
descriptive space, not how they are experienced by the driver of
the car or the body subject or the person who speaks or writes: it
is a matter of referential accuracy and consistency rather than of
felt sense.

Different as these examples may seem to be at first glance, they are not a merely
casual collection. I take them to be three levels or aspects of one very basic circumstance, depending on whether we are focusing on mode of expression ("symbolism"), form of thinking ("laws of thought"), or the character of the descriptum
or referent (car motor, arterial system, language). In all three cases, exact conceptual edges are demanded or at least expected. Those who are invested in precision
and regularity would claim that these three instances specify exemplary ways of
finding or bringing patterns of order into human discourse. Those less invested in
this pursuit might grant that they hold as formal or practical or referential frameworks for much that we think and experience and say—as minimal conditions of
conceptual coherence—and yet that these frameworks do not take us to the core
of what matters: a core that is intrinsically qualitative, having to do with the experiential sense of what we feel, think, and say, and having more to do with *how* we
undergo these frameworks than *what* we take them to be (their strictly identifiable
content in its cognitive or semantic, physiological or mechanical kernel). These latter persons may grant that formal or practical fineness characterizes purely structural aspects of language as well as of much human activity and thought, but would
still insist that this fineness cannot do justice to the nexus of implicatory meanings
that compose human experience as it is undergone by the subjects who are actually
engaged in such experience. To assert the importance of this direct experience
is not to impugn the validity of the symbolic media, the laws of thought, or the
systematic understandings of mechanical operations, corporeal physiology, and
linguistic utterance. On the contrary, it is to accept the benefit of the precision required of the edges at play in these various areas of human accomplishment but
also to insist on the value of, but then to insist that the experiential component.

   We encounter a very different situation when the not-fine or indeterminate
edges of discourse and thinking are valorized as such—both for their own sake
and for that which they portend. In this case, three characteristic circumstances
stand out.

   ەʒ  an essential indeterminacy accrues to the language employed: this
        language draws on the polyvalence if not the outright ambiguity of
        words. Merleau-Ponty and Nancy may be considered paradigmatic

in their valuing of such language in philosophy, but everyday discourse, as Wittgenstein and Cavell have both stressed, is itself constituted through and through by such indeterminacies: as when we say something like "see you around" (the precise where and when are only vaguely indicated) or "I had dinner with someone" (where the someone in question is left unspecified). Despite their indeterminateness, both expressions are perfectly intelligible as they are uttered in ordinary speech; we know what they mean even if their exact referents are left undetermined.

⌇  Certain concepts by which we express our thoughts are intrinsically vague. As we have seen earlier in this book, Husserl calls these concepts "morphological," meaning that they are more concerned with the approximate configuration of something than with its analytical or formal essence. To Husserl's examples (being "notched," "umbelliform") I would add "boundary-like" (as contrasted with "border-like"), "marginal," and "threshold-like." In these latter cases, not just my discourse but my very thinking is imbued with indeterminacy: the edges of such concepts, thought or spoken, are blurred in such a way that they cannot be made fully determinate without losing their special serviceability.

⌇  The very things we are thinking of or discoursing about: these can be themselves indeterminate, characterized through and through by their resistance to precise specification. After Hegel, Merleau-Ponty is the premier thinker of the deep indeterminacy of things: a basic axiom for him is that "the indeterminate is a positive phenomenon."[8]

This second grouping of diverse situations of experience, thought, and discourse opens a curtain on edges that are less than fine: indeed, such nonprecise edges are *demanded* if certain kinds of thinking, sensing, and discoursing are to be possible. At stake here is the conviction that these edges are perfectly valid; they are not failures of precision, as the orthodoxy of logocentric thought presumes, but are fully functional and indeed required in their own singular ways and in the contexts wherein they figure.

## V

"Proximally and for the most part"—as Heidegger liked to put it[9]—most of us find ourselves in between the two extremes I have just sketched out. We cope well, or well enough, thinking and talking in this middle realm. This being so, we are likely to find ourselves in agreement with Derrida's deconstruction of the false binaries of Western philosophy that have been prevalent since Aristotle's commitment to hylomorphic models of life and mind, and after Merleau-Ponty's equally trenchant assessment of traditional dichotomies such as mind versus matter, or empiricism versus intellectualism. In this light, is not the very distinction between fine and amorphous edges another instance of such a binary? Should we not be content to continue living—thinking, perceiving, feeling—in the intermediate zone that lies between these extremities of edge?

A move to such a middle domain should not be merely a matter of convenience or compromise. Nor should it seek to deny or dissolve the distinctive differences between the two poles of the fine and the amorphous. Rather, these poles can be seen as providing a relational framework for all that lies between them. They are valuable precisely *as extremities* that lay out the full field of edges that fit between them. Their extremity entails that precisely because most edges are neither absolutely fine nor altogether amorphous they are able to configure the worlds they act to inform and shape. This is to say that the majority of edges are shapeful if inexact, and it is in just this respect that they are such active presences. (They are inexact to the degree that they do not satisfy certain formal standards of measurement brought to bear upon them; only mathematically specifiable edges, for example, the edges of Euclidean shapes, are consistently exact.[10]) It follows that the fine/amorphous distinction can be considered as providing upper and lower bounds for edges as different as those found in gaps, rills, neighborhoods, the earth's horizons, and clouds floating by in the sky.

To characterize this situation differently, every occupant of the vast middle kingdom of edges manifests some factor of each pole, albeit in considerably varying ratios. The edges of my own lived body provide a case in point: they have a certain determinacy—I am intimately acquainted with its characteristic contours to the point of its continually reliable recognition (I cannot doubt that this is my own body I am looking at in the mirror)—yet these very same edges are also indeterminate in their inherent habitualities and their potentials for change. Much the same is true of our psychical being, whose edges range from rigid (in schizoid states) to flexible (as in the case of the spontaneous self, e.g., Winnicott's "true self"). In the region extending from the fine to the amorphous, edges are prized neither for their precision alone nor for their imprecision as such but for being positioned such that a variety of intermediate edge-situations can arise therefrom.

This space of the in-between is akin to what Deleuze and Guattari call "smooth space," through which diverse currents flow in highly diversified patterns. Coinhering in such space are quite disparate entities and events, as well as the experiences we have of them and the discourses and symbolisms by which they are articulated. In *A Thousand Plateaus*, in which the model of smooth space is set forth, leading examples of such in-betweenness—"intermezzos" in Deleuze

and Guattari's term—include becoming-animal and becoming-woman, whereby
entire species and gender differences conjoin in a middle space animated by
dynamic processes. That is to say, the presumptively definite and exclusive edges
that distinguish man from woman, or humans from animals, are no longer separative and exclusive. We here move to a space in which what matters is a process
of subtle *becoming-other*: of gradually dissolving traits of being standardly male as
these give way to certain accustomed ways of being female, and vice versa; the
same ambiguity obtains for the dyad of human / animal. Such othering of accepted
edge differentials is neither so precise as to invite exact measurement nor so diffuse as to defy any identification or specification.

What matters most in such intermediate situations and others akin to them
(such as the character of human skin as at once absorptive and protective) is the
open and shifting character of generation and transmission across edges that are
neither altogether fine nor wholly without contour. It is on, at, and through such
inexact edges that what might be thought incompossible—human and animal,
man and woman, what is inside and outside the skin—come into close conjunction. This is a distinctive in-between situation in a smooth space wherein the
contours of disparate beings shade into each other in an intertanglement of differences that are not just compatible with each other but also actively cocreative.

Such intermixing of edges in a shared space is not always a later stage of
development. Sometimes it is the primary state. In the Commons in its original
form in England and New England, animals and humans mingled in a plot of land
around a town that was set aside for grazing and planting, a plot that was owned in
common rather than by individual citizens. The Commons was a margin that had
sufficient room to allow diverse creatures to live together in mutually sustaining
ways. Together, they coconstituted a smooth space in which not only humans
and animals but also earth and sky, soil and shrubs, and much else combined
forces to the benefit of all involved. The Commons' own outer edges were not
strictly delimited by fences or walls, yet they were perfectly well known by the residents of the local community: known in their approximate, not their exact, location. The Commons was in effect a species of "transitional space" (in Winnicott's
term). In this space, otherwise divergent kinds of beings found a middle ground
of support and sustenance.[11] In such a space, what matters most is not the manifest disparity between the things thereby conjoined but the fact that their edges
connect across their very differences—and in a place that they commonly occupy.
This would not be possible if these edges were too definite or too indefinite:
instead, it is thanks to their very inexactitude that the diverse inhabitants of a
Commons coexist as well as they do. As coparticipants in a comparatively capacious common space, they can be quite different in kind and still connect with
each other in effective and meaningful ways.

In order to intermingle in this intermezzo, the edges of things and events need not be chockablock or tightly conjoined. Spaces between edges create areas of leeway. What ancient philosophers termed *diastémata* ("spatial intervals") are integral to the commixture of edges that fall between the extremes of the austerely fine and the altogether amorphous. In such a situation edges articulate across diastematic differences. In a circumstance such as the Commons, instead of being in literal contact, the edges of very different kinds of things—cows and humans, birds and snakes, plants and trees, earth and sky—communicate across intervals that range from infinitesimal to broad and deep. They need not transform into one another in the sort of radical transmutation envisioned by Deleuze and Guattari—who are concerned with a very basic "becoming other"—but they do constitute a closely knit community of diverse beings.

I am here arguing that we are not confined to an exclusive choice between edges that are too fine—so refined or subtle as to lose their intrinsic force and significance—and edges that are so shapeless as to no longer figure or function as edges at all. Between these antipodes there is an entire realm of diversely situated inexact edges that is as accessible as it is varied. In this realm of continual transition are to be found whole ranges of edges that are the basis of many disparate ways of thinking and feeling, and of practical as well as creative actions. If too acute, the edges will act to exclude each other, as in a city planner's map that does not account for concrete movements in and out of neighborhoods. But the edges in such situations must have sufficient shape to allow for their intercalation—an intercalation that need not be literally edge-to-edge, as with the parts of a motor—but may benefit from intervals left between that enable a special elasticity, a give-and-take that animates them across their differences. In all such cases, the result is a dynamic field of flows and counterflows. No such flowing, indeed no freedom for even minimal movement, can happen if the edges that populate these situations are too fiercely constrictive, as in many prison cells, or too open-ended, as in an endless and trackless desert.

## VI

My argument so far has proceeded from a critique of inappropriately exact edges to the staking out of an intermediate space located between such edges and sheerly amorphous ones. The fine and the amorphous turn out to be the epicenters of active fields in which synergies of inexact edges emerge in the form of unanticipated becomings. These fields are the source of what I have been calling *edge-worlds* throughout this book. The dynamism and rich variety of these worlds, each of which is subtended by such fields, take place between the poles of overly fine and undershaped edges.

Despite their manifest differences, these two extreme poles share one important trait. Each represents the point where edges themselves begin to vanish as efficacious presences. If a given edge is too fine—too subtle, too sharp, too acute for the context in which it exists—it loses its force as edge. Husserl's vanishing knife blade is a case in point; so is a remark in a conversation whose subtlety is inapropos, as when someone insists on "a distinction that makes no difference." For all concrete purposes, the disappearing blade and the overly refined conversational point have failed in their role as edges: they are nonstarters in their respective edge-worlds. Similarly, a too amorphous edge—blunt to the point of being too obtuse, too diffuse, too sprawling vis-à-vis a given context or topic—is decommissioned as an effective edge. We confront here a circumstance in which opposed extremes—each taking edge to a certain limit—share a common fate in which the force and function of edge itself is lost.

This observation has two concrete consequences for the project I have undertaken in this book. The first is structural: any given field of edges is not flanked by two ultimate edge extremes in such a way that everything in between has to be construed in terms of one or the other, or by way of their admixture. We are at quite another place from that which we find with, say, birth and death, regarded as the two extremities of life. Each passing stage of life can be understood as moving away from the fact of birth and as approaching ever closer to death, or as an ever-changing mixture of the two: as "livingdying."[12] Birth and death are in effect the terminal states of a single lifetime, each stage of which can be understood in relation to one or the other, or to both. In contrast, neither the extremely fine nor the densely dull serve as fixed terms that definitively delimit the dynamic edge fields I have been discussing here, much less as offering paradigmatic cases for understanding all the other edges in these fields. They are instead the vanishing points of this same field—the points where its animated edgefulness ceases because it is becoming too much or too little. Rather than being definitive perimeters in the manner of birth and death, these are effervescing peripheries.

The second consequence of recognizing the special status of the hyperfine and the excessively amorphous is still more important. It can be stated thus: *to be an edge at all is to possess a certain minimal rigor of structure and force.* This minimal requirement for being an edge has been at play throughout this book, even if it has taken different forms at different stages. It is most manifest in the case of physical things whose very materiality guarantees that these things will have edges possessing what Peirce called *Secondness*, that is, inherent causal force: such edges push back our touch and direct our sight. The surgeon's knife—thanks to its acutely honed edge—possesses just the right rigor to make surgical incisions. It is for this very reason that the edges of physical things such as knives are so often taken as paradigmatic for all edges—a point I have addressed more than once in the course of this book. But if the edges of physical things come to be too refined, they lose all Secondness and are lost to perception; the same is true if they are so amorphous as to lose their gripping power or even to fail to hold our apprehension—melting altogether into what underlies them or disappearing into what succeeds them.

The edges of events have their own rigor, primarily that of beginning and ending: they are self-defining as it were. They unfold at their own pace, engendering a certain rhythm of phases, the edges of which are essential to identifying them as singular events. As with the edges of physical things, too subtle endings (or beginnings or intermediate phases) will dissolve into the course of the events themselves rather than providing for them an active gestalt that allows them to be demarcated in time and history.

Another instance of this same minimal but requisite rigor is to be found in the edges of our body—not just because this body is a material thing but also because of its intrinsic singularity, the way it is uniquely configured by its own edges: my body cannot be confused with your body. The fact that the edges of the lived body are for the most part soft to the touch does not diminish the specificity of such edges, neither at the level of the species (where a diverse but recognizable phenotype is at play) nor at the level of the individual body as distinguishably different in each instance. In parallel with bodily edges, those pertaining to the earth are unique, radically singular. Here, too, we have a physical body, but now a massive one. Nevertheless, this very massiveness has its own distinctive outer edges that are neither too subtle nor too blunt to be perceived: they have the requisite specificity of structure to be evident in the outer shape of the earth as seen in photographs taken from outer space as well as in the curvature of the horizon as glimpsed from a boat in a low trough at sea.

And what of the edges of the psyche? Here we are far from corporeal edges, though there are certainly psychical *events* that have their own edges (having emotions, entertaining ideas, and so on). We detect configurations of the psyche in patterns that are commonly designated as "character," "persona," and "personality," or in troubled syndromes such as the schizoid personality and the schizophrenic self. Even short of these particular psychical consolidations, we find within the psyche edge-bearing infrastructures of the soul. Indeed, my description of various plateaus of psychical life, as outlined in chapter 8—those on which thinking and feeling of many kinds occur—points to conditions and states that have their own Secondness. Enough at least to permit their being described in terms of inner and outer psychical edges and to be *felt* in certain particular ways—as when I feel a distinct enthusiasm for something, or repelled by an undesired result of an election, or when I engage in a creative line of thought.

## VII

From this last discussion we may conclude that edges, to be efficacious as edges, must possess at least these five traits: consistency, resistance, constancy, closure, and culmination. (1) An edge has to exhibit a certain *consistency* of configuration; a configuration that was utterly inconsistent, allowing no shape or structure at all to be detected, would not allow us to grasp it as an edge, much less to make use of it. (2) To be an edge is to be capable of exerting a certain *resistance* to efforts to alter it. It can be reshaped when enough force is applied to it but must be resistant enough to count as the edge of that thing (or event, body, psyche, earth) and to persist until it is forced to change character. (3) By the same token, it has to display a certain *constancy* if only to allow us to identify it, even if only momentarily; it may well change its shape over time, but then it will become a different edge of a different thing or event. (Some edges, such as those of ocean waves, change constantly but remain recognizable by their generic shapes.) (4) Finally, every edge has to effect *closure* of some significant sort: it must close off or terminate that of which it is the edge, and to do so in a way that allows its perception as that very edge. (5) Common to the edge of anything is the fact that it clings to that for which it acts as edge in such a way as to culminate it. This holds true, however tenuous the clinging may be (notably in the case of psychic states) and however rapidly it changes (as in rapidly altering cloud formations). In all these cases, the edge brings its bearer to a completeness it would not have without it. An edge of any sort at once configures and reflects the space and time occupied by that of which it is the edge, orienting it within the region in which it is located. This same edge marks out the subject of the edge—*what* is edged—in such a way that we can apprehend it, employ it, discuss it, and remember it as such. Outliers by their structure and position, edges are recognitory signs for everything that coheres as a thing or event, body or psyche, earth or sky.

Candidates for edges that exhibit into the extremes of fineness or bluntness fail to exhibit these five traits. For that very reason, they are edges by default, or better "edges" in name only. They serve only as abstract or projected epicenters for ever-proliferating fields of edges of many kinds. They are in effect exoskeletons for these fields but are not integral parts of the fields themselves. The edges that matter are to be found in the heterogeneous synergetic realm that lies between these two extremes.

## VIII

Let us return for a last time to the title of these late reflections: "Not to Put Too Fine an Edge on Things." I have not taken on this theme straightforwardly but have been proceeding by indirection. But the question comes back: should one not attempt to put a fine edge on things in the end if not in the beginning? We might allow a certain generosity in the opening stage of a given description, but should we not pin things down eventually? It is this insistent question that haunts much of modernity as well as my own project in this book: is not my own peri-phenomenological task just that of putting a *fine edge* on edges themselves?

Is this not indeed the very goal of a careful peri-phenomenological investigation of edges?

My raising this question at this late point betrays a certain skepticism on my part about the passion for precision that has so often been an obsessive concern in Western thought—a passion whose detailed history John Dewey sought to recount in *The Quest for Certainty*. Its high priests would include Plato when engaged in the method of division in the *Sophist*, Aristotle in his *Prior* and *Posterior Analytics*, Descartes in the *Discourse on Method*, members of the Vienna Circle in its early days, and still others. Efforts to formalize philosophy by turning it into an axiomatics or formal semantics—or others kinds of systematic enterprise—continue today. These various ventures have been tempered by the advent of ordinary language philosophy, which has underlined those aspects of everyday usage that resist just such formalizing and systematizing.

It was doubtless John Austin, writing in the wake of Wittgenstein, who threw the most disruptive curve ball into these efforts to achieve extreme rigor by demonstrating the powerful and pervasive nonreferential uses of words in their illocutionary and perlocutionary force. By opening up the performative dimension of language, Austin was pointing to situations in which formal exactitude of description in the constative or propositional mode is either not possible or not appropriate, since what is often at stake is the actual effects of words on human actions—effects that are highly variable depending on the actors and the context in each instance, making it difficult to generalize over all pertinent cases. The title of Austin's William James lectures of 1955, *How to Do Things with Words*, indicates the direction he was taking: "how" is more important than "what" or "why," and the semantic range of "things" is extended by the very indefiniteness of what they mean. There is no attempt on Austin's part to say just what "things" signify for him, though the reader is clear that they are not physical objects. Austin's implicit reasoning seems to be this: if the things we mean are only indefinitely describable, we cannot expect the terms that describe them to be altogether exact. From this I infer that the edges of these same things do not lend themselves to formally precise description either.

In affirming this, we are a long way from Descartes's demand for clarity and distinctness as the twin criteria of ideas we can trust in the pursuit of knowledge. The point is not just that "clarity is not enough" (the famous title of a late-twentieth-century book), much less that we should not seek a false clarity that in fact illuminates nothing.[13] Rather, we should acknowledge that there is a right time for clarity, and a right version of it in any given domain of knowledge, in view of the inescapable contextuality of knowing. Recall here how Freud, in discovering the unconscious (than which nothing more indistinct or unthing-like can be imagined), sought the apt language for it—if not in the symbolism he devised in his "Project for a Scientific

Psychology" (a task he soon abandoned), then in the most apt verbal descriptions he could devise, as these are set forth in the final chapter of *The Interpretation of Dreams*, in the essay "The Unconscious," and in later writings. It is striking how different are these successive descriptions given by the man who is credited with having discovered the unconscious. They do not show that the unconscious is hopelessly amorphous, altogether outside the scope of discussion in natural language, but rather that its description will vary depending on the presuppositions and purposes of an investigator's efforts at a given phase of his search.

Aristotle put it best: we should seek only as much precision as a given field of inquiry permits, and in accordance with the *kind* of objects that populate that field.[14] Appropriate precision is all that we should ever expect, thus all we should ever pursue. The ideal of "perfect clarity" is misleading; for any given domain and occasion, apposite clarity is all that is called for. If we should not put too fine an edge on things, this is because the things themselves, *die Sachen selbst*, do not call for a precision that exceeds what their phenomenal surfaces and their inherent edges offer to our apprehension and thus to our description. Asking for more than this is demanding too much; asking for less than this is insufficient. The aim of description should be to delineate things as they show themselves—just this and no more. Doing so is not to put too fine an edge on things; it is to invoke, in suitable words, the edges the things themselves manifest—where "the things themselves" include edges of all the diverse types I have described in this book.

Clarity and precision, then, are subordinate to something more important in descriptive enterprises of many kinds: this is to be true to the phenomenal and peri-phenomenal appearings of things, including the edges through which they show themselves to us. We need to be true to things not only in words—indispensable as these are—but also in images and performances. In his dramatic depiction of Hamlet, Shakespeare delineates the complexities of human self-doubt more insightfully than does any attempt to give a strictly behavioral or massively statistical analysis of this same state. His effort is less to get to the formal essence of such doubting than it is to evoke what this tortured mental state feels like from within: its felt sense. In conveying this, Shakespeare leaves considerable space for what is unclear when one is in the throes of this mental state. He respects its inherent uncertainty, its very obscurity. In this regard, he was already accomplishing what William James recommended in his *Principles of Psychology* three centuries later: "It is, in short, the re-instatement of the vague to its proper place in our mental life which I am so anxious to press on the attention [of my readers]."[15]

The point is certainly not to seek the obscure for its own sake. To do so leads to an equal but opposite error to that of being obsessed with precision as such. We should not flee from the demanding arms of the precise into the easy embrace of the imprecise. Much less should we seek "the obscure by the more obscure": this way lies obscurantism. But above all it is misguided to insist on a standard of exactitude that distorts the lived experience of something, for this way lies the kind of fallacy operative in the notion of the "objective body" in Merleau-Ponty's term. Such a body may be represented as reducible to quantifiable variables, but it fails to characterize what the lived body itself undergoes—in its edges as in its core.

The point is to pursue precision when this is called for by the subject matter itself and its context and to tolerate less-than-precise description when this is appropriate to the very character of what we are investigating. When we are in pursuit of a deeper understanding of something, we should eschew merely casual descriptions. By the same token, we must also refuse to put too fine a point on the description of something if this distorts an account that is true to the descriptum itself. The aim is not to impose but to respect: "respect" in an epistemic rather than a narrowly ethical sense of this term. We fail to respect something when our account of it reduces it to something else than what we experience; say, when we convert kinesthetic bodily experiences into quantified sensations.[16] An account of such sensations may be scientifically valid and useful, but it does not answer to the actually felt experience of kinesthesia. Pursuing the too fine often means subscribing to an ideology of precision at the expense of what the things themselves suggest we should say about them. Instead, we should listen to what they have to say before we have our say. Between the things to be described and our description of them, the former is the first among equals.

This is not to claim that the two domains of experience (the exact and the inexact) are crisply distinguishable from each other, but they are not infinitely distant either. The boundary between them is informal and indeterminate and shifting, thus reflecting their ever-changing interaction. Not just the edges of things, or the edges of words, but the edge between these two major kinds of edge is here at stake. This edge constitutes the verge of the interworld they together compose. At this verge, and through it, things and words commingle. Efforts at description (including peri-phenomenological investigations) should suit closely that which they describe—not fit them as a hand in a glove but accrue to them and reflect them. Appositely descriptive words join forces with that which they delineate: most notably for us, the edges of things or events, bodies or psyches, earth or sky. After they do their descriptive work, they join forces with the things described by becoming sedimented into subsequent experiences of these things, even as the things themselves leave adumbrative traces in the words that describe them.

No wonder we can do all kinds of things with words, if it is true that the things themselves are always already saturated with verbal discourse and vice versa. We are once again in the land of the in-between: now in the intermezzo that stretches between thing-world and word-world and back again. The two worlds form an animated common space of dynamic interplay between words and things.

This is where things are indeed done *with* words but also, in turn, where things are done *to* words. In this book, the abiding focus has been the world of edges insofar as edges can be captured in peri-phenomenological descriptions, and leave their traces in them in turn. One of my major aims has been to demonstrate various ways of doing things with edges by way of the words that closely describe them. A book about edges is about the way that edges can be brought into words that are neither too precise nor too vague but that are true to the edges themselves.

Instead of forcing the doxographical brunt of our beliefs or the logological bearing of our words onto things, we need to look for and listen to the edges that belong to the things themselves: the things that populate the various edge-worlds we share with humans and other living and nonliving things. It behooves us to give witness to the diverse edges of things in the open realm where they first come forward to our attention, and to attempt to describe them as such. What matters most is what edges offer to us, not what we impose upon them, least of all our ideologies of exactitude.

This is not to deny that beliefs and words alike—along with feelings and imaginings and perceivings—may be integral parts of the act of witnessing edges. Our goal should be to let things (from the most accessible physical things to the most elusive psychical feelings and thoughts) present themselves to us without straitjacketing them in overly constrictive concepts or passing them over in idle talk or burying them in misleading beliefs. Our descriptive task is to let the edges of things appear and call to us, move and affect us—from within their own dense nexus, their own ways of being implicated in the interworlds we inhabit with them.

We must learn to question the presumed primacy of formally precise or measurably exact edges, however necessary such edges may be in certain contexts. Without sinking into a miasma of words or concepts or images, we need to be receptive to a field energized by edges that connect and carry forward rather than block or occlude. To do this, we have to learn how not to impose fixed ideas of edges on things but learn instead how to appreciate the deep rhythms in the edges we encounter in the pack and welter that make up our daily (and nightly) lives. It is from an immersion in these edges that things appear and speak to us. When we are receptive to such manifestations, we can replace the formality of border-like precision with the flow of open boundaries that move at their own pace and take on their own shape. Then edges can be the "cracks" by which the light gets in, as Leonard Cohen puts it: the light that enables a more lucid understanding of the multifarious edge-worlds of which we form part. By means of these same edges, creative thought emerges and (in Deleuze's words) what is "good and great in humanity" can arise. Unthinking both unduly rigid and excessively loose models of edge, we can rethink what edges can be when they are allowed to occupy their own space and to move and change in accordance with their own time. In this way we will be drawn out of our all too cloistered and distracted lives, becoming more aware of worlds not of our own making. It is a matter of recognizing and rejoining the ecstasy of the edge.[17]

## Notes

1. The three "waves" (in Plato's metaphor) refer to the radical suggestions of Socrates in discussion with Glaucon: the equal education of men and women, the holding of women and children in common, and the rule of philosophers. See Plato, *Republic* 457b–d, 472a, and 473c.

2. See Plato, *Sophist* 226a–231b.

3. At the limit, such an edge is reabsorbed into place itself, and has to be imagined or posited for it. What is remarkable is how rarely this is the case. In the very great majority of instances, an edge or set of edges can be discerned. For a discussion of the major differences between formal French and "wild" English gardens, see Edward S. Casey, *Getting Back into Place*, 2nd ed. (Indiana University Press, 2009), chapter 6, "Building Sites and Cultivating Places."

4. Maurice Merleau-Ponty, "Indirect Language and the Voices of Silence," in *Signs*, trans. R. McCleary (Evanston, IL: Northwestern University Press, 1964), p. 41: "This meaning arising at the edge of signs (*au bord des signes*), this immanence of the whole in the parts, is found throughout the history of culture." My citation in the main text departs slightly from this translation.

5. Timothy Williamson, *Vagueness* (Oxford: Oxford University Press, 2000), as cited by Richard Rorty in an essay in the *London Review of Books* (January 2005); see also Roy Sorenson, *Vagueness and Contradiction* (Oxford: Clarendon, 2001), especially chapter 1, "Absolute Borderline Cases."

6. On this episode in Husserl's youth, see Herbert Spiegelberg, *The Phenomenological Movement: A Historical Introduction* (The Hague: Nijhoff, 1965), vol. 1, chapter 2.

7. T. S. Eliot, "Death by Water," a section title of "The Waste Land."

8. Merleau-Ponty, *Phenomenology of Perception*, trans. Landes, p. 7: "We must recognize the indeterminate as a positive phenomenon."

9. *Zunächst und zumeist* is a recurrent phrase in *Being and Time*.

10. It is to be noted that what I have just called "standards of measurement" are not themselves exact in any absolute sense; they are exact only in relation to other standards and in terms of certain criteria, not in themselves. Only mathematical measures are both exact and nonrelative. I owe this clarification to Lissa McCullough.

11. For an engaging discussion of the relevance of the Commons to contemporary life, see Lewis Hyde, *Common as Air: Revolution, Art, and Ownership* (New York: Farrar, Straus, & Giroux, 2011).

12. I cite this phrase from Charles Scott, who gave a paper with this title at the annual meeting of the Society for Phenomenology and Existential Philosophy in 2014.

13. See H. D. Lewis, ed., *Clarity Is not Enough: Essays in Criticism of Linguistic Philosophy* (London: Allen & Unwin, 1963).

14. "It belongs to an educated person to look for just such precision in each kind of discourse as the nature of the thing that one is concerned with admits" (*Nichomachean Ethics*, book 1, chapter 3, 1094b). The use of "thing" (*pragma*) is striking in this statement.

15. William James, *The Principles of Psychology* (New York: Dover, 1950; reprint of 1890 edition), 1:254. James said this at a particular moment of late-modern history, in 1890, when the aspirations of laboratory-based physiological psychology were running as high as those of neurologically based psychology and philosophy are today. (It was from this matrix of epistemic ideals that Freud had emerged in his early training in medicine; and it was this same matrix that Bergson questioned in the first chapter of his *Time and Free Will*, published in 1889.)

16. This is of course a major theme of Merleau-Ponty in his *Phenomenology of Perception*. See especially the introduction (chapter 1), and part 1, chapters 1 and 2.

17. I wish to thank Andrés Colapinto for his very close reading and incisive critique of this chapter.

# Postlude: Why Edges Matter in Their Very Heterodoxicality

> Every cultural act lives essentially on the boundaries, and derives its seriousness and significance from this fact. Separated from these boundaries it loses ground and becomes vacuous, arrogant, degenerates and dies.
> —Mikhail Bakhtin, *Art and Answerability: Early Philosophical Essays*

I would not have written this book had I not been convinced, first, that edges are an important and ubiquitous feature of the worlds we inhabit at every stage of life, and second, that they have been systematically neglected by philosophers, including phenomenologists.[1] If my effort has been even minimally successful, it has persuaded the reader of the truth of the first claim, which concern the pervasive presence of edges in our ongoing lives. As to the second, the paucity of the treatment of edges in the philosophical literature speaks for itself. Still the reader may ask, why an entire book on edges? Why all the fuss about edges? In this postlude I address the general significance of edges in human lives and in philosophy in the face of indifference or skepticism about their importance; I then turn to a meditation on several heterodoxical propositions that must be confronted before this book can begin to draw to a close.

## I

Consider the well-researched fact that human infants after fourteen months will pause at a "visual cliff"—such as a drop-off from the floor on which they are crawling as it is viewed through a transparent glass pane continuous with the floor on which they are positioned.[2] They are *arrested* by their first perception of this particular edge and will not move farther over it even though they would be perfectly safe were they to do so. This indicates a deep—perhaps even "hardwired"—awareness of the significance of edges very early in life. After that, the presence of edges in human experience becomes so consequential and so massive that it would be virtually impossible to trace out the exact evolution of their perception: not even Piaget has studied this in his classical book on children's perception of space.[3] One thing is clear: as we grow up and develop, we must learn how to negotiate a vast array of edges in which we are enmeshed in our daily lives. An edgeless circumstance is a very rare event. Perhaps only when swimming underwater do we approximate to such an absence of edges, though even here we glimpse edges of a certain murky sort: those of the walls of the swimming pool we are in or, if we are in the ocean, various strands of kelp or coral reefs.

To be in an entirely unedged world is as rare as it is dangerous, as those lost in a dense fog realize: once when driving to Stonington, Maine, late in the evening I could not make out the edges of the highway I was on and had to pull over for the night for fear of running off the road. Short of an extremity such as this, we are guided and oriented by edges, which indicate to us which way to go and which not. We count on edges as the orientational markers of ongoing experience. Edges tell us both what kind of things we are encountering and where we are going; they convey just enough information for us to be able to recognize and assess what is before and around us—or, if we cannot do so due to their ambiguity, we tend to draw closer to make out the edge-structure more reliably. Informative edges belong to ordinary physical things, to faces and whole bodies, to entire places and ongoing events, to landscapes and waterscapes and the earth itself. Edges are both altogether ordinary—being everywhere we look or touch, hear or smell— yet they are also quite literally extraordinary. Even as they take us into the heart of our everyday life-world, they also take us out of it into other worlds—into other places and times as these are adumbrated by the edges of our current world. We exist in one edge-world after another, oftentimes several at once, as was already evident in my experience of walking on 110th Street in New York and as happens to each of us all the time.

Most of the time our attention goes toward edges that act as "subjective lures" (in Whitehead's term), as if we were seeking guidance from them. But we also *come from* edges, and when we do they may possess a very special lever- age. I have in mind the way that coming from a marginal position, far from being a disadvantage (which it certainly is when forced upon us), can act to disrupt a staid and settled center and engender alternative directions that possess consider- able creative force. Evidence for this comes especially from the arts, where it has been said that "across the board, the margins and not the center tend to be the places of greatest cultural innovation."[4] Exemplary instances abound, one of which was the Dada movement as it took form in the ambience of the Café Voltaire in Zurich during World War I. There Tristan Tzara, a Romanian immigrant, along with other immigrant artists, precipitated a radically new conception of art whose repercussions are still being felt. As Costica Bradatan has written, "It must have been Tzara's marginality that enabled him to do what he did: founding an artistic movement meant to deride systematically a civilization whose blind trust in instrumental rationality and fetishization of technology had pushed it into one of the most destructive wars the world had ever seen. For Dadaism the center—be it artistic, philosophical, intellectual, economic or political—was not worthy of anything but mockery."[5] The Dada movement has clear affinities with the broader phenomenon known as "outsider art," whose very name makes the point here at issue: creative change often comes from the edges, undermining what is conventional and taken for granted, thereby clearing the way for what is novel.[6]

Actively occupying the edge is important not only in art but also in the evolution of species on earth. In chapter 5, we learned that in Darwin's view many of the most significant evolutionary advances occur when members of certain animal species live *at the edge* of their communities. There they must be resourceful in adapting to new and previously unknown places or they will perish. Their lives are at risk, and this calls for creatively adaptive actions. Each of the Galapagos islands was in effect "a little world within itself"[7]—in effect, a self-sustaining edge-world. Making the adaptive best of being located at the far edges results in evolutionary advances that come to benefit the species as a whole. Once again, then, the force for innovative change comes from the margin—from the edge.

## II

Granting the creative potential for humans and tortoises alike when living in the margins of more settled situations, why should such eccentric edges matter *philosophically*? Indeed, why should edges of any kind matter to philosophers? Does not the conspicuous neglect of edges in philosophy suggest their comparative insignificance? The issue comes to a crux in the philosophical analysis of perception, a topic of intense interest ever since Plato's inaugural account in the *Theatetus*. In that area of philosophical work the emphasis is on questions of knowledge and truth, and only rarely on the infrastructures of the perceived world itself. Edges, if noticed at all, are taken for granted and passed over. Yet a careful inspection of perceptual experience reveals that edges are integral to whatever we perceive by means of our sensuously alert bodies.

Edges are significant in perception in one quite specific way: as essential to the fact that perceived things exist in space and time. Regarding space, the fact that everything physical comes edged helps to demonstrate that even if space itself is infinite—in whichever sense of "infinite" we may choose to emphasize—things that appear in space are ineluctably finite. They *must* be so if they terminate in the edges that are their effective cutting-off points, without which they would no longer be distinct things at all: and not to be distinct is not to be a thing. Distinctness, thinghood, and edgedness are covalent concepts. Physical things are condensed modules of spatiality that represent the effective foreclosure of open space, and they are located in those particular stretches of space that are their places. As for time, we have found that events construed as exemplary temporal happenings come edged as well, especially at their beginnings and endings but also at intermediate points as well. To the extent that perceived things are part of events, they possess temporal as well as spatial edges.

In short, the role of edges in perception, as this is specified spatially and temporally, is of central significance and for this reason calls for the attention of philosophers, who cannot afford to ignore them if they pretend to offer a comprehensive account of human experience, including its perceptual parameters.

In *The World at a Glance*, I maintained that the glance presents another instance of unjustifiable oversight by philosophers; now, in *The World on Edge*, I am making a parallel argument for edges. On my assessment, edge and glance are both integral to perceptual experience. The time has come for a more complete acknowledgment of the philosophical importance of both of these overlooked phenomena in perception. Each turns out on closer inspection to be far from "peripheral," if this word implies something insignificant or trivial. But if the peripheral is taken as a collective noun that connotes many ways of being off-center, it is from peripherality itself that the glance and the edge give rise to the pervasive and ramifying effects I have traced out for both of these peri-phenomena. Even if it is at first tempting to consider them to be extrinsic or secondary to what is central in perception, they end by being intrinsic and primary to the very perceptual experiences in which they figure: each works from the sides of these experiences—sides that prove indispensable to them.

## III

And yet all the fuss I have made about edges in this book, if not much ado about nothing, is it not about something that is almost nothing! Already in the prelude to this book, I claimed edges are "next to nothing." They are where something protrusive begins to vanish, and this is as true of a place or an event as it is of a material thing or the human body or even the psyche. It holds for external as well as internal edges. Edges exist where something that is thrust forward is at the same time on the verge of disappearing. This is so despite the fact that edges are also the very place where that same something—for example, the edge of a knife or the tip of a pencil—takes effect: where (and whereby) the knife actually cuts into a piece of fruit, and where (and whereby) a pencil can write down a sentence.

The fact is that edges are incongruous entities: even as they assert themselves with decided force and specific effect, they dwindle in material volume or spatial extent as well as in temporal outreach. The moment of efficacity is also the moment of decreasing mass: an edge "delimits and enables"—both at once.[8] As enabling, this mass is effectual; as delimited, this same mass is in the process of expiring. It is as if there were an inverse ratio between the felt or perceived mass as dwindling and the way this mass influences that with which it is contiguous or that into which it reaches. In the case of edges, the How Much (how much mass, weight, extent, duration) and the With What (with what efficacy, force, causal power, effect) are in a curious compensatory relationship: the less of one, the more of the other.

The relationship between the delimited and the enabling is not just an odd juxtaposition of terms; it is still more puzzling than this. For it is precisely *from within that which is diminishing* that force is exerted. If the knife's edge had too much unshaped material mass—if this mass were not shaped in a certain way and to a certain degree—its blade would not be sharp enough to cut into or through things as it is designed to do; nor could I write intelligibly if I tried to do so with a too blunt pencil. The distinctive virtue of each instrument—its aptitude for accomplishing its specific purpose—vis-à-vis its appointed task comes from its very paucity of mass or volume.[9] For this same paucity is essential to the distinctive configuration of the edge with which it exerts its force.

The point I am making here is not just paradoxical: it is *heterodoxical*. It has to do not just with two contrary or conflicting beliefs posited alongside one another—as *para-doxa* literally signifies—but also with two quite disparate phenomena (*heteros* means "other") yoked together in a disjunctive conjunction. This is not "heterodoxy," that is, an intentionally oppositional belief held in opposition to an established orthodoxy. We have to do, rather, with two heterogeneous factors in which effectiveness in the realization of a particular function or task derives from the very fact of diminished substance.

This heterodoxical circumstance is not limited to the edges of knives or the points of pencils. It is ingredient in expansive contexts such as the experience of landscape or abstract art. In the case of landscape, it concerns how various natural phenomena—"natural" in the senses discussed in chapters 3 and 4—exhibit edges that give a landscape vista a special shape and scope. By marking the endings of fields or plains, a modest stretch of grass or a few trees act to usher in a more encompassing vista: to introduce it as it were.[10] If they were more demanding visually or took up too much pictorial space, they would hinder a more expansive view. Their very sparseness is a source of strength in opening onto a larger landscape. In abstract art, taken as a paradigmatic display of artifice, edges display a peculiar power to draw and hold aesthetic attention, whether in the form of early Cubist paintings by Braque or Picasso, or in Mondrian's stark studies, or in the dark sculptural complexes of Louise Nevelson, or the lighter-toned sculpted woodworks of Martin Puryear. In each of these diverse works we witness an interplay between linear and color-saturated structures that set up the theme or *motif* of the work as perceived at first glance; but our lingering look is drawn by these introductory edges into another order of perception, that of the work as such, the work as a whole. The edges glimpsed at first and up front cannot be too massive or too strident or else this more complete perception will be compromised. Properly presented, they are indispensable to this perception: they become more fully efficacious there thanks precisely to their delimited annunciatory status.

A second heterodoxical situation is found in the fact that *a single edge is where many dimensionalities converge*: not just material and spatial and eventmental ones, but also those that are social, ethical, historical, personal, and interpersonal. We witness this, for example, in the concrete circumstance of hospitality, where certain bare gestures of welcoming bear multiple intentionalities and meanings. Opening a door or gate and extending a welcoming hand to the person seeking entry constitute minimal conditions for the full flowering of hospitality, a practice that embodies an entire history of hospitality within a given culture or tradition. This is not to mention the ethics of the interaction—how, in what spirit, I as host treat an arriving guest. The seemingly simple act of opening my door or gate also incorporates a number of aspects that are dense culturally and historically. By embodying this density, each discrete edge in this situation contributes to the effective enactment of hospitality.[11]

The subtly edged event of hospitality is thus a telling instance of the second heterodox: namely, that every edge bears a number of intersecting directions of interest and intended use, as well as whole traditions of significance. But this holds even for a bare knife edge, whose exact shape reflects the tasks it is meant to perform as well as a certain tradition of kitchenware design. The same slim edge incorporates a whole legacy of prior usage as being just this kind of knife (say, one employed to cut certain foodstuffs, such as bread or fruit). Its very action becomes multiplex when, in addition to cutting outright, this action is extended to paring, pruning, or shearing. Inflected as well is its own history as a unique material thing.

For instance, just *this* pearl-handled knife was originally in my aunt's kitchen; she gave it to me when I was first setting up house and I have kept it around ever since in the several places where I have lived. It has been sharpened and resharpened many times. All of these multiple facticities and historicities dance on the cutting edge of its one thin blade. It is as if the economy of means evident in this edge had been designed so as to be able to contain all these diverse dimensions. But there is no conscious calculation here, just a conjunction of the requirements of practicality, the availability of certain materials for manufacture (iron, steel, other alloys), all within concrete contexts of cooking and consumption. In the pearl handle of this knife, there is also a decorative factor that has its own history. The bare blade and the handle of this knife both carry an entire webwork of meanings and applications.

In between gestures of hospitality and the uses of a kitchen knife lies a spectrum of intermediate cases. Each is exemplary of the heterodoxical situation whereby something exiguous carries an outsize load of causalities and significations. The fact that some edges are primarily "natural," that is, belong to an uncontrived physical world that has come about in accordance with its own resources, laws, and processes, does not exempt them from bearing up under—indeed *bearing*—complexities of origin and nuances of sense. Take the edge of an inland lake in Maine such as Moosehead Lake: this is the expression of many centuries of geological and meteorological history, beginning with the recession of the last great glacier that covered this part of the world 18,000 years ago, and continuing into the present period of rapidly changing climate. Each stretch of the lake's edge bears the marks of this dense natural history in the form of moraine deposited there, the character of the surrounding soils, the grasses and plants that grow seasonally around the lake, and the lake's water as it impinges on the lake's own shores.

At the same shores are also found traces of human interventions in the lake's recent history—among them docks for boating and swimming, canoes and kayaks and power boats, fishing nets, and the like. These populate the lake's edge at several junctures, sometimes overwhelming it to a point where the naturally given edge is obscured, buried beneath the detritus of constructed and imposed edges wrought by human beings in their passion for leisurely pursuits. Nevertheless, the two kinds of edges here at stake, natural and artifactual, remain distinguishable *as kinds* even if they have become intermeshed in ordinary perception. Whether considered apart or taken together, each of these kinds of edges bears out the truth of the second heterodox: that a great deal can pivot on very little.

In all these ways and others, *much hangs on the edge*. Borne up by the slender thread of an edge is a surfeit of overdetermined and overdetermining structures and meanings. Whatever the central bulk and inherent mass of something may be—and whatever its historical, cultural, or social roots—it is in and through its edges that this bulk and mass, along with its genesis in time and history, are brought to bear. From the slender substance of these edges—ever more slender as they move to a point of termination—an array of active forces and lasting effects proceeds. This is the deeper truth that is shared by the first two heterodoxes, which show themselves to be closely related ways of understanding both the generation and the efficacy of the occupants of the edge-world. Each demonstrates that in the realm of edge diminutive mass and volume is consonant with having considerable effects and reflecting a great deal of history.

## IV

There is a third heterodoxical truth to be considered: *edges, although next to nothing in their constitution, bring about proximity to many things.* Even as they are diminished in their substantial being, they extend into their immediate environs and beyond. I remark here not on the actual *effect* of the edge by way of its sheer force—the brunt of the first heterodox—but on its many ramifications, whether causally efficacious or not. The very reduction of an edge's sheer mass and volume allows it to insinuate itself all the more fully into its surrounding world, to fit into multiple contexts in that world, or when not literally fitting, to adumbrate things and events that are external to the edge itself. Such adumbration is the edge-wise equivalent of intentionality in the classical sense of Brentano and Husserl. But where for these latter thinkers intentionality is exclusively a matter of conscious mind attending to its own content (its *noema* in Husserl's term), in the case of all but psychical edges, we are dealing with a specifically *material intentionality*.[12] It is as if the materiality of an edge, far from being merely inertial, directs itself toward a world at which it aims and to which it draws near—and to which it draws us close as well: us as its perceivers and participants. In this respect, edges are comparable to antennae that point outward and enter into entanglement with surrounding things, people, and states of affairs.

In this signal feature of their being, edges are not unlike earth in Heidegger's conception, an elemental factor that thrusts itself beyond itself. The earth is not simply what is closed in and buried but a dynamic force that exists in an active struggle with the world, the domain of history and language: "The earth is not simply the Closed but that which rises up as self-closing. . . . Earth juts through the world and world grounds itself on the earth."[13] So, too, do edges jut into the worlds of which they are a part, extending into these same worlds in ways that give them direction and shape they would otherwise lack. In this action, edges reach out beyond where they literally end.

In their lean economy, *edges explicate:* they fold out, unfold. They act to reach into what does not belong to them strictly as edges—that is, what is of another order. Unmindingly, they intend that order. Their lightness of being is coeval with, and indicative of, a material manifold of becomings. Moreover, they have concrete effects on these becomings. The fixed edge of a reservoir, for example, has every-thing to do with the shape and volume of the water that is collected there as a material form of becoming. The water is shaped into becoming the contents of the reservoir; it takes on its exact volume thanks to the shape of the container in which it is located. Even a tenuous or soft edge can be an effective presence in the realm of becoming. Thresholds and margins are cases in point: even if not linear in structure and far from being fixed (they may be continually changing), they bear on and refer to what lies on their other side—which they serve to signal or suggest. In this way, they act to bring out what occurs on this other side, reaching from here to what is over there and prefiguring it.

We recognize here the familiar action of boundaries, which in their very porosity encourage flows of several sorts to occur *through* them. The presence of "ecozones" between nations—as at the border between Peru and Bolivia—acts to facilitate the flow of humans and animals and plant species across them. They stand in stark contrast with the defensive and preventive nature of strictly supervised borders, especially as these are materialized in border walls designed to arrest the free movement of undocumented migrants, as at the United States–Mexico border wall at La Frontera. In this latter case the permeability and outreach of boundary-like edges is deliberately curtailed by the construction of a physical barrier between those on one side and those on the other. The result is thwarted movement and dashed dreams. Even here, however, adumbration across the edge may occur: a reference to what is happening on the other side of the border, as when border artists who are confined to one side of the border depict life on its other side by painting on their side of the wall scenes of this life—the very life to which the wall denies access to those without proper papers for crossing.[14]

Apart from a situation such as we find at La Frontera—extreme in the forced choices its imposes on those situated in the vicinity of the border wall—in many other cases edges ingress adroitly into what lies beyond them. A given edge sends its prefiguring presence into what surrounds it by a form of forward influence. Its effects are not limited to those caused by its literal contact with environing things or events. They can proceed by an action of foreshadowing, as when a glass of wine is raised in starting to make a toast but is not sipped until the toast has been given. Edges portend in many other ways as well. Walking in a city, the edges of my body bear forward in anticipation of my destination. The bodies of those who participated in the Women's March of January 21, 2017, leaned forward toward Trump Tower as they made their way up Fifth Ave.

The material intentionality of edges is realized through what can be called *apperceptive transfer*. I have argued elsewhere that apperception needs to be recognized as an important supplement to ordinary perception; it entails a subtle form or level of perception that apprehends nuanced structures missed in the course of perceiving things or events outright, at a molar level. Apperception is most characteristically enacted by the subtleties of the glance, but it is also at play in the experience of edges in their nuanced self-eclipsing character, when we catch sight of their exfoliation into their near and far circumambience.[15] Thanks to such self-transcendence, edges take us into environing dynamic fields, which we apperceive rather than perceive point blank. But they do so only from within the confinement that they embody in their role as ending, circumscribing, and delimiting. From being next to nothing—from their very dwindling down—they allow us to come not just into something in particular but also into whole domains of things and events: whole worlds. From within their very enclosure, they transfer us elsewhere. This is nothing if not heterodoxical.

In this regard, every edge is a leading edge. Such is the transferential power of edges: as apperceived in their minute and even delicate transactions, they take us across themselves into what is not of their being but that can become part of our experience from here on. Next to nothing themselves, they bring us close to everything in the circumambient world into which they carry us.

## V

Already in the prelude to this book I remarked that the being of edges consists in their vanishing. At that early point, this stood as a bald assertion; now, in nearing the end of this book, I am able to explore it more carefully. No matter how definitive the edge of a certain kind of thing may be—think of a razor's edge—and no matter how effective it may be in its enactment, it is also always coming to an end. In the case of the edges of physical things, they move away from the very surfaces whose closure they provide; as we have just seen, the primary thrust of their material intentionality is outward beyond these surfaces toward that with which they interact. This is already indicated in the fact that their most salient characteristic is often their convex angularity, which contributes to their conspicuous presence in everyday life: we sometimes stumble over edges. It is in their insistent extrusion or literal extroversion that we meet and know most edges in daily experience: a fact not lost on babies groping along new surfaces, or those who walk with canes. With notable exceptions (such as ingrown fingernails), most edges are pitched *out*. Yet in their very outgoingness they run out of means to continue; *they expire in their ecstasy*. This is a recurrent structure that we have encountered a number of times in the course of this book. Despite its being rarely noticed, it is indispensable to the being of edges and integral to their basic action.

This heterodoxical situation can be elucidated by expanding on a theme I have discussed elsewhere as "the logic of the less."[16] Edges, despite their inherent diminishment—their becoming *less* (less than replete) and always partial (there is no total edge)[17]—possess an unsuspected power. This power displays itself in many contexts: personal, collective, social, political, ethical, and aesthetic. In such contexts, they come to have more influence than their inobtrusive presence in our lives might seem to permit or predict. Even as they taper away or suddenly shear off, they are things to contend with in the actual world, being expansive and sometimes explosive forces there, as when the edges of an automobile destroyed by a car bomb tear into the bodies of those nearby, or when the narrow edge of a closely contested political victory gives rise to a hegemonic regime change on the part of the victor, as occurred in the United States in November, 2016.[18] Their destiny in human and biological life-worlds is to extend themselves beyond their ostensible limits (limited to being the close-fitting edges of preexisting surfaces and ongoing events) into what surrounds them, with various differential effects. The Maginot Line that was constructed in the 1930s to protect the French against German invasion was much more than a cartographical posit, a line on a map. It was an elaborate and expensive fortification that embodied a defensive posture for an entire nation, one that made it all the more tempting to destroy or evade. Imagined as invulnerable by the French, it was experienced as a provocative affront by

Nazi generals, who outflanked it and invaded France by way of Belgium. From this instance and countless others, we see that edges *expose themselves:* they extend themselves outside their delimited presence and invite response from what lies around and beyond them.

At the same time and as an equally integral part of their being, *edges run out.* They "run out" in both senses of this expression: they exhaust themselves and they leave themselves. As self-exhausting, they come to an end, often a peremptory one. As leaving themselves, they outrun their literal limits. These two aspects of edges trace out a main axis of the logic of the less. To run out is to become depleted of materiality or energy, but this is compatible with having an effective after-presence in a surrounding space and becoming an influence there. This is what I meant just above in saying that they "expire in their ecstasy": they burst out even as they run out.

Another aspect of the logic of the less is that edges are subject to scrutiny as if they were the merely passive objects of our looks, yet they also assert themselves as *there to be seen,* prominently enough to attract notice. It is almost as if edges make themselves lesser (weaker, less fortified) so as to be stronger—more effective than if they were outsized, bulky, or blunt.

The logic of the less signifies just this: *in being less, an entity or event is more.* Here the emphasis should be placed on the *is,* the copula of the affirmation of existence (and of identity, as we shall see shortly). So considered, the less does not merely gain something separately more, more mass or more force, as it were. *The less is itself, in itself and by itself, more.* By way of being less, it *is* more. Not just more than we had expected (a matter of calculation) but qualitatively more, intrinsically more: *more as such.*

How can this be? As I have remarked several times in this book, edges are always already petering out and perishing. They are less than what they seem to be when they catch our eye as saliencies emerging from a sheer surface. This intrinsic lesser being is the fate of edges of every kind, whether of things or events, places or bodies or psyches. Yet such diminution in extent or spread (in the case of psychic edges, in trackable internal process) does not mean loss in efficacy, merit, or value. On the contrary, edges are all the more effective for being the exiguous entities they are—where I take *exiguous* to signify a less than complete presence, diminutive compared with more robust things or places or processes. Despite being exiguous—or rather, *because of it*—edges are all the more efficacious in their action and effects. In the realm of edges there is no loss, much less imperfection, in being less. On the contrary, what is less is indispensable to being an edge at all—in the first and the last place.

It is in holding fast to its destiny as a lesser being that an edge is all the more effective: *in being less, it is all the more efficacious.* And the more efficacious it is—the more it makes a difference—the more it is itself. *It is more itself precisely as less.* It is more itself intensively and qualitatively, that is to say, more *itself in itself*: where "in itself" connotes being itself in a manner that does not depend on contextual factors but rather on its own resources and strengths. This is so even if these resources and strengths are in the process of perishing.

A skeptic may respond, is not the less simply, and strictly, *relative to the more*—by definition? This is certainly so if we restrict ourselves to the formal, definitional meaning of these terms, that is, matters of measurable size. But what I am proposing in the case of edges is something more radical: *the equation of the less with the more*. Or more exactly I am asserting their *adequation*, their qualitative equality, as is symbolized by an equal sign with a tilde placed over it ($\cong$) to indicate that the equation is effective even and precisely as qualitative. The equation in question is not one in which every aspect of each is equivalent to every aspect of the other, without remainder. Instead of perfect coincidence, we are considering a situation in which there can be shortfall as well as overshot, yet one that retains a significant core of qualitative sameness.

This kind of sameness is compatible with difference. Indeed, as Heidegger insists, sameness, fully considered, does not exclude difference but thrives from it and is even constituted by it: "The same [*das Selbe*] is not the merely identical [*das Gleiche*]. In the merely identical, the different disappears. In the same the different appears, and appears all the more pressingly, the more resolutely thinking is concerned with the same matter in the same way."[19] Thus in saying that for edges less is more, I do not intend this *is* as a matter of formal or quantitative self-identity, as in the equation $a = a$. I refer rather to a more informal identity that is at play in saying that things "are (more or less) the same," that is, they share the same qualities albeit differentially. They participate together in these qualities; they are bivalent partners in sameness. In this spirit we can think of the less and the more as adequational partners in the constitution of the same things—and of edges in particular.

Otherwise put, the less and the more of an edge, though qualitatively the same, are not simply or numerically *one*. I prefer to regard them as alternative foci or epicenters within a One that is itself an alternative expression of the Same. This is to say that an extraordinary entity like an edge is at once less and more (and in particular, it is more in being less), and in this way it is one and the same edge.

## VI

Since this discussion is beginning to wax abstract, let us back up and consider some concrete ways in which edges are at once less and more—and both at once in significant ways that allow them to be alternative expressions of the same.

*Intercalation of edges belonging to two (or more) entities.* When we refer to edges as "close-fitting," we have in mind a situation in which the edges of one entity connect intimately with those of another. In order to fit well, such edges must be significantly less than, say, those of a solid sheet of something; their being is subtractive in comparison with this latter, which in itself offers no edges suitable for connection. A flat piece of plywood is edge-connective only when it is stacked up against a comparably flat second sheet—in which case, there is contiguity, but not the kind of morphological fit that is present when my body climbs into a close-fitting wetsuit in order to swim in cold water. In the latter case, my bodily edges (hips and chest and shoulders) fit into the shape of the suit as determined by its style and materials of composition. One set of edges (of the trunk of my body, my arms and legs) coexists closely with another set (belonging to the suit itself). In this conjoint intercalation, the rubber wetsuit with my body in it involves a tight mutual fitting that contrasts markedly with the way one rectangular board is casually placed up against the flat surface of another. In both cases, there is contact and edge-to-edge connection. But when my body slips into a wetsuit of suitable size there is, in addition, a close contiguity of the edges of each as they fit into one another: a matter of mutual fit.

This happens only because of a factor of the less—less of a body mass than were I bloated in the manner of Aristophanes's imagined rotund human beings in Plato's *Symposium*[20]—that allows for the neat fit that amounts to being more: more in that the two entities whose edges interconnect now form one complete entity, that is, my-body-in-a-wetsuit. This *more* is not more as measured by merely quantitative indicators—more mass, weight, or volume—but rather takes the form of a new entity that is in effect two-in-one or, alternately expressed, different-in-the-same. Because my body mass is less than bloated and can fit into a wetsuit that fits me, once suited I become more—more than my unsuited self and able to become more myself-as-swimmer-in-cold-waters.

*Edges in a fluid medium.* But the *more* in question is not restricted to this last kind of situation, in which two entities connect by way of a close fit between the definite edges of each. In another circumstance, the edges of a physical thing are in touch with a surrounding medium that has no definite edges of its own. I have in mind a circumstance such as that of marsh grasses in the midst of tidal waters. The long thin edges of these grasses (such as Spartina) have evolved to absorb nutrients from these waters in efficient ways that strengthen these grasses while combing the waters in such a way as to moderate and regulate them during the influx and outflow of tides. Taken together, the marsh grasses and the tidal waters form a unity that is in effect an entity of 2+; that is, more than either taken separately, yet not their simple addition qua separate entities (1+1=2). Without edges that establish an intimacy of interaction, there would be just one solid substance and one fluid medium, indifferently juxtaposed like a rock in water. Instead, an active environment, an entire microworld, arises from the interplay of the edges of marsh grasses with the medium of water that surrounds them on all sides: a two-way entanglement in which each influences the other and the two together create a shared unitary world: a whole marsh world. This world is one even though it is composed from (at least) two constituents that in their interaction constitute more than the sheer addition of one to the other.

*Intermedia interaction.* I do not mean to imply that edges accrue to discrete physical things alone: these may be the most conspicuous, but they are far from exhausting the field of candidates for the *less = more* adequation. What I have just called the "medium" has its own kind of edges.[21] In many circumstances these are deeply compenetrative with the edges of other media.[22] The compenetration does not require a close fit. I have in mind the way in which incoming and out-going tidal waters themselves meet at their fringes, achieving an ever-shifting equi-poise in which currents of one flow into the other, disappearing into each other as separate entities.[23] There are countless other instances of this subtle but thor-ough *intermediation.* They include atmospheric commixtures of multiple airs and gasses. In such instances, the merging of one medium with another is such that there is no effective remainder or trace—nothing beyond a slight discoloration or odor, if even that. (Hence their insidious character in the case of poisonous gases.) The result is one continuous medium that is the direct expression of the merging of edges: one and the same being has been engendered from nuanced differences in media, issuing in a *more* that has come directly from the *less* of discrete outer edges: once again, a 2+ situation.

*Psychical interpenetration.* Not altogether unlike the mixing of media through their edges, psychical events also interpenetrate in subtle and thorough manners. In both cases, the edges are noticeably "soft," pliable and nonlinear—and known to be such. Psychical edges are internal to psychical being, to conscious, precon-scious, and unconscious processes and states. And they are internal to each other—so much so that it is often difficult to detect precise differences between them, as one memory gives way to another, one thought becomes another under our very (mental) eyes. As I have emphasized in chapter 9, in this realm all is in flux, all is transitional. Edges are here subordinate to the processes and transitions to which they belong. We find ourselves at an antipode from the circumstance of the wet-suit, in which a certain stability of edges is required for formfitting to occur: in this case, the edges of a human body and those of the rubber suit into which it is inserted. This is not to deny that there are phases of psychical processes that announce themselves as terminal or initiatory, that embody the opening or clos-ing of a given psychical event: as when we sense the dawning of a memory or the conclusion of a thought. But such edge states, though distinct enough to be iden-tified separately, join up with other such states to bring about a virtual monism of consciousness; which is to say, *one* psychical stream composed of many psychical phases and states. With the significant exception of traumatic experiences, these states are woven into the tapestry of ongoing mental processes, a tapestry that is as close to seamless as human experience allows. Ultimately, for each psychically alive being, there is one and the same psychical process: the same even as it differs from moment to moment, phase to phase, state to state. The one-and-the-sameness of this process incorporates the differences between its constituent moments. The lesser being of these moments is essential to the full being of the full psychical process: they do not just add up to make this more what it is, they *are the more* already: each part of the process being in a certain manner the whole of process itself, thanks to condensing and reflecting it.

In all four instances, then, we witness distinctive ways in which the lesser being of edges occasions the being more of the whole of which these edges figure as parts. Such edges are at one with the becoming whole that their very ingrediency helps to realize. Despite the considerable descriptive differences among the four cases in point, in each instance we see sameness arising from difference and compatible with it, and oneness from two or more constituents. This oneness is not a simple additive whole but is immanent in these very constituents considered as "total parts" in which the whole inheres. Despite the literal partiality of edges, a whole entity or place or event is at stake at each stage and not just at the end: the marsh itself, a tidal scene, a pervasive atmosphere, a flowing psychical stream. More generally, *one* and the *same* issues from the *many* and the *different*; *more* comes from *less*—a less that is becoming more, all the more the same and precisely from the different. The exiguousness of edges, their very slightness, far from being a disintegrative or subtractive force, contributes directly to the moreness of a whole of which these edges are indispensable and integral parts. Not only are such edges adept in their functionality (e.g., their fit), but they also help to realize outcomes that exceed what their comparative slenderness would allow or predict on a purely quantitative assessment. And they do so by already incorporating—thus rendering immanent—the more or whole of which they are such integral parts.

Not only does less *become* more in these instances. Less *is* more: not just a constituent ingredient in the more but something that already contains the more even if in adumbrative format. The body in the wetsuit is already the swimmer in cold waters; the diffuse gases are the atmosphere they help to constitute; the reeds and the water are the marsh they together make up; the phases of psychical process are the process itself.

Thus we see how the edge considered as a being of the less (less in many ways but especially in being less than perfectly plenary) can be *more just as less*: more in its very role as lesser. The less does not transform itself into the more as into something different: it is already more—more effective and more transformative—in and through its very operation as less: which is to say, as an edge. This is the converse of the situation in which the less is tributary from the more, as in Freud's claim concerning the Rat Man's obsessive self-doubt: "he who doubts his own love doubts every lesser thing."[24] Here Freud posits an ideal primary state of unambivalent love for another human being, failure to realize which results from a series of acts of doubting, each concerned with something more trivial than the last. In this case the less is directly derivative from the more, taken as an initial state of wholeness. This circumstance can be diagrammed thus:

more > less > still less > even less yet . . . ad indefinitum

Whereas the paradigm I am pursuing is quite different:

less = more . . . less = more . . . ad indefinitum

Instead of a diminution from more to less, edges present us with something else: not with the diametrical opposite of this situation—going incrementally from less to more—but with the more radical circumstance in which less *is* more. To make this latter claim is tantamount to acknowledging the inherently augmentative, whole-making power of the edge.

## VII

We find in daily discourse and everyday life many at least partial parallels to this situation, in which the ordinary proves to be extraordinary. By the things we say or the actions we take, we often engage in the logic of the less-as-more. To begin with, there are a number of expressions in ordinary language that exemplify or at least suggest this logic. Here are four of these.

*The cutting edge.* Normally, this means being at the vanguard, where the edge itself may be modest in extent yet makes all the difference to the future of a given enterprise; but it also implies that if an edge is able to cut into something substantial (such as an already existing project, a standing institution), it manifests a power that one would not predict from its diminutive being: think of the frail 82-year-old nun Megan Rice, who with several others broke into the nuclear facility in Tennessee and poured blood on critical machinery there.[25]

*The underdog has the advantage.* The very person who starts from behind or suffers from certain handicaps may, coming precisely from this disadvantaged position, gain an unexpected advantage in a given competitive situation (athletic, political, and so forth). Hans-Georg Gadamer, though a polio victim in his early youth, won tennis championships in Germany as a young man—not to mention his later triumphs as a philosopher.

*Coming from behind.* This is closely related to the underdog situation, but now the situation is one in which one starts badly and yet manages to win a race; as with the tortoise in the fable of the tortoise and the hare.

*Edging others out.* Here the idea is not that of coming from far behind but rather that of being close to leading—so close that it is just a matter of pulling ahead by an extra effort in the last stretch, even if this means only slightly outperforming others. This occurs in the home stretch of many foot races. It also happens in academia, when someone from a small set of assistant professors, all similarly talented, comes to gain tenure first by virtue of publishing a single article that outshines those of her colleagues.

In all these ordinary locutions, the context is that of success in endeavors in which winning out is at stake or at least significant improvement takes place. This context is also understood in the usual interpretation of the popular saying that "less is more," where *more* signifies something overt or measurable, easily detectable or recognizable by others such as public success. This is why I have gone to such lengths to give a different interpretation of the same formula—one that is not dependent on quantifiable effects or degree of public recognition but that takes into account other criteria such as significance or lasting effect, as realized by forming or reflecting a greater whole.

In the case of still other analogies, matters become more complex and subtle. In these, we can no longer fall back on worldly and public criteria of success or progress; something else is at issue.

*Part/whole relations.* We have considered this relation under the heading of bodily edges, which often illustrate this relationship in which a part (a gesture, a form of posture) condenses the whole and takes on a potency or "independence" (in Rilke's word) akin to that of the whole of which it is a part. In this case, the part is a lesser thing compared to the literal, total whole, yet it has an inherent strength that allows it to stand in for the whole, or rather, to bring it about that *the whole is already in the part*, which is to say, that *the more inhabits the less*. Thus my whole body is present in its various edges, being compressed and expressed there. When I say "this is *my* knee," I am at one with my knee, wholly in it: the knee is me.

*Glance/look relations.* The human glance is only one way of looking, and one that seems at first to be partial or even trivial; yet it contains a remarkable power of its own that renders it one of the most effective modes of human looking— in many ways more perceptive than the more highly valorized acts of gazing and observing when it comes to certain basic activities such as knowledge acquisition, ethical action, and artistic creation. In merely glancing around us an entire world is gained: a world not as fully accessible in other modalities of vision, such as the objectifying gaze, which risks losing the world into whose detailed structure it peers so intently. A gaze such as the medical gaze may miss the whole even as it scrutinizes the part.[26] But I can glance at the other's body and see it instantly as unmistakably my friend David's body and that of no one else.

Other contemporary thinkers have recommended their own versions of the logic of the less. Deleuze and Guattari in *A Thousand Plateaus* propose two ideas significantly parallel to this logic. First, they posit that nomadic actions, despite their seeming disarray and disorganization, can succeed in vanquishing a hegemonic state apparatus by means of concerted guerilla action in the very face of massive imperialist and colonialist powers: for example, in French Algeria, Vietnam, Iraq, and Afghanistan. Second, they discuss the unsuspected potency in the modern era of what they designate as "minor sciences" vis-à-vis the "royal sciences"—where the latter are represented by physics, chemistry, and biology, and the former by hydraulics or metallurgy or tidology. The informal and sometimes amateur character of these last three enterprises carries with it a special kind of leverage, along with a unique mode of understanding the surrounding world—a leverage and an understanding which the officially sanctioned sciences fail to accomplish on their own restricted terms.[27] In both instances, then, what is tempting to regard as less objectively potent or epistemically discerning proves to be more effective and more insightful in ways that a settled state apparatus and an ensconced royal science fail to realize.

## VIII

Edges are inherently bivalent. They are so in two major ways: as intermediary and yet intense; as immanent but also transcendent.

Edges are *intermediary* as between thing and non-thing, as coming into being and leaving it, and as being between substance and medium. Edges are interim entities and agents: as internal, they come between parts of a thing or event; as external, they stand between that which they outline and what surrounds it. (Hence my invocation of the intermediacy of edges in city spaces.) Thanks to being intermediary, edges intervene as active and insistent presences that link parts of things and entire situations. At the same time, edges are intense as condensed expressions of closure and finitude. Without a certain intensity—if only as a perceived contour—an edge cannot function as edge. Thanks to being intense, an edge stands in: it literally *insists* ("sits in") on its being where it is and what it is.

Edges are *immanent* as endoskeletal structures: say, the edges of the individual keys on my computer keyboard as these form an implicit pattern for my eyes and fingers. But edges are also *transcendent* as going out and up: as in the outer edges of my computer regarded as a physical object. In the first capacity, they are inherent in the thing or region or happening *into* which the edged entity or event recedes and finds its place: the "plane of immanence" to adapt a term of Deleuze's.[28] In the second capacity, edges exceed their own base: they are literally ecstatic. They are prominences, literal preeminences, with respect to that base; they go outward or upward, transcendently, from within their own self-inherent or immanent being. (We recognize here another way of construing their material intentionality.) In this basic dual directionality, edges can be considered transcendences in immanence.

Every edge comes double-edged, two-in-one: as intense *and* intermediary, transcendent *and* immanent; but also as outgoing *and* incoming, adventuresome *and* abiding, jutting out *and* receding, existing *and* perishing—and more *and* less. The duplicity of edges is ingredient in actions that distinguish and diverge even as they unite and link.

The bivalence of edges is everywhere evident. Formally considered, edges form lines as well as angles that are dihedral: literally "two-sided" in two-dimensional representations. More concretely, they form part of a *to/from* structure: into the edge-bearer from the edges of its surfaces. But they also belong to a *from/to* structure—from the edge-bearer extending outward to other things or events. If they are an integral part of a more encompassing three-dimensional life-world, this is due to their deft steerage into this world. It is as if edges were the dexterous phantom limbs of things and events. Edges are at once the protentional outreachings of these things and events as well as their retentional inreachings.

Edges realize a decided doubling within the world as we experience it. They go out and up even as they act to anchor in and down. This insistent two-way dialectic keeps them slim, *lesser*, and thus in a position to spring forth by actions of attaching and connecting, cutting and separating. In this way the economy of edges becomes apparent along with their potentiality for acute experimentalism. Thanks to their outpost location, edges are perpetually on the frontier of experience, where they exceed the bulk and substance of the things or places or events that subtend them, eclipsing their hulking core, their inertial center. In this way they are *more* than these same things and places and events. But they are more not in sheer physical mass or measurable duration in time but rather as rooted in the lesser being of the infrastructures of these various edge-bearing vehicles. Between the immanent center of edgeful effectuation and the transcending of this center there is energetic exchange at all times.

Edges prove to be the intermezzi of the world as we know it. They are beings of the between—*truchements*, "go-betweens." They go back and forth between one thing and other things, one place and many places, one event and several events, one bodily or psychical process and numerous others. Their mythical prototype is as much Hermes as it is Janus, since edges not only look forward and backward at once but they inhabit the crossroads of human experience, ingredient in this experience throughout. Hermes was the god of crossings, the mercurial messenger between the Olympian gods and human beings. Moving fleet-footed between the two, he was their ultimate mediatrix. Edges may not be in direct touch with the gods, but they are as connective as Hermes in their interstitial powers: they "cross and dip" in the creative interplay of things.[29] They span the intervals, infinitesimal as well as extensive, that exist between that which they connect. Edges play back and forth between surfaces as well as on them; they show themselves on the sleeves of things and on the forefront and back end of events as they actualize a complex dialectic of the human and nonhuman dimensions of things and events, places and bodies, earth and psyche, sun and sky.

Edges are the insistent and existent intermediaries that hold whole life-worlds together even as they emerge into their own and defy these worlds by creating edge-worlds with their own parameters. They are linkage and resistance, being both conjunctive and scissioning. Edges join and disjoin, combine and break off. In shifting back and forth rapidly between these and other opposed extremes, they require the speed of Hermes even as they reflect the double face of Janus, who looks forward and backward at once. With edges we have before us two actions (retreating and extruding), two directions (backward and forward), two vectors (in and out), and two basic parameters (less and more). All these pairs are in turn members of an indefinite dyad of like and unlike, one and many, same and different.

## Notes

1. The exceptions can be counted on two hands, and none of these is a study of edges as such: Avrum Stroll, *Surfaces* (Minneapolis: University of Minnesota Press, 1988); Jean-Luc Nancy, *Being Singular Plural*, trans. Robert D. Richardson and Anne E. O'Byrne (Stanford: Stanford University Press, 2000); Jacques Derrida, "Parergon," in *The Truth in Painting*, trans. Geoff Bennington and Ian McLeod (Chicago: University of Chicago Press, 1987), pp. 37–82, "Finis" in *Aporias*, trans. Thomas Dutoit (Stanford: Stanford University press, 1993), pp. 1–42, and "*Ousia* and *Grammē*: A Note on a Note from *Being and Time*," in *Margins of Philosophy*, ed. Alan Bass (Chicago: University of Chicago Press, 1982), pp. 29–68; Husserl's "The Origin of Geometry" in *The Crisis of European Sciences and Transcendental Phenomenology*, trans. David Carr (Evanston, IL: Northwestern University Press, 1970), pp. 353–78, which gave rise to the commentaries of Derrida (*Edmund Husserl's "Origin of Geometry": An Introduction*, trans. John P. Leavey [Lincoln: University of Nebraska Press, 1989]) and Merleau-Ponty (*Husserl at the Limits of Phenomenology*, ed. Leonard Lawlor and Bettina Bergo [Evanston, IL: Northwestern University Press, 2002]). See also my short essay, "Going to the Edge," in *The Oxford Literary Review* 36, no. 2 (2014): pp. 191–95, for a discussion of edge in Derrida's work overall.

2. See Eleanor J. Gibson and Richard D. Walk, "The 'Visual Cliff,'" in *Scientific American* 202 (1960): pp. 67–71. Cited in James J. Gibson, *An Ecological Approach to Visual Perception* (Atlantic Highlands, NJ: Lawrence Erlbaum, 1986).

3. See Jean Piaget, *The Child's Conception of Space* (London: Routledge, 1956).

4. Peter Gelderloos, "Precarity in Paradox: The Barcelona Model," *New York Times*, June 28, 2015.

5. On the Dada movement, see the article by Costica Bradatan in the column *The Stone*, "Change Comes from the Margins," *New York Times*, June 30, 2015.

6. Outsider art—the art of those who are institutionalized as "insane"—was first brought to full public attention by Jean Dubuffet, the French artist who created a museum in Switzerland devoted to their work. See Roger Cardinal, *Outsider Art* (New York: Praeger, 1972).

7. Charles Darwin, *The Origin of Species by Means of Natural Selection*, ed. Joseph Carroll (Peterborough, Ontario: Broadview Texts, 2003), p. 454. Darwin adds that the same is true of "the mocking thrush, finches, and numerous plants" (p. 458).

8. This phrase is from an unpublished essay by Bret Davis, "Knowing Limits: Toward a Nonwillful Perspectivism with Nietzsche, Heidegger, and Zen." Commenting on Heidegger's discussion of *peras* in "Building Dwelling Thinking," Davis writes, "*Horizon* derives from *horizein*, meaning 'to bound or limit,' and from *horos*, meaning 'boundary.' The horizon, however, *not only delimits but also enables* by orienting our circle-of-vision (*Gesichtskreis*)" (my italics).

9. Note that by "mass" in the last two paragraphs, I am not using the term in the sense of classical physical mechanics; I am using the term as meaning perceived volume but with sufficient heft and weight to exert a force on other things.

10. This is referred to as *repoussoir* ("set off," "contrast") in art-historical discourse on landscape painting. For a more complete analysis, see my *Representing Place: Landscape Painting and Maps* (Minneapolis: University of Minnesota Press, 2002), pp. 61, 79–80, 161, 163.

11. I have explored the circumstance of hospitality in my essay "Strangers at the Edge of Hospitality," as published in Richard Kearney and Kascha Semonovitch, *Phenomenologies of the Stranger: Between Hostility and Hospitality* (New York: Fordham University Press, 2011).

12. Between the intentionality of consciousness and material intentionality is "corporeal intentionality" (in Merleau-Ponty's term): the intentionality of the lived body. This third form of intentionality itself operates through the edges of the body—for instance, in expressive bodily gestures, as discussed in chapter 8. To this extent, I consider it to be continuous with material intentionality, which includes the intentionality of animate as well as inanimate things.

13. Heidegger, "The Origin of the Work of Art," in *Poetry Language Thought*, ed. and trans. A. Hofstadter (New York: Harper & Row, 1971), p. 54.

14. For a discussion of the role of art at the United States–Mexico border wall, see Casey and Watkins, *Up Against the Wall: Re-Imagining the U.S.–Mexico Border Wall*, chapter 8: "Border-Wall Art as Limit Acts." Another alleviation of the border wall is found in the Sabal Palm Sanctuary in the Lower Rio Grande region, where a natural preserve has been kept and nurtured in the very presence of the wall, offering to various natural species if not to human beings a place of open transition. For a description of this situation, see chapter 3.

15. On apperception, see Edward S. Casey, *The World at a Glance* (Bloomington: Indiana University Press, 2002), pp. 260–62 and 476–79, especially p. 478: "The appearances we apperceive are not fixed attributes or permanent properties of things but moving figures dancing on surfaces, forms mutating under our very eyes, a world in continual

transformation rather than a sum of established items." The "world in continual transformation" I would now characterize as an edge-world of ongoing changes.

16. See Casey, *The World at a Glance*, especially pp. 439–48, where I discuss "the Logic of the Less" in ways that are at once parallel to, yet distinct from, the same logic as it obtains in the case of edges.

17. Is there an absolute edge? D. G. Leahy has argued that there is in a religious context in his remarkable essay, "To Create the Absolute Edge," *Journal of the American Academy of Religion* 57, no. 4 (Winter 1989): 773–89.

18. I refer to the victory of Donald Trump over Hilary Clinton for the American presidency. The margin of difference was so close that the popular vote was the converse of the Electoral College count. Yet from this narrow base, a radically different governmental agenda from that which Clinton's victory would have meant will emerge in the years to come.

19. Martin Heidegger, *Identity and Difference*, trans. Joan Stambaugh (New York: Harper and Row, 1969), p. 45. I have here altered "difference" to "different."

20. Plato, *Symposium* 190a.

21. For a technical definition of "medium" as well as "surface" and "edge," see James J. Gibson, *An Ecological Approach to Visual Perception*, Glossary.

22. Exceptions include oil and water, notorious for their unmixability—which does not exclude the real possibility that the former can pollute the latter when certain of its ingredients break loose at a molecular level.

23. Recall my analysis of the waters at Sand Beach in Stonington described in chapter 5, along with the photo given in the corresponding figure.

24. Sigmund Freud, "Notes Upon a Case of Obsessional Neurosis," in *The Standard Edition of the Complete Psychological Works*, Volume 10 (1909), trans. James Strachey (London: Hogarth, 1955), pp. 151–318. The phrase "his own love" refers to the Rat Man's love for significant others, especially his love of his father, about whom he was obsessively ambivalent.

25. See the *New York Times* article on this event, "The Nun Who Broke Into the Nuclear Sanctum," by William J. Broad, August 11, 2012.

26. See Casey, *The World at a Glance*, especially chapter 4, "The Hegemony of the Gaze," and the afterword, "Families of the Glance and the Gaze." The medical gaze is treated in Michel Foucault, *The Birth of the Clinic: An Archaeology of Medical Perception*, trans. Alan M. Sheridan Smith (New York: Vintage, 1994).

27. For both of these lines of inquiry, see Gilles Deleuze and Felix Guattari, *A Thousand Plateaus*, trans. Brian Massumi (Minneapolis: University of Minnesota Press, 2005), chapter 12, "Nomadology."

28. On the plane of immanence, see Deleuze and Guattari, *A Thousand Plateaus*, pp. 154 and 266–67, as well as Deleuze and Guattari, *What Is Philosophy?*, trans. Hugh Tomlinson and Graham Burchell (New York: Columbia University Press, 1994), chapter 2, pp. 35–60.

29. See Eugene Gendlin, "Crossing and Dipping: Some Terms for Approaching the Interface Between Natural Understanding and Logical Formulation," in *Mind and Machines* 5, no. 4 (November 1995): pp. 547–60. Available on the Focusing Institute website: http://www.focusing.org/gendlin.html. See also Eugene Gendlin, *Saying What We Mean: Toward a Responsive Order*, ed. E. S. Casey & D. Schoeller (Evanston: Northwestern University Press, 2017).

# Epilogue: Life on the Edge of Danger, Disaster, and Doom

> In the self-organizing reality everything is always on edge. There is only edge.
> —George Quasha (email communication of January 11, 2016)

All life is lived on edge, as I am repeatedly reminded by the ambulances and fire trucks that scream their way through traffic below my apartment on 110th Street. As living bodies, we exist on *this* side—the near side—of the manifold edges that structure our immediate life-world. Minimally but essentially, life is a biological fact sustained by anabolic and catabolic processes. It is *bios* in the original sense: life that is vital, sensitive, and adaptive to its immediate milieu. With every new situation in life comes a new set of edges to cope with. Many of these offer little challenge, such as minor changes in weather or in the energy level of our own body on a given day. Our ongoing habitual body enables us to adjust with minimal effort to these modestly altered edge conditions. But every life is subject to disease of many sorts, sometimes endemic (as with endogenously generated cancer), sometimes due to infection (plagues, epidemics, and other noxious influences); liable to accidents (falls, collisions) and violent assaults; and always vulnerable to unanticipated edges of danger that can undermine and undo life itself.

From the place of our own bodily being, rendered sensitive by our skin and our various sensory organs, we experience the mass of edges that make up the world around us, the multitude of exterior edges. The singular edges of my unique body-complex, my perceptual profile, exist under the impress of an always impending edge-world. This world stands quite literally at the edge of my life; its impingement on me is something I cannot ever fully control. My life is always at serious risk of annihilation, whether accidentally or by the hostile actions of others. Whatever the cause, I find myself continually subject to the threat of no longer existing. This alarming realization obtains not just for myself, but for others as well: one feels poignantly their being at high risk—whether a friend is a patient in the ICU unit of a hospital, my brother is driving in heavy traffic in Los Angeles, or my partner is swimming in a tempestuous ocean. When not perilous, life is uncertain, always precarious to some degree.

Sartre interprets this situation as generating a special form of existential anxiety in which one's in-itself and for-itself dimensions realize a queasy equilibrium. As a purely in-itself being, I am just a thing that can all too quickly fall to my fate, like a stone subject to gravity. As a for-itself, I am free to do any number of things: to hurl myself into the abyss, to draw back decisively, or to pause in an anxious and unresolved state of not knowing what to do. On Sartre's assessment, this circumstance is far from being merely contingent; all of human existence is afflicted with the vertiginous—if one is honest about the fragility of one's basic state of being-in-the-world.[1] As this book draws to a close, I shall address this fateful fact by underlining the extreme and ultimate urgencies of life lived on tenterhooks.

I do this not in an effort to end on a negative note, but rather to fill out the larger picture of the diverse edges-worlds we inhabit. In earlier parts of this book, we have witnessed a number of salutary edge situations, especially those that come under the generic heading of permeable boundaries and that also include cusps and verges, thresholds, and peripheries. Each of these is well suited to usher in the new and the promising—to give rise to what is constructive rather than to what is unduly constrictive. We have witnessed a number of concrete cases in point: green zones on international borders, "gateways" in resilient communities, horizons of landscapes that give onto open territory, and so on. But edges also precipitate us into what Freud called "danger situations" that may undermine our well-being. It is to these that this epilogue attends.

## I

The riskiness of human existence is at stake in Heidegger's claim that human beings' default position is that of a *Verfallensein* from which there is no effective escape. Attempting to flee from the existential fate of falling, human beings seek what is leveled down and predictable, but these latter offer only temporary reprieve from the falling that afflicts human beings at the deepest ontological level. Human existence is nothing if not subject to harm. We live a life continually on the verge of harm.[2] Moreover, Emmanuel Levinas and Judith Butler both argue that the other person's vulnerability is more profound—more ethically and politically significant—than one's own. For Levinas, this means that others call for my unflagging recognition of their destitution. Butler is concerned especially with the precariousness of those who are subject to being killed or gravely wounded in wars, whose suffering remains unacknowledged—above all by the marauding forces that overtake them.[3]

Many civilian victims of war perish anonymously, left dead or dying by the assaulting forces; all too often they become numbers on a tally maintained by the attacking army. They are in no position to make their own precarity known to the invading forces, who are by and large indifferent to their fate. As anonymous victims of war, the civilian dead are ungrieved by the aggressors, never having had a chance to articulate the urgent imperative that they not be harmed in their abject defenselessness.[4] Every human being lives at risk of death by accident or disease—since "to be born is to be capable of dying" in the German proverb[5]—but those singled out by Butler live in danger zones that lie directly in the path of military actions. The ethical imperative not to kill other human beings is countermanded by the temptation on the part of the attacking forces to annihilate everyone in the path of a given military operation, civilians and soldiers alike; each person in such a situation exists in a state of continual high risk of death.

War exponentially increases the precariousness of human life in quite specific ways. Butler is especially concerned with the effects of wars that could and should have been prevented, such as those initiated in the last fifteen years by the United States in the Middle East and Central Asia. She points to this country's propensity to inhibit public mourning by rendering invisible the faces of the victims of wars it has created and pursued, including those of our own soldiers killed in combat.[6] Thus not only undue violence but also unacknowledged, unmournable suffering and death are at stake. The fragile edge of human life is made grotesquely manifest in the violent destruction, death, injury, starvation, and terror to which war exposes all who fall in its path—and it becomes all the more problematic when these horrors of war are minimized and concealed from citizens of the marauding nation. In putting everyone in its wake at risk, war enacts the edge of precarity itself—a perilous perimeter where the edge of life itself is at stake: life that is all too soon forgotten in the confusion and devastation wrought by war.

Death is the ultimate edge of human life, beyond which there is no other: it is "the undiscovered country from whose bourn no traveler returns."[7] These celebrated words of Hamlet indicate death's abrupt absoluteness, its irremissibility, from which there is no way back. As a *bourn*, it is a form of border in the strong sense with which we are now familiar: an edge that is both definable and definitive. Death is a one-way street: a *sens unique*. With the exception of certain anomalous cases,[8] death cannot be retraversed once it has been passed over. This is not to deny that in certain respects death also serves as a boundary: those dying can enter death in many ways, from gentle to violent, and this range indicates that death is not accurately analogous to a line that is simply crossed over or not. There is such a thing as "easeful death" in which the person dying enters the state of death painlessly. It is perhaps with reference to this possibility that Hamlet also says, "to die: to sleep—to sleep, perchance to dream" (3.1.63–64). In dying we may not simply enter into a comatose or mindless state of oblivion, but just might experience a dream-like state, whether pleasant or nightmarish: "there's the rub, / For in that sleep of death what dreams may come / When we have shuffled off this mortal coil / Must give us pause" (3.1.64–67).

Death is not merely the final edge of life; it, too, comes double-edged. It is at once a border and a boundary—a border in being a condition that cannot be reversed or crossed back over; a boundary in being a state that we can enter in a variety of ways, no one of which is imperative or even paradigmatic. Death is no simple way of being, nor is it a merely biological process (even if it stems from the failure of the body's physiology). It is a complex form of becoming in which humans reach the final edge of life, whether they are explicitly conscious of it or not.

## II

Beyond biological death, with its existential edge, there is another kind of death: social death. This is the death one undergoes when cut off from all contact with other human beings. In referring to social death, I have in mind a quite different experience from any kind of voluntary isolation, such as that practiced by hermits who choose to sequester themselves far from human settlements in caves or huts, as well as those who go into a prolonged retreat on their own, such as the practice of Dark Retreat in Tibetan Buddhism. Each of these is an elective activity that can be terminated when desired. The case of solitary confinement is very different. Here one is involuntarily and forcefully sequestered as punishment for a presumed crime. In "solitary" one is constricted to a single cell with no human contact: neither with guards nor with other prisoners. One is forced to live alone in sensory deprivation in a small walled cell, sometimes for years (four decades in the case of Albert Woodcock of the Angola Three) with no possibility to alter one's isolated state; being free to exit is just what is forbidden: this is the ultimate situation of No Exit.

The effect of this extreme state is to be cut off from any form of vital community—and it is just this that causes the most profound suffering. Complete social isolation is an intolerable state of existence. In her book *Solitary Confinement*, Lisa Guenther reports that many prisoners become psychotic if held alone for a period as short as forty-eight hours, suffering from "insomnia, anxiety, panic, withdrawal, hypersensitivity, ruminations, cognitive dysfunction, hallucinations, loss of control, irritability, aggression, rage, paranoia, hopelessness, lethargy, depression, a sense of impending emotional breakdown."[9] Indeed, it can be argued that one's entire being is changed by this form of severe sequestration; as one victim of solitary confinement put it, "solitary confinement can alter the ontological makeup of a stone."[10] The effect is one of "living death," which Guenther analyzes into *civil death* and *social death*. Civil death entails the deprivation of one's basic rights (the right to vote, for example). Social death means being removed from any significant contact with others. There is a destruction of one's coherent, customary social world.[11] A prisoner in solitary reports, "You feel as if the world has ended, but you somehow survived."[12] The world thus lost is a world populated with other living beings (including members of other species) with whom one could be in continuous contact: it is this world-of-others that is eliminated in the social death induced by solitary confinement.

Try to imagine for a moment what solitary confinement is like. In a solitary cell, your body has virtually *nowhere to move* and certainly *nowhere to go*: you might be able to take two paces in one direction and three in another—if there is space enough for this. The cell itself is stocked with the minimal furniture allowed: a bare pallet bed, a simple sink, a toilet bowl. Your body is *up against the wall* at all times. You are not just hemmed in by the cell's stolid walls; any bodily movement is arrested by these same walls, whether built of concrete or steel, and you are forced to stay put within this strict enclosure. Even if you do not literally bump into or butt against the walls—in extreme fatigue or a fit of rage—you are oppressed at all times by walls that prevent any possibility of passing through them or going beyond them.

The solitary cell is rigid in its rectilinearity and unyielding in its constrictive rigor. The solitary prisoner lives in a row of interlocked edge-enclosures, starting with individual cells (as small as six by eight feet, often with no windows) that are arranged in corridors, which are contained in whole cell blocks surrounded by high walls and surveillance towers. This prisoner has no access to other spaces, not even "the yard" where nonsolitary prisoners are allowed to exercise and mix. Crucially, all the many edges that delimit the life of the solitary prisoner—edges crammed inside one another like Russian dolls—are the hardest of hard edges. The solitary prisoner is left with nothing but an enmeshment of edges that determine every movement he makes, edges of surfaces that are always already in place, implacably immovable. No matter how strong it may be, his physical body is no match for such edges and surfaces, which keep him in *one and only one place* or more exactly *one site*. This is indeed a situation of no exit: in Sartre's phrase *huis clos*— literally, closed doors.

Nelson Mandela describes his experience in a solitary cell as follows: "I could walk the length of my cell in three paces. When I lay down, I could feel the wall with my feet and my head grazed the concrete at the other side. The width was about six feet, and the walls were at least two feet thick. . . . That small cramped space was to be my home for I knew not how long."[13] The last phrase is especially significant. For the experience of a closed-off life has a temporal dimension that is as intolerable as that of spatial confinement. Mandela remarks that "each day is like the one before; each week like the one before it, so that the months and years blend into each other."[14] For the solitary prisoner, days and weeks lose their difference; they merge into a single, unbearable, undifferentiated mass. Solitary confinement is life lived on the edge of a severely constricted space and a bleakly unlimited time. There are too many restrictive spatial edges to allow for freely undertaken physical movements and social interactions, and there are too few distinctive temporal edges to temper a sense of unending time.[15] In both ways solitary confinement is likely to induce a sense of despair and doom. The prisoner is pinioned in a claustrophobic world of fiercely reinforced edges.[16]

## III

When we speak of "the edge of doom," we rarely pause to ponder what this may mean: which doom, what edge? In ordinary parlance, the phrase "going to the edge of doom" signifies doing or experiencing something *to an ultimate extreme*—notably, to the point of exhaustion, the end-state of human energies. Or else, more portentously, it alludes to something descending upon us that will crush us in some devastating way and that offers no prospect of egress. In its heavier reaches, "doom" signifies a darkly decisive way in which human beings will experience the end of things, the end of time, including the end of life. And not just one's own life: that of others, too. These dreaded end-states are projected as coming about by way of unrelenting and indiscriminate forces. For all those affected by them, these forces are experienced as arbitrary, violent, and inexorable.

Doom can take many forms. The most personal is one's own death, especially when this is the result of being afflicted by a dire diagnosis, such as pancreatic cancer in an advanced state. Another is an addiction in which one is caught up and from which one cannot seem to escape.[17] Or else the election of a political leader whom one does not trust and whom one considers reckless and likely to precipitate widespread suffering among the very people who elected him. But for the most part doom is felt to descend on us from an impersonal elsewhere against which we feel ourselves defenseless: a pestilence to which we are likely to succumb, an economic depression that undermines our ability to live in comparative ease, an oncoming war we are unable to prevent. And the sense of doom is even more intense when these dreaded prospects take us by surprise, coming from we know not where, often arriving without early warning signs, suddenly and sometimes savagely.

In the last thirty years, a doom-laden syndrome has become manifest in which many of the earth's peoples have become ensnared. At stake is the loss of their land, their home, or their livelihood, as well as their natural resources, especially water and clean air. These losses, analyzed by Saskia Sassen in her book *Expulsions: Brutality and Complexity in the Global Economy*, result from a series of converging factors: international capital committed to financial derivatives, extraction of minerals and fossil fuels, and extensive land grabs. The convergence of these factors is accompanied by an increasing indebtedness on the part of nations who are paying off forced debts (often incurred from loans by the World Bank or the International Monetary Fund), and this in turn has led to the slashing of social programs and to undercutting long-term stable employment. The afflicted countries range from Sudan and Gabon to Greece to Indonesia. International corporations, predatory nations, and individual financiers and entrepreneurs profit immensely from a situation in which such countries, in their impoverished state, are compelled to sell land and water rights at very low prices. The tacit collusions between these various marauding forces, "assemblages of powerful actors, markets, technologies, and governments," are extremely complex, but the effect is cruelly straightforward: "savage sorting," as Sassen calls it.[18] Many thousands of people in the brutalized countries wake up to find their land sold out from under them, their jobs eliminated, their pensions turned to dust, and the atmosphere around them contaminated by chemicals and other pollutants: a situation of "dead water and dead land."[19]

Revealingly, Sassen calls this immensely destructive complex of phenomena a "systemic edge," by which she means that what could easily be regarded as separate forces are actually in a covertly collusive relationship that acts to undermine the lives of ordinary people living in the afflicted nations—that puts these lives on edge. The fate of these people is often that of "expulsion," forced removal from their longstanding way of life and from the places they have inhabited for generations. "Today's systemic edge is a space of expulsions," writes Sassen, "in contrast to the Keynesian epoch where the systemic edge was a space of incorporation."[20] A post–World War II ethic of inclusion and respect for basic human rights has given way to a contemporary space of exclusion and of the deprivation of these rights. Those experiencing the brunt of this exclusionary edge suffer from a sense of doom from which there is no effective exit. They are altogether cornered by this edge. For a desperate situation such as this there can be no adequate preparation, no guaranteed prevention, and no viable escape. Most often, there is no choice but to submit to the onset of events over which one has no effective control: no choice but to acknowledge the "slings and arrows of outrageous fortune" in Shakespeare's all too prophetic words, and to submit to the forces of fate.

A sense of hopeless entrapment makes ordinary residents into international refugees who seek to escape failing economies and deadly political conflict— uprooted people who experience concrete forms of approaching doom, leading many to flee overland or at sea, often at great risk. From one form of doom they are often cast into the arms of another: as witnessed by the many drownings of African and Middle Eastern migrants in the Mediterranean in recent years. Even if the refugees or migrants reach the new country they seek, they may be forced by that country to return to the scene of violence they were fleeing—as at La Frontera or in Syria—where an even darker fate may well await them in punishment for having left in the first place.

## IV

The most comprehensive impending doom at this historical moment stems from the more and more frequent disasters emerging as a direct consequence of climate change. This urgent situation has occasioned a feeling of helplessness and a new kind of depressive melancholy.[21] There is a widely shared sense that *it is coming*— an environmental doomsday induced by accelerating mass extinctions of animal and plant species, the flooding that will overtake whole countries, uncontrollable hurricanes and tsunamis along with violent changes in weather that will have devastating consequences for all life on the planet. The fact that climate scientists are overwhelmingly in accord that such dark scenarios are virtually certain to occur only adds to the increasing conviction that all life on Earth is now imperiled by the relentless onslaught of ever more extensive environmental traumas. An endangered Earth finds itself on the edge of doom.

The sense of peril engendered by the climate crisis is not something experienced only by individuals. This is a brink faced by everyone everywhere on Earth: we are all perched on the same high cliff of imminent climate disaster. Short of nuclear holocaust, such disaster is the most drastic form living on precarious edges can take. It is not unlike solitary confinement in that eventually the entire human race—along with all other living beings on Earth—will be consigned to a collective prison, a penitentiary of environmental degradation, a prison *from without*, so to speak, from which there is no escape. This is the fate that awaits us if current projections of climate science prove accurate. The climate crisis is the ultimate crisis: it threatens to destroy life in the oceans and the atmosphere as well as on land. It presents us with a circumstance in which biological life, always fragile and on edge, will be faced with a new and final challenge: how to remain robust enough to survive the extremities of climate chaos. This is a challenge that brings us to the very edge of life on earth, since it concerns the quite conceivable ending of this life.

With a mounting climate crisis, we move into a perilous phase in which earthly life itself is on the threshold of elimination. If we are not to resign ourselves to this fate, it is up to us and subsequent generations to forge a new vision for a viable future, however demanding may be the concrete steps required to realize such a vision. Can an imaginative pursuit of more resourceful ways of coping with the crisis bring enabling edges to our increasingly disabled earth and create a more resilient edge-world? Can we rise to this challenge for which there is neither precedent nor exact parallel in any previous era of life on earth?

## V

Each doom-bearing event brings its own edge. For there is no doom without edge, or rather two edges: one edge that gives access to it *as doom* and another that marks the ending of the state of doom itself.[22] On the one hand, there is the opening stage of doom, the *near side* of an emerging doom; on the other, there is doom's *far side*—its trailing off, no longer having the full force it once had, the fading of its biting edge. A tornado heading for the center of Topeka, Kansas, in 1966, was viewed from a nearby hill by many residents of the city, who were powerless to avoid the threat of the racing dark funnel. They watched it as it headed toward the city center, where it destroyed hundreds of buildings, after which they saw it moving into the open landscape on the far edge of town. The ominous arm of the tornado, its swirling cone, was witnessed both oncoming and outgoing. For those in the city center who may not have seen it coming, it struck suddenly with blinding force, but even here there was an opening and a closing phase experienced in a span of minutes.

This literal duplicity of the edge of doom is an essential feature found in each of the edge situations outlined above—whether this be the course of a natural disaster, a situation of forced expulsion, the suffocating sense of being addicted to artificial substances, or the imminent loss of one's land and livelihood. The power of doom is concentrated between the two phases of this double edge, a power that is responsible for the intensity of its force and the felt sense of its unavoidability. Unlike other acute forms of edge that cut off sharply and definitively—the edge of a geometric figure or a printed page, for example, or a separation barrier, or the wall of a solitary cell—the edge of doom *unfolds*, opening out as it develops, just as the tornado's funnel moved inexorably toward the center of Topeka. By the same token, it also *enfolds* that which it overtakes, incorporating it into the course of its action and the mass of its force, as when the same tornado descended upon the buildings it ravaged. This enfolding can be so complete and overwhelming, that we experience it as the undergoing of the doom-bearing event itself, given that it is what overcomes us most decisively if we find ourselves at the heart of the disaster that has been unleashed. It catches us coming and going, engendering affects ranging from awe to terror—in this respect resembling the experience of the sublime as described by Burke and Kant.

In addition to its double-edged character, there are three other basic features of the edge of doom: its heavy brunt, its singularity, and its felt momentum.

(1) Although many risks and perils of our day-to-day world come to us as being "as sharp as the edge of a knife" (in the Northwest Indian saying I have cited before)—occurring as quickly as a sudden automobile accident—the doom that hangs over us is more like a bludgeon than a knife. We are subject to its brunt, brute force more than to its acutely cutting character. We stagger before and under it: we cannot come to terms with it: *our* terms are not *its* terms. The tornado will make its own way no matter how much we may wish and pray otherwise: it cannot be deterred.[23] Not only can we not redirect it, we cannot dodge it if we are directly in its overbearing path. This is likewise true of earthquakes and tsunamis—and, in the human realm, of the intricate and pervasive global exploitations and

expulsions described by Sassen; in relation to these, hapless individuals find themselves powerless to divert their overdetermined course.

(2) Each doom is singular, not only because it is experienced by myself uniquely as *my fate* (or, by extension, as *our fate*, the fate of a people), but because it is intrinsically unique *as an event*.[24] The destructive force of each tornado is unique even if all tornados share certain meteorological features in common. Because of their singularity, dooms cannot be compared: what happens in Gabon is not the same as what transpires in the Congo, even if they stem from the same collusion of global forces. Once fully underway, such dooms can only be endured, one at a time. The doom whose edges I submit to is *this* doom, not any or every doom: this singular doom afflicts me, or us.

(3) Brunt-bearing and singular, the doom I experience overwhelms me by its internal momentum, irreducible to the measurable momentum of a physical object in motion that was paradigmatic in early modern classical mechanics. It is the immeasurably momentous character of the doom that takes me over: the tornado that overtakes the city, the sudden loss of my land and access to water, the deaths of my beloved friends. I experience the singularity of my fate in the impact of the besetment, which allows me no choice but to witness it, if I am at a certain safe distance, or to submit to it abjectly, if I am caught up in it so directly as to have to let it happen.

Rather than anxiety or alarm, the psychical state that ensues when doom breaks out is more akin to a state of deep melancholy that is akin to resignation. This is not the melancholy that follows upon the unmourned loss of life in war, as in Butler's analysis. It arises instead from the sense of a forced ending—of time, of life, of a world or indeed *the* world—from which there is no way back. Instead of being led to address and improve my own condition, as in the experience of certain limited emergencies, I am more likely to be moved to abject despair.[25] I find myself moving beyond my resilient and resourceful self—moved *somewhere else*, to another place, to the locus of doom itself. I am at this locus and nowhere else, and from there I cannot discern any effective exit.

Truth be told, we are on a precarious edge as soon as we are born, with the first breath we draw, at each subsequent moment, unto the eventual end that we designate as death. We are subject to danger not only in wartime but also in peacetime: the untoward awaits us at every turn. In broad daylight, as in the night, peril lurks: there is no perfectly safe venue. We like to think that we are protected from the most difficult of fates—but dangers may arrive at any time in any form, few of which we can fully anticipate. Living in modern times offers no assurance against disasters—as witnessed by nuclear proliferation, dirty bombs, and drone warfare—and it is not clear that we are leading any less precarious lives overall than did our ancestors. We live on perpetually exposed edges.

Peirce regarded Chance as the first stage and still continuing basis of everything more stable, notably Habit and Law. We live subject to chance occurrences and outcomes. No wonder we are anxious beings who experience ourselves as *unheimlich* on earth: not-at-home even when in our accustomed home place, profoundly uneasy even in the most familiar surroundings. Precarity spreads to every corner of our lives. It thrives on the edges where we live and have our being. To be on edge is to be precariously positioned and there is no form of existing, human or otherwise, that is not so situated. Our human world and the worlds of other species are made from edges that structure and support ongoing life, but that also act to confuse, mislead, and endanger this same life.

What I have called the *edge-world* is not only a world composed of intricate patterns and permutations of edges; it is also a world that is itself on edge. As a consequence, each of us is pitched on a thousand edges—edges on which we shake and tremble even as we pretend to go about our lives undisturbed. Our equanimity is only skin-deep; underneath it the abysses gape open, not just at the far edge of the known world or at the base of a precipice. We are denizens of a world on edge, and we are ourselves creatures of exposed edges. This is not just a matter of being accident-prone or vulnerable as individuals. We carry risk to others, endangering *their* lives as well as our own. Whole populations of human beings have been decimated by their fellow humans. Many animal and bird species have been rendered extinct because of human actions in the Anthropocene. Now we are on the verge of making ourselves extinct if humanly induced climate change takes its full vengeance.

There is no way to exist on earth, no alternative path, other than to follow the edges that guide us even as they expose us to risk at every turn. We must take such exposure into account, learning how to identify those edges that are likely to lead us astray: each of us exists on a perpetual visual cliff. Some edges bring us to an unwelcome fate for which we are not adequately prepared: on these I have focused in this epilogue. Instead of trying to forget them or merely regret them, we must think on them, reflecting on what they portend. Becoming wary of certain edges, we can come to trust other edges that will configure our life-worlds in ways that are both more constructive and more creative. These more auspicious edges point the way for us, incisively even if not infallibly. Thoughtfully traversed, they are able to liberate us, indicating directions with the potential to save us from our own destructive and self-destructive ventures.

The deep bivalence of edges—their capacity to take us into trouble as well as to alleviate and amplify our lives—calls forth our full powers of discernment. From such discernment we can better envision pathways into a future of apposite action. This future will have its own edges, but they are more likely to be bound-ary-like and threshold-traversing than border-like and perimeter-clutching. This book has suggested numerous ways in which such forward-looking edges—fortuitous as well as forged—emerge in our lives if we will acknowledge and nur-ture them: edges of paintings and musical compositions, edges of Commons, gateways in cities, bodily edges that allow us to embrace the world more fully, psy-chical edges that help us to feel more deeply, and edges of the earth that we care for with respect and foresight.

"You learn the most by watching the edges," goes the Inuit saying cited ear-lier. Such edge watching is in part a practical activity of becoming more acutely aware of the formative role of edges in our lives: becoming better able to recog-nize their variety as well as their many combinations. But it is in larger part a mat-ter of learning to think on the edge—to *think edge*—so that we may come to act more effectively and live more insightfully in a world on edge.[26]

## Notes

1. For Sartre's analysis of existential vertigo, see "The Origin of Nothingness," chap-ter 5 of *Being and Nothingness*, trans. Hazel E. Barnes (New York: Washington Square Press, 1992), pp. 21–46.

2. On falling, see Martin Heidegger, *Being and Time*, trans. Joan Stambaugh (Albany: State University of New York Press, 1996), "Falling Prey and Thrownness," pp. 164–68, and "The Temporality of Falling Prey," pp. 317–20. Heidegger is not speaking of physical situa-tions of falling but of all the ways in which human beings fall into inauthenticity. These ways are so massive and multiple that inauthenticity itself is the basic state of human beings, with authentic actions being "existentiell modifications" of this state of *Uneigentlichkeit*.

3. See Butler's essay "Precarious Life" in her book *Precarious Life: The Powers of Mourn-ing and Violence* (London: Verso, 2004), pp. 128–51. One of Butler's main concerns is the fact that unacknowledged atrocities involve deaths that in their anonymity cannot be grieved.

4. Butler's primary example is that of the children and the other citizens of Iraq and Afghanistan who were killed in the wake of the intervention of US forces in those coun-tries from 2003 until the present. But she is also concerned with other comparable circum-stances, such as that of the many Palestinians killed by Israeli soldiers since 1948. For the most complete articulation of this point of view, see Butler's essay "Violence, Mourning, Politics," in *Precarious Life*, pp. 19–49.

5. For Heidegger's elaboration of this adage, see Heidegger, *Being and Time*, p. 343: "Dasein stretches along between birth and death." He writes, "Factical Dasein exists as born, and, born, it is already dying in the sense of being-toward-death."

6. Recourse to the faces of the victims of war violence—faces that on the Levinasian paradigm are uniquely capable of conveying the prohibition against outright murder—has been largely denied to the American public, thereby muting critique and implicitly sanc-tioning the continuation of violence against "the enemy." See the latter half of Butler's

essay "Precarious Life," pp. 140–51, especially these words: "The erasure of that suffering [of innocent victims of war] through the prohibition of images and representations more generally circumscribes the sphere of appearance, what we can see and what we can know. . . . The task at hand is to establish modes of public seeing and hearing that might well respond to the cry of the [suffering] human within the sphere of appearance. . . . We might consider this as one of the philosophical and representational implications of war, because politics—and power—work in part through regulating what can appear, what can be heard" (pp. 146–47).

7. *Hamlet* 3.1.81–82.

8. I refer to cases in which a person is convinced that he has died but then finds himself suddenly alive again. Michael Quill of Santa Monica has described such an experience, which occurred just after an automobile accident. But the liminal state he experienced took place entirely at the level of losing and gaining consciousness; it would be another matter to claim that his *life*—his biological, vital life—was lost and then regained (conversation of June 30, 2014). Strictly speaking, such a loss occurs only in circumstances of resuscitation. For a discussion of details of resuscitation—the ultimate edge-state as medically determined—see Elaine Scarry, *Thinking in an Emergency* (New York: Norton, 2011), pp. 19–34.

9. Psychologists for Social Responsibility (PsySR), "PsySR Open Letter on PFC Bradley Manning's Solitary Confinement," January 3, 2011. This is part of a letter written to Robert Gates as Defense Secretary that argued that PFC Bradley (now Chelsea) Manning's being held in solitary confinement at Quantico Marine Corps Base for (at the time) over six months constituted "cruel, unusual and inhumane treatment in violation of U.S. law." The letter states that those held in solitary for longer than ten days invariably had very seriously debilitating effects. They conclude that "solitary confinement can have severely deleterious effects on the psychological well-being of those subjected to it" (cited from "PsySR Open Letter").

10. Jack Henry Abbott, *In the Belly of the Beast: Letters from Prison* (New York: Vintage, 1991), p. 45; cited in Guenther, *Solitary Confinement*, p. xi.

11. This is the thesis of Elaine Scarry in *The Body in Pain* (New York: Oxford University Press, 1985), which proposes that the most destructive effect of torture, beyond the physical pain and psychical fear, is the loss of a meaningful life-world. Solitary confinement can be considered a special form of torture, and it, too, involves world-loss, in this case the loss of the social world.

12. Jeremy Pinson, cited in Guenther, *Solitary Confinement*, p. xii.

13. Nelson Mandela, *Long Walk to Freedom* (New York: Little, Brown, 1994), p. 384.

14. Mandela, *Long Walk to Freedom*, p. 389. Mandela also observes that "time slows down in prison; the days seem endless" (ibid.).

15. Such countability is a helpful structuring of the passage of time. Such moments help the prisoner realize and mark out how long he has been in prison and how much longer remains, even when condemned to a life sentence. Without such demarcation he is *lost in time*. Here I use the pronoun *he* advisedly, given that more men than women are kept in solitary confinement in the United States. But women are by no means spared this fate; in California prisons women's solitary confinement has seen a dramatic increase in recent years.

For documentation and an eloquent plea for being considered along with men, see *The Fire Inside: Newsletter for the California Coalition for Women Prisoners* 49 (Fall 2013/Winter 2014).

16. For these remarks, I have drawn in part upon my essay "Skin Deep: Bodies Edging into Place," in *Carnal Hermeneutics*, ed. Richard Kearney and Brian Treanor (New York: Fordham University Press, 2015), pp. 159–72.

17. It is just because of this sense of inescapability and inexorability that the most effective way out of many serious addictions has come from Alcoholics Anonymous, which insists that the addicted person change their life in fundamental ways, reposing confidence in the superior force of a divine being. I am here simplifying what is often a much more complicated situation in which the addicted person may feel foreclosure of life at one level but a hope for and projection of becoming unaddicted at another level. Self-deceptive or defensive as this latter attitude sometimes is, it may also prepare the path to rehabilitation.

18. Saskia Sassen, *Expulsions: Brutality and Complexity in the Global Economy* (Cambridge: Harvard University Press, 2014), p. 4; the earlier citation in this sentence is from p. 220.

19. Ibid., p. 222.

20. Ibid., p. 221.

21. Climate change–induced depression has given rise to a new form of therapeutic practice, "eco-therapy." See, for instance, *Ecotherapy: Healing with Nature in Mind*, ed. Linda Buzzell-Saltzman and Craig Chalquist (San Francisco: Sierra Club Books, 2009), and *Ecotherapy Newsletter*, http://www.ecotherapyheals.com.

22. A notable exception seems to be the "eternal damnation" of Catholic doctrine—an unending inferno from which there is no exit, only unmitigated suffering. In certain respects, it is the apocalyptic correlate of solitary confinement.

23. The Native Americans who once lived in the Topeka region considered it to be protected from tornadoes by a mound located on the southwest edge of the modern town: "Burnett's Mound" as it came to be called. But the tornado I have described leapt over this hill and descended directly onto the city.

24. I underline "as an event" since I am here arguing that the edge of doom has a structure of its own. This structure—its double edge and the three traits under discussion just now—allows comparison between different occurrences of doom; but *as a happening* each case of doom is experienced as singular and unique.

25. For a discerning discussion of emergency situations and lessons to be learned from them, see Scarry, *Thinking in an Emergency*, chapter 2: "Four Models of Emergency Thinking."

26. For a close analysis of thinking on the edge, see the afterward/forward, "Thinking Edges, Edges of Thinking."

# Afterward/Forward: Thinking Edges, Edges of Thinking

We live in a world poised precariously on the edge of oncoming disasters, any one of which is enough to transform and even threaten life on earth. As I have emphasized in the epilogue, we are on the edge of environmental doom at this very moment, due to the effects of climate change around the globe. In California alone, heat and aridity have brought about a major drought that threatens the state not only with a dearth of water but also with fires in the mountains and hills. When I stood looking west into the ocean at Moro Bay as described in the prelude to this book, I was mindful of the plume of radioactivity that was then making its way from Fukushima to this highly vulnerable coast, which is bracing for anticipated earthquakes and tsunamis of its own. This is not to mention the vast vortex in the Pacific Ocean, the Great Patch in which innumerable fish are choking on the plastic bags humans have heedlessly discarded on the west coast of North America. And *we* are choking, too: the very atmosphere in which humans and animals everywhere live and breathe is laden with noxious pollutants and radioactive debris. There is also the brink on which the world has been tottering since the bombings of Nagasaki and Hiroshima, inaugurating an era of atomic and nuclear weapons—an era that is even more dangerously imminent now that drones can carry dirty bombs almost anywhere on the globe. This litany of impending disasters characterizes a world that for some time now has been under siege in the wake of industrialization and fossil fuel extraction.

Each of these situations is *diastremic*: a looming disaster in an extreme form. Worse yet, each is of a proportion that discourages direct action, because none of these diastremes is anything we can easily get a handle on, conceptually or practically. Climate change, late capitalism, nuclear fission, and fossil fuel exploitation are notoriously difficult to address. None is an *object* in anything like the Kantian sense of a discrete object of ordinary experience; all are "hyperobjects," using Timothy Morton's term—a word that captures the gist of our increasingly hyperbolic age.[1] The unencompassability of these and other diastremes, their having no discernible end or limit, their edgelessness, has put us on edge: and all the more so when those who deny humanly induced climate change assume positions of political power. The critical fact is that we—you and I—*belong to that same perilous edge*. We stand and we stagger on it, whatever comforting tales some may tell. The world as we know it is on the edge of disappearing, and we are on that same edge: no one, nothing, can escape it. I am not invoking *Apocalypse Now*, nor am I predicting the Absolute End in the manner of a postmodern Cassandra or Tiresias. I am talking about the end of the world as we humans—and all other sentient beings—have known it. We may not be able to reverse global warming (though we can mitigate it), or entirely eliminate the risks of nuclear contamination, but it is likely that we do have some time left. How much, no one knows; but during the time remaining we can at the very least *think on the edge*—think over and think through the pandemic that we are all ensnared in and that we have brought about ourselves. Being so much on the edge of disaster, we can at least reflect on it: indeed, we must do so, for not to do so is to indulge in irresponsible and self-defeating negligence.

Not just think *about it*—that is being done by myriad others at this historical moment, some of them strategically situated to think about what to do about it constructively if not salvifically. Lending thought to the current state of emergency, our task is to *think through what it means to think on it*. Accordingly, in this final moment of the book I shall engage philosophical, or, as I prefer to call it, *reflective thinking*, construed as itself a form of thinking on the edge. But what does it mean to think on the edge? I shall explore this seemingly innocent formula with particular emphasis on the edge on which reflective thinking itself takes place.

### I

A preliminary question: *Where are we*? Where are we *really*? James Joyce spoke of being "whenabouts in space." What about "whereabouts in time" (also mentioned by Joyce)? *About where* are we *at this* time? As I write these words, it's close to 6:00 p.m. on Sunday, March 20, 2016, and I'm in New York City. But these are not the whereabouts and whenabouts that really matter. It does not help to determine that we are at a certain punctual place or time, except for purposes of orientation or reportage. This way lies clock time and world time as well as meters and miles: all of which entail precise linear edges. More worthy of pursuit are the *where* and *when* whose edges defy exact measurement—which are intrinsically indefinite. It is of little significance to say that Riverside Park, in which I hope to take a meditative walk later today, is so many meters wide or long. Much more significant experientially is the physiognomy of the park, its ever-changing contour, and the way that it settles into the Hudson River below and to the west: a body of water that flows in a time of its own keeping.

Ever unearthly, human beings have devised a schizoid world, confining themselves to an exclusive choice between the punctuality of clocks and the linearity of maps on the one hand and the infinite void (cosmic, metaphysical, theological) on the other. The spatiality and temporality that matter lie in between—in the shoals of time and the tides of space and their human counterparts in moods and thoughts that seem to come and go at their own pace.

To think that we are limited to living on an axis where the point and the line dominate is to live among the hard edges that are expressions of what Whitehead called Simple Locations in time and space—the Fallacy of Misplaced Concreteness engendered in early modern thinking—a grievous error from which we postmoderns still suffer. Our headlong recourse to the phantasmagoria of virtual worlds made accessible by the internet can be regarded as an effort to escape the suffocation brought on by the strictly located hard edges of the "reality principle" to which our egological selves are geared to respond. The world of "determinate presence" is Heidegger's term for the inferno of hard and sharp edges that has plagued Western civilization from its first formulations of the nature of being. "The world is as sharp as the edge of a knife," goes the indigenous saying I have cited several times in this book.[2] So it has indeed come to be with ever-increasing intensity in recent times. But the world is also otherwise; it sports other edges, on other occasions.

These occasions include unfathomable dreamtime and immeasurable dreamspace, wandering reveries, and ecstatic bodily experiences. They feature soft edges that reflect experiences of dreaming, falling into reverie, and going outside ourselves into we know not what (or conversely, being inhabited by forces whose provenance we cannot detect). In each case, we are concerned with edges for which no exact metric is forthcoming. Yet such occasions are not defective for being less than fully determinate. Far from it—their very virtue, their distinctive mark, is the way they at once facilitate and express the drift, the direction, of a dream, a reverie, an inspired bodily gesture. Their edges morph as they evolve in space and time, and in any given case they are *inexact*.[3]

Reflective thinking is another member of this same series. When we think reflectively, we enter into an edge-world having its own distinctive topography: its own landscape or seascape, its own contours and local features, its own shapes and surfaces, each with a distinctive set of edges. In such thinking, we take a walk on the shores of our own act of reflection. There is an ancient recognition of the close relationship between thinking and walking: *solvitur ambulando*, "to be solved by walking." The gist of this Latin dictum has been affirmed by thinkers as diverse as Rousseau, Thoreau, and Heidegger. Putting the body in motion is not just a favorable prelude to thinking; it is to jump-start thinking itself, to start thinking in an especially ruminative way.[4] For us, the question is: through what edges does such thinking move, what are its most characteristic outer and inner shores?

My premise throughout this book has been that the edges of things and places and events, and of much else besides, far from being secondary and external, are primary: they are formative features of that of which they are the edges. Far from edges being only the final stage of something, the finishing touch, they are also where that something *begins*. We come to things and happenings from the edges of our sensory being (our senses being mostly located at the outer edges of our

bodies) so as to rejoin the edges of what impinges on us in the near-space of our
immediate ambit as well as the far-space of the distance (where we often cannot
perceive anything other than profiles and silhouettes of things). Our animal existence proceeds from edge to edge in the interworld of intercalated edges, those
of our sensing bodies and those of our sensed environs as intermeshed in a living
matrix. Much the same is true of our existence as thinking creatures.

## II

In *What Is Called Thinking?* Martin Heidegger proposes that what is most "thought-
worthy" is precisely what has evaded reflective thought: "what must be thought
about, turns away from man. It withdraws from him."[5] The withdrawal occurred
long ago with the beginning of philosophical thinking itself, though at no determinate date. Instead of thinking this radically withdrawn content—or better,
*event*[6]—as such, humans can only *point to it* in its very withdrawal; and this is accomplished by gestures that act not as indicative signs but as hints (*Winken*) that
"stay without interpretation."[7]

Just here the *edge* enters Heidegger's discourse. If we are not to remain permanently in "the foothills of thought," we need to take a leap: "The leap takes us
abruptly to where everything is different, so different that it strikes us as strange.
Abrupt means the sudden sheer descent or rise that marks the chasm's edge.
Though we may not founder in such a leap, what the leap takes us to will con-
found us."[8] As if to compensate for—if not to tame—such strangeness, Heidegger
emphasizes that the very withdrawal of what is thought-worthy brings with it "its
own, incomparable nearness."[9] Such nearness is achieved by an activity of "handicraft" or "handiwork." "Thinking itself," he adds, "is man's simplest, and therefore
hardest, handiwork if it would be accomplished at its proper time."[10]

So the thinker, on Heidegger's conception, is confronted with two forms of
the farness of thought—its withdrawal and its strangeness—and two modes of
closeness: "the enigmatic and therefore mutable nearness of its appeal"[11] as well
as the proximal character of thinking regarded as handiwork. What calls to be
thought, "what gives us to think,"[12] lies between the farness and the nearness of
thought and constitutes their shared edge. What kind of an edge is this? It is *a
margin of difference*. Not only a margin where difference appears, or a margin that
has a differently configured edge (say, proximal versus distal), but a margin that is
itself the product of difference, that is the expression of the sheer differentiation
between the thinker and the to-be-thought. This differentiation is the outcome of
the dramatic moment when philosophical thinking leaps into what is foreign to it,
*other* than it, encountering the contour of the strange. Just here, at this edge, we
encounter the decisive turning to thought. For it is *on the edge* of thinking, in the
margin of difference, that the advent of thinking is to be found.

Heidegger here limits his options to the mediocre thinking of leveled-down everyday thinking and the leap out of such thinking: "the leap alone takes us into the neighborhood where thinking resides."[13] This stark dyadic choice fails to capture the deepest challenge of thinking, which is to *stay on the edge*, perched there uneasily, indefinitely suspended and without any prospect of egress from that edge.

Gilles Deleuze falls into an equally untenable dilemma—that between the self-assured thinking of "common sense" and of "good will" and the extremity of a radical thinking that begins in the experience of shock, in an encounter with what forces us to think, and finally in a leap.[14] For Deleuze, we need to be shocked into thinking from out of the mediocrity of tranquilized *bon sens*. Too much previous thought in the West has been subjected to the post-Cartesian regime of representation in which what prevails is "the same and the similar," a regime that "profoundly betrays what it means to think."[15] This regime presumes an innate capacity to think on the part of human beings, thanks to which they "naturally" aim at the truth conceived as received wisdom in any given situation.[16] Deleuze's effort is to unseat this unquestioned presumption and to replace it with a model in which what gives rise to thought is not found in anything located within the process of thinking itself but in something *other*, something so alien that "it can only perplex us when we encounter it."[17] This something other "forces us to think . . . [in] a fundamental *encounter*."[18] This encounter occurs only at the level of the sensible, not as based on sheer sensory givenness but as a *sign* that compels thinking, above all the sign of a "problem" that sets us thinking in the first place.[19]

Both Deleuze and Heidegger posit situations in which there are only two alternatives: the even tranquility of everyday common beliefs—those held by "the they" (*das man*) and the person of good philosophical faith and common sense (which is to say, *everyman*)—and the precipitous circumstance of confronting one's stupidity in a mortifying moment in which one realizes just how wrong or ignorant one has been up to that point. What we encounter in that moment, in Deleuze's graphic description, "are the demons, the sign-bearers: powers of the leap, the interval, the intensive and the instant."[20] Both thinkers assume that such a sudden encounter with the demonic or the chasm of difference is the only viable alternative to the narcotization induced by common sense and good will in the routines of leveled down living. Each, strikingly, moves to the *leap* as the only way out of the stultifying sea of false serenity. *Beyond the sedentary, there is only the saltatory.* Both thereby overlook a third way. This is the way I want here to explore: that of *thinking on the edge*.

## III

The thinking I have in mind is neither desultory nor saltatory. It does not consist in the meandering induced by thinking any thoughts whatsoever—that way lies pointless thinking, or better thinking besides the point—but it also does not require a decisive leap across a chasm, the melodrama of thinking as set forth by Heidegger and Deleuze. It consists rather in a patient staying on the edge of a challenge to thinking, probing that edge on a plateau that is unique to reflective thinking.[21] This plateau is not pregiven; it is generated by the act of thinking itself. It amounts to clearing the space requisite for thinking through what one can call a "question": a question insistently calling for an answer.[22] Reflective thinking is not merely an encounter with a problem whose effect is to make us feel stupid, in Deleuze's valorized sense; it is the careful probing of a compelling question in the space and time of its own devising, without rushing to a premature answer. It remains on the plateau, the butte, or mesa *on which* reflective thinking emerges: just there, right there, and nowhere else. This is thinking on the edge.

Any butte or mesa has its own edges and thus brings with it its own saltatory dimension. The *saltus* or leap is not from one preconstituted edge to another, as happens in the hard-edge world of determinate perception and movement—or, for that matter, as found in dogmatic common sense or reassuring good sense. The leap of thinking on the edge *creates its own edges even as it leaps*. It goes from edges of its own earlier making to still other edges of its further devising. It is not just edge-savvy but edge-creative; it is not only a matter of *knowing* edges or focusing on them but also of *bringing them into being*. Thinking, we might say, generates *the becoming of edges themselves*, the edges of radical thought. Some of these are familiar from previous acts of thinking, but many of them are new in their very emergence. Thinking on the edge is neither nomadic (wandering among given edges) nor sheerly sequential (as in a free-association train of thought) nor is it formally structured (as in a classical syllogism). What then *is* it? What kind of thinking and what kind of edge are at stake here?

### IV

A stellar instance of the thinking I have in mind is found in Heidegger himself, a thinker who spent a lifetime thinking and rethinking the question of Being, staying on the edge of his own thinking and creating ever new edges from which to think Being differently. Another instance is exemplified by Paul Cézanne, who sometimes worked on a single painting—intermittently—for twenty years. He was *thinking on the edge* of his subject and of his medium by painting from that edge. If Mont Sainte-Victoire was one of his favorite "motifs," it was seen and reseen many times—in many different paintings and many times in the evolution of a single painting—so that what he came to think of that mountain emerged in the medium of paint. Painting (and repainting) was the plateau on which he worked, and the materiality of that plateau took the form of oil paint (and sometimes watercolor).

Heidegger and Cézanne each thought on the edge, despite their manifest differences in concrete activity and focus of concern. Each pointed to the necessity of an edge of thinking that is just broad enough to contain the thinking they had to do—on a butte sufficiently broad to support this same thinking but no wider than its own outer edges. They put themselves in the place of thinking by creating it and its edges anew with each painting or book they undertook.

## V

What is thinking anyway? We commonly say that it is *having thoughts, entertaining ideas.* This means allowing thought-acts to occur: "mental episodes" in which whatever is thought in such acts or episodes (the "idea" or "ideas") is held consciously in mind, however briefly. I am here referring to ordinary acts of cogitation—*cogitationes,* in Descartes's term.[23] Having thoughts in this way is quite literally superficial: they occur on the conscious *superficies* or surface of the mind, where "the mind" is little other than a container of ideas.

Conscious thought episodes of this sort are precisely what Heidegger did *not* have in mind when he opened his lecture course titled *What Is Called Thinking?* by saying that *"Most thought-provoking is that we are still not thinking."*[24] The thinking he has in mind is the thinking of Being, a rather extraordinary kind of thinking that has its own history, having arisen among the early Greeks and having been repeatedly forgotten or repressed, even from the start, but reglimpsed from time to time, most recently by Heidegger himself. This is ontological thinking: thinking in and of the realm of Being—if not of Being itself, and then of its disparate manifestations in poetry and architecture, painting and sculpture, and in rare philosophical or theological texts.[25]

Rather than pursuing the question of Being, I shall here focus on a form of concrete reflective thinking that occurs in philosophy and in other undertakings, including activities of everyday life. Such thinking consists in *thinking over* or *thinking through* certain thoughts. Rather than such thinking being something highly specialized and requiring certification by so-called professional thinkers, such as logicians and semioticians, we are often thinking this way even in the most ordinary circumstances. It happens whenever we become "pensive" or "thoughtful" for whatever reason, whether this occurs in existential crises or during deliberations about what we want to do with our life from here on—indeed, whenever we find ourselves thinking in the context of some urgency. Sometimes explicitly philosophical concepts are useful in such thinking, but often they are not: we are *just thinking*, thinking things over or through in our own way. To think *over* connotes gathering our thoughts in order to ponder their merit; thinking them *through* emphasizes the process of going through them successively in order to arrive at a new realization. In neither case is the aim anything practical per se—it is not a matter of thinking in order to do *x* or *y* better or more efficiently—even if our reflection may well have arisen from practical exigencies, from what Dewey called a "problematic situation."

I hold that such thinking as I have here in mind *is* philosophical thinking; it has philosophical import, even if it is not formally ordered or guided by explicit goals or styles that bear the mark of established philosophical schools or trends. Its source is the same as in other forms of cogitation: thoughts that pass unbidden through our minds, albeit not always with a high resolution. Most often, such thoughts glide in and out of our daily waking activities, whatever their provenance. They are definitely among the thoughts that the thirteenth-century Zen master Dogen (1200–1253) had in mind when he gave instructions for doing zazen meditation practice. Dogen gives this account of the following incident:

> A monk asked Yaoshan, "In steadfast sitting, what do you think?"
> Yaoshan said, "Think not thinking."
> The monk asked, "How do you think not thinking?"
> Yaoshan replied, "Beyond thinking."[26]

It is clear that Yaoshan is not here recommending that there be *no thinking* at all in zazen, that is, achieving an altogether empty mind. Rather, he is suggesting that the most important dimension of zazen is not the choice between thinking and not thinking (having thoughts versus having none at all) but engagement in a third state: "beyond thinking" or, better yet, "nonthinking," which is a standard translation of the Japanese term *hi-shiryō*. *Hi-shiryō* signifies letting thinking happen or not happen, not striving to attain one or the other—especially not one versus the other. It is on the basis of nonthinking that the very distinction between thinking and not thinking becomes possible: "in order to think not thinking, nonthinking is always used."[27] Nonthinking is *not* not thinking; not thinking signifies having no thoughts at all; nonthinking is a state of mind that makes thinking itself possible; it is a basic state that gives rise to explicit thinking as well as to not-thinking. It can be schematically represented thus:

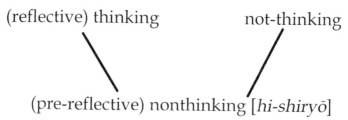

FIGURE 20. Schema of Thinking, Not-Thinking, and Nonthinking according to Dogon.

Unlike not thinking, the domain of nonthinking does not exclude the incursion of everyday thoughts, the kind that arise in the practicing person's mind, supported by sitting meditation but not restricted to this situation. These thoughts are of many sorts: idle, practical, or obsessive. But nonthinking as I construe it also includes acts of thinking that can be characterized as *prereflective*: those that precede acts of express reflection. As Bret Davis suggests in an alternative translation of *hi-shiryō*, such thinking emerges from "beneath thinking" in its more express and reflective forms.[28] *Hi-shiryō* facilitates reflective thinking and is a condition of possibility for its emergence. As a consequence, nonthinking takes us to what precedes any choice, indeed any difference, between reflective thinking and not thinking.

Thinking of any kind, whether as reflective or prereflective, has to have a place in which to occur. This place is precisely what I have been calling a "plateau" for thinking.[29] Thinking as reflective calls for an especially intimate place of enactment: there and there alone one is at one with one's thoughts, whatever their ultimate antecedence or their eventual effect. Or rather we should say *here and here alone*: for it is a matter of thinking that occurs in its own near-space, close-up, so as to be all the more effectively on the narrow path of thinking that is on the way to the far north of thought itself, its outer horizon. *Hi-shiryō* is the name of the path from which reflective thinking takes its rise. Dogen was the first to point to this path or way, but each thinker must undertake it herself and in her own distinctive way.[30]

This path requires its own space in which to unfold. Considered as beneath or "before" reflective thinking ("before thinking" is another construal of *hi-shiryō*),[31] nonthinking in Dogen's positively valorized sense has to be enacted *somewhere*; it has to have its proper place or scene of emergence. Dogen already said as much: "Do not treasure or belittle what is near, but be intimate with it."[32]

When underway on the path of nonthinking, even if we are beneath or before reflective thinking, *we are already thinking*. In particular, we are *thinking on the edge*, that is to say, prereflectively thinking in a *topos noetos* (a "mental place") that belongs to such thinking as its own near-space, its own place of enactment. And to posit such a place is *to think of thinking in a new way*. For it means that all thinking, reflective as well as prereflective, requires its own plateau with its own edges.

In saying this, I do not mean to imply that the place of nonthinking is anything literally extraordinary. It is "always fully realizable . . . in each singular moment of our being unceasingly under way."[33] It presents itself continually as a task to be undertaken in the very midst of the quotidian: it is thinking that is "always presencing beneath our feet."[34] (Notice: *beneath our feet*, not in the head, as Descartes or Kant would insist.) Those thinkers who identify themselves as "logicians" promote thinking in a concerted, *head*-strong way when they offer elegant means to resolve certain stateable problems or paradoxes. Dogen is telling us that significant thinking of a very different sort may come to happen under our feet—from the ground up.

Such thinking is a "practice of thoughtful discrimination,"[35] and it requires the undergirding of bodily posture and practice, which is where the here and now happens for the thinker, whether seated in zazen or at a desk in a study. Bodily praxis is an integral part of both what I have been calling "reflective thinking" and what Dogen terms "nonthinking." Reflective thinking is made possible by the prereflective activity of sitting or some other concrete form of being on the path of hi-shiryō. We think seated or in motion, and in both cases we do so by means of our entire prereflective existence. In this sense, every reflective thinker is also a nonthinker who is at once a body and a mind immersed in his or her life-world.[36]

To think at the base level identified by Dogen is to be poised on a plateau that is often no more than a bare ridge. It is to think on the edge. It is perilous, yet it subtends reflective thinking from below, von unten: so far below that it can also be experienced as an abyss.[37] It is not the 1001st plateau, but the place from which thinkers of a certain profundity think and write. I would wager that almost all original philosophical thinking, whether systematic (such as Aristotle's *Metaphysics* or Hegel's *Science of Logic*) or paradoxical (Heraclitus, Nicolas of Cusa, Kierkegaard, and Dogen himself), emerges from some such subtending space. Free ranging as human thought may become, it is always linked to a place *from which* it comes. This is the place of hi-shiryō. The more soaring the speculation, the more the need for a place from which it takes its rise and to which it is likely to return. This place is neither a foundation nor a ground; it is nothing substantial, *it is an edge.*

Such an edge-place (a place that is an edge) is a nonplace—no place at all if "place" is restricted to an exact position as determined by geometric coordinates or identified with sheer spatial extent. The place/nonplace from which reflective thinking springs does not have determinate dimensions. It is akin to the indefinitely bounded shoal into which a beach disappears, stretching out under the ocean. Such an indeterminate place, the place of prereflective nonthinking, is the ultimate *upon which* (*woraufhin*) where reflective thinking can occur.[38]

"If [you] attain this place," asserts Dogen, "then, in accordance with everyday activity, there is the presencing of truth."[39]

## VI

This place is the plateau of "thinking on the edge." Thinking not merely *of* or *about* the edge, or on the other side of it, but at it—*on it*—in the near and narrow space of the plateau it provides and the path that opens out from it. Such a space, such an edge, is presumed by all the forms of thinking I have been discussing: by reflective, prereflective, and nonreflective or mundane thinking (which is equivalent to not-thinking); but also by nonthinking itself. This effective edge is the narrow space whereupon all these modes of thinking happen. It stands under them all. It also furnishes the basis for the *pausing* that is essential to taking thought of a reflective cast. As such, it is the temporal equivalent of the spatiality of the plateau that supports reflective thinking. "Il faut pauser," said Louis XIV in his small treatise on how to walk appreciatively through the gardens of Versailles. (Voltaire was only echoing the Sun King when he famously counseled the readers of *Candide*: "cultiver vos jardins"—which we might here translate as "cultivate your reflective practice in place.") The Zen meditator and the reflective thinker alike advise us to pause on the edge of thought, in an open place that induces released reflective thinking.[40] For both, it is a matter of cultivating a basic attitude of *letting-be*, or perhaps better, of *letting-go*: letting one's thoughts go outward even as they are underwritten from below by one's bodily posture in a closely fitting edged place. This place, like a shoal, underlies the surges of active thinking of many sorts.

Not despite this underlayer but through it, we encounter the continuous plateau on which reflective thinking occurs. On this plateau, what Western Apaches call "smooth mind" emerges. The Apache word for "smooth mind"—the basic state in which wisdom occurs—connotes a cleared space. "Like cleared plots of land," writes Keith Basso, "smooth minds are unobstructed—uncluttered and unfettered—a quality which permits them to observe and reason with penetrating clarity."[41] It needs to be emphasized that the plateau here at stake need not be literally smooth, despite the common core of the semantic group of words that include "place," "plot," "platform," and "plateau." It may also contain rills that literally complicate thinking on the edge; edges within this edge introduce wrinkles into otherwise smooth thinking: a thinking that often consists in the form of gathering thoughts and discriminating among them.

Proceeding along this same edge, new thoughts can occur at any moment; often the most creative ones arrive unexpectedly like breaking waves, seemingly random thoughts that arrive athwart the path of thinking as it has been traversed up to that point. Such thoughts *come in from the edges* of the plateau of reflective thinking—from beneath this plateau, from the depths of *hi-shiryō*. In Dogen's own metaphorics, they come in from the open seas of nonthinking: "Just as the sky or the ocean remains there, regardless of whether or not there are passing clouds or waves, the nonthinking mind remains there, regardless of whether or not we are thinking, not-thinking, or thinking of not-thinking."[42] The great reservoir of nonthinking underlies *all* thinking, including what I have been calling reflective thinking. From this reservoir, stray thoughts cut across the course that reflective thinking has taken so far, vagrant thoughts that may surprise us.[43] To be open to such lateral and sometimes wild thoughts, an occasional pause—sitting meditation, a walk, a siesta, virtually any activity in one's near-space—prepares the way, allowing us to be receptive to these unanticipated ingressions.

What counts in thinking on the edge is not to get to the end of a given line of thought—to complete that thought, as if it had a finish line, a dead end—but to be on the way of thinking itself, *reflecting in the way*, wherever it may lead: "This is where the place [of the presencing of truth] is, and the Way (*dô*) achieves its circulation."[44]

## VII

My concern in this afterward / forward has been to draw attention to the special *spatiality* of the edge on which reflective thinking occurs. Too often such thinking is considered exclusively in its temporal dimension—as, say, a mere succession of thoughts, a sequence of cogitations in time, as in Hegel's invocation of "the *slow* labor of the Negative" or Aristotle's insistence that leisure time is required to do philosophy. It is my conviction that the spatiality of thinking, especially reflective thinking, has been neglected, thereby preventing a full understanding of the deeper dynamics of such thinking. I am here attempting to rectify the balance by drawing attention to the implicit spatial, or rather *placial*, dimensions of the very activity in which thinkers continually engage, whether they are fully aware of it or not. It is in this context that I am singling out the importance of the edge on which such thinking happens.

In so doing, I am extending my own earlier work on place to a new region, that of reflective thinking on the edge. This is an odd threesome, you might say—thinking and place and edge—yet it is one whose conjunction is very much in the spirit of Bachelard's *Poetics of Space*, a book that explores the disparate realms of poetry and space in the context of literary reverie. I am intending something similar here by combining Dogen's idea of thinking-as-nonthinking with place considered as the scene where the edges of thought emerge.

Whenabouts in space and whereabouts in time are we, after all? Joyce's chiasmatic confounding of time and space can be understood as expressing the time-space of reflective thought that takes place on the prereflective plateau that lies beneath or before reflective thinking of the sort that is operative in creative and thoughtful philosophy and painting—and in many other domains.

The contemporary world remains very much on the edge—above all, on the edge of its own destruction: if not by nuclear fission, then from rising oceans and the other effects of climate change. No one can pretend to know of easy ways to remove us from the precarity that has become our common lot. But we can at least think together, indeed we *must* think together, in order to reflect more fully on the fateful circumstance in which all humans, in fact all species of living being, now find themselves. Can we think anew about thinking itself as a prelude to coming up with answers to the much vaster problem of what looks to be the earth's endgame? Can we think the world on edge by occupying the edges of thinking more effectively? Can we have the courage to think on the edge by bringing ourselves to the edges of our own thought?

Thinking reflectively in this direction, we might pull in a catch of new insights and different strategies—a set of unaccustomed thoughts—thanks to the reflective equivalent of "the net that draws up both quivering fish and seaweed from the seabed," in Merleau-Ponty's vivid image.[45] This book has been an experiment in thinking about the manifold edges of human experience: it is *an exploration of thinking on the edge about edges themselves.* For to come to grips with the disparate edges in our lives, we need to put our thinking on its own edge—to put it on the qui vive so that we can more decisively perform a periphenomenology of edges of many kinds, and thereby achieve their more exact description. On the basis of this description, we can be better prepared to cope more adroitly with the diastremes in which we, along with the earth itself, are now caught up.[46]

## Notes

1. Timothy Morton, *Hyperobjects: Philosophy and Ecology after the End of the World* (Minneapolis: University of Minnesota Press, 2013).

2. Cited by Gary Snyder, *The Practice of the Wild* (San Francisco: North Point Press, 1990), p. 19.

3. Strictly speaking, the term should be "anexact" to emphasize that the edges of dreams and reveries and bodily experiences do not merely resist determinate standards of measurement but escape the very effort to measure them with *any* known metric. For more discussion, see part 4, "A Last Lesson."

4. On this topic, see Henry David Thoreau's classic essay, "Walking," and Rebecca Solnit, *Wanderlust: A History of Walking* (New York: Penguin, 2000), especially part 1, "The Pace of Thoughts."

5. Martin Heidegger, *What Is Called Thinking?*, trans. J. Glenn Gray (New York: Harper, 1976), p. 8.

6. Heidegger specifies, "Withdrawal is an event" (ibid., p. 9).

7. Ibid., p. 10.

8. Ibid., p. 12. "Chasm's edge" translates *"Rand der Kluft."* Elsewhere, Heidegger specifies that the leap is *over* the ontological difference between Being and beings. See Heidegger, *Contributions to Philosophy*, trans. R. Rojcewicz and Daniela Vallega-Neu (Bloomington: Indiana University Press, 2012) p. 197.

9. Ibid., p. 17.

10. Ibid., pp. 16–17.

11. Ibid., p. 17.

12. Ibid., p. 6.

13. Ibid., p. 12.

14. Although paying homage to Heidegger for his "profound texts" on thinking (*Difference and Repetition*, trans. Paul Patton [New York: Columbia University Press, 1994], p. 144), Deleuze ends up arguing that Heidegger falls prey to the reductive logic of the Same: "he retains the primacy of the Same, even if this is supposed to include and comprehend difference as such—whence the metaphors of gift which are substituted for those of violence" (ibid., p. 321n11).

15. Ibid., p. 167.

16. Deleuze, *Difference and Repetition*, p. 131: "The most general form of representation is thus found in the element of a common sense understood as an upright nature and a good will." At stake in this image of thought is a tenacious prephilosophical presupposition of the right-directedness of philosophical thought: "According to this image, thought has an affinity with the true. . . . It is *in terms of* this image that everybody knows and is presumed to know what it means to think. . . . We may call this image of thought a dogmatic, orthodox or moral image" (ibid.).

17. Ibid., p. 132.

18. Ibid., p. 139.

19. What we encounter in the perceived world, "the being of the sensible," "moves the soul, 'perplexes it'—in other words forces it to pose a problem: as though the object of the encounter, the sign, were the bearer of a problem—as though it were a problem" (*Difference and Repetition*, p. 140).

20. *Difference and Repetition*, p. 145. What moves us to think is "the contingency of an encounter with that which forces thought to raise up and educate the absolute necessity of an act of thought or a passion to think" (p. 139). Note also: "'everyone' knows well that men in fact think rarely, and more often under the impulse of a shock than in the excitement of a taste for thinking" (p. 132).

21. Thinking on this plateau is an instance of what Merleau-Ponty calls "hyper-reflection." On hyper-reflection (*sur-réflexion*), see Maurice Merleau-Ponty, *The Visible and the Invisible*, trans. Alphonso Lingis (Evanston: Northwestern University Press, 1973), pp. 38 and 46.

22. I have in mind here R. G. Collingwood's "logic of question and answer" as set forth in *An Autobiography* (Oxford: Oxford University Press, 1939).

23. Thus for Descartes thinking occurs by consciously held cogitations. Freud concurs, stating unequivocally in *The Interpretation of Dreams* that the dream-work, which operates unconsciously, "does not think, calculate, or judge in any way at all; it restricts itself to giving things a new form" (Sigmund Freud, *The Interpretation of Dreams*, trans. J. Strachey [New York: Avon, 1965], p. 545). He denies that there is an "independent intellectual activity" in dreaming (pp. 489–99). Thus thinking is for him, as for Descartes, entirely and only a conscious process.

24. M. Heidegger, *What Is Called Thinking?*, p. 4.

25. The thinking of Being is not for Heidegger a straightforward project, as if it were a search for anything like an object. It is neither an activity nor a matter of passive reception. Nor is Being something *unknown* in the manner of the unconscious, much less an object of consciousness. All of these divisive binaries are assiduously avoided in Heidegger's condensed apothegm: "there is Being (*es gibt Sein*)." Even the locution "the thinking of Being" has to be read as allowing for both the subjective and the objective genitive, so that such thinking belongs as much to Being as to the thinker of Being. I thank Bret Davis for suggesting some of these clarifications.

26. Zen Master Dogen, *Beyond Thinking: A Guide to Zen Meditation*, ed. Kasuaki Tanahashi (Boston: Shambala Press, 2004), p. 37.

27. Ibid., p. 37.

28. I follow Davis's lead here: "*Hi-shiryō* is sometimes more freely translated as 'beyond thinking'—yet, in keeping with the orientation of a radical 'backward step' to what Nishitani Keiji calls 'the absolute near-side,' it would be better understood as 'beneath thinking'" (Bret W. Davis, "The Enlightening Practice of Nonthinking: Unfolding Dōgen's *Fukanzazengi*," in *Engaging Dōgen's Zen: The Philosophy of Practice as Awakening*, ed. Tetzuzen Jason M. Wirth, Shūdō Brian Schroeder, and Kanpū Bret W. Davis [Somerville, MA: Wisdom Publications, 2016]).

29. Alternatively, it can be considered a *porch* of thinking, the very *perch* on which it occurs—with all the precariousness that the psychological state of "being on edge" implies—but now construed as characterizing the very scene of thinking, its atrium or forestage.

30. As Bret Davis puts it, for Dogen "truth presences completely right here and right now, and this living moment (*nikon*) of being-time is all there is ever to life, and to death" (Bret W. Davis, "The Presencing of Truth: Dogen's *Genjokoani*," in *Buddhist Philosophy: Essential Readings*," ed. J. Garfield and W. Edelgass [Oxford University Press, 2009], p. 255; hereafter cited as "The Presencing of Truth").

31. Bret Davis, communication of March 7, 2013.

32. Dogen, *Beyond Thinking*, p. 39. He says the same of far-space: "Do not treasure or belittle what is far away, but be intimate with it" (ibid.).

33. Davis, "The Presencing of Truth," p. 256.

34. Ibid., p. 255. See also the phrase "right here beneath your feet" as used by Davis, p. 258.

35. Bret W. Davis, "The Philosophy of Zen Master Dogen: Egoless Perspectivism," in *The Oxford Handbook of World Philosophy*, ed. J. L. Garfield and W. Edelgass (Oxford University Press, 2011), p. 352. Hereafter cited as "The Philosophy of Dogen."

36. Dogen says that in zazen one sits "within body-mind," and he posits "the oneness of body-mind (*shinjin ichinyo*)"; cited by Davis, "The Philosophy of Dogen," p. 355.

37. The phrase *von unten* (from below) is employed by Karl Jaspers in his *Philosophie*.

38. *Woraufhin* is Heidegger's adverbial term in *Being and Time* for the matrix from within which an instrumental complex is engendered.

39. Davis, "The Presencing of Truth," p. 258.

40. By "released reflective thinking," I have in mind an activity akin to Heidegger's notions of *Besinnung* ("reflective thought") and *Gelassenheit* ("letting be").

41. Keith H. Basso, *Wisdom Sits in Places: Landscape and Language among the Western Apache* (Albuquerque: University of New Mexico Press, 1996), p. 131. Smooth mind allows one to "reflect on" and "think of" things that matter; it is the basis of the precept that "you must think about it and keep on thinking about it" (pp. 138, 140, 127).

42. Davis, "The Enlightening Practice of Nonthinking," p. 20. This reservoir is "an essentially indeterminate field of nondual awareness, a field which underlies or encompasses the determinations of thinking, not-thinking, and thinking of not-thinking" (p. 21).

43. Here is the proper place for the Heideggerian-Deleuzian saltatory model, which mistakes the part for the whole by putting the entire emphasis on the leap or *saltus* that occasions surprise.

44. Davis, "The Presencing of Truth," p. 258.

45. Maurice Merleau-Ponty, *Phenomenology of Perception*, trans. D. Landes (New York: Routledge, 2012), p. lxxix.

46. This afterward/forward is a much-revised version of an invited lecture, "Thinking on the Edge," delivered on March 20, 2014, at the annual meeting of the Comparative and Continental Philosophy Circle in Santa Barbara, California. By calling this last component of the book "Afterward/Forward," I mean to point to the way it draws together much of what precedes it while also looking ahead to what is to come when reflective thinking is engaged.

# INDEX

EDWARD S. CASEY is Distinguished Professor of Philosophy at SUNY, Stony Brook. He is the author of numerous books, including *Getting Back into Place* (Indiana University Press, 1993; 2nd ed. 2009), *Imagining* (Indiana University Press, 1976; 2nd ed. 2000), and *Remembering* (Indiana University Press, 1987; 2nd ed. 2000). *The World on Edge* is a sequel to his book *The World at a Glance* (Indiana University Press, 2007).